TRANSPARENCY IN THE WTO
SPS AND TBT AGREEMENTS

Transparency of trade regulations among all WTO Members is essential for open, fair and predictable trade relations. A myriad of different regulations apply across WTO Members and have the potential to affect international trade. The Agreements on the Application of Sanitary and Phytosanitary Measures and on Technical Barriers to Trade offer the most comprehensive frameworks in the WTO within which to address the costs arising from regulatory diversity, by providing for regulatory transparency and co-operation. This book gives a detailed account of the legal principles of the two Agreements, an in-depth discussion of dialogue between WTO Members and an overview of the few cases that end up in formal dispute settlement. It shows that the strength of the WTO legal and institutional system goes well beyond its dispute settlement system, with transparency enabling implementation of WTO obligations as a result of better information sharing and co-operation among Members themselves, through non-judicial means.

MARIANNA B. KARTTUNEN has worked as a policy analyst within the OECD Regulatory Policy Division, focusing on international regulatory co-operation, since February 2016. In this position, she has carried out innovative policy work on international regulatory co-operation, including leading the first in-depth country reviews on the subject. Previously, she held a position as policy adviser at the OECD G8-G20 Sherpa Office and conducted research at the Trade and Environment Division of the WTO. Karttunen has a PhD in law from the European University Institute and has published in leading journals on international trade law.

CAMBRIDGE INTERNATIONAL TRADE
AND ECONOMIC LAW

Series Editors

Dr Lorand Bartels
University of Cambridge
Professor Thomas Cottier
University of Berne
Professor Tomer Broude
Hebrew University of Jerusalem
Professor Andrea K. Bjorklund
McGill University, Montréal

Processes of economic regionalisation and globalisation have intensified over the last decades, accompanied by increases in the regulation of international trade and economics at the levels of international, regional and national laws. At the same time, significant challenges have arisen with respect to economic liberalization, rule-based systems of trade and investment, and their political and social impacts. The subject matter of this series is international economic law, in this contemporary context. Its core is the regulation of international trade, investment, finance and cognate areas such as intellectual property and competition policy. The series publishes books on related regulatory areas, in particular human rights, labour, environment and culture, as well as sustainable development. These areas are horizontally interconnected and vertically linked at the international, regional and national levels. The series also includes works on governance, dealing with the structure and operation of international organisations related to the field of international economic law, and the way they interact with other subjects of international and national law. The series aims to include excellent legal doctrinal treatises, as well as cutting-edge interdisciplinary works that engage law and the social sciences and humanities.

Books in the Series

*Transparency in the WTO SPS and TBT Agreements:
The Real Jewel in the WTO's Crown*
Marianna B. Karttunen

Emerging Powers in International Economic Law
Sonia E. Rolland and David M. Trubek

*Commitments and Flexibilities in the WTO Agreement
on Subsidies and Countervailing Measures*
Jose Guilherme Moreno Caiado

*The Return of the Home State to Investor–State
Disputes: Bringing Back Diplomatic Protection?*
Rodrigo Polanco

The Public International Law of Trade in Legal Services
David Collins

*Industrial Policy and the World Trade Organization:
Between Legal Constraints and Flexibilities*
Sherzod Shadikhodjaev

*The Prudential Carve-Out for Financial Services: Rationale and
Practice in the GATS and Preferential Trade Agreements*
Carlo Maria Cantore

Judicial Acts and Investment Treaty Arbitration
Berk Demirkol

*Distributive Justice and World Trade Law: A Political
Theory of International Trade Regulation*
Oisin Suttle

Freedom of Transit and Access to Gas Pipeline Networks under WTO Law
Vitalily Pogoretskyy

Reclaiming Development in the World Trading System, 2nd edition
Yong-Shik Lee

Developing Countries and Preferential Services Trade
Charlotte Sieber-Gasser

*WTO Dispute Settlement and the TRIPS Agreement: Applying
Intellectual Property Standards in a Trade Law Framework*
Matthew Kennedy

Establishing Judicial Authority in International Economic Law
Edited by Joanna Jemielniak, Laura Nielsen and Henrik Palmer Olsen

*Trade, Investment, Innovation and their Impact on
Access to Medicines: An Asian Perspective*
Locknie Hsu

The Law, Economics and Politics of International Standardisation
Panagiotis Delimatsis

The WTO and International Investment Law: Converging Systems
Jürgen Kurtz

*Export Restrictions on Critical Minerals and Metals:
Testing the Adequacy of WTO Disciplines*
Ilaria Espa

*Optimal Regulation and the Law of International Trade: The
Interface between the Right to Regulate and WTO Law*
Boris Rigod

The Social Foundations of World Trade: Norms, Community and Constitution
Sungjoon Cho

Public Participation and Legitimacy in the WTO
Yves Bonzon

The Challenge of Safeguards in the WTO
Fernando Piérola

General Interests of Host States in International Investment Law
Edited by Giorgio Sacerdoti, with Pia Acconci,
Mara Valenti and Anna De Luca

*The Law of Development Cooperation: A Comparative
Analysis of the World Bank, the EU and Germany*
Philipp Dann

*WTO Disciplines on Subsidies and Countervailing Measures:
Balancing Policy Space and Legal Constraints*
Dominic Coppens

*Domestic Judicial Review of Trade Remedies:
Experiences of the Most Active WTO Members*
Edited by Müslüm Yilmaz

*The Relevant Market in International Economic Law:
A Comparative Antitrust and GATT Analysis*
Christian A. Melischek

*International Organizations in WTO Dispute
Settlement: How Much Institutional Sensitivity?*
Marina Foltea

*Public Services and International Trade Liberalization:
Human Rights and Gender Implications*
Barnali Choudhury

*The Law and Politics of WTO Waivers: Stability and
Flexibility in Public International Law*
Isabel Feichtner

African Regional Trade Agreements as Legal Regimes
James Thuo Gathii

*Liberalizing International Trade after Doha: Multilateral,
Plurilateral, Regional, and Unilateral Initiatives*
David A. Gantz

*Processes and Production Methods (PPMs) in WTO
Law: Interfacing Trade and Social Goals*
Christiane R. Conrad

Non-discrimination in International Trade in Services: 'Likeness' in WTO/GATS
Nicolas F. Diebold

The Law, Economics and Politics of Retaliation in WTO Dispute Settlement
Edited by Chad P. Bown and Joost Pauwelyn

The Multilateralization of International Investment Law
Stephan W. Schill

*Trade Policy Flexibility and Enforcement in the
WTO: A Law and Economics Analysis*
Simon A.B. Schropp

TRANSPARENCY IN THE WTO SPS AND TBT AGREEMENTS

The Real Jewel in the WTO's Crown

MARIANNA B. KARTTUNEN

OECD

CAMBRIDGE
UNIVERSITY PRESS

University Printing House, Cambridge CB2 8BS, United Kingdom

One Liberty Plaza, 20th Floor, New York, NY 10006, USA

477 Williamstown Road, Port Melbourne, VIC 3207, Australia

314–321, 3rd Floor, Plot 3, Splendor Forum, Jasola District Centre, New Delhi - 110025, India

103 Penang Road, #05-06/07, Visioncrest Commercial, Singapore 238467

Cambridge University Press is part of the University of Cambridge.

It furthers the University's mission by disseminating knowledge in the pursuit of education, learning and research at the highest international levels of excellence.

www.cambridge.org
Information on this title: www.cambridge.org/9781108732376
DOI: 10.1017/9781108762946

© Marianna B. Karttunen 2020

This publication is in copyright. Subject to statutory exception and to the provisions of relevant collective licensing agreements, no reproduction of any part may take place without the written permission of Cambridge University Press.

First published 2020
First paperback edition 2022

A catalogue record for this publication is available from the British Library

ISBN 978-1-108-48645-3 Hardback
ISBN 978-1-108-73237-6 Paperback

Cambridge University Press has no responsibility for the persistence or accuracy of URLs for external or third-party internet websites referred to in this publication, and does not guarantee that any content on such websites is, or will remain, accurate or appropriate.

To Nicolas and Léonard, in memory
of the oceans we have crossed together
and in anticipation of the many yet to come

CONTENTS

List of Figures   xii
List of Tables   xiv
Foreword   xv
Acknowledgements   xvii
List of Abbreviations   xx
Table of Cases   xxii
Country Classification   xxvii

Introduction   1
   I Why Have Transparency Obligations within the WTO System?   2
   II An Overview of Transparency within the WTO   4
   III Transparency in the SPS and TBT Agreements: A Case Study of Right-to-Know, Targeted and Interactive Transparency in the WTO   8
   IV Important Fields of Study outside the Scope of This Book   11
   V An Overview of the Book's Structure   19

PART I   **Why the SPS and TBT Agreements? A Legal Framework in Support of Regulatory Quality**   21

   1 **The Legal Principles Applying to Domestic Regulations under the SPS and TBT Agreements: Finding a Balance between Regulatory Autonomy and Free Trade**   23
      I The Scope of the SPS and TBT Agreements   25
      II The Justification of Domestic Measures   30
      III The Prohibition of Discrimination within the Limits of Regulatory Autonomy   38

CONTENTS

2 Transparency as a Core Principle under the SPS and TBT Agreements   46
    I   The Purpose of Transparency under the SPS and TBT Agreements: Information, Predictability and Dialogue   47
    II   The Scope of Transparency Obligations: Proposed Regulations Diverging from International Standards with a Significant Effect on Trade   51
    III   A Typology of Transparency Tools under the SPS and TBT Agreements: Decentralised, Centralised and Collaborative Transparency   62

3 International Regulatory Co-operation under the SPS and TBT Agreements   100
    I   What Is International Regulatory Co-operation?   101
    II   International Regulatory Co-operation Encouraged under the SPS and TBT Agreements   104
    III   International Regulatory Co-operation Enabled by the SPS and TBT Institutional Framework   118

Conclusion of Part I   129

PART II Transparency as a Substitute for Dispute Settlement: The Most Effective Compliance Tool in the WTO?   131

4 The Steps in the WTO Disputing Pyramid: From Domestic Measures to Disputes   137
    I   The Base of the Pyramid: Centralised Access to the Measures of All WTO Members   138
    II   From Centralised Information to Regulatory Dialogue   155
    III   Behind the Scenes: The Private Sector's Role in Measuring the Impacts of Domestic Regulations   166

5 The Content of the WTO Disputing Pyramid: What Do Members Need to Know to Prevent Disputes from Arising?   174
    I   The Trend Underlying STCs: Understanding Domestic Regulation among WTO Members   175
    II   The Broader Content of STCs: Transparency, Regulatory Co-operation and Practical Impediments to Trade   178
    III   When Is Transparency Enough? Those Cases that Do not Escalate to Formal Dispute Settlement   207

Conclusion of Part II   214

PART III Transparency as a Complement to
Dispute Settlement: Information and Dialogue
towards a Mutually Acceptable Solution   217

6   Transparency and Disputes: Where Is the Difference?   219
    I   From STCs to Requests for Consultations:
        A Systematic Sequence?   220
    II SPS and TBT Requests for Consultations:
        An Overview of Transparency Steps   233

7   Climbing the WTO Disputing Pyramid: The Challenges
    Leading up to Disputes   247
    I   Information about WTO-Inconsistent Measures   250
    II   The Resources Required to Access Adjudication   253
    III The Lack of Alternative Fora in which
         to Address Trade Frictions   260

8   Access to the WTO Disputing Pyramid: The 'Transparency
    Staircase'   265
    I   Information about Other Members' Regulations   266
    II   Resources   272
    III Alternative Fora and Negotiating Capacity   273

9   Is the Current Interaction between Transparency
    and Dispute Settlement the Best It Can Be?   274
    I   Improving the Availability of Information   278
    II Enhancing the Scope and Benefits
        of Regulatory Co-operation   286

    Conclusion of Part III   292

    Conclusion   294
    Appendices   301
    References   304
    Index   316

FIGURES

2.1 STCs discussed per TBT Committee meeting, 2008–2017 98
2.2 STCs discussed per SPS Committee meeting, 2008–2017 98
3.1 Applying GRPs to the lifecycle of TBT and SPS measures 117
3.2 Opportunities for co-operation throughout policy cycle 120
P2.1 Disputing pyramid 134
P2.2 SPS and TBT disputing pyramid, from transparency to dispute settlement, 1995–2018 135
4.1 Total TBT notifications, 1995–2018 140
4.2 Total SPS notifications, 1995–2018 140
4.3 Share of TBT notifications subject to follow-up, 1995–2015 141
4.4 TBT notifications, by development status, 1995–2015 142
4.5 SPS notifications, by development status, 1995–2015 143
4.6 Average time period left for comments after TBT notifications by Members, 1996–2018 143
4.7 Share of SPS STCs raised against non-notified measures, 2010–2014 151
4.8 Share of TBT STCs raised against non-notified measures, 1995–2018 152
4.9 Share of SPS STCs raised against non-notified measures by country group, 2010–2014 153
4.10 Share of TBT STCs raised against non-notified measures by country group, 2010–2014 153
4.11 Trends in TBT notifications and STCs, 1995–2018 157
4.12 Trends in SPS notifications and STCs, 1995–2018 158
4.13 Number of TBT STCs relating to non-notified measures 159
4.14 Number of SPS STCs relating to non-notified measures 160
4.15 Number of EU comments on notifications and STCs raised, 2003–2014 161
4.16 Number of EU measures subject to comments on notifications and to STCs, 2003–2014 161
4.17 TBT STCs and bilateral discussions 164
4.18 SPS STCs and bilateral discussions 164
5.1 Types of issue raised in SPS STCs, as share of total SPS STCs, 2010–2014 176
5.2 Types of issue raised in TBT STCs, as share of total TBT STCs, 2010–2014 176
5.3 STCs about actual or potential trade effects 178

LIST OF FIGURES

6.1 SPS requests for consultations preceded by STCs, 1995–2018   221
6.2 TBT requests for consultations preceded by STCs, 1995–2018   224
6.3 Issues raised in TBT STCs and requests for consultations   225
6.4 Issues raised in SPS STCs and requests for consultations   225

TABLES

4.1 Members submitting notifications through TBT NSS, 2014–2015   146
4.2 Countries submitting comments on EU notifications, 2010–2014   156
6.1 Participation in SPS STCs, 2010–2014   230
6.2 Participation in SPS requests for consultations, 1995–2018   231
6.3 Participation in TBT STCs, 2010–2014   234
6.4 Participation in TBT requests for consultations, 1995–2018   235
6.5 WTO disputes with major SPS claims   236
6.6 WTO disputes with major TBT claims   238
7.1 Complainants and respondents in SPS requests for consultations, 1995–2018   255
7.2 Complainants and respondents in TBT requests for consultations, 1995–2018   255
8.1 SPS and TBT transparency mechanisms in response to information needed in the pre-litigation phase   267

FOREWORD

The relationship between transparency and adjudication has been the focus of analysis for economists, political scientists and lawyers alike. Marianna Karttunen has brought all this work under one roof and added her own perspective. This is nothing short of the most comprehensive and penetrating volume discussing transparency in the new-generation agreements dealing with domestic policies, the WTO Agreements on the Application of Sanitary and Phytosanitary Measures (the SPS Agreement, or SPS) and on Technical Barriers to Trade (the TBT Agreement, or TBT). The author has provided a one-stop shop in which the rationale for transparency is adequately explained and its impact on litigation is clarified.

The SPS and TBT Agreements are used in fact as a test bed for the author to examine the validity of theories regarding the relationship between transparency and adjudication, and more precisely whether they are complements or substitutes, or both. Specific trade concerns (STCs), a hybrid between transparency and adjudication, provided her with the most appropriate tool to explore this relationship. An ever-increasing number of STCs has led to an ever-decreasing number of TBT/SPS disputes. The latter, nevertheless, could also be the result of increased predictability of case law as a result of jurisprudential evolution and/or the increasing number of free trade areas (FTAs) with provisions on this score, as well as many other factors.

One thing is clear though: STCs have contributed in reducing trade friction and there is wide acceptance of the usefulness of STCs – otherwise why contemplate emulating this mechanism in other areas/agreements dealing with non-tariff barriers?

What the author masterfully shows with her work is how STCs have become the antechamber for a better understanding of regulatory choices and how they have enhanced regulatory co-operation. Even within a context of negative (shallow) integration, like the WTO, with no institutional watchdog overlooking consistency of national policies, never mind positive integration, STCs have managed to provide a pathway that allows affected third parties to become familiar with national preferences.

A lot still remains to be done and the author points, in the last chapter of Part III of this volume, to the work that lies ahead, suggesting ways of addressing current observed inadequacies. This volume is must-read work not only for those who want to familiarise themselves with the TBT/SPS systems of transparency and adjudication but also every one interested in exploring the relationship between transparency and adjudication in general.

Petros C. Mavroidis
Edwin B. Parker Professor of Law
Columbia Law School, New York

ACKNOWLEDGEMENTS

This book – adapted from the PhD dissertation I defended in December 2016 – would never have seen the light of day without the immense support I received from my family, friends and colleagues.

I am most indebted to Petros C. Mavroidis for his devoted supervision and endless encouragement. It is thanks to his vision and masterful knowledge of the WTO that I came to appreciate the importance and complexity of transparency within the multilateral trading system. It was a great privilege to benefit from his guidance, and I owe him my profound gratitude for making my PhD research such a fascinating and pleasurable experience.

From the very early stages of my research, I also benefited from invaluable advice from Robert Wolfe. I am very grateful to him for his precious counsel, our numerous exchanges and his continued enthusiasm about my research.

I also wish to thank Bernard Hoekman and André Sapir for their careful consideration of my dissertation as part of my examination board and for their insightful reports, which have been of great assistance in the preparation of this book.

The European University Institute offered me an extraordinary setting in which to conduct research and write, not least thanks to the wonderful colleagues whom I met there. I remain very appreciative of Jonathan Chevry's recommendation to embark on the beautiful Tuscan adventure and thank all the great friends I made along the way for making this researcher's life less lonely. I thank my dearest friend and colleague Leticia Díez Sanchez, whose admirable passion for multidisciplinary research inspired me to explore new perspectives and whose insights influenced me greatly throughout my thesis. I am also very thankful to have been part of the 'Franco-Finnish writing group' led by Nicola Hargreaves, with François Delerue, Harri Ruohomäki and the lovely Frau Papazian. I thank them all for their time, patience and useful feedback. Many thanks also to Katia Soboul for her kind support, and to Laurence Duranel for her help in submitting my final draft and preparing my defence.

My research benefited greatly from the privilege of an internship at the WTO Trade and Environment Division, working on technical barriers to trade. During this experience, Úna Flanagan, Devin McDaniels and Erik Wijkström taught me immense amounts about the reality of the work within the WTO Secretariat. I am extremely grateful for their guidance and support during my internship and ever since.

I thank Erik Wijkström in particular for facilitating my contact with delegations to the TBT Committee, and hence helping me to interview Ms Barreda, Ms Beharry, Mr Brits, Mr Buvinic Alarcon, M Corrêa, Ms Ikonya, M Opiyo, M Parent, Mr Sacchetti, Mr Srivastava, Mr Sun and Mr Zubkov. These interviews were part of my survey on the role of the private sector in ensuring transparency of TBT measures. They were crucial for my understanding of transparency in practice and I reiterate my thanks to all respondents.

More broadly, throughout my thesis, I conducted a number of interviews that influenced me greatly. In this context, I would like to thank Véronique Bastien, Alejandro Jara, Iza Lejárraga, Lauro Locks, Niall Meagher, Roland Mollerus, Denise Prévost, David Shark, Gretchen Stanton, Ludivine Tamiotti and Christiane Wolff for sharing their invaluable experience and insights with me.

When transforming my thesis into a book, I received very kind support from the editing and publishing teams at Cambridge University Press, in particular Marianne Nield and Chloe Quinn. I am also very thankful to Vanessa Plaister for her thorough copy-editing, and her patience and understanding throughout the process.

Finally, I wish to thank all those who accompanied me in my transition to and return from my postgraduate degree.

I must start by thanking my first economics professor Yvan Berrebi, without whom the world of international organisations would still be a distant fantasy for me. I am deeply saddened not to be able to share this book with him and I will remember very dearly his endless support from high school years until the end of my graduate studies.

I owe a heartfelt thank you to my past and present OECD colleagues from whom I learned so much in the very first steps of my career and who have given me a warm welcome back. I am extremely grateful to Céline Kauffmann, who has not only taught me enormously about international regulatory co-operation but also given me immeasurable support in the last phases of the drafting of both the PhD and the final book manuscript. I thank Mercy DeMenno for her valuable insights, helping me to take the leap in submitting my manuscript proposal and embarking on the exciting publication process. I also thank my dear Hélène François for her attentive listening, her patient advice and her generous friendship.

Most of all, I thank my family, who gave me the ambition and courage to undertake a doctoral degree and supported me in the additional endeavour of transforming it into a book. My husband Nicolas Saint Bris has remained positive and supportive throughout my emotional PhD rollercoaster, offering infinite patience and understanding. This book will always remind me of happy memories of our wedding and our lives in Florence, Nairobi, Geneva and finally Paris, until the very last moments before the arrival of our little Léonard. I am ever so grateful that he never ceased to believe in me. My admiration for my parents Muriel and Anssi Karttunen has pushed me to constantly aim for greater dreams. They are the root of my confidence in the future and I thank them for always standing by my side, helping me through difficult times and praising my achievements. Finally, these acknowledgements would not be complete without a tribute to my beloved Hamlet, who has brought to me only joy (and a few rubber toys).

Despite the sincere gratitude I express to everyone mentioned, the views and mistakes in this book are exclusively my own.

ABBREVIATIONS

ACWL	Advisory Centre on WTO Law
APEC	Asia-Pacific Economic Co-operation
AQSIQ	General Administration of Quality Supervision, Inspection and Quarantine (China)
ASCM	Agreement on Subsidies and Countervailing Measures (WTO)
ASF	African swine fever
BRICS	Brazil, Russia, India, China and South Africa
BTA	bilateral trade agreement
CAP	conformity assessment procedure
CETA	Comprehensive Economic and Trade Agreement (EU–Canada)
COOL	certain country of origin labelling
CPTPP	Comprehensive and Progressive Agreement for Trans-Pacific Partnership
DSB	Dispute Settlement Body (WTO)
DSU	Dispute Settlement Understanding (WTO)
ECJ	European Court of Justice
EU	European Union
FDA	Food and Drug Administration (US)
FTA	free trade agreement
GATS	General Agreement on Trade in Services
GATT	General Agreement on Tariffs and Trade
GCC	Gulf Co-operation Council
GDP	gross domestic product
G-Mark	Gulf Conformity Mark (GCC)
GMOs	genetically modified organisms
GMP	Good Manufacturing Practices (Brazil)
GNP	gross national production
GRPs	Good Regulatory Practices
IEC	International Electrotechnical Commission
IGO	intergovernmental organisation

LIST OF ABBREVIATIONS

IMS	Information Management System (WTO)
IPPC	International Plant Protection Convention
IRC	International Regulatory Co-operation (OECD)
ISO	International Organization for Standardization
ITC	International Trade Centre
LDCs	least-developed countries
MRA	mutual recognition agreement
MRLs	maximum residual limits
NAMA	non-agricultural market access
NGO	non-governmental organisation
NSS	Notification Submission System (WTO)
OECD	Organisation for Economic Co-operation and Development
OIE	World Organisation for Animal Health
PPMs	processes and production methods
PRA	pest risk analysis
PTA	preferential trade agreement
REACH	registration, evaluation, authorisation and restriction of chemicals
RIA	regulatory impact assessment
RTA	regional trade agreement
SPS	sanitary and phytosanitary
SPS Agreement	Agreement on the Application of Sanitary and Phytosanitary Measures (WTO)
STC	specific trade concern
TBT	technical barrier to trade
TBT Agreement	Agreement on Technical Barriers to Trade (WTO)
TFA	Trade Facilitation Agreement (WTO)
TPP	Trans-Pacific Partnership
TPRB	Trade Policy Review Body
TPRM	Trade Policy Review Mechanism
TPR	trade policy review
TRIPS	Agreement on Trade-Related Aspects of Intellectual Property Rights (WTO)
TTIP	Transatlantic Trade and Investment Partnership
UNDESA	United Nations Department of Economic and Social Affairs
USDA	US Department of Agriculture
USMCA	United States–Mexico–Canada Agreement
WHO	World Health Organization
WIRSPA	West Indies Rum and Spirits Producers' Association
WTO	World Trade Organization

TABLE OF CASES

Australia – Apples	Appellate Body Report, Australia – Measures Affecting the Importation of Apples from New Zealand, WT/DS367/AB/R, adopted 17 December 2010, DSR 2010:V, p. 2175
Australia – Apples	Panel Report, Australia – Measures Affecting the Importation of Apples from New Zealand, WT/DS367/R, adopted 17 December 2010, as modified by Appellate Body Report WT/DS367/AB/R, DSR 2010:VI, p. 2371
Australia – Salmon	Appellate Body Report, Australia – Measures Affecting Importation of Salmon, WT/DS18/AB/R, adopted 6 November 1998, DSR 1998:VIII, p. 3327
Australia – Salmon	Panel Report, Australia – Measures Affecting Importation of Salmon – Recourse to Article 21.5 of the DSU by Canada, WT/DS18/RW, adopted 20 March 2000, DSR 2000:IV, p. 2031
Australia – Salmon	Panel Report, Australia – Measures Affecting Importation of Salmon, WT/DS18/R and Corr.1, adopted 6 November 1998, as modified by Appellate Body Report WT/DS18/AB/R, DSR 1998:VIII, p. 3407
Canada – Aircraft	Appellate Body Report, Canada – Measures Affecting the Export of Civilian Aircraft, WT/DS70/AB/R, adopted 20 August 1999, DSR 1999:III, p. 1377
Chile – Price Band System	Appellate Body Report, Chile – Price Band System and Safeguard Measures Relating to Certain Agricultural Products, WT/DS207/AB/R, adopted 23 October 2002, DSR 2002:VIII, p. 3045 (Corr.1, DSR 2006:XII, p. 5473)

EC – Approval and Marketing of Biotech Products	Panel Reports, European Communities – Measures Affecting the Approval and Marketing of Biotech Products, WT/DS291/R, Add.1 to Add.9 and Corr.1 / WT/DS292/R, Add.1 to Add.9 and Corr.1 / WT/DS293/R, Add.1 to Add.9 and Corr.1, adopted 21 November 2006, DSR 2006:III, p. 847
EC – Asbestos	Appellate Body Report, European Communities – Measures Affecting Asbestos and Asbestos-Containing Products, WT/DS135/AB/R, adopted 5 April 2001, DSR 2001:VII, p. 3243
EC – Hormones	Appellate Body Report, European Communities – Measures Concerning Meat and Meat Products (Hormones), WT/DS26/AB/R, WT/DS48/AB/R, adopted 13 February 1998, DSR 1998:I, p. 135
EC – Hormones	Panel Reports, European Communities – Measures Concerning Meat and Meat Products (Hormones), WT/DS48/R/CAN (Canada) / WT/DS26/R/USA (US), adopted 13 February 1998, as modified by Appellate Body Report WT/DS26/AB/R, WT/DS48/AB/R, DSR 1998:II, p. 235 / DSR 1998:II, p. 699
EC – IT Products	Panel Reports, European Communities and Its Member States – Tariff Treatment of Certain Information Technology Products, WT/DS375/R / WT/DS376/R / WT/DS377/R, adopted 21 September 2010, DSR 2010:III, p. 933
EC – Sardines	Appellate Body Report, European Communities – Trade Description of Sardines, WT/DS231/AB/R, adopted 23 October 2002, DSR 2002:VIII, p. 3359
EC – Sardines	Panel Report, European Communities – Trade Description of Sardines, WT/DS231/R and Corr.1, adopted 23 October 2002, as modified by Appellate Body Report WT/DS231/AB/R, DSR 2002:VIII, p. 3451
EC – Selected Customs Matters	Panel Report, European Communities – Selected Customs Matters, WT/DS315/R, adopted 11 December 2006, as modified by Appellate Body Report WT/DS315/AB/R, DSR 2006:IX, p. 3915

EC – Seal Products	Appellate Body Reports, European Communities – Measures Prohibiting the Importation and Marketing of Seal Products, WT/DS400/AB/R / WT/DS401/AB/R, adopted 18 June 2014, DSR 2014:I, p. 7
EC – Seal Products	Panel Reports, European Communities – Measures Prohibiting the Importation and Marketing of Seal Products, WT/DS400/R and Add.1 / WT/DS401/R and Add.1, adopted 18 June 2014, as modified by Appellate Body Reports WT/DS400/AB/R / WT/DS401/AB/R, DSR 2014:II, p. 365
India – Agricultural Products	Appellate Body Report, India – Measures Concerning the Importation of Certain Agricultural Products, WT/DS430/AB/R, adopted 19 June 2015, DSR 2015:V, p. 2459
India – Agricultural Products	Panel Report, India – Measures Concerning the Importation of Certain Agricultural Products, WT/DS430/R and Add.1, adopted 19 June 2015, as modified by Appellate Body Report WT/DS430/AB/R, DSR 2015:V, p. 2663
Japan – Agricultural Products II	Appellate Body Report, Japan – Measures Affecting Agricultural Products, WT/DS76/AB/R, adopted 19 March 1999, DSR 1999:I, p. 277
Japan – Agricultural Products II	Panel Report, Japan – Measures Affecting Agricultural Products, WT/DS76/R, adopted 19 March 1999, as modified by Appellate Body Report WT/DS76/AB/R, DSR 1999:I, p. 315
Japan – Apples	Appellate Body Report, Japan – Measures Affecting the Importation of Apples, WT/DS245/AB/R, adopted 10 December 2003, DSR 2003:IX, p. 4391
Japan – Apples	Panel Report, Japan – Measures Affecting the Importation of Apples, WT/DS245/R, adopted 10 December 2003
Japan – Film	Panel Report, Japan – Measures Affecting Consumer Photographic Film and Paper, WT/DS44/R, adopted 22 April 1998, DSR 1998:IV, p. 1179
Korea – Alcoholic Beverages	Panel Report, Korea – Taxes on Alcoholic Beverages, WT/DS75/R, WT/DS84/R, adopted 17 February 1999, as modified by Appellate Body Report WT/DS75/AB/R, WT/DS84/AB/R, DSR 1999:I, p. 44

Korea – Bovine Meat (Canada)	Panel Report, Korea – Measures Affecting the Importation of Bovine Meat and Meat Products from Canada, WT/DS391/R, 3 July 2012, unadopted
Korea – Radionuclides	Appellate Body Report, Korea – Import Bans, and Testing and Certification Requirements for Radionuclides, WT/DS495/AB/R and Add.1, circulated to WTO Members 11 April 2019 [adoption pending]
Russia – Pigs (EU)	Appellate Body Report, Russian Federation – Measures on the Importation of Live Pigs, Pork and Other Pig Products from the European Union, WT/DS475/AB/R and Add.1, adopted 21 March 2017, DSR 2017:I, p. 207
Russia – Pigs (EU)	Panel Report, Russian Federation – Measures on the Importation of Live Pigs, Pork and Other Pig Products from the European Union, WT/DS475/R and Add.1, adopted 21 March 2017, as modified by Appellate Body Report WT/DS475/AB/R, DSR 2017:II, p. 361
US – Animals	Panel Report, United States – Measures Affecting the Importation of Animals, Meat and Other Animal Products from Argentina, WT/DS447/R and Add.1, adopted 31 August 2015, DSR 2015:VIII, p. 4085
US – Clove Cigarettes	Appellate Body Report, United States – Measures Affecting the Production and Sale of Clove Cigarettes, WT/DS406/AB/R, adopted 24 April 2012, DSR 2012:XI, p. 5751
US – Clove Cigarettes	Panel Report, United States – Measures Affecting the Production and Sale of Clove Cigarettes, WT/DS406/R, adopted 24 April 2012, as modified by Appellate Body Report WT/DS406/AB/R, DSR 2012:XI, p. 5865
US – COOL	Appellate Body Reports, United States – Certain Country of Origin Labelling (COOL) Requirements, WT/DS384/AB/R / WT/DS386/AB/R, adopted 23 July 2012, DSR 2012:V, p. 2449

US – COOL	Panel Reports, United States – Certain Country of Origin Labelling (COOL) Requirements, WT/DS384/R / WT/DS386/R, adopted 23 July 2012, as modified by Appellate Body Reports WT/DS384/AB/R / WT/DS386/AB/R, DSR 2012:VI, p. 2745
US – Poultry (China)	Panel Report, United States – Certain Measures Affecting Imports of Poultry from China, WT/DS392/R, adopted 25 October 2010, DSR 2010:V, p. 1909
US – Shrimp	Appellate Body Report, United States – Import Prohibition of Certain Shrimp and Shrimp Products, WT/DS58/AB/R, adopted 6 November 1998, DSR 1998:VII, p. 2755
US – Tuna II (Mexico)	Appellate Body Report, United States – Measures Concerning the Importation, Marketing and Sale of Tuna and Tuna Products, WT/DS381/AB/R, adopted 13 June 2012, DSR 2012:IV, p. 1837
US – Tuna II (Mexico)	Panel Report, United States – Measures Concerning the Importation, Marketing and Sale of Tuna and Tuna Products, WT/DS381/R, adopted 13 June 2012, as modified by Appellate Body Report WT/DS381/AB/R, DSR 2012:IV, p. 2013
US – Underwear	Appellate Body Report, United States – Restrictions on Imports of Cotton and Man-Made Fibre Underwear, WT/DS24/AB/R, adopted 25 February 1997, DSR 1997:I, p. 11
US – Underwear	Panel Report, United States – Restrictions on Imports of Cotton and Man-Made Fibre Underwear, WT/DS24/R, adopted 25 February 1997, as modified by Appellate Body Report WT/DS24/AB/R, DSR 1997:I, p. 31
US – Wool Shirts and Blouses	Appellate Body Report, United States – Measure Affecting Imports of Woven Wool Shirts and Blouses from India, WT/DS33/AB/R, adopted 23 May 1997, and Corr.1, DSR 1997:I, p. 323

COUNTRY CLASSIFICATION

This country classification is used throughout the book to reflect the WTO Members active in the WTO transparency and dispute settlement mechanisms, beyond the traditional division between developed and developing countries and least-developed countries. It adds nuance to definitions of developed and developing countries, and therefore aims to distinguish those who truly engage in the system from those who remain passive.

BRICS   Brazil; Russia; India; China; South Africa

DEV   (Developing countries) Albania; Antigua and Barbuda; Argentina; Armenia; Bahrain; Barbados; Belize; Bolivia; Botswana; Brunei Darussalam; Cabo Verde; Cameroon; Colombia; Congo; Costa Rica; Côte d'Ivoire; Cuba; Cyprus; Dominica; Dominican Republic; Ecuador; Egypt; El Salvador; Fiji; Gabon; Georgia; Ghana; Grenada; Guatemala; Guyana; Honduras; Indonesia; Jamaica; Jordan; Kenya; State of Kuwait; Kyrgyz Republic; Macao; Malaysia; Maldives; Malta; Mauritius; Moldova; Mongolia; Montenegro; Morocco; Namibia; Nicaragua; Nigeria; Oman; Pakistan; Panama; Papua New Guinea; Paraguay; Peru; Philippines; Qatar; Saint Kitts and Nevis; Saint Lucia; Saint Vincent and the Grenadines; Samoa; Saudi Arabia; Sri Lanka; Suriname; Swaziland; Chinese Taipei; Tajikistan; Thailand; The Former Yugoslav Republic of Macedonia; Tonga; Trinidad and Tobago; Tunisia; Ukraine; United Arab Emirates; Uruguay; Venezuela; Viet Nam; Zimbabwe

G2   EU; US

IND   (OECD Members and other industrialised countries) Australia; Canada; Chile; Hong Kong, China; Iceland; Israel; Japan; Korea; Luxembourg; Liechtenstein; Mexico; New Zealand; Norway; Singapore; Switzerland; Turkey

LDCs[1]   (Least-developed countries) Afghanistan; Angola; Bangladesh; Benin; Burkina Faso; Burundi; Cambodia; Central African Republic; Chad; Democratic Republic of the Congo; Djibouti; The Gambia; Guinea; Guinea-Bissau; Haiti; Lao People's Democratic Republic; Lesotho; Madagascar; Malawi; Mali; Mauritania; Mozambique; Myanmar; Nepal; Niger; Rwanda; Senegal; Sierra Leone; Solomon Islands; Tanzania; Togo; Uganda; Vanuatu; Yemen; Zambia

[1] This list comprises the WTO Members who are considered LDCs according to the United Nations Conference on Trade and Development (UNCTAD). http://unctad.org/en/pages/aldc/Least%20Developed%20Countries/UN-list-of-Least-Developed-Countries.aspx.

Introduction

> If the broad light of day could be let in upon men's actions, it would purify them as the sun disinfects.
>
> Louis D. Brandeis (1891)

With these words, Associate Supreme Court Justice Louis Brandeis gave voice to the pioneers introducing transparency into the American legal system. His metaphor of sunlight and its 'disinfectant' benefits has been cited extensively in domestic law in favour of transparency policies and their potential advantages. Recently, Mavroidis and Wolfe have applied this image in the context of the World Trade Organization (WTO), noting that 'transparency contributes more to social order than does coercion' and that '[t]ransparency ought to improve the operation of the trading system by allowing verification by all Members that national law, policy, and implementation achieve the objective intended by the agreements'.[1]

Taking this now-famous image as its starting point, this book explores the provisions set out in two WTO agreements that establish an obligation of transparency, aiming to 'purify' or 'disinfect' domestic trade regulations. In other words, it examines the provisions that encourage WTO Members to share information in a way that results in better compliance with WTO obligations.

This book argues that, in the specific contexts of the WTO Agreements on the Application of Sanitary and Phytosanitary Measures (the SPS Agreement, or SPS) and on Technical Barriers to Trade (the TBT Agreement, or TBT), transparency has a crucial role to play, acting both as a substitute for and a complement to dispute settlement. On the one hand, Members use it to ensure that trade policies are predictable, to improve the quality of domestic policies by means of co-operation and to address

---

[1] Petros C. Mavroidis and Robert Wolfe, 'From Sunshine to a Common Agent: The Evolving Understanding of Transparency in the WTO', RSCAS Research Paper No. PP 2015/01/Columbia Public Law Research Paper No. 14-461, 25 April 2015, 9. http://papers.ssrn.com/abstract=2569178.

trade frictions before they escalate to the level of formal dispute. As such, transparency is a substitute for dispute settlement because it defuses tensions and prevents formal disputes from arising. On the other hand, in those few cases in which frictions persist, the information gathered at the different levels of transparency can support Members raising a dispute. Transparency in relation to SPS and TBT measures is essential if all Members are to be able to settle such cases and to pursue dialogue alongside formal dispute proceedings. Transparency therefore complements dispute settlement by equalising Members' access to the WTO Dispute Settlement Body (DSB).

The underlying aim of this book is to show that the strength of the WTO legal system goes beyond its dispute settlement mechanisms. Indeed, while the DSB is a unique achievement in terms of enforcing obligations among sovereign States, the transparency obligations established under the SPS and TBT Agreements allow Members themselves to co-operate and monitor their own and others' implementation of the same. As such, the transparency framework established under the SPS and TBT Agreements is particularly relevant in ensuring coherence among domestic regulations without requiring the convergence of domestic policies.

I Why Have Transparency Obligations within the WTO System?

The multilateral trading system is characterised today by a fragmentation of production cycles across different countries and companies in what is commonly referred to as 'global value chains', multiplying the regulations applicable to the goods and services traded. Consider cigarettes. At the very outset, tobacco plants may be subject to measures restricting genetic engineering or the pesticides used in their production, such restrictions aiming to protect the environment and limit the effects on human health. The chemicals and additives used during processing of the tobacco leaves may be subject to specific limitations, aiming to mitigate the impact their use may have on human health and safety. The design of the cigarettes' packaging may also be subject to certain conditions requiring labels that inform consumers of the risks that cigarettes pose to their health. Finally, imported cigarettes may be subject to a tariff, aiming to control their flow into the country.

From a trade perspective, all these measures represent obvious added costs for the companies producing the cigarettes and seeking to sell them in different markets. The tariff imposed at the border when cigarettes are imported is the most typical form of 'trade barrier' addressed by signatories to the General Agreement on Tariffs and Trade (GATT) since 1947 and its level is the subject of negotiations among the parties. The legality of such tariffs is therefore relatively simple to determine, because it depends on the concessions agreed to by the country in question. In the case of the cigarettes, the other three types of measure described, which aim to protect the environment, protect human health or mandate consumer information, concern conditions for the sale of cigarettes in a specific market and therefore represent measures 'beyond the border'. In the GATT of 1947, they were restricted only to the extent that they were discriminatory. In other words, Members could decide on whichever policies they thought relevant as long as they applied them equally to both domestic and foreign producers. However, as countries became increasingly conscious of the significant costs of trade that domestic regulations could represent, additional agreements were negotiated and concluded under the auspices of what became the WTO in 1995.[2]

The SPS Agreement and the TBT Agreement are two particularly relevant WTO instruments in relation to our cigarettes example. Broadly speaking, the SPS Agreement applies to domestic regulations aiming to protect human, animal and plant life and health, while the TBT Agreement applies to measures aiming to protect human, animal or plant life or health and the environment, or to prevent deceptive practices. Both Agreements underline WTO Members' freedom to adopt domestic measures to fulfil these objectives, while setting out some conditions that aim to preclude such measures being unnecessarily restrictive of international trade or discriminatory against foreign producers.

This 'negative integration' approach – whereby Members agree to fulfil certain obligations, but remain free to determine what specific policies to apply domestically – results in a highly heterogeneous regulatory environment, with as many regulations and policy issues as there are countries, all of which have the potential to affect trade.

To mitigate the unnecessary trade costs resulting from that heterogeneity, the drafters of the SPS and TBT Agreements introduced a transparency framework that fosters coherence between Members' policies by facilitating regulatory co-operation at the early stages of the domestic policy cycle. A system of information and dialogue centred on the WTO Secretariat

---

[2] GATT Contracting Parties became conscious of the 'non-tariff barrier' problem at the end of the 1960s, realising that, beyond those measures that were outright illegal, there were also a number of 'legal' non-tariff barriers that called into question the scope of the GATT. See Robert E. Hudec, *The GATT Legal System and World Trade Diplomacy* (Salem, NH: Butterworth Legal, 1990), 231–2.

and available to all 164 WTO Members positions SPS and TBT transparency as a crucial factor both aligning domestic approaches when possible and ensuring the quality of domestic measures, as well as granting public access to information when different policies might be proposed.

In this sense, the 'transparency' on which this book focuses is about the sharing of domestic regulations and the rights that this entails for other Members, as expressed in the notions of 'regulatory transparency' or 'reasoned transparency'.

At the domestic level, *regulatory* transparency can be defined as 'the capacity of regulated entities to express views on, identify, and understand their obligations under the rule of law'.[3] The regulatory transparency mandated under the WTO system not only implies parity of benefits across regulated entities but also allows WTO Members to exercise their rights to identify, express views on and understand their obligations to other Members and interested parties.

Regulatory transparency therefore involves something more than a simple disclosure of information, aiming instead to engender a deeper understanding. Coglianese describes this as *'reasoned* transparency' – something more than what he calls simple 'fishbowl transparency' – and this deeper transparency 'demands that government officials offer explicit explanations for their actions'.[4] For Coglianese, '[s]ound explanations will be based on application of normative principles to the facts and evidence accumulated by decision makers – and will show why other alternative courses of action were rejected'.[5] Only with these 'sound explanations' will the observer achieve insights into the decision-makers' rationale.

II An Overview of Transparency within the WTO

To illustrate the variety of transparency tools available within the WTO, we can describe the different forms of transparency as a three-generation process through which transparency mechanisms adapt to the growing range of areas covered by WTO agreements, benefiting from the institutionalisation of the WTO, while also following trends in transparency

---

[3] Evdokia Moïsé, 'Transparency Mechanisms and Non-tariff Measures', OECD Trade Policy Papers No. 111, 1 April 2011, 26. www.oecd-ilibrary.org/content/workingpaper/5kgf0rzzwfq3-en.

[4] Cary Coglianese, 'The Transparency President? The Obama Administration and Open Government', *Governance* 22, no. 4 (2009): 529–44.

[5] Ibid.

policies at the national level.[6] It is important to note that this classification into three generations does not denote any hierarchy between the transparency measures; rather, the measures 'have proven complementary and overlapping'.[7]

A   Right-to-Know Transparency: The Availability of Information

The first-generation transparency provisions are those that respond to a 'right to know', essentially requiring open access to government practice, so that governments can be accountable for their actions. In the GATT integration process, this corresponds to those transparency measures that emerged during the early stages of the GATT. With the GATT's focus then on reducing tariff barriers, the transparency mechanism most referred to at that time was publication of the ceilings that the Contracting Parties negotiated for their import tariffs, known as 'schedules of concessions'.

Article X GATT on the publication and administration of laws – today considered to be the general transparency provision – was also included in the GATT 1947, but it played a limited role in terms of transparency, equivalent only to the first 'right to know' laws in the United States.[8] Panels referred to it as a 'subsidiary' claim[9] and Contracting Parties preferred to base their claims on more 'substantive' provisions, such as Article XI on quantitative restrictions.[10]

---

[6] The three generations are mainly developed in Archon Fung, *Full Disclosure: The Perils and Promise of Transparency* (New York: Cambridge University Press, 2007). Wolfe has analysed WTO transparency provisions in light of these three generations: Robert Wolfe and Terry Collins-Williams, 'Transparency as a Trade Policy Tool: The WTO's Cloudy Windows', *World Trade Review* 9, no. 4 (2010): 551–81; Robert Wolfe, 'Letting the Sun Shine in at the WTO: How Transparency Brings the Trading System to Life', Staff Working Paper No. ERSD-2013-03, 22 November 2013. http://papers.ssrn.com/sol3/Delivery.cfm?abstractid=2229741. See also Mavroidis and Wolfe, 'From Sunshine to a Common Agent'.

[7] Fung, *Full Disclosure*, 25.

[8] Article X is said to have been adopted on the basis of a proposal made by the United States in 1946, with very similar language as that in the original US draft, inspired by its recently adopted national legislation – in particular, the US Administrative Process Act (APA) of 1946, cf. §§553 et seq.: Sylvia Ostry, 'China and the WTO Transparency Issue', *UCLA Journal of International Law and Foreign Affairs* 3, no. 1 (1998): 1–22. On right-to-know laws, see Fung, *Full Disclosure*.

[9] For example, GATT Panel Report, *Japanese Measures on Imports of Leather*, BISD 31S/94, adopted 15 May 1984 (*Japan – Leather II (US)*), esp. §57.

[10] Padideh Ala'i, 'From the Periphery to the Center? The Evolving WTO Jurisprudence on Transparency and Good Governance', *Contributions to Books*, 6 February 2010. http://works.bepress.com/padideh_alai/3.

This first-generation transparency within the WTO can also be described as 'decentralised' transparency, whereby governments are required to publish their measures with an effect on trade[11] and interested Members are expected to look for the information themselves, making access to information a costly and time-consuming process.

While first-generation transparency is essential to create a predictable trading environment, its effect on the quality of the regulation remains limited. Indeed, while some traders with in-house lawyers who closely follow the official gazettes in relevant countries may become acquainted with the published measures, in practice the majority of traders find out about changes to legislation only when researching the regulatory environment in any given country – or when their products are stopped at the border for non-compliance with the new requirements.

A more accessible source of information is therefore key if traders around the world are to be well aware of the regulations with which they must comply in each different export market. The WTO provides a privileged platform on which to centralise such information – particularly through second-generation 'targeted' transparency.

B Targeted Transparency: Access to Information

Second-generation, or 'targeted', transparency 'mandates access to precisely defined and structured factual information from private or public sources with the aim of furthering particular policy objectives'[12] and aims to provide 'facts that people want in time, places, and ways that enable them to act'.[13]

In the WTO, the second generation of transparency rose to prominence after the reforms of the Uruguay Round (1986–1994), which triggered a paradigm shift in transparency, benefiting from the establishment of the WTO. Notification obligations became more systematic and were followed up with reviews by special 'committees' within the WTO Secretariat.

---

[11] For example, Art. X GATT. The interpretation of this article has also evolved, however, from what was considered to be only a subsidiary claim under the GATT to become a 'principle of fundamental importance – that of promoting full disclosure of governmental acts affecting Members and private persons and enterprises, whether of domestic or foreign nationality': Appellate Body Report, *US – Underwear*, §20. On this evolution, see Padideh Ala'i, 'From the Periphery to the Center? The Evolving WTO Jurisprudence on Transparency and Good Governance', *Journal of International Economic Law* 11, no. 4 (2008): 779–802.

[12] Fung, *Full Disclosure*, 25.

[13] Ibid., xv.

The Trade Policy Review Mechanism (TPRM) was established, with the specific goal of contributing 'to the smoother functioning of the multilateral trading system, by achieving greater transparency in, and understanding of, the trade policies and practices of Members'.[14] The creation of the TPRM was a fundamental step by means of which the WTO guaranteed, from a central position in its institutional framework, transparency of the multilateral trading system. More broadly, the TPRM was to ensure transparency in and an understanding of trade policies and practices among all Members, improving their likely adherence to their obligations under the WTO.[15] With this major innovation, the WTO Secretariat started to increasingly 'centralise' information, assuming some responsibility for gathering the information, providing a platform for Members to discuss the measures disclosed and even eventually offering recognition of the impact of those measures on the multilateral trading system.[16]

Many new agreements were also concluded under the WTO framework, most of them including general transparency provisions, with a wide range of specific transparency requirements. This led to the further centralisation of information with the WTO Secretariat that is in evidence today. This centralised transparency covers very different types of measure and may, for example, require Members to notify their measures to the WTO Secretariat,[17] to report on their measures and submit their trade policy landscape to review by a special body,[18] or to notify any other Members not yet notified of the measures.[19]

C Interactive Transparency: Information Enabling Dialogue

Third-generation, or 'collaborative', transparency – also known as 'interactive' transparency – is based on 'efficiency of procuring information'.[20] While they aimed at improving transparency by means of centralised information, some WTO agreements also introduced transparency provisions that enable dialogue between WTO Members. The SPS and TBT Agreements are among them, requiring Members to allow

---

[14] Marrakesh Agreement, Annex III, para. A.
[15] See Annex III, para. A(i), WTO.
[16] I owe this distinction between 'centralised' and 'decentralised' transparency to conversations with Petros C. Mavroidis.
[17] For example, Art. 63.2 TRIPS.
[18] For example, Annex III, para. C(v), GATT.
[19] For example, Art. III.5 GATS.
[20] Mavroidis and Wolfe, 'From Sunshine to a Common Agent', 3.

reasonable time for comments on notifications, to take these comments into consideration and to discuss these comments, for example.[21] To this end, the SPS and TBT Agreements require Members to establish enquiry points.[22] In addition, practice has evolved enabling such dialogue among Members within the SPS and TBT Committees. As such, Members now raise in those spaces specific trade concerns (STCs) about other Members' trade policies or practices. This is critical progress towards improving the accessibility of the information, facilitating and reducing the cost of accessing information when Members and other interested parties need to find answers.

More recently, practice has evolved to make use of the opportunities offered by new information technologies, empowering information users to improve the information source by contributing to public platforms and ensuring timely updates. This evolution started in the WTO in the early 2000s, when the WTO Secretariat encouraged Members to use online tools to publish and notify trade measures in various sectors. The aim is now less about 'producing information' and more about 'communicating information, listening to the views of stakeholders, and improving WTO decision-making procedures'.[23] While these new tools came into being after other transparency mechanisms and hence can be seen as part of the third generation of transparency, the way in which they are used in practice suggests that they enable centralised (second-generation) transparency more than they do interactive transparency.

III Transparency in the SPS and TBT Agreements: A Case Study of Right-to-Know, Targeted and Interactive Transparency in the WTO

The SPS and TBT Agreements are the most revealing illustration of the three-generation transparency system at work in the WTO's highly developed transparency framework, thanks to both the obligations set out in the Agreements themselves and substantive Committee practices aiming to improve transparency. Notifications under both SPS and TBT together represent around 90 per cent of all notifications submitted to

---

[21] See Annex B, para. 5(b)–(d), SPS; Art. 2.9.2 and 2.9.4 TBT.
[22] Article X.1 TBT; Annex B, para. 3, SPS.
[23] Wolfe, 'Letting the Sun Shine in at the WTO', 13.

III TRANSPARENCY IN THE SPS AND TBT AGREEMENTS 9

the WTO for trade in goods.[24] Therefore not only is transparency highly developed under the SPS and TBT Agreements but also Members are actively fulfilling their transparency obligations under these two in comparison with other WTO agreements.

The activity of Members under the SPS and TBT Agreements offers important insights into the functions of transparency as a tool in ensuring that domestic regulatory frameworks comply with WTO obligations. Transparency in the SPS and TBT Agreements is arguably all the more unique in that it bridges the wide gap between supranational obligations at the WTO level and the everyday regulatory processes of Members' domestic authorities. Not only do the transparency provisions facilitate the essential sharing of information on Members' national policies, but also their role in compliance means that the provisions can preclude the need for dispute settlement.

The WTO's dispute settlement system is hailed as the 'jewel' in its crown – that is, as one of the WTO's major achievements. It is a compulsory third-party adjudication system that is unique in inter-state relations and essential for the enforcement of all WTO instruments.

According to Article 3.2 of the WTO's Dispute Settlement Understanding (DSU):

> The dispute settlement system of the WTO is a central element in providing security and predictability to the multilateral trading system. The Members recognise that it serves to preserve the rights and obligations of Members under the covered agreements, and to clarify the existing provisions of those agreements in accordance with customary rules of interpretation of public international law.

However, like any judicial system, not only is it costly to use, requiring that Members have access to information and resources if they are to argue a case before the DSB in Geneva, but also any such case may have political consequences. A more flexible and accessible mechanism that allows Members to address trade frictions without resorting to adjudication is therefore desirable and this is precisely how the WTO wields its transparency requirements. While it may not draw on the authority of a third-party adjudicator, the system of transparency mechanisms can fulfil the three functions of providing security and predictability in the multilateral trading system, preserving Members' rights and obligations, and clarifying existing provisions.

[24] These figures come from http://i-tip.wto.org/. The exact data from this website might be incomplete because it does not coincide exactly with that of the specific http://tbtims.wto.org and http://spsims.wto.org, but the shares of notifications do seem to be relatively accurate.

10   INTRODUCTION

The first links between transparency and dispute settlement in the WTO were established in the TPRM during the Uruguay Round.[25] The texts defining the TPRM[26] – confirmed by case law[27] – underline that it should not serve the purposes of the WTO's dispute settlement procedures and yet several authors have pointed out its potential to enhance enforcement of WTO obligations, doing just that.

Mavroidis predicted that, although its effect was still limited at the time of its adoption, 'if the TPRM progresses to become a more integrated scheme, the boundary between transparency and legal assessment will become more indistinguishable and, ultimately, the latter will replace the former'.[28] Qureshi argued that transparency is a 'precondition' and a 'facet' of enforcement (which he defined as a technique for facilitating adherence), and that the 'TPRM constitutes a significant attempt at surmounting the problem of adherence to the WTO code'.[29]

The transparency mechanisms of the SPS and TBT Agreements go further in ensuring implementation than the already major benefits of the TPRM by encouraging Members to consult whenever they are concerned by a specific measure. In particular, in this book the empirical study of the uses made of transparency will demonstrate that it has become an important tool to ensure implementation of Members' obligations under the SPS and TBT Agreements. On the one hand, it is useful for regulating Members, who can gather feedback on their draft measures and ensure that they better align with their substantive obligations. On the other hand, it allows Members to monitor their trading partners' domestic approaches and alert those partners when the trade effect seems overly burdensome, contrary to all Members' obligations under the SPS and TBT Agreements.

Finally, when trade frictions persist and a third party needs to intervene, the transparency framework must indeed give way to the WTO's dispute

---

[25] The TPRM was provisionally effective as of 12 April 1989, when the Negotiating Group on the Functioning of the GATT System (responsible for negotiating the terms of a surveillance scheme for the GATT) reached an agreement. It became fully part of the WTO institution with the establishment of the Organization at the end of the Uruguay Round.
[26] The TPRM is not 'intended to serve as a basis for the enforcement of specific obligations under the Agreement or for dispute settlement procedures, or to impose new policy commitments on Members': Annex III, para. A:2, GATT.
[27] See *Canada – Aircraft*; *Chile – Price Band System*.
[28] Petros C. Mavroidis, 'Surveillance Schemes: The GATT's New Trade Policy Review Mechanism', *Michigan Journal of International Law* 13, no. 2 (1991): 374.
[29] Asif H. Qureshi, 'The New GATT Trade Policy Review Mechanism: An Exercise in Transparency or "Enforcement"?', *Journal of World Trade* 24, no. 3 (1990): 142–60.

settlement system. However, observers have noted that there are several factors that precondition resort to dispute settlement and that these all entail significant costs. Briefly put, resorting to dispute settlement requires the ability to identify a WTO-inconsistent measure, to estimate its trade effects, and to evaluate the costs and benefits of litigation. Meeting these conditions themselves involves considerable costs, which can act as a deterrent for a large proportion of Members – particularly those who have never litigated in the WTO before and for whom the 'start-up' costs will be especially high. The extensive information on and understanding of other Members' domestic policies that the SPS and TBT transparency tools facilitate may help Members to overcome these start-up costs, and hence may contribute to equalising access to the dispute settlement system.

To summarise, in a perfectly transparent system, all Members would, in the first instance, have equal opportunities to try to solve issues at an informal level, either bilaterally or in Committee meetings. Second, Members would have equal insight into and knowledge of other Members' trade regimes and potentially trade-restrictive measures, and each would therefore have a similar chance to weigh the opportunity costs of litigating or not. And finally, if it decides to pursue litigation and having progressed through the three generations of transparency, any WTO Member should have accumulated the necessary information with which to build a solid legal case against another Member whose measure is affecting trade.

IV Important Fields of Study outside the Scope of This Book

This book focuses exclusively on the framework for transparency set out in the SPS and TBT Agreements, highlighting the specific context in which these transparency tools have developed. This focus means that closely related issues are excluded from the scope of the book. First of all, while necessarily influenced by trends in international law, the study of transparency under the SPS and TBT Agreements falls within the exclusive remits of WTO law and policy. But other WTO instruments also include transparency provisions and practices – in particular, Article X GATT and the TPRM. These two transparency tools play an essential role in ensuring transparency in the multilateral trading system, but have sufficiently different functions and scopes of application such that they deserve to be studied distinctly from the SPS and TBT Agreements. They will therefore not be studied here nor will we focus in depth on the consequences of the WTO's transparency obligations and practices at the domestic level.

A Transparency as an Important Trend in International Law

In the era of the internet – that is, of free access to information, digital data flows and immediacy – transparency has become an essential theme in all aspects of our private and public lives. Citizens share every aspect of their daily lives with their social networks and with the companies that operate these networks, search engines or their mobile phones. At the same time, citizens expect the same transparency from the public bodies that govern them. Access-to-information laws have flourished throughout the world and citizens increasingly demand participation in democratic processes, where a few years ago governments were only just beginning to open their rule-making processes to targeted stakeholder groups. In this context, there has been increasing literature about institutional transparency, both in the WTO[30] and more broadly in other fields of international law.[31] This literature shows that, like other disciplines, international law has been influenced by the increasing demand for transparency and has had to move away from the traditional closed-door culture that characterised diplomatic negotiations. In this sense, the institutions, processes and mechanisms of international law are becoming much more transparent, although they remain reactive rather than proactive.[32] This book is, of course, influenced by this overall trend towards a 'reign' of transparency and a battle against secrecy. Nevertheless, it focuses on the very specific function that the transparency of Members' domestic regulations plays in the implementation of the WTO's SPS and TBT Agreements. It therefore excludes from its scope discussions about transparency within or among international organisations themselves – and the WTO, in particular – in their negotiations and rule-making practices.

B Article X GATT: Disclosure and Due Process

Article X GATT is the basis of transparency requirements in the multilateral trading system. Today, as the only article of the GATT dedicated to transparency, it is considered to be a general transparency obligation.[33]

---

[30] Panagiotis Delimatsis, 'Institutional Transparency in the WTO', in Andrea Bianchi and Anne Peters, eds, *Transparency in International Law* (Cambridge: Cambridge University Press, 2013), 112–41.

[31] Andrea Bianchi and Anne Peters, eds, *Transparency in International Law* (Cambridge: Cambridge University Press, 2013), 112–41.

[32] Anne Peters, 'Towards Transparency as a Global Norm', in Andrea Bianchi and Anne Peters, eds, *Transparency in International Law* (Cambridge: Cambridge University Press, 2013), 536.

[33] Petros C. Mavroidis, *The Law of the World Trade Organization (WTO): Documents, Cases & Analysis*, 2nd edn, American Casebook Series (St. Paul, MN: West, 2013).

IV FIELDS OF STUDY OUTSIDE THE SCOPE OF THIS BOOK   13

As such, it is the baseline for transparency in the WTO, and it is therefore closely related to transparency obligations under the SPS and TBT Agreements.

Like transparency under the SPS and TBT Agreements, Article X GATT can also be seen as penetrating the domestic rule-making processes of WTO Members. Indeed, it requires both the prompt publication and the uniform, reasonable and impartial administration of trade regulations, and as such it presents these two obligations as intertwined, under the broader umbrella of 'due process'.

The objectives of Article X GATT, set out slightly differently in each paragraph, take the obligations to publish and administer trade regulations beyond simple procedure, with a common intention of ensuring their predictability, uniformity and impartiality through transparency. The two first paragraphs of Article X require accurate information to be provided to governments and traders, and mandate the predictability of the Member's trade policy environment. Article X:3 requires that Members administer their trade measures in a uniform, reasonable and impartial way, and maintain or establish a review procedure – all of which amounts to 'certain minimum standards for transparency and procedural fairness in the administration of trade regulations'.[34]

Alone, Article X GATT can be seen as an incentive for governments to establish transparent legal and regulatory environments as a basis for regulatory policy,[35] in this way serving as the 'oldest good governance provision of the WTO Agreements'.[36] It is also considered to be a useful tool for preventing corruption and illicit payments in international trade relations.[37] Case law has proven that the obligations resulting from Article X are no longer merely a 'subsidiary matter', as some panels claimed under the GATT.[38] As its objectives suggest, it is more ambitious in scope than a procedural requirement. The panels and the WTO's Appellate Body have increasingly applied Article X, in a movement described as 'from the periphery to the center'[39] – that is, from a secondary procedural obligation to a 'principle of fundamental importance'.[40] Ala'i underlines that

---

[34] Appellate Body Report, *US – Shrimp*, §41.
[35] See e.g. OECD Recommendation of the Council on Regulatory Policy and Governance, Principle 2. www.oecd.org/gov/regulatory-policy/49990817.pdf.
[36] Ala'i, 'From the Periphery to the Center?', 801.
[37] Krista Nadakavukaren Schefer, 'Corruption and the WTO Legal System', *Journal of World Trade* 43, no. 4 (2009): 737–70.
[38] For example, GATT Panel Report, *Japan – Leather II (US)*, §57.
[39] Ala'i, 'From the Periphery to the Center?'.
[40] Appellate Body Report, *US – Underwear*, §21.

the number of cases with claims concerning Article X have grown 'exponentially' since the GATT period ended with the creation of the WTO – an increase that the author explains as resulting from an increasing reliance by WTO Members on good governance principles such as transparency and a shift away from a system based merely on tariffs.[41] Going further on the implications of Article X for domestic legal frameworks, Chen argues that Article X GATT is 'intrusive', because of its 'capacity for direct impact on the field of members' administrative law', with a chance that it might 'undermine members' exercising of their sovereignty'.[42]

Article X GATT is an important predecessor to the transparency obligations under the SPS and TBT Agreements, and establishes our expectations for transparency in the WTO in general. It is therefore referred to occasionally in this study of the SPS and TBT obligations, when relevant. However, Article X differs significantly from the SPS and TBT Agreements in that it imposes an obligation on WTO Members *individually*, without the unique and essential characteristic of SPS and TBT transparency – that is, that it creates obligations and opportunities for *dialogue among Members* on domestic measures. In the same vein, Article X GATT does not result in the centralisation of information – an essential characteristic of the SPS and TBT transparency systems. Because of these fundamental differences, and insofar as this book explores the unique role they have in supporting the SPS and TBT Agreements' effect of rationalising domestic regulatory processes, Article X GATT falls outside the scope of this book.

C The TPRM: Guarding Transparency within the Multilateral Trading System

The TPRM plays a natural role as a 'guardian' of transparency within the multilateral trading system. It aims at transparency in and an understanding of Members' trade policies and practices, towards improved adherence to WTO obligations, and in this sense it is closely linked with the functions of SPS and TBT transparency. However, the TPRM has its own institutional set-up and, accordingly, its own limitations, which is why it is excluded from the scope of this book. In particular, trade policy reviews are closer to the sort of 'traditional' peer review process

---

[41] Ala'i, 'From the Periphery to the Center?'.
[42] Sijie Chen, 'China's Compliance with WTO Systemic Obligations: Institution-Related Impediments to Effective Implementation of GATT Article X', *Amsterdam Law Forum* 4, no. 4 (2012): 26–50.

conducted in other international organisations than they are to the discussions conducted within the SPS and TBT Committees.[43] In practice, the Trade Policy Review Body (TPRB) prepares TPRM reports on the basis of one report by the WTO Secretariat and another by the reviewed Member.[44] The TPRM explicitly excludes any relationship between the TPRM and the WTO's dispute settlement mechanisms, highlighting that it is not intended to serve as a basis for enforcement of specific obligations, for dispute settlement procedures or for the imposition of new policy commitments on Members.[45] Indeed, the TPRM is not triggered by another WTO Member, but by the WTO Secretariat, nor was the TPRM intended to create any binding legal obligation, contrary to decisions arising from the DSB.[46]

Several criticisms have been made of the TPRM's specific institutional set-up and procedures, such as the high resources it demands of the Secretariat in carrying out its reviews[47] or its limited benefits for developing countries.[48] In particular, in a recent comprehensive study of the TPRM, Kende shows that even though it is generally perceived as a successful peer review mechanism, reviews under the TPRM are often overly repetitive and diplomatic, lacking sufficient depth to support countries in reform efforts.[49]

The procedures by which the TPRB conducts its 'peer reviews' are therefore very different from the flexible mechanism of STCs that has developed organically into a multilateral dialogue open to all WTO Members. It is because these STCs are Member-driven that they can result in open discussions on the compliance of domestic measures with legal rights and obligations under the SPS and TBT Agreements. The measures discussed are often in draft form, engendering international dialogue throughout the

---

[43] On peer reviews in other international organisations, see Fabrizio Pagani, 'Peer Review: A Tool for Co-operation and Change' (OECD, 11 September 2002), SG/LEG(2002)1. www.oecd.org/dac/peer-reviews/1955285.pdf.

[44] For further description, see Peter Van den Bossche and Werner Zdouc, *The Law and Policy of the World Trade Organization* (Cambridge: Cambridge University Press, 2013), 95.

[45] Ibid.

[46] Mavroidis, 'Surveillance Schemes', 398.

[47] This criticism was voiced e.g. by Sam Laird, 'The WTO's Trade Policy Review Mechanism: From Through the Looking Glass', *The World Economy* 22, no. 6 (2003): 741–64. See also Mathias Kende, *The Trade Policy Review Mechanism: A Critical Analysis*, International Economic Law (Oxford: Oxford University Press, 2018), 2, who still considered the 'relatively constant human resources and possibly diminishing budgetary means' to be an issue.

[48] Arunabha Ghosh, 'Developing Countries in the WTO Trade Policy Review Mechanism', *World Trade Review* 9, no. 3 (2010): 419–55.

[49] Kende, *The Trade Policy Review Mechanism*.

domestic regulatory process and allowing all WTO Members to offer their views on domestic regulations in development. Therefore, while the TPRM undoubtedly has important lessons for transparency in the frameworks of the SPS and TBT Agreements, particularly in terms of how to enhance its effectiveness, the mechanism itself remains outside of the scope of this book.

D WTO Transparency and Its Consequences for Domestic Frameworks

This book argues that, thanks to the well-developed transparency framework under the SPS and TBT Agreements, WTO Members have a privileged opportunity to engage in regulatory dialogue and co-operation. This allows WTO members to manage conflicts before they are raised in dispute settlement and supports them in gathering additional information and pursuing dialogue when formal disputes do arise. From this perspective, the discussions that take place between Members either through bilateral comments on notifications or within the SPS or TBT Committees may have an important impact on domestic regulatory processes and policy debates.

Essential research on specific TBT discussions confirms that a direct causal relationship between discussions in the WTO context and changes at the domestic level is not easy to demonstrate. In particular, Gruszczynski highlights the difficulties of estimating the actual effects of TBT Committee discussions on domestic processes.[50] He shows that TBT Committee discussions improved awareness within the European Union (EU) of the negative implications for other WTO Members of its complex regulatory framework on the registration, evaluation, authorisation and restriction of chemicals (REACH),[51] and served as a catalyst for subsequent bilateral consultations, overall allowing for a process of learning both specifically by the EU and among WTO Members more

---

[50] Lukasz Gruszczynski, 'The REACH Regulation and the TBT Agreement: The Role of the TBT Committee in Regulatory Processes', in Tracey Epps and M. J. Trebilcock, eds, *Research Handbook on the WTO and Technical Barriers to Trade* (Cheltenham: Edward Elgar, 2013), 424–53.

[51] Regulation (EC) No. 1907/2006 of the European Parliament and of the Council of 18 December 2006 concerning the Registration, Evaluation, Authorisation and Restriction of Chemicals (REACH), establishing a European Chemicals Agency, amending 1999/45/EC and repealing Council Regulation (EEC) No. 793/93 and Commission Regulation (EC) No. 1488/94, as well as Council Directive 76/769/EEC and Commission Directives 91/155/EEC, 93/67/EEC, 93/105/EC and 2000/21/EC, OJ L 396, 30.12.2006, 1–849, as subsequently amended.

IV FIELDS OF STUDY OUTSIDE THE SCOPE OF THIS BOOK 17

generally.[52] However, he points out that other WTO Members raised several additional concerns in the Committee meetings that the EU did not incorporate, illustrating the limits of the Committee discussions. Indeed, the factors influencing a regulatory procedure may come from various sources and the weights of the different factors in the final regulatory outcome are difficult to determine. This is particularly the case for such complex reform as that of the EU's REACH Regulation, which involved, among other efforts, internet consultations, bilateral dialogue with major trading partners and stakeholder engagement with the EU Commission itself.[53]

The current book does not pretend to give evidence of the actual effects of STC discussions on domestic regulations; rather, it focuses on the discussions that take place within the WTO Committees, their relationship with WTO obligations and the dispute settlement process. The empirical evidence presented is therefore limited to the content of discussions at the international level, among WTO Members, with the objective of identifying how the SPS and TBT transparency frameworks allow Members to address the issues they face when implementing their TBT and SPS obligations and to engage in the permanent platform for dialogue rather than resort to legal disputes. The effects of these discussions on domestic regulation would warrant a separate in-depth study of an individual country and regulation, to include a close empirical study of domestic rule-making processes. Such research would be very welcome to complement the general findings of this book.

E Transparency Provisions in Bilateral and Regional Trade Agreements: Innovative Language, but Limited Institutional Frameworks

Transparency regimes in regional trade agreements (RTAs) have an important potential to reduce trade costs between countries.[54] In some circumstances, transparency in RTAs or bilateral trade agreements (BTAs) is covered under more in-depth provisions, in agreement-specific and other chapters. In the SPS and TBT chapters of RTAs, such provisions

---

[52] Gruszczynski, 'The REACH Regulation and the TBT Agreement', 11.
[53] Ibid., 10.
[54] Iza Lejárraga, 'Multilateralising Regionalism: Strengthening Transparency Disciplines in Trade', OECD Trade Policy Paper No. 152, 26 June 2013. doi:10.1787/5k44t7k99xzq-en.

typically add to the texts of the WTO's SPS and TBT Agreements with language that reflects recommendations issued by the SPS and TBT Committees.[55] In addition, BTAs and RTAs increasingly include horizontal transparency chapters governing all sectors and areas covered by the trade agreement.[56] And, quite significantly, BTAs and RTAs also set up institutional bodies – whether broad governing bodies, thematic subcommittees or fora specifically for regulatory co-operation[57] – that may themselves serve as ways of managing conflicts before they escalate into formal dispute.[58]

In this way, a new generation of trade agreements suggests that WTO Members have learned from the benefits of transparency in the WTO context and are willing to take transparency a step further. From that perspective, references will be made to such recent provisions in this book insofar as they present interesting angles on the SPS and TBT Agreements. Nevertheless, it is worth noting that transparency in these trade agreements is very distinct in two respects from the WTO transparency framework, to an extent that would justify a separate study. On the one hand, the RTAs are, by definition, limited to only a few parties. They may result in improved transparency for the public in general, but sometimes they entail notifications and create a dialogue only among the parties themselves. The results of this transparency are therefore much more limited in facilitating transparent domestic regulations as a public good. On the other hand, the RTAs do not benefit from the same institutional knowledge and framework as that of the WTO, including regular meetings between all WTO Members and the support of the WTO Secretariat. Even though RTAs may set up committees that arguably do have important effects similar to those of the SPS and TBT Committees, those effects are necessarily more limited in scope than those of the WTO, which benefit from centralised transparency about all Members' regulations.

---

[55] For examples, see Chapter 2.
[56] Lejárraga identifies 53 RTAs signed by the OECD and major emerging economies with such horizontal transparency chapters, noting that this approach is particularly prevalent in the RTAs of the United States, New Zealand and Canada: Lejárraga, 'Multilateralising Regionalism', 26.
[57] See e.g. the Regulatory Co-operation Forum set up under Art. 21.5 CETA.
[58] Margherita Melillo, 'Informal Dispute Resolution in Preferential Trade Agreements', *Journal of World Trade* 53, no. 1 (2019): 95–127.

V An Overview of the Book's Structure

In its effort to present the transparency framework and practices under the SPS and TBT Agreements and to identify the role that transparency plays in the WTO's legal and institutional system in relation to dispute settlement, this book starts with a study of the legal regime of the SPS and TBT Agreements. Part I will explain what provisions in the two Agreements specifically mandate a comprehensive transparency framework and why and how Members are given an incentive to use, throughout their domestic regulatory processes, the transparency and regulatory dialogue mechanisms established under the SPS and TBT Agreements.

Part II concentrates on Members' practices when fulfilling their transparency obligations under the SPS and TBT Agreements. A description of the use of the different transparency mechanisms and an in-depth analysis of the discussions that take place in the SPS and TBT Committees allows us to examine trends in Members' multilateral regulatory dialogue and the effects that this has on managing disputes.

Finally, in Part III we compare the regulatory dialogue that takes place thanks to transparency tools with the formal disputes that are argued before the DSB. In this part, we see how transparency and dispute settlement serve complementary purposes. Ultimately, the different transparency tools available to WTO Members may support them when they decide to engage with formal dispute settlement, thus granting all Members equal access to WTO adjudication.

PART I

Why the SPS and TBT Agreements?
A Legal Framework in Support of Regulatory Quality

The world today is inherently interconnected, largely thanks to an immense growth in global trade volumes during the second half of the twentieth century. With goods and services often crossing borders several times a day, to be sold from one country to another, national sovereign States must adopt laws and regulations that reflect their national policy priorities, cultural backgrounds and specific needs.

While the volume of tariffs and quantitative restrictions has progressively eased since the signature of the General Agreement on Tariffs and Trade (GATT) in 1947, pernicious barriers remain – the result of regulations that differ among importing and exporting countries. Unlike tariffs, these regulations cannot simply be eliminated. Indeed, such regulations are essential to delivering legitimate domestic policy objectives such as citizens' welfare, the protection of animals and plants, and the protection of the environment, among other things. Certain conditions can nevertheless be applied to ensure that restrictions to trade under these regulations remain proportionate to their legitimate domestic policy objectives.

The GATT included only limited provisions aiming to tackle regulatory barriers among signatory States. Consistent with a principle of negative integration, it left Members competent to choose the policies they deemed most appropriate, requiring only that they should not restrict trade with protectionist measures. The WTO Agreements on the Application of Sanitary and Phytosanitary Measures (SPS Agreement, or SPS) and on Technical Barriers to Trade (TBT Agreement, or TBT) go much further in this regard, providing not only detailed requirements governing the domestic treatment of foreign products but also obligations that apply to domestic regulations in absolute terms, requiring that they be of a certain 'quality'. While negative integration means that there is no directly substantive obligation governing the regulations to be adopted, the SPS and TBT Agreements encourage domestic regulators to take the cross-border effects into account when drafting such instruments and reduce regulatory diversity.

Chapter 1 will highlight the particularities of the SPS and TBT legal regimes to the extent that they address non-tariff barriers to trade by imposing requirements on domestic rule-makers.

The SPS and TBT regimes call for developed provisions regarding transparency, intended to address the 'open-ended' character of the obligations. Chapter 2 will focus on the existing transparency framework set out in the Agreements, presenting the legal obligations and related practices that have evolved as a result of its implementation.

In addition to these substantive obligations and thanks to the information that can be gathered as a consequence of the transparency requirements, the two Agreements not only encourage regulatory dialogue among Members but also provide a framework for regulatory co-operation. Chapter 3 will expand the picture presented in Chapters 1 and 2, explaining the rationale and methods by which regulatory co-operation is effected under the TBT and SPS Agreements.

Overall, this part of the book argues that implementation of the legal and institutional regimes established in the SPS and TBT Agreements is Member-driven. Because they are imposed under 'incomplete contracts'[1] and with only limited information, the substantive transparency obligations and related practices within the SPS and TBT Committees position regulatory dialogue as a way in which Members can work together towards the most appropriate domestic measures. Ultimately, the robust transparency framework under the Agreements asks that WTO Members monitor the legality of each other's domestic regulations and asks them to co-operate to ensure their effective implementation.

---

[1] Bernard Hoekman and Petros C. Mavroidis, 'The Dark Side of the Moon: "Completing" the WTO Contract through Adjudication', November 2012, 14. http://globalgovernanceprogramme.eui.eu/wp-content/uploads/2012/11/Hoekman-Mavroidis-MESSERLIN-FEST_FIN.pdf.

1

The Legal Principles Applying to Domestic Regulations under the SPS and TBT Agreements

Finding a Balance between Regulatory Autonomy and Free Trade

The General Agreement on Tariffs and Trade (GATT) is based on the principle of regulatory autonomy, allowing Members to choose whichever measure best delivers their policy objectives. It is interested in domestic regulations only to the extent that they discriminate against foreign products. A certain number of exceptions listed in Article XX GATT allow Members to justify domestic measures that are otherwise discriminatory or trade-restrictive. Such regulations, which may aim at objectives such as protecting human, animal and plant life or health, upholding public morals or preserving exhaustible natural resources, among others, are subject to WTO law only when another WTO Member challenges their legality before the WTO's Dispute Settlement Body (DSB). Such disputes are determined on a case-by-case basis under the conditions set out in Article XX.

Once countries have mutually conceded their tariffs, there is a risk that they may otherwise try to secure advantage for domestic producers, for instance by means of regulations that impose costs on foreign producers.[1] A principle of non-discrimination is therefore not sufficient to guarantee that domestic measures will not be protectionist. The Agreements on the Application of Sanitary and Phytosanitary Measures (SPS Agreement, or SPS) and on Technical Barriers to Trade (TBT Agreement, or TBT) address this shortcoming under the GATT. Unlike the GATT, the two Agreements provide for a much more comprehensive test that Members must themselves apply during their regulatory process.

---

[1] Petros C. Mavroidis, *Trade in Goods* (Oxford: Oxford University Press, 2012), 672; M. J. Trebilcock, Robert Howse and Antonia Eliason, *The Regulation of International Trade*, 4th edn (Abingdon/New York: Routledge, 2013), 136–7.

The SPS and TBT Agreements do not include 'exceptions' that allow a WTO Member to justify a measure that fails to meet the Member's obligations under the Agreements. Public policy objectives, including the protection of human health and safety, and of the environment, are embedded in the Agreements' general objectives. As a result, WTO Members' regulatory autonomy is reaffirmed and protected, and the burden of proving that a Member's practices constitute excessive restriction of trade lies with the complaining party.

This chapter will look at those provisions under the SPS and TBT Agreements that require Members to balance their own public policy objectives with the WTO's trade liberalisation objectives. This weighing of objectives results in obligations under the Agreements that measure the 'quality' of the domestic regulations themselves.[2] The Agreements therefore not only provide for domestic regulation that achieves a certain result but also prescribe Members' conduct in the regulatory processes towards that result.[3]

Looking at the provisions from the perspective of the domestic regulators can offer insight into the rationale underpinning the transparency framework set out in the SPS and TBT Agreements and practices within the SPS and TBT Committees. These provisions require a difficult balancing of Members' autonomy and obligations. This balancing applies to all measures that come within the scope of the SPS and TBT Agreements (see section I), and it is particularly stark in Members' obligations to justify domestic measures (see section II) and not to discriminate between domestic and foreign products (see section III). As a result, the regulating authorities face the daunting task of both complying with the SPS and TBT Agreements and pursuing their own policy objectives, while complaining Members face the challenge of identifying both the policy objective and alternative options if they are to evidence violations under the WTO Agreements. This chapter aims to highlight the role of transparency and the regulatory dialogue that it facilitates, which will be the subject of subsequent chapters, in clarifying the policy objective underpinning domestic regulations and ensuring that the means chosen to achieve that objective is consistent with a Member's WTO obligations.

---

[2] Petros C. Mavroidis, 'Regulatory Cooperation: Lessons from the WTO and the World Trade Regime', E15 Initiative Policy Options Paper, 22 January 2016. www3.weforum.org/docs/E15/WEF_Regulatory_Cooperation_Lessons_WTO_WTR_report_2015_1401.pdf.
[3] Mavroidis, *Trade in Goods*.

I   The Scope of the SPS and TBT Agreements

The scope of the SPS and TBT Agreements in itself justifies an extensive dialogue between Members about those domestic measures falling within it. Such measures extend beyond economic considerations into politically sensitive matters relating to a State's protection of human, plant or animal health or safety, consumer protection and information, or protection of the environment. These issues are all the more sensitive given that Members' approaches may differ and some trading partners may perceive a Member's approach to be more burdensome than necessary.

A   Measures under the SPS Agreement: Defined by Their Purpose

The measures that fall within the scope of the SPS Agreement are defined by their purpose rather than their type. The SPS Agreement applies if a measure pursues policy objectives aiming to protect human or animal life or health. The regulating Member must therefore pay attention to its obligations when drafting any such measure, not only when asked to justify it before an adjudicator.

The scope of the SPS Agreement is defined in Article 1.1, which specifies that it applies to all 'sanitary and phytosanitary measures which may, directly or indirectly, affect international trade'. As such, the SPS Agreement applies to a broad range of domestic measures, without drawing a distinction among the types of measure as does the TBT Agreement. Annex A to the SPS Agreement, which provides a list of definitions, confirms that the single criterion that brings a domestic document within the scope of the SPS Agreement is its objective. Paragraph 1 provides that a 'Sanitary or phytosanitary measure' is:

... Any measure applied:
(a) to protect animal or plant life or health within the territory of the Member from risks arising from the entry, establishment or spread of pests, diseases, disease-carrying organisms or disease-causing organisms;
(b) to protect human or animal life or health within the territory of the Member from risks arising from additives, contaminants, toxins or disease-causing organisms in foods, beverages or feedstuffs;
(c) to protect human life or health within the territory of the Member from risks arising from diseases carried by animals, plants or products thereof, or from the entry, establishment or spread of pests; or
(d) to prevent or limit other damage within the territory of the Member from the entry, establishment or spread of pests.
[...]

Because the objective is the determining factor that brings the measure within the scope of the SPS Agreement, a regulating Member cannot simply state that a measure is an SPS measure. In *Australia – Apples*, the WTO's Appellate Body specified that WTO panels should look instead at a range of circumstances to establish whether a measure is an SPS measure:

> Whether a measure is 'applied … to protect' in the sense of Annex A(1)(a) must be ascertained not only from the objectives of the measure as expressed by the responding party, but also from the text and structure of the relevant measure, its surrounding regulatory context, and the way in which it is designed and applied. For any given measure to fall within the scope of Annex A(1)(a), scrutiny of such circumstances must reveal a clear and objective relationship between that measure and the specific purposes enumerated in Annex A(1)(a).[4]

Thus the legal nature of the measure has no bearing on its qualification as an SPS measure. This is implied in Annex A, paragraph 1, which refers to 'Any measure', and has been confirmed by the Appellate Body:

> Taken together, the words 'include' and 'all relevant' therefore suggest that measures of a type not expressly listed may nevertheless constitute SPS measures when they are 'relevant', that is, when they are 'applied' for a purpose that corresponds to one of those listed in subparagraphs (a) through (d). Conversely, the fact that an instrument is of a type listed in the last sentence of Annex A (1) is not, in itself, sufficient to bring such an instrument within the ambit of the SPS Agreement.[5]

The objective of an SPS measure is therefore legitimate by definition. In this way, it is already clear that the material scope of the SPS Agreement is dynamically different from that of the GATT, under which the objectives of a measure enter into consideration only when the regulating Member argues that a WTO-inconsistent measure is justified by an exception as listed in Article XX GATT.

The panel in *EC – Hormones* further underlined this point:

> We note in this respect that the general approach adopted in Article XX(b) of GATT is fundamentally different from the approach adopted in the SPS Agreement. Article XX(b), which is not limited to sanitary or phytosanitary measures, provides for a general exception which can be invoked to justify any violation of another GATT provision. The SPS Agreement, on the other hand, provides for specific obligations to be met in order for a Member to enact or maintain specific types of measures, namely sanitary and phytosanitary measures.[6]

[4] Appellate Body Report, *Australia – Apples*, §173.
[5] Ibid., §175.
[6] Panel Reports, *EC – Hormones*, §8.39.

In other words, the objective of the measure – as expressed explicitly *and* in the text and structure of the measure – is the key factor in determining whether it falls within the scope of the SPS Agreement. Identifying this explicit and more 'implicit' objective is a challenge for any complaining parties, however, and we shall see that this is an issue that is often raised in SPS Committee discussions by WTO Members 'concerned' with SPS measures.

B Measures under the TBT Agreement: Technical Regulations, Conformity Assessment Procedures and Standards

The TBT Agreement differs from the SPS Agreement in that it covers three different types of measure to which it applies different legal frameworks: technical regulations, conformity assessment procedures (CAPs), and standards. These three types of measure have objectives that go well beyond international trade, as the scopes of the two Agreements suggest. The measures are nonetheless of particular relevance for international trade, because a product's compliance with the Agreements is a condition of its access to a market. However, simply stating that a measure is a technical regulation, a CAP or a standard is not enough to bring it within the scope of the TBT Agreement; in the case of a dispute, the WTO adjudicator will look closely at its characteristics to confirm whether a measure is a TBT measure.

1 Technical Regulations

The TBT Agreement defines technical regulations on the basis of their scope of application and their effect.

Annex 1, paragraph 1, to the TBT Agreement defines a 'Technical regulation' as a '[d]ocument which lays down product characteristics or their related processes and production methods, including the applicable administrative provisions, with which compliance is mandatory. It may also include or deal exclusively with terminology, symbols, packaging, marking or labelling requirements as they apply to a product, process or production method.'

In addition, the WTO's Appellate Body has specified three characteristics that define technical regulations as understood under Annex 1:

- the document must apply to an identifiable product or group of products;
- the document must set out one or more product characteristics; and
- compliance with the document must be mandatory.[7]

---

[7] Appellate Body Report, *EC – Sardines*, §§175–6.

The definition of 'technical regulation' under the TBT Agreement does not preclude the 'document' being a domestic legal instrument. It is therefore not clear whether it applies to regulations in the domestic sense – that is, instruments enacted under the authority of the executive branch – or in a more generic sense to regulations as normative texts. Indeed, the Appellate Body notes the broad character of the term 'document' referred to by Annex 1, paragraph 1: 'Annex 1.1 defines the term "technical regulation" by reference to a "document", which is defined quite broadly as "something written, inscribed, etc., which furnishes evidence or information upon any subject". The use of the term "document" could therefore cover a broad range of instruments or apply to a variety of measures.'[8]

In *EC – Seal Products*, the Appellate Body expanded on its previous reasoning:

> The first sentence of Annex 1.1 delineates the scope of measures that can be characterised as a technical regulation by referring to a document that 'lays down product characteristics or their related processes and production methods, including the applicable administrative provisions'. The verb 'lay down' is defined as 'establish, formulate definitely (a principle, a rule); prescribe (a course of action, limits, etc.)'. Annex 1.1 further describes a technical regulation by reference to a 'document' and makes clear that it is 'compliance' with the content of the document laying down product characteristics or their related PPMs [processes and production methods] that must be found to be 'mandatory'. Accordingly, *the scope of Annex 1.1 appears to be limited to those documents that establish or prescribe something and thus have a certain normative content.*[9]

The main indication under case law that qualifies a measure as a technical regulation is its 'normative content'. In principle, this includes regulations of any nature according to domestic law. Therefore, if the legal nature of the document is not a determining factor, the main characteristic of a technical regulation that distinguishes it from other TBT measures is its mandatory effect.

The meaning of 'mandatory' has been interpreted widely under case law, making the scope of technical regulations unpredictable. Nonetheless, the Appellate Body has specified that a document need not be mandatory in its language to be a technical regulation, but rather in its 'effect'.[10] In this regard, to determine whether a measure is or is not a technical regulation, a Member will need to 'investigate' whether it

---

[8] Appellate Body Report, *US – Tuna II (Mexico)*, §185.
[9] Appellate Body Report, *EC – Seal Products*, §5.10, emphasis added.
[10] Appellate Body Report, *EC – Asbestos*, §68.

may impose mandatory requirements even if it is not, formally speaking, legally binding.[11] As we shall see later in this chapter, bilateral discussions or discussions in the TBT Committee are typically a valuable opportunity for a Member concerned with another Member's domestic measure to seek further information and to clarify its actual effect, helping the parties to identify whether or not it is a technical regulation.

2 Conformity Assessment Procedures

Conformity assessment procedures provide confidence that a certain requirement set out in a technical regulation or standard will be respected. Annex 1, paragraph 3, to the TBT Agreement defines a CAP as '[a]ny procedure used, directly or indirectly, to determine that relevant requirements in technical regulations or standards are fulfilled'. There are a number of ways of providing or demonstrating conformity, each of which involves different actors. The TBT Agreement adds to paragraph 3 an explanatory note listing examples of CAPs: 'Conformity assessment procedures include, *inter alia*, procedures for sampling, testing and inspection; evaluation, verification and assurance of conformity; registration, accreditation and approval as well as their combinations.' Two common procedures are *not* included in this list: certification and a supplier's declaration of conformity.

In practice, CAPs represent significant costs for exporting companies, who must demonstrate compliance to gain access to a new market, and so the TBT Agreement offers several ways in which they can avoid unnecessary costs. The objective of the CAPs provisions is to make sure that what the importing Member requires of the exporting Member to comply with its regulations is neither too burdensome nor discriminatory.

Balancing these requirements demands some trust between the two parties. As we shall see in Part II, recent evidence shows that Members frequently discuss CAPs within the TBT Committee.[12] The subjective nature of the CAP – that is, of one Member's judgement of another's compliance – underpins the need for dialogue among Members.

---

[11] For a critique of this position by the Appellate Body and the confusion created by this very broad approach to the concept of 'mandatory', see Meredith Crowley and Robert Howse, '*Tuna – Dolphin II*: A Legal and Economic Analysis of the Appellate Body Report', *World Trade Review* 13, no. 2 (2014): 324.

[12] Marianna Karttunen and Devin McDaniels, 'Trade, Testing and Toasters: Conformity Assessment Procedures and the TBT Committee', *Journal of World Trade* 50, no. 5 (2016): 755–92.

3 Standards

Under the TBT Agreement, 'standards' may cover a similar scope of issues to technical regulations. Indeed, a 'standard' is defined in Annex 1, paragraph 2, to the TBT Agreement as a:

> Document approved by a recognized body, that provides, for common and repeated use, rules, guidelines or characteristics for products or related processes and production methods, with which compliance is not mandatory. It may also include or deal exclusively with terminology, symbols, packaging, marking or labelling requirements as they apply to a product, process or production method.

According to this definition, both standards and technical regulations can be 'normative' documents. The key feature that distinguishes the one from the other is that standards are voluntary and technical regulations are mandatory in effect.

In addition, whereas the governmental nature of technical regulations is implied, it is not a given for standards: they may be adopted by a 'recognised body', including by 'non-governmental standardising bodies', as long as those bodies have a 'legal power'.[13] This does not, however, include standards that are entirely 'private', developed by private companies.

Nevertheless, such 'private' standards may still have an impact on market access or participation in supply chains by preventing unnecessary barriers to trade.[14] If they are developed within the TBT framework and in line with the Code of Good Practice for the Preparation, Adoption and Application of Standards set out in Annex 3 to the TBT Agreement, this could lend such standards credibility. Debates in the SPS Committee have long sought to define the thin line between 'standards' and 'private standards', and hence whether or not such standards fall within the scope of the SPS Agreement.[15]

II The Justification of Domestic Measures

To prevent domestic measures from having arbitrary impact on foreign traders, the SPS and TBT Agreements require domestic measures to be justified – namely, to be 'necessary' to the policy objective pursued.

---

[13] Article 4.1 and Annex 1, para. 8, TBT, respectively.
[14] Petros C. Mavroidis and Robert Wolfe, 'Private Standards and the WTO: Reclusive No More', RSCAS Research Paper No. 2016/17, 2016. https://cadmus.eui.eu/bitstream/handle/1814/40384/RSCAS_2016_17.pdf?sequence=1.
[15] WTO, 'Actions Regarding SPS-Related Private Standards' (G/SPS/55, 6 April 2011).

The SPS Agreement requires both necessity and a scientific basis for SPS measures (section A), whereas the TBT Agreement focuses on the necessity of domestic measures to legitimate policy objectives (section B).

The requirement that measures be 'necessary' is not a central principle in the GATT. It is included only in Article XX GATT, to activate the general exceptions to GATT obligations on grounds of public morals and the protection of human, animal or plant life or health.[16] This exception is therefore to be used only as a defence and the burden of proving the necessity of non-compliance lies with the defendant.[17]

Under the SPS and TBT Agreements, the necessity of a measure is no longer a negative exception, but rather is positively embedded in all measures that WTO Members might adopt. In other words, Members have the right to adopt those measures that are necessary to fulfil their policy objectives (in the areas covered by the Agreements).

Necessity is therefore the core principle that determines whether a measure violates the SPS or TBT Agreements. It is, however, based on an inherently subjective starting point: the 'legitimacy' of an objective is judged relative to domestic policy priorities and, even within the country, it is judged by a certain regulatory authority. Within the WTO, the two Agreements provide a framework under which necessity can be evaluated, each taking a different approach, focusing on 'rationalising' the regulatory process a Member must follow when developing an SPS or TBT measure, while leaving the Member competent to determine its policy objective.

The 'necessity' requirement does not mean, however, that Members will automatically apply the most economically efficient measure. Indeed, it focuses on the necessity of the objectives and effects of the measure more than on the measure's efficiency in delivering those effects. Nevertheless, taking necessity into account when developing an SPS or TBT measure is still likely to result in its efficiency.[18] In this sense, necessity introduces a certain requirement of 'regulatory quality', contributing to a drive towards evidence-based policy-making.

---

[16] Article XX(a) and (b) GATT.
[17] On the burden of proof in the case of exceptions, see Appellate Body Report, *US - Underwear*, §7.16; Appellate Body Report, *US - Wool Shirts and Blouses*; Joanne Scott, *The WTO Agreement on Sanitary and Phytosanitary Measures: A Commentary*, Oxford Commentaries on the GATT/WTO Agreements (Oxford: Oxford University Press, 2009), 77.
[18] Bernard M. Hoekman and Michel M. Kostecki, *The Political Economy of the World Trading System: The WTO and Beyond* (Oxford: Oxford University Press, 2009), 85.

A   The SPS Agreement: The Necessity and Scientific Basis of Domestic Measures

The SPS Agreement recognises the regulatory autonomy of Members in language that is even clearer than that of the TBT Agreement. In addition to the provisions set out in its Preamble, Article 2.1 of the SPS Agreement recognises Members' 'right to take sanitary and phytosanitary measures necessary for the protection of human, animal or plant life or health'. The word 'necessary' already appearing in this right to regulate, the SPS Agreement goes on to specify that Members may apply SPS measures 'only to the extent necessary to protect human, animal or plant life or health' and as long as they are 'based on scientific principles'.

There are therefore two different limitations placed on Members' rights to regulate under the SPS Agreement: the necessity of a measure and its basis in scientific evidence.

1   Necessity

The 'necessity' of SPS measures is provided for in Article 2.2 of the SPS Agreement and refined in Article 5.6. Indeed, while the former sets out the principle that only 'necessary' measures can be adopted, the latter adds the requirement that Members should assess whether there is a regulatory alternative that might achieve the same aim and, if so, take into account its 'technical and economic feasibility'. Thus Article 2.2 relates to the way in which a measure is applied, whereas Article 5.6 relates to the substance of the measure. The consequences of this distinction in practice are still unclear,[19] but case law indicates that the two articles are to be read in conjunction.[20]

In *Australia – Salmon*, the Appellate Body provided three cumulative criteria for assessing the necessity of a measure under Article 5.6 – namely, that the measure '(1) is reasonably available taking into account technical and economic feasibility; (2) achieves the Member's appropriate level of sanitary or phytosanitary protection; and (3) is significantly less restrictive to trade than the SPS measure contested'.[21]

---

[19] Gabrielle Marceau and Joel P. Trachtman, 'A Map of the World Trade Organization Law of Domestic Regulation of Goods: The Technical Barriers to Trade Agreement, the Sanitary and Phytosanitary Measures Agreement, and the General Agreement on Tariffs and Trade', *Journal of World Trade* 48, no. 2 (2014): 351–432.

[20] Article 5.6 is to be read together with Art. 2.2, which establishes the general principle: 'We consider, in particular, that the more specific language of Article 5.6 should be read in light of the more general language in Article 2.2.' See Panel Report, *Japan – Agricultural Products II*, §8.71.

[21] Appellate Body Report, *Australia – Salmon*, §194.

Assessment of the 'appropriate' level of protection is subjective, of course, and depends on the objective pursued and the level of risk with which the Member adopting the SPS measure is comfortable. The SPS Agreement considers it to be up to the regulating Member to determine what it considers 'appropriate'. In this sense, the Appellate Body has confirmed that this is a *'prerogative'* of the regulating Member[22] and that risk-averse Members might even decide that the appropriate level of protection involves taking 'zero risk'.[23] Members must be able to define their perception of the appropriate level of protection, but do not need to do so in quantitative terms.[24]

2 Scientific Evidence

The SPS Agreement includes an additional protection against measures being based on arbitrary policy by setting out several 'science-based obligations'.[25] It requires Members to base their measures on scientific principles (Art. 2.2 SPS), which they shall determine through risk assessment (Art. 5.1 SPS), and it requires that they maintain the measure according to scientific evidence (Art. 5.2 SPS). The Appellate Body has clarified that Article 2.2 sets out the general principle requiring scientific evidence, whereas Articles 5.1 and 5.2 are rather specific applications of that basic obligation.

These innovative principles can be criticised, however, both because the WTO may not be the appropriate forum in which to impose a single scientific viewpoint and because the tools introduced can be considered excessively rigid in relation to rapidly evolving scientific findings.[26] However, in line with the negative integration that is characteristic of WTO agreements in general, these obligations should not be seen as imposing any positive obligations on Members. On the contrary, they can be seen as raising the bar to ensure better standards and regulations by 'enhancing the quality of rational democratic deliberation about risk and its control'.[27] Indeed, Scott notes that the WTO's DSB has largely

---

[22] Ibid., §199, emphasis original.
[23] Appellate Body Report, *EC – Hormones*, §172.
[24] Appellate Body Report, *Australia – Salmon*, §206.
[25] Scott, *The WTO Agreement on Sanitary and Phytosanitary Measures*, 76.
[26] Ibid., 77.
[27] Robert Howse, 'Democracy, Science, and Free Trade: Risk Regulation on Trial at the World Trade Organization', *Michigan Law Review* 98, no. 7 (1999): 2329. Howse argues further that the provisions of the SPS Agreement should be 'understood not as usurping legitimate democratic choices for stricter regulations, but as enhancing the quality of rational democratic deliberation about risk and its control. ... If rational deliberation is an important element in making democratic outcomes legitimate, then providing some role for scientific principles and evidence in the regulatory process may enhance, rather than undermine, democratic control of risk.'

interpreted these provisions as 'procedural'[28] and, broadly speaking, the Appellate Body insists on methodological requirements that distinguish 'science' from 'non-science'.[29]

Nevertheless, even if their reliance on scientific evidence is mostly procedural, WTO Members each have different approaches to science and to risk.[30] From this perspective, achieving a consensus among Members on what constitutes 'sufficient' scientific evidence is generally impossible and so the intervention of a third-party adjudicator who can posit an authoritative interpretation of the SPS Agreement is essential.

Regrettably, case law offers little clarity in this regard and the WTO's adjudicators have not fully seized the opportunity to 'rationalise' the scientific evidence base for SPS measures. In particular, the Appellate Body considers that a measure may be based on scientific principles – and therefore compliant with Article 2.2 – even if there has been no risk assessment.[31] In so concluding, it draws a distinction between the scientific principles and the 'rational' process through which they are adopted,[32] and what constitutes 'sufficient' evidence remains relatively vague, leaving space for uncertainty.[33] As we shall see in Part II, this uncertainty surrounding the interpretation of scientific evidence obligations is among the few characteristics that remain difficult to address informally in bilateral or Committee discussions – and hence Members tend to turn to the WTO's adjudicators for an official interpretation.

B   The TBT Agreement: The Need to Fulfil a Legitimate Policy Objective

The TBT Agreement imposes on Members the obligation not to adopt a technical regulation unless it is necessary and prescribes that, if enacted, the measure should be no more restrictive than is necessary.[34]

---

[28] Scott, *The WTO Agreement on Sanitary and Phytosanitary Measures*, 78.
[29] See, in particular, Appellate Body Report, *Australia – Apples*, §§215 and 221. On this, see Petros C. Mavroidis, *The Regulation of International Trade, Vol. 1: GATT* (Cambridge, MA/London: MIT Press, 2016), 477.
[30] Mavroidis, *The Regulation of International Trade*, 472.
[31] See Appellate Body Report, *Australia – Salmon*, §§137–8.
[32] On this, see criticism by Mavroidis, *The Regulation of International Trade*, 472.
[33] Marie Denise Prévost, *Balancing Trade and Health in the SPS Agreement: The Development Dimension* (Nijmegen: Wolf Legal, 2009), esp. 592.
[34] Mavroidis, *The Regulation of International Trade*, 419–20.

According to Article 2.2 of the TBT Agreement:

> Members shall ensure that technical regulations are not prepared, adopted or applied with a view to or with the effect of creating unnecessary obstacles to international trade. For this purpose, technical regulations shall not be more trade-restrictive than necessary to fulfil a legitimate objective, taking account of the risks non-fulfilment would create. Such legitimate objectives are, *inter alia*: national security requirements; the prevention of deceptive practices; protection of human health or safety, animal or plant life or health, or the environment. In assessing such risks, relevant elements of consideration are, *inter alia*: available scientific and technical information, related processing technology or intended end-uses of products.

Neither the objective of technical regulations nor their effect must result in unnecessary obstacles to trade and the benchmark against which to determine the necessity of a measure, according to Article 2.2, is a non-exhaustive list of legitimate objectives.[35]

Very little guidance is given on how to define the 'necessity' of a measure and Members maintain significant autonomy in this regard. The main elements offered in the TBT Agreement are that the necessity of a measure can be determined by assessing the 'legitimate objective' it pursues, in relation to the non-exhaustive list of objectives included in Article 2.2, and by considering the risks that would exist if the measure were not adopted. In addition, while the TBT Agreement does not require TBT measures to be adopted on the basis of scientific evidence, it does acknowledge that elements justifying the necessity of a measure may include 'scientific and technical information'.

In *US – Tuna II (Mexico)*, the Appellate Body defined three factors that might determine the necessity of a measure under the TBT Agreement:

> A panel should begin by considering factors that include: (i) the degree of contribution made by the measure to the legitimate objective at issue; (ii) the trade-restrictiveness of the measure; and (iii) the nature of the risks at issue and the gravity of consequences that would arise from non-fulfilment of the objective(s) pursued by the Member through the measure. In most cases, a comparison of the challenged measure and possible alternative measures should be undertaken.[36]

In other words, to determine the necessity of a challenged measure, panels are to analyse in some depth the efficiency of the measure in achieving the sought objective and compare it with alternative measures – in

---

[35] Appellate Body Report, *US – COOL*, §372; Appellate Body Report, *US – Tuna II (Mexico)*, §313.
[36] Appellate Body Report, *US – Tuna II (Mexico)*, §322.

particular, in light of the outcome if the challenged measure had not been adopted.

1 Measures Pursuing Legitimate Objectives

Members are free to determine the domestic policy objectives they pursue. Article 2.2 of the TBT Agreement provides a list of legitimate objectives that go beyond those set out in the SPS Agreement and mentions these '*inter alia*'. It therefore establishes a presumption that the objectives cited in Article 2.2 are legitimate, but leaves open the possibility that Members might pursue policy objectives that are not on the list.[37]

Members are also free to determine the level of protection they consider appropriate:

> [The TBT Agreement] recognizes that a Member shall not be prevented from taking measures necessary to achieve its legitimate objectives 'at the levels it considers appropriate', subject to the requirement that such measures are not applied in a manner that would constitute a means of arbitrary or unjustifiable discrimination between countries where the same conditions prevail or a disguised restriction on international trade, and are otherwise in accordance with the TBT Agreement. As we see it, a WTO Member, by preparing, adopting, and applying a measure in order to pursue a legitimate objective, articulates either implicitly or explicitly the level at which it seeks to pursue that particular legitimate objective.[38]

It is therefore the complaining party that must demonstrate evidence proving that the measure is excessive in relation to the protection at which it aims. Indeed, in *US – Clove Cigarettes*, the Appellate Body affirmed that it was the complaining party that 'carrie[d] the burden of providing us with evidence and argumentation on what is the level of protection sought by the United States, and why banning clove cigarettes greatly exceeds the level of protection sought'.[39]

Although it is indeed logical that the complaining Member should prove the excessive effect of a contested measure, it is more difficult for that Member to gather evidence of the level of protection sought than it is for the regulating Member itself to supply it.[40] Hence the importance, prior to adjudication, of transparency and dialogue with the regulating Member about measures and the level of protection sought.

---

[37] Ibid.
[38] Ibid., §315.
[39] Appellate Body Report, *US – Clove Cigarettes*, §7.373.
[40] For a criticism of this approach, see Mavroidis, *Trade in Goods*.

2 The Risks that Non-fulfilment Would Create

In relation to the obligation that a regulating Member must assess the risks of not fulfilling its policy objective, the TBT Agreement requires States to consider alternative policy options – particularly, a policy of non-intervention.

The Appellate Body has said that '[t]he obligation... suggests that the comparison of the challenged measure with a possible alternative measure should be made in light of the nature of the risks at issue and the gravity of the consequences that would arise from non-fulfilment of the legitimate objective'.[41] In other words, panels are expected to conduct an in-depth analysis of the alternative scenarios.

This consideration of alternative scenarios can be compared with the *ex ante* regulatory impact assessment (RIA) that is required before a Member develops a measure, which exercise involves considering regulatory and non-regulatory alternatives and conducting cost–benefit analyses of different options.[42] If panels were to engage in such assessment, they would be expected to conduct very detailed economic analysis.[43] This could be welcome, to the extent that a panel is able to go to such lengths, in that it might help to rationalise regulatory interventions – but, in practice, panels have adopted a more qualitative approach.[44] As a result, it is left up to Members to use the evidence they have at hand to demonstrate that their measures are 'necessary'.

As we will see in Part II, 'necessity' remains important to Members when deciding upon the appropriate measure. Even though the language of the TBT Agreement itself and the accompanying case law are not precise enough to ensure that the most efficient measure is always adopted, discussing 'necessity' within the transparency framework and particularly within the TBT Committee allows Members to collaborate in the search for cost-efficient measures and helps them to rationalise policy interventions through dialogue, rather than through prescriptive legal principles.

Given the general logic of the SPS and TBT Agreements, which aim first and foremost at preventing WTO Members from developing regulatory measures that restrict international trade, the core obligation is that measures must be necessary. They are presumed to be necessary if they are based on international standards and the regulating Member should otherwise

---

[41] Appellate Body Report, *US – Tuna II (Mexico)*, §321.
[42] See Principle 4.3 of OECD, 'Recommendation of the Council on Regulatory Policy and Governance', 2012. www.oecd.org/gov/regulatory-policy/49990817.pdf.
[43] Mavroidis, *The Regulation of International Trade*, 422.
[44] See Appellate Body Report, *US – Tuna II (Mexico)*, §§328–30. On this, see also Mavroidis, *The Regulation of International Trade*, 422; Boris Rigod, *Optimal Regulation and the Law of International Trade* (Cambridge: Cambridge University Press, 2015), 178–9.

demonstrate them to be such. The obligation of non-discrimination constitutes a 'coherent whole' in combination with the necessity obligation and can be seen as sequential to the discussion of necessity: if a measure is necessary, then it should also be applied in a non-discriminatory manner.[45]

III The Prohibition of Discrimination within the Limits of Regulatory Autonomy

Like the GATT, both the SPS and TBT Agreements include a non-discrimination obligation. However, the obligation under the Agreements differs from the general GATT obligation. The non-discrimination obligation under the SPS Agreement is worded differently from that under the GATT and has therefore resulted in specific interpretations by WTO adjudicators (section A). Non-discrimination under the TBT Agreement has been interpreted similarly to that under the GATT, while acknowledging that, in the TBT context, certain situations justify 'legitimate regulatory distinctions' (section B).

A Non-discrimination under the SPS Agreement

The SPS Agreement includes an obligation of non-discrimination, which, although worded differently, is similar to that under the GATT and the TBT Agreement. However, the SPS Agreement adds a requirement specific to SPS subject matter, requiring all WTO Members to apply a consistent level of protection against risks to human life or health, or to animal and plant life or health, as well as to avoid discrimination or disguised restrictions to trade.

1 The Non-discrimination Test

According to Article 2.3 of the SPS Agreement, Members must neither adopt nor apply measures that result in discrimination between other Members, as well as between other Members and themselves:

> Members shall ensure that their sanitary and phytosanitary measures do not arbitrarily or unjustifiably discriminate between Members where identical or similar conditions prevail, including between their own territory and that of other Members. Sanitary and phytosanitary measures shall not be applied in a manner which would constitute a disguised restriction on international trade.

---

[45] Petros C. Mavroidis, 'Last Mile for Tuna (to a Safe Harbour): What Is the TBT Agreement All About?', *European Journal of International Law* 30, no. 1 (2019): 299.

III THE PROHIBITION OF DISCRIMINATION

The language defining the non-discrimination principle under the SPS Agreement differs from that of the GATT and the TBT Agreement. The language of Article 2.3 of the SPS Agreement resembles that of Article XX GATT on the general exception for the protection of human, animal or plant life or health more than it does that of Article III GATT or even Article 2.1 of the TBT Agreement. Indeed, strikingly, the terms 'like products' and 'less favourable treatment' – which are the basis of the tests for discrimination in case law under the GATT and the TBT Agreement – are absent from the SPS Agreement, and the subjects of comparison are 'Members' as opposed to products.

This results in a more broadly applicable obligation that is not only more difficult to comply with but also more difficult to prove violated. The test to determine whether there is discrimination according to Article 2.3 of the SPS Agreement was set out by a WTO panel in *Australia – Salmon* and it involves proving three cumulative points – namely, that:

- the measure discriminates between the territories of Members other than the Member imposing the measure, or between the territory of the Member imposing the measure and that of another Member;
- the discrimination is arbitrary or unjustifiable; and
- identical or similar conditions prevail in the territories of the Members compared.[46]

The first criterion is particularly broad and means that, unlike the GATT and the TBT Agreement, the competitive relationship between products is not the starting point in determining discriminatory treatment under the SPS Agreement. Indeed, the panel considered the obligation to apply to both similar and different products.[47] Therefore the test focuses more on the conditions that apply to the products than on the products themselves in any determination of whether the discrimination is unjustified.[48]

2 Consistency of the Protection

As an additional 'condition' imposed on Members' regulatory autonomy, the SPS Agreement establishes a certain threshold for regulatory quality beyond only a measure's trade effects. Article 5.5 of the SPS Agreement requires a Member to avoid 'unjustifiable distinctions in the levels it considers to be appropriate in different situations, if such distinctions

---

[46] Panel Report, *Australia – Salmon (Recourse to Article 21.5 of the DSU by Canada)*, §7.111.
[47] Ibid., §7.112.
[48] For more details on this, see Prévost, 'Balancing Trade and Health in the SPS Agreement'; Marceau and Trachtman, 'A Map of the World Trade Organization Law of Domestic Regulation of Goods', 351–432.

result in discrimination or a disguised restriction on international trade'. The primary objective of this 'consistency' requirement is to avoid discrimination or disguised restrictions to trade, as explicitly mentioned in Article 5.5. Nevertheless, by imposing a consistent level of protection against risks to human, animal and plant health or safety throughout Members' policies, the SPS Agreement imposes on domestic regulators the principle of coherence that they are encouraged to consider throughout their regulatory interventions: 'Where appropriate promote regulatory coherence through co-ordination mechanisms between the supranational, the national and sub-national levels of government. Identify cross-cutting regulatory issues at all levels of government, to promote coherence between regulatory approaches and avoid duplication or conflict of regulations.'[49]

In practice, this obligation is difficult to implement and to enforce, and hence the SPS Committee adopted a set of guidelines to help regulating Members to determine whether a proposed regulation may result in a violation of Article 5.5.[50] Two key elements of the obligation under Article 5.5 stand out as a common thread throughout the guidelines: the regulating Member's obligation to apply the concept of appropriate level of protection consistently and the obligation to avoid arbitrary or unjustifiable distinctions among the levels of regulation considered appropriate.[51]

The SPS Committee underlines that the consistency requirement has impact at the very early stages of the regulatory process, even before a Member identifies the relevant measure:

> The determination of the appropriate level of protection is an element in the decision-making process which logically precedes the selection and use of one or more sanitary or phytosanitary measures. The following guidelines therefore address the application of the concept of the appropriate level of protection, and subsequently its practical implementation.[52]

Thus this requirement introduces an international aspect at the very earliest stages of the domestic regulatory cycle, aiming to avoid arbitrary or discriminatory behaviour at the outset when choosing the level at which to protect human health and safety. In this sense, even before the level of protection is judged right or wrong, the SPS Agreement aims to prevent the regulating Member from manifesting discriminatory intent.

---

[49] Organisation for Economic Co-operation and Development, 'Recommendation of the Council on Regulatory Policy and Governance', 2012, Principle 10. www.oecd.org/gov/regulatory-policy/49990817.pdf.
[50] See WTO, 'Guidelines to Further the Practical Implementation of Article 5.5' (G/SPS/15, 2000).
[51] See ibid., Introduction.
[52] Ibid., 2.

Transparency is essential if regulating Members are to demonstrate consistent levels of protection among different policies. The SPS guidelines therefore start with a call for Members to indicate, 'in a sufficiently clear manner', what level of protection they consider appropriate, 'either in a published statement or other text generally available to interested parties'.[53]

To determine the 'appropriate' character of protection, the guidelines invite Members to compare their levels of protection and thereby to ensure that their own are not arbitrary or unjustifiable. If differing levels of protection are found to be arbitrary or unjustifiable, the regulating Member is then to examine whether its regulation may result in discrimination or a disguised restriction on international trade.

The SPS Committee guidelines list 'warning signals' that may constitute 'discrimination or a disguised restriction on international trade' – namely:

- 'substantial differences in the levels of protection considered to be appropriate in different situations';
- 'the existence of arbitrary or unjustifiable differences in the levels of protection considered by a Member as appropriate in different situations';
- 'the absence of a scientific justification for a sanitary or phytosanitary measure applied allegedly to achieve the appropriate level of protection, or the fact that a measure is not based on a risk assessment as appropriate to the circumstances (either because there is no risk assessment or because there is an insufficient risk assessment)'.[54]

In addition, the guidelines underline the importance of *reasoned* transparency in the adoption of SPS measures and, more specifically, of dialogue among the regulators determining the level of protection as a way of ensuring the consistency of regulations:

> A Member should establish clear and effective communication and information flows within and between the authorities responsible for the determination of appropriate levels of protection. An important element in seeking to ensure that decisions on an appropriate level of protection meet the provisions of Article 5.5 is information and communication. The authorities responsible for the preparation and implementation of such decisions should be aware of relevant decisions taken by that Member in other cases, and particularly in situations comparable to the one at hand.[55]

---

[53] Ibid.
[54] Ibid., 3.
[55] Ibid., §A3.

Therefore, going beyond requiring Members to take into account the external impacts of their levels of protection and read together with the Committee guidelines, Article 5.5 of the SPS Agreement establishes a consistency requirement that encourages coherence among domestic regulatory choices and which may have domestic benefits that reach beyond trade effects.

Neither the GATT nor the TBT Agreement includes any such requirement – although Marceau and Trachtman argue that *Korea – Bovine Meat (Canada)* introduces a soft consistency requirement into the Article XX GATT necessity test that might also be transposed into the necessity test under Article 2.2 of the TBT Agreement.[56]

B Non-discrimination under the TBT Agreement

The non-discrimination provision of the TBT Agreement uses similar language to that found in Article III GATT. To establish that a measure is discriminatory under the TBT Agreement:

(i) the measure needs to be a technical regulation;[57]
(ii) the imported and domestic products need to be 'like products' (which the WTO's Appellate Body defines using the same criteria as those applied under the GATT, based on the competitive relationship between the products at stake);[58] and
(iii) the imported products must be accorded 'less favourable treatment' than the like domestic products.

However, the main difference between the text of the TBT Agreement and that of the GATT lies in the absence of a separate TBT article on exceptions to the obligations. This absence seems justified by the importance attributed to the regulatory autonomy of Members – a principle set out in the Preamble to the TBT Agreement and limited only by certain obligations, including that Members do not discriminate against other Members or between a Member and themselves.

---

[56] Marceau and Trachtman, 'A Map of the World Trade Organization Law of Domestic Regulation of Goods'.
[57] A similar obligation applies to CAPs and standards.
[58] '… the very concept of "treatment no less favourable", which is expressed in the same words in Article III:4 of the GATT 1994 and in Article 2.1 of the *TBT Agreement*, informs the determination of likeness, suggesting that likeness is about the "nature and extent of a competitive relationship between and among products" ': Appellate Body Report, *US – Clove Cigarettes*, §111.

The Appellate Body noted this absence of a general exception clause in the TBT Agreement in its report on *US – Clove Cigarettes*, but without drawing any general conclusions.[59] It merely considered that the balance the GATT held between non-discrimination and the general exceptions was directly embedded in Article 2.1 of the TBT Agreement 'itself, read in the light of its context and its object and purpose'.[60]

The Appellate Body's reports have been highly criticised on this basis. One particular criticism is that, by directly 'importing' the test for determining 'likeness' from GATT case law, in which it is based on consumer preference, the Appellate Body fails to reflect the TBT Agreement's focus on regulatory barriers, for instance by taking into account the regulator's perspective rather than that of the consumer in determining likeness.[61]

In *US – Clove Cigarettes*, however, the Appellate Body does interpret non-discrimination in the TBT Agreement in a way that facilitates regulatory autonomy, by introducing the concept of a 'legitimate regulatory distinction'. The Appellate Body therefore underlines that certain differences of treatment may be justified:

> The object and purpose of the TBT Agreement is to strike a balance between, on the one hand, the objective of trade liberalization and, on the other hand, Members' right to regulate. This object and purpose therefore suggests that Article 2.1 should not be interpreted as prohibiting any detrimental impact on competitive opportunities for imports in cases where such detrimental impact on imports stems exclusively from legitimate regulatory distinctions.[62]

The concept of legitimate regulatory distinction is, in theory, an additional legal protection granting Members regulatory autonomy, allowing them to justify different regulatory approaches in different circumstances. Nevertheless, the criteria with which the Appellate Body decides on the legitimacy of a regulatory distinction is particularly difficult to predict. Any regulating Member invoking such a defence needs to demonstrate that the detrimental effect stems

---

[59] 'Finally, we observe that the *TBT Agreement* does not contain among its provisions a general exceptions clause. This may be contrasted with the GATT 1994, which contains a general exceptions clause in Article XX': Appellate Body Report, *US – Clove Cigarettes*, §101.
[60] Ibid., §109.
[61] Petros C. Mavroidis, 'Driftin' Too Far from Shore: Why the Test for Compliance with the TBT Agreement Developed by the WTO Appellate Body Is Wrong, and What Should the AB Have Done Instead', *World Trade Review* 12, no. 3 (2013): 509–31.
[62] Appellate Body Report, *US – Clove Cigarettes*, §174.

exclusively from the legitimate regulatory distinction, as set out by the Appellate Body in *US – Clove Cigarettes* and further confirmed in *US – Tuna II (Mexico)*.[63] Mavroidis notes that this is all the more difficult to demonstrate given that necessary policies do, by definition, impose some level of burden on international trade: Members are not required to adopt the first best measure, but merely 'necessary' measures.[64] The Appellate Body's compliance report in *US – Tuna II (Mexico)* did not help to clarify the concept or the ways in which a Member might demonstrate the causality between the detrimental impact and the legitimacy of the regulatory distinction.[65] In this context, it is all the more important that transparency is guaranteed throughout the regulatory process to highlight the evidence basis of regulations and to prove non-discriminatory intent.

Overall, the obligations of non-discrimination and necessity, as set out in the SPS and TBT Agreements, require Members to consider the likely cross-border effects when developing their domestic measures. This is an important first step towards starting to mitigate the negative effects of regulatory heterogeneity throughout the multilateral trading system. Nevertheless, the obligations remain 'fuzzy',[66] in that methodologies for identifying the most appropriate measure are not apparent and regulating Members may still struggle to find it. The transparency and regulatory co-operation framework set up by the SPS and TBT Agreements and the related Committee practices are therefore particularly important

---

[63] Appellate Body Report, *US – Tuna II (Mexico)*, §297.
[64] Mavroidis, 'Last Mile for Tuna (to a Safe Harbour)', 294.
[65] See commentaries to Art. 21.5 in Appellate Body Report, *United States – Measures Concerning the Importation, Marketing and Sale of Tuna and Tuna Products*, WT/DS381/AB/RW, 20 November 2015 (Compliance (Art. 21.5)). For example, Mavroidis, 'Last Mile for Tuna (to a Safe Harbour)'; Robert Howse, 'The *Tuna/Dolphin* Appellate Body 21.5 Ruling: A Decision That Could Threaten the Integrity and Efficiency of WTO Dispute Settlement', *International Economic Law and Policy Blog* (blog), 2015. https://worldtradelaw.typepad.com/ielpblog/2015/11/the-tunadolphin-appellate-body-215-ruling-a-decision-that-could-threaten-the-integrity-and-efficiency-of-wto-dispute-settl.html; Cary Coglianese and André Sapir, 'Risk and Regulatory Calibration: WTO Compliance Review of the US Dolphin-Safe Tuna Labeling Regime', *World Trade Review* 16, no. 2 (2017): 327–48.
[66] Hoekman and Kostecki note that 'the disciplines of many WTO agreements are often fuzzy, ambiguous or simply not defined. As a result there can easily be legitimate uncertainty regarding the appropriate interpretations of a provision in a specific context': Hoekman and Kostecki, *The Political Economy of the World Trading System*, 85.

to complement these open-ended obligations, to help rationalise regulatory interventions and to further reduce the unnecessary trade costs of regulatory divergence. Finally, in the event that trade frictions exist, transparency and regulatory dialogue are essential in clarifying the rationale behind a measure and the evidence-based process that was followed in its adoption, so that all parties can determine whether or not the measure complies with the SPS and TBT Agreements.

2

Transparency as a Core Principle under the SPS and TBT Agreements

Transparency provisions play an essential role in ensuring the effective implementation of the WTO Agreements on the Application of Sanitary and Phytosanitary Measures (SPS Agreement, or SPS) and on Technical Barriers to Trade (TBT Agreement, or TBT). Transparency provisions open up access to information on other Members' domestic measures and, to a certain extent, also their rationale. As such, Members' compliance with transparency obligations is key if trading partners are to identify which laws and regulations affect trade significantly, and to estimate whether or not those laws and regulations have been adopted in line with SPS and TBT obligations.

This chapter presents the transparency requirements under the SPS and TBT Agreements and the role that these requirements may play in allowing Members to share information on and insight into their policies at an early stage in the regulatory process.

Both the SPS and the TBT Agreements cite transparency as an important element in the domestic regulatory process, but the structure of the transparency requirements is different in the two Agreements. The TBT Agreement includes most of its transparency obligations in the same articles as those that cover other core obligations,[1] underlining the connection between the transparency mechanisms and the common goals of clear regulations and parity among them. The SPS Agreement includes most of its detailed requirements in an annex, with only one brief article in the body text of the Agreement providing

---

[1] The TBT Agreement includes separate articles on transparency for technical regulations (Art. 2 TBT), standards (Annex 3 TBT) and conformity assessment procedures (CAPs) (Art. 5 TBT). We shall not look at the transparency of standards, which differs slightly from that of technical regulations and CAPs, which represent the bulk of Members' transparency practice under the TBT Agreement.

for notification and information sharing.[2] The language used in both Agreements is almost identical, however, justifying a chapter studying the two jointly.

To some extent, bilateral trade agreements (BTAs) and regional trade agreements (RTAs) concluded since the SPS and TBT Agreements have built on the existing transparency provisions. These developments are referred to in what follows insofar as they illuminate evolving practice within the WTO.

I   The Purpose of Transparency under the SPS and TBT Agreements: Information, Predictability and Dialogue

Both the SPS and TBT Agreements use very similar language, largely inspired by the Tokyo Round 'Standards Code' (especially Article 2.5 et seq.). Transparency provisions in both of the Agreements pursue three complementary objectives: making regulations known and publicly available (section A); allowing other Members, particularly developing countries, time to adapt to newly adopted measures (section B); and allowing interested parties to comment on new regulatory drafts, thus opening up dialogue throughout the regulatory process (section C).[3]

The first two objectives are close to those pursued by transparency provisions in other WTO texts. Although the SPS and TBT transparency provisions differ considerably from those found elsewhere in the WTO, the early drafts of the negotiations towards the General Agreement on Tariffs and Trade (GATT) show that the GATT negotiators also considered similar objectives, pointing towards the origins of the SPS and TBT transparency provisions.

A   Information: Making Regulations Known and Publicly Available to Interested Parties

Making regulations known and publicly available is the most obvious obligation pursued by transparency: a domestic measure must be disclosed in such a way that relevant parties can become acquainted with it.

---

[2] Annex B and Art. 7 SPS.
[3] Ludivine Tamiotti, 'Article 2 TBT Agreement', in Rüdiger Wolfrum, Peter-Tobias Stoll and Anja Seibert-Fohr, eds, *WTO: Technical Barriers and SPS Measures*, vol. III, Max Planck Commentaries on World Trade Law (Leiden/Boston, MA: Martinus Nijhoff, 2007), 210–34.

This objective is apparent in the SPS and TBT Agreements, both of which explicitly require a measure to be published for that reason.[4] The WTO's Appellate Body has confirmed that enhancing the transparency of SPS regulations adopted or maintained by other Members is the object and purpose of Annex B, paragraph 1, to the SPS Agreement, which sets out a publication requirement, aiming to enable 'interested parties to become acquainted with' a measure.[5]

The language with which each of the two Agreements defines the extent of the obligation to publish differs slightly: the TBT Agreement pursues the objective of providing information to private parties ('interested parties in other Members'), while the SPS Agreement aims to make information available among Members ('interested Members'). The extension of the obligation to 'interested parties' under the TBT Agreement allows for a broad application of transparency, reaching beyond Members to encompass non-governmental stakeholders, enabling them to play an active part in the gathering and dissemination of information.

The notification procedures under the SPS and TBT Agreements are key to ensuring that information about domestic measures is made genuinely available. In its case law, the WTO has confirmed the distinction between making information available and the TBT obligation to provide information to all WTO Members via the notification procedure. In *US – Clove Cigarettes*, the United States argued that it did not need to notify because all the information was publicly available. The panel rejected this line of reasoning, underlining that:

> In our view, regardless of the merits of the United States' arguments, the obligation set out in Article 2.9.2 of the *TBT Agreement* is straightforward: WTO Members must notify other Members through the WTO Secretariat of the product coverage, the objective and the rationale of their proposed technical regulations, at an early appropriate stage. The United States has failed to do so in respect of Section 907(a)(1)(A).[6]

In other words, the panel in this case distinguished between the mere existence of publicly available information and the unique characteristic of TBT notifications that, at an early appropriate stage, provide information to all WTO Members about the product's coverage, as well as the objective and the rationale of proposed technical regulations, and ensure that all this information is made accessible from a centralised source via the WTO Secretariat.

---

[4] See e.g. 2.9.1 and 5.6.1 TBT.
[5] Appellate Body Report, *Japan – Agricultural Products II*, §10.
[6] Panel Report, *US – Clove Cigarettes*, §7.541.

I   THE PURPOSE OF TRANSPARENCY

The objective of guaranteeing the public availability of information on domestic regulations was already being raised in the early years of GATT negotiations. The first draft of the GATT included a proposal by the United States requiring publication of domestic measures and their centralisation: 'Copies of ... laws, regulations, decisions, rulings and agreements shall be communicated promptly to the Organization.'[7] Although this proposal was omitted from the final text of Article X GATT, the obligation of notification provided for in both the SPS and TBT Agreements[8] is in line with the early draft, as is the obligation to submit statements on the implementation and administration of the TBT Agreement.[9] The provisions of the SPS and TBT Agreements are more limited in scope than the initial proposal for the GATT, because they apply only to SPS and TBT measures, as well as to only draft and not final adopted measures. Nevertheless, the centralisation of information by the WTO Secretariat – through notifications, committee discussions, and statements on the implementation and administration of the TBT Agreement in particular – contributes to the objective that information on Members' domestic measures be made genuinely publicly available.

B   Predictability: Allowing Traders Time to Adapt to the New Measures

The second objective of transparency under the two Agreements consists of ensuring that the costs that changes in regulatory requirements will entail for traders are predictable. It is directly linked to the broader purpose of avoiding unnecessary obstacles to trade by embedding foreseeability into the domestic requirements of all WTO Members.

Both Agreements include in their transparency obligations the requirement to give traders sufficient time to adapt to new measures. The requirement is explicit in the call for a 'reasonable interval between the publication of ... regulations and their entry into force'.[10] It is also apparent in the provision requiring the publication of a notice before the regulation is adopted. This is important if traders are to be able to predict the different types of cost that exporting to a certain country will entail – particularly the specification costs incurred when adapting a product to meet the regulatory requirements in the export market.

---

[7] E/PC/T/33, 28.
[8] Articles 2.9 and 5.6 TBT; Art. 5.B and Annex B, SPS.
[9] Article 15.2 TBT.
[10] Articles 2.12 and 5.9 TBT; Annex B, para. 2, SPS.

The original US proposal for the GATT article on transparency included a more detailed provision in this regard, excluding the application of new requirements to 'products of any other Members already en route at the time of publication thereof'.[11] This text was not agreed upon, however, and such a detailed obligation was included neither in the GATT nor in the SPS and TBT Agreements.

C Dialogue on Draft Measures between Members to Encourage Regulatory Coherence

The third and fundamental objective of the transparency under the SPS and TBT Agreements is to encourage dialogue between Members on proposed measures before their entry into force, which may support the development of coherent measures across WTO Members. The two Agreements require that Members allow, without discrimination, 'reasonable time for other Members to make comments in writing'.[12] The right to comment in response to notifications is an essential aspect of transparency under the SPS and TBT Agreements, discussed in five paragraphs of each,[13] and provided for in relation to both 'regular' and emergency notifications.

The requirement in an international agreement to consider comments on draft measures (via WTO notifications) is a unique transparency tool that allows Members to participate in other Members' regulatory process. The TBT Committee itself recognised that notification procedures 'provide Members with the opportunity to influence final requirements of other Members, and could enhance harmonisation as well as lead to the transfer of technology'.[14]

The panel in *US – Clove Cigarettes* confirmed that the opportunity to comment is at the heart of the notification procedure under the TBT Agreement:

> In our view, Article 2.9.2 (as it is also the case with Article 5.6.2 for conformity assessment procedures) is at the core of the *TBT Agreement*'s transparency provisions: the very purpose of the notification is to provide opportunity for comment before the proposed measure enters into force, when there is time for changes to be made before 'it is too late'.[15]

---

[11] Article 21.3 of the London Draft: see E/PC/T/33, 28.
[12] Articles 2.9.4 and 5.6.4 TBT; Art. 5.d SPS.
[13] Articles 2.9.2–2.9.4, 2.10.3 and 2.10.4 TBT; Annex B, paras 5.b–d and 6.b–c, SPS.
[14] WTO, 'Third Triennial Review of the Operation and Implementation of the Agreement on Technical Barriers to Trade' (G/TBT/13, 2003), 3.
[15] Panel Report, *US – Clove Cigarettes*, §7.536.

The SPS Committee notes that these consultations on draft measures at the WTO level may also help to reinforce transparency and enhance consultation processes domestically – namely, by expanding the reach of the consultation internationally and allowing other countries to have input on proposed domestic measures.[16]

The scope of the notification process is designed to enable regulatory dialogue regarding draft measures. Notifications are required for measures that do not adopt international standards and which may have a significant effect on other Members' trade, and thus this is also when the right to comment on notifications is most relevant. In addition, as we will see later in the chapter, comments should be provided at a time when they may be truly useful for other countries in reducing unnecessary trade costs: comments can be made on draft measures even when international standards have not been adopted.

The obligation to notify applies to draft measures, thus focusing on *ex ante* transparency. This is a key characteristic of the SPS and TBT Agreements, which differs from the *ex post* transparency that applies under GATT 1947. In concentrating on the *preparation* of measures and consultation among all Members, the SPS and TBT transparency framework minimises the need for further transparency after adoption. While it might be said that this reduces the visibility of existing trade policies, the two Agreements aim more at fostering dialogue between Members on proposed measures than at providing complete information on the existing regulatory environment.

Ultimately, by ensuring that there is regulatory dialogue and co-operation between Members, this right under the SPS and TBT Agreements aims to ensure that, in the absence of harmonisation, all new measures are consistent with the WTO Agreements and do not create unnecessary barriers to trade. In other words, the right aims to mitigate divergences among Members' regulatory approaches.

II   The Scope of Transparency Obligations: Proposed Regulations Diverging from International Standards with a Significant Effect on Trade

Transparency obligations under the SPS and TBT Agreements do not cover all domestic measures; they apply only to measures that fall within the scope of the SPS and TBT Agreements and which have an effect on trade. The

---

[16] WTO, 'How to Apply the Transparency Provisions of the SPS Agreement: A Handbook Prepared by the WTO Secretariat', September 2002, 11. www.wto.org/english/tratop_e/sps_e/spshand_e.pdf.

scope of the SPS and TBT Agreements is particularly important if WTO Members – and, most specifically, the regulators subject to the transparency framework – are to know which measures they are meant to be transparent about. To comply with these transparency obligations, the authorities responsible for notifying to the WTO must be aware of the drafts that regulators throughout their country are preparing and must be able to determine whether those drafts fall within the scope of the two Agreements. This entails significant co-ordination among authorities at the domestic level.

Articles 2.9 and 5.6 of the TBT Agreement set out the scope of the basic *ex ante* transparency obligations under the two Agreements: publication of a notice, notifications, provision of copies and time for comments. Members must comply with these obligations when they plan to adopt a measure that is not based on international standards and if it may have a significant effect on trade.

Annex B to the SPS Agreement is slightly different in this regard and separates out the transparency obligations under different headings. The two criteria applied under the TBT Agreement's core transparency obligations fall, in the SPS Agreement, under the heading 'Notification Procedures' (Annex B, para. 5, SBS). The content below this heading is, however, the same as the obligations listed under Articles 2.9 and 5.6 of the TBT Agreement. In practice, there is no reason to believe that the transparency obligations under the two Agreements should be interpreted differently.

A Proposed Regulations: An Emphasis on Ex Ante Transparency

The most significant transparency obligations apply mainly to *proposed* rather than *adopted* measures. The TBT Agreement applies to 'proposed regulations' and 'proposed conformity assessment procedures',[17] while the SPS Agreement applies to 'SPS measures' and 'SPS regulations'.[18] Neither the main body of the SPS Agreement nor Annex B explicitly refers to proposed regulations as the TBT Agreement does, but the obligations do imply the notification of draft measures, because notification must take place 'at an early stage, when amendments can still be introduced and comments taken into account'.[19]

---

[17] Articles 2.9 and 5.6 TBT, respectively.
[18] Article 7 and Annex B SPS, respectively.
[19] Annex B, para. 5.b, SPS. This is also confirmed in the SPS Committee's transparency guidelines: see WTO, 'How to Apply the Transparency Provisions of the SPS Agreement'.

II THE SCOPE OF TRANSPARENCY OBLIGATIONS   53

This is significantly different from other WTO transparency obligations. Indeed, throughout other WTO agreements, *ex post* transparency – that is, the transparency of existing measures – is the dominant transparency paradigm. Under the Understanding Regarding Notification, Consultation, Dispute Settlement and Surveillance adopted in 1979, Contracting Parties to the GATT undertook to notify other Contracting Parties, as far as possible, 'of their adoption of trade measures affecting the operation of the General Agreement'.[20] This general commitment to notify did not, however, apply directly to draft measures. The Parties agreed that they 'should endeavour to notify such measures in advance of implementation',[21] but this does not require there to be notification before the adoption of a measure and the language encouraging notification before implementation is relatively weak. The Understanding then acknowledges that, when this is not possible, 'such measures should be notified *ex post facto*'.[22]

Under the SPS and TBT Agreements, on the other hand, *ex post* transparency is a marginal aspect of the wide range of transparency obligations established. There is no legal notification obligation for adopted regulations nor is there an obligation to respond to enquiries or to take into account comments on adopted regulations. Adopted measures must be publicly available, but they do not benefit from the centralised character of notification obligations. The transparency framework under the SPS and TBT Agreements therefore applies to regulations to come rather than to existing regulations. While this is a key attribute of SPS and TBT transparency, characterised mainly by the opening of a dialogue regarding domestic draft measures, it also largely limits the benefits of notifications to this dialogue. The predictability and accessibility of existing regulatory frameworks is ensured only by means of consultation on regulatory drafts. The transparency requirements that apply to adopted measures are far less thorough. The TBT Committee's 2018 triennial review offered WTO Members an opportunity to renew their recommendation that all Members also notify 'the adopted final text of technical regulations and conformity assessment procedures'.[23]

---

[20] GATT Understanding Regarding Notification, Consultation, Dispute Settlement and Surveillance (L/4907, 28 November 1979), para. 3.
[21] Ibid.
[22] Ibid. The complete sentence reads: 'In other cases, where prior notification has not been possible, such measures should be notified promptly *ex post facto*.'
[23] WTO, 'Eighth Triennial Review of the Operation and Implementation of the Agreement on Technical Barriers to Trade under Article 15.4' (G/TBT/41, 19 November 2018), 20.

B Proposed Regulations: A Broad Range of Measures Falling within the Transparency Framework

There is a broad variety of measures covered under the SPS and TBT transparency obligations. Both Agreements require transparency of 'regulations', defined very broadly. While the more measures disclosed, the better for foreign trading partners, in practice this may entail difficulty for all domestic authorities if they are to keep up with the WTO obligations while pursuing their day jobs. The role of domestic enquiry points, at which we look later in this chapter, is therefore essential in raising awareness of the WTO obligation at the national level and ensuring that different authorities notify the WTO of the measures they adopt.

1   SPS Measures or Regulations

Transparency under the SPS Agreement, as interpreted by the WTO's Appellate Body, covers many types of measure, as long as they pursue the objectives of the SPS Agreement.

Article 7 of the SPS Agreement requires transparency of SPS 'measures', while Annex B uses the term SPS 'regulations'. The two seem very closely related, with the difference being that SPS 'regulations' are generally applicable.[24] Annex B, paragraph 1, to the SPS Agreement includes a footnote defining regulations as 'measures such as laws, decrees or ordinances which are applicable generally'. The Appellate Body considers the list of measures in the footnote to be non-exhaustive, as implied by the phrase 'such as', and further notes that the transparency obligation 'also includes, in our opinion, other instruments which are applicable generally and are similar in character to the instruments explicitly referred to in the illustrative list of the footnote to paragraph 1 of Annex B'.[25] This precision aligns the SPS transparency requirements with those under the GATT publication obligation, which applies to all '[l]aws, regulations, judicial decisions and administrative rulings of general application'.[26]

---

[24] The SPS Committee notes the two separate terms, but minimises the difference in meaning between the two: 'The SPS Agreement uses the terms "measures" and "regulations" somewhat interchangeably. Readers should note that regardless of the term used, the Agreement is referring to any sanitary or phytosanitary measure such as laws, decrees, or ordinances applied to protection of human, animal or plant life or health as defined under paragraph 1 of Annex A to the SPS Agreement.' (WTO, 'How to Apply the Transparency Provisions of the SPS Agreement', 11, fn. 2).

[25] Appellate Body Report, *Japan – Agricultural Products II*, §105.

[26] See e.g. Art. X:1 GATT.

II THE SCOPE OF TRANSPARENCY OBLIGATIONS

SPS measures may have a limited application, for example affecting only certain specific regions in the case of a disease epidemic. However, this does not preclude measures taken in such circumstances being of 'general application'. In the context of the GATT, panels have considered that measures of 'general application' should also be interpreted widely, as long as the impact of the measure applies beyond a specific case. In particular, such measures should cover a 'range of situations or cases, rather than being limited in their scope of application',[27] affecting 'an unidentified number of economic operators, including domestic and foreign producers',[28] 'not limited to a single import or importer'.[29] The measures of 'general application' may also include 'administrative rulings in individual cases' as long as they 'establish or revise principles or criteria applicable in future cases'.[30] In this last case, however, the burden of proof lies with the defendant.[31]

2 The TBT Agreement: Technical Regulations, Conformity Assessment Procedures and Standards

As noted earlier, the TBT Agreement applies to a specific range of domestic measures – namely, technical regulations, CAPs and standards. In this sense, the scope of transparency under the TBT Agreement is more precisely defined than that under the SPS Agreement and does not seem to extend to judicial decisions.

While the transparency requirements are similar for technical regulations and CAPs, they differ slightly for standards.

a The Transparency of Technical Regulations and Conformity Assessment Procedures Under the TBT Agreement, the transparency obligation applies to all regulations or CAPs in the same way as it does to other measures under the Agreement.

In practice, Members tend to notify all administrative acts, regulations, standards and guidelines – perhaps because the specifics of technical regulations are more generally included in administrative acts implementing primary statutes. Nevertheless, several Members also

---

[27] Panel Report, *EC – Selected Customs Matters*, §7.116.
[28] Panel Report, *US – Underwear*, §7.65.
[29] Panel Report, *EC – IT Products*, §7.159.
[30] Panel Report, *Japan – Film*, §10.388.
[31] Ibid.

notify statutes, confirming the breadth of documents that Members consider to be 'technical regulations', regardless of their domestic legal character.[32]

Members sometimes avoid the risk of 'self-incrimination' that notifications can pose by expressing in the notification that it is for transparency purposes only and not to respond to a notification obligation under the Agreements. This is the case, for instance, in the European Union's notification on genetically modified foods: 'This notification is for transparency purposes and does not prejudge the position of the European Union on the applicability of the TBT Agreement to the notified measures, or on the nature and effects of the measure itself.'[33]

b **The Transparency of Standards** The transparency obligations also apply to standards, although not quite as they do to technical regulations and CAPs. The scope of the transparency obligation for standards is in line with the definition of standards themselves: it covers voluntary standards that have been adopted by a standardising body.[34]

As mentioned in Chapter 1, it is the Code of Good Practice for the Preparation, Adoption and Application of Standards set out in Annex 3 to the TBT Agreement that introduces the principles applicable to standardising bodies. As it does for technical regulations and CAPs, the Code of Good Practice provides for the centralisation of information on standards and a special period for comments before a standard can be adopted. The Code ends with a provision requiring standardising bodies to afford 'sympathetic consideration to, and adequate opportunity for consultation'.[35]

Given that standards are not developed by WTO Members directly but by standardising bodies – whether governmental or non-governmental – and that these standards are voluntary and not binding, it is not the WTO Secretariat that centralises the information, but an information centre

---

[32] In recent years, see e.g. notifications by Albania (G/TBT/N/ALB/68), Canada (G/TBT/N/CAN/405), Chile (G/TBT/N/CHL/292; G/TBT/N/CHL/289), Ireland (G/TBT/N/IRL/1), Italy (G/TBT/N/ITA/16), Latvia (G/TBT/N/14) and Ukraine (G/TBT/N/UKR/89).
[33] G/TBT/N/EU/284.
[34] These principles regarding the transparency of international standards are separate from those relating to technical regulations and CAPs because of the voluntary nature of standards. Standards therefore do not come within the scope of the obligations presented in the rest of this section.
[35] Annex 3, paras L–N, TBT.

jointly operated by the International Organization for Standardization (ISO) and the International Electrotechnical Commission (IEC) – that is, the ISO/IEC Information Centre.[36]

C   The Absence of International Standards: Information about Only Those Measures Presumed to Be Divergent

If regulations conform with international standards, we can presume that they will not create an unnecessary barrier to trade.[37] Transparency helps to ensure that a new regulation does not pursue protectionist objectives under cover of a legitimate objective. Therefore, if the regulation conforms with international standards, there is presumably less need for transparency. The legitimacy of the Member's objectives is not as clear when the new regulation is not based on an international standard, whether because it does not exist or because the Member chooses not to follow it. In this instance only, then, the TBT and SPS Agreements require the publication of a notice, notification and response to enquiries or comments.

The international standard criterion can be criticised as excluding certain potentially trade-restrictive measures from notification.[38] Indeed, it relies on the premise that measures adopted on the basis of international standards are clearer and more predictable than others because Members all have the same access to and awareness of international standards. However, even measures adopted on the basis of international standards may involve adaptation costs for traders and not all Members may wholly understand existing international standards.[39] Indeed, international standards are mentioned in an increasing number of trade concerns: measures based on international standards do not necessarily conform with them. Countries may use different methodologies when basing their domestic measures on international

---

[36] Annex 3, para. J, TBT.
[37] Article 2.5 TBT; Art. 3.2 SPS.
[38] Joanne Scott, *The WTO Agreement on Sanitary and Phytosanitary Measures: A Commentary*. Oxford Commentaries on the GATT/WTO Agreements (Oxford: Oxford University Press, 2009).
[39] Prévost notes that 'several Members at lower levels of development, in practice, have difficulties participating effectively in international standard setting activities, and the resulting standards may therefore not reflect their needs and concerns': Marie Denise Prévost, 'Transparency Obligations under the TBT Agreement', in Tracey Epps and M. J. Trebilcock, eds, *Research Handbook on the WTO and Technical Barriers to Trade*, Research Handbooks on the WTO (Cheltenham: Edward Elgar, 2013), 127.

standards, spanning referring to, recognising or incorporating them. Few countries take a systematic approach to incorporating international standards into their domestic legislation: among OECD countries, only a third have a standardised approach.[40] WTO Members may therefore end up with different domestic regulations despite their common 'basis' on a single standard.

Taking this into account, both the SPS and TBT Committees have encouraged Members to notify measures even when they are said to comply with international standards. The SPS Committee has encouraged Members to notify even those regulations that are substantially the same as international standards if the regulations have a significant effect on trade.[41] The notification format that the Committee recommends therefore includes a section asking the Member to identify any relevant international standard(s).[42] The WTO Secretariat is required to report annually to the Committee on the proportion of Members' notifications that relate to the adoption of international standards, guidelines and recommendations; since 2008, the date of the SPS Committee recommendation, that figure has increased considerably.[43] In 2018, 44 per cent of all SPS notifications identified an international standard as relevant to the notified measure,[44] largely indicating 'conformity' with the indicated standard (35 per cent).[45] Members can consequently be seen to be going beyond the obligations set out in the SPS Agreement, seeking to raise awareness of the majority of, if not all, new measures.

---

[40] OECD, *OECD Regulatory Policy Outlook 2018* (Paris: OECD, 2018), 136. www.oecd.org/governance/oecd-regulatory-policy-outlook-2018-9789264303072-en.htm.

[41] WTO, 'Recommended Procedures for Implementing the Transparency Obligations of the SPS Agreement (Article 7)' (G/SPS/7/Rev.3, 2008). Canada, the EU and New Zealand had supported the elimination of this criterion for notifications under the SPS Agreement, arguing that a new regulation can result in obstacles to trade for exporting countries even when the measure is based on an international standard: see G/SPS/W/157, paras 8–10; G/SPS/W/158, para. 4.7; G/SPS/W/159.

[42] See section 8 of the regular SPS notification template: WTO, 'Notification Template' (G/SPS/N, undated). www.wto.org/english/tratop_e/sps_e/transparency_toolkit_e.htm.

[43] See G/SPS/GEN/804/Rev.1-7.

[44] Of 1,717 SPS notifications, 747 indicated an international standard as a basis for the notified measure: http://spsims.wto.org/.

[45] Of 747 notifications indicating an international standard as a basis, 587 notifications were said to 'conform' to an international standard (i.e. 79 per cent): http://spsims.wto.org/. This conclusion is based on the premise that the content notified by Members is accurate. It is, of course, possible that Members may indicate that their measure conforms to an international standard even though it does not, but such bad faith notifications are not accounted for in these statistics because they are difficult to identify.

The TBT Committee has also encouraged Members to notify in the absence of international standards and to indicate in their notification 'whether or not they consider that a relevant international standard exists and, if appropriate, to provide information about deviations'.[46] However, the WTO Secretariat does not report to the TBT Committee on the volume of notifications based on international standards and therefore there is no data publicly available in this regard.

It is noteworthy here that some BTAs and RTAs concluded under the SPS and TBT Agreements have responded to this 'shortcoming' by requiring their parties to notify measures based on international standards. This may benefit all WTO Members if the parties to the RTA agree that the notifications are to be submitted to the WTO Secretariat and not only to the other parties to the RTA. In particular, the United States–Mexico–Canada Agreement (USMCA) requires parties to notify technical regulations and CAPs related to international standards as long as the measure has a significant effect on trade.[47] In addition, the USMCA specifies that, when submitting emergency notifications on technical regulations or CAPs, the parties should specify the precise international standard, guide or recommendation with which the proposed text accords.[48] In fact, the SPS chapter of the USMCA requires parties to notify using the WTO Notification Submission System (NSS), which means that the additional information that the three parties to the USMCA (Canada, Mexico and the United States) may include in these notifications will be delivered to and hence will benefit all WTO Members.[49]

D A Significant Effect on Trade: Information about Measures of Relevance in the WTO Context

Transparency, as envisaged in the WTO SPS and TBT Agreements, is important to ensure there is no unnecessary restriction on trade. When a measure has no particular effect on trade, it is not necessary to ensure that Members have knowledge of and access to it. However, if it may have a significant effect, then the draft regulation must be published. Both the

---

[46] WTO, 'Fifth Triennial Review of the Operation and Implementation of the Agreement on Technical Barriers to Trade under Article 15.4' (G/TBT/26, 2009), para. 36.
[47] Article 11.7.11 USMCA (technical barriers to trade); Art. 9.13.4 USMCA (sanitary and phytosanitary measures).
[48] Article 11.7.12 USMCA (technical barriers to trade).
[49] The TBT chapter is less explicit in this regard, but it does also require parties to transmit notifications contemporaneously to the enquiry points of each of the USMCA party and the WTO Secretariat. It can be assumed that the same information would be shared among the USMCA parties and all WTO Members.

SPS and TBT Committees have noted that the phrase 'significant effect' includes 'both import-enhancing and import-reducing effects on the trade of other Members',[50] 'as long as such effects are significant'.[51]

The TBT Committee specifies that this significance should relate to 'a specific product or a group of products, or products in general', and particularly to trade 'between two or more Members'.[52] For example, when asked about the significant effect on US–Indonesian trade of an American prohibition of clove cigarettes, a WTO panel considered that because the vast majority of clove cigarettes in the United States were imported from Indonesia, the value of which amounted to approximately USD 15 million in 2008, there was indeed a 'significant' effect.[53]

This condition applies to the publication of a notice, notification and response to enquiries or comments before a measure is adopted and hence the significant trade effect needs only to be potential. Indeed, the language of Article 2 of the TBT Agreement speaks of cases in which a technical regulation '*may* have a significant effect on trade of other Members'. The panel in *US – Clove Cigarettes* confirmed, in this regard, that a notice must be published even if a technical regulation has no actual effect on trade.

The same wording is used in Annex B, paragraph 5, to the SPS Agreement, which also anticipates publication of those measures that may have a significant trade effect. The panel in *Japan – Apples* set out two tests that will determine whether or not this is the case, looking first at whether market access conditions have changed for the exporting Member[54] and second at whether the conditions are significantly different – that is, 'whether the change has resulted in any increase in production, packaging and sales costs, such as more onerous treatment requirements or more time-consuming administrative formalities'.[55]

---

[50] WTO, 'Decisions and Recommendations Adopted by the WTO Committee on Technical Barriers to Trade since 1995' (G/TBT/1/Rev.12, 2015), para. 4.3.1.1; WTO, 'Recommended Procedures for Implementing the Transparency Obligations' (G/SPS/7/Rev.3, 2008), para. 10.
[51] WTO, 'Recommended Procedures for Implementing the Transparency Obligations', para. 10.
[52] WTO, 'Decisions and Recommendations Adopted by the WTO Committee on Technical Barriers to Trade since 1995' (G/TBT/1/Rev.10, 2011).
[53] Panel Report, *US – Clove Cigarettes*.
[54] In other words, 'would the exported product (apple fruit from the United States in this case) still be permitted to enter Japan if they complied with the prescription contained in the previous regulations?': Panel Report, *Japan – Apples*, §8.314.
[55] Ibid.

The SPS and TBT Committees have also set out a list of factors that Members should take into account when assessing whether a measure affects trade with other Members.[56]

Such an assessment may be difficult for the Member adopting a new measure, which Member must know which other Members are interested in importing the affected product into the domestic market and in what ways their companies will have to modify their practices to import under the new legislation. Taking these difficulties into account, the TBT Committee has encouraged Members to notify measures in all instances in which they are not certain whether or not a measure may have 'significant effects on trade'.[57]

One way of determining the impacts of trade is via the use of regulatory policy tools. In particular, engaging in public consultation and conducting regulatory impact assessments (RIAs) during development of a domestic measure may help regulators to gather evidence about the potential impacts of the draft text. In this sense, comments on notifications, insofar as they offer insights from foreign trading partners, may help to flag unintended impacts on international trade costs. *Ex ante* RIAs – which allow Members to evaluate the costs of regulatory or non-regulatory alternatives and identify the most cost-effective option with which to achieve the policy objective – can also be a way of evaluating the costs of such alternatives to trade.

With 'significant effect on trade' calling for notification, the SPS Committee has granted Members permission not to open a 60-day period for comment when a measure is 'trade-facilitating'.[58] The WTO's Recommended Procedures for Implementing the Transparency Obligations of the SPS Agreement mention that such '[t]rade-facilitating

---

[56] WTO, 'Questionnaire on Transparency under the SPS Agreement' (G/SPS/GEN/1382, 2 February 2015); WTO, 'Recommended Procedures for Implementing the Transparency Obligations' (G/SPS/7/Rev.3, 2008), para. 10: 'To assess whether the sanitary or phytosanitary regulation may have a significant effect on trade, the Member concerned should consider relevant available information such as: the value or other importance of imports to the importing and/or exporting Members concerned, whether from other Members individually or collectively; the potential development of such imports; and difficulties for producers in other Members, particularly in developing country Members, to comply with the proposed sanitary or phytosanitary regulations. The concept of a significant effect on trade of other Members should include both import-enhancing and import-reducing effects on the trade of other Members, as long as such effects are significant.' See also WTO, 'Decisions and Recommendations Adopted by the WTO Committee on Technical Barriers to Trade since 1995' (G/TBT/1/Rev.12, 2015), para. 4.3.1.1.

[57] WTO, 'Sixth Triennial Review of the Operation and Implementation of the Agreement on Technical Barriers to Trade under Article 15.4' (G/TBT/32, 2012), para. 12.

[58] WTO, 'Overview Regarding the Level of Implementation of the Transparency Provisions of the SPS Agreement' (G/SPS/GEN/804/Rev.12, 17 October 2019), para. 3.31.

measures could include, inter alia, the raising of the level of maximum residue limits of certain pesticides in certain products, the lifting of a ban on imports, or the simplification or elimination of certain certification/approval procedures'.[59] In 2019, 38 per cent of regular notifications were listed by Members as 'trade-facilitating'.[60]

III A Typology of Transparency Tools under the SPS and TBT Agreements: Decentralised, Centralised and Collaborative Transparency

The variety of transparency provisions and practices that exist within the SPS and TBT frameworks has resulted in a comprehensive system of transparency of domestic regulations among WTO Members. There are, however, different ways of classifying the different transparency tools that exist. The WTO Secretariat has divided the transparency obligations under the TBT Agreement into 'three pillars': publishing, notifying and responding to enquiries.[61] Wolfe divides the transparency obligations across the WTO into three 'generations',[62] following the conceptual framework established by Fung at the domestic level.[63] However, the idea of a generational chronology does not match the order in which the transparency mechanisms have emerged at the domestic level. This section will therefore analyse the transparency mechanisms in terms of their function, in line with Fung and Wolfe, but without following their chronological approach.

In practice, 'right-to-know' transparency enables decentralised access to information merely through the act of disclosure. In the WTO, it is ensured by the obligation that all proposed and adopted measures be published (section A). 'Centralised' transparency allows Members not only to access information but also to understand it. In the SPS and TBT Agreements, it is ensured by the requirement that Members notify certain measures

---

[59] WTO, 'Recommended Procedures for Implementing the Transparency Obligations', para. 3.
[60] WTO, 'Overview Regarding the Level of Implementation of the Transparency Provisions of the SPS Agreement', para. 3.31. Data from 1 January to 15 September 2019.
[61] WTO TBT Committee, 'Minutes of the Meeting Held on 29 June 2001' (G/TBT/M/24, 14 August 2001), Annex 1, §1.
[62] Robert Wolfe, 'Letting the Sun Shine in at the WTO: How Transparency Brings the Trading System to Life', Staff Working Paper No. ERSD-2013-03, 22 November 2013. http://papers.ssrn.com/sol3/Delivery.cfm?abstractid=2229741.
[63] Archon Fung, *Full Disclosure: The Perils and Promise of Transparency* (New York: Cambridge University Press, 2007).

III A TYPOLOGY OF TRANSPARENCY TOOLS   63

to the WTO Secretariat in a specific format and at a specific time (section B) – namely, those measures that have the potential to cause tensions between Members. Finally, 'collaborative' transparency is the most unique characteristic of transparency under the SPS and TBT framework: it not only ensures that Members have access to and understanding of domestic regulations but also fosters a genuine dialogue between WTO Members. This type of transparency includes the right to comment on notified measures, the requirement to establish specific authorities to receive enquiries about domestic regulations and the practice of 'specific trade concerns' (STCs) that has developed in the two Committees (section C).

New technologies are increasingly used to enhance the effectiveness of the different forms of transparency. In this section, these technologies will be presented alongside the relevant obligations that they support.

A 'Right-to-Know' Transparency: When Members and Private Traders May Become Aware

Right-to-know transparency is essentially ensured through the obligation of publication. Publication is a basic requirement that exists in most democratic legal systems today and it is the first step in guaranteeing genuine transparency – and hence the foundation on which all other transparency tools build. In this sense, publication within the WTO functions as a useful reminder for some countries and a factor driving positive reform for others.

Transparency under the SPS and TBT Agreements is in line with that provided for in other WTO agreements and other legal systems. By adding specific publication requirements to the general GATT obligation, however, the SPS and TBT Agreements extend the scope of the guarantee of transparency. There are two publication requirements set out under the SPS and TBT Agreements, both of which are key to ensuring that there is comprehensive transparency throughout the domestic regulatory process: the publication of a notice and the publication of adopted measures.

1 The Publication of a Notice

In the domestic regulatory process, the publication of a notice of a draft technical regulation, standard or CAP[64] is the first TBT and SPS transparency requirement with which regulators need to comply, before they submit notifications of draft regulations. It can be understood as the 'forward planning' tool in regulatory policy.

[64] Articles 2.9.1 and 5.6.1 TBT; Annex B, para. 5.a, SPS.

The obligation to publish a notice concerns draft measures and may help to identify in advance those measures that have the potential of affecting trade. It therefore applies in the two instances explained earlier: when the regulation is not based on an international standard and when the measure has a significant effect on trade.

a The Content and Location of the Obligation to Publish a Notice The obligation to publish a notice included in Article 2.9.1 of the TBT Agreement can serve as a 'hook' to encourage Members to engage in dialogue before beginning to draft a measure.[65] As such, this could be the basis for a highly co-operative regulatory process, starting very early on in the development of the domestic measure.

There is no definition of what a 'notice' makes reference to and the Committees give little guidance in this respect. The TBT Committee has noted that there is 'no uniformity between Members as to how this notice is to be published'[66] and therefore it decided to examine how interested parties might best become acquainted with Members' notices.

The TBT Committee has required Members to include information on the relevant publications in their 'statements of implementation' under Article 15.2 of the TBT Agreement.[67] In particular, the Committee requires Members to specify:

> ... the names of the publications used to announce that work is proceeding on draft technical regulations or standards and procedures for assessment of conformity and those in which the texts of technical regulations and standards or procedures for assessment of conformity are published under Articles 2.9.1, 2.11; 3.1 (in relation to 2.9.1 and 2.11); 5.6.1, 5.8; 7.1, 8.1 and 9.2 (in relation to 5.6.1 and 5.8); and paragraphs J, L and O of Annex 3 of the Agreement.[68]

On this basis, the WTO Secretariat, under its own initiative, gathers the names of the publications that Members specify in their 'statements of

---

[65] Erik Wijkström, 'The Third Pillar: Behind the Scenes, WTO Committee Work Delivers', *E15 Initiative*, 15 December 2015.
[66] WTO, 'Fourth Triennial Review of the Operation and Implementation of the Agreement on Technical Barriers to Trade under Article 15.4' (G/TBT/19, 14 November 2006), para. 51.
[67] Under Art. 15.2 TBT, Members are required to submit a statement listing the measures taken to ensure the implementation and administration of the TBT Agreement. See WTO, 'Decisions and Recommendations Adopted by the WTO Committee on Technical Barriers to Trade since 1995' (G/TBT/1/Rev.12, 2015), 18.
[68] WTO, 'Decisions and Recommendations Adopted by the WTO Committee on Technical Barriers to Trade since 1995' (G/TBT/1/Rev.10, 2011), 17.

implementation'. It then lists this information in a periodically updated table, made publicly available under the designation 'G/TBT/GEN/39' (and revisions). The latest version of the list, at time of writing, was published in 2011 (G/TBT/GEN/39/Rev.5). Publications were listed for 104 Members (out of a total of 160), of which only 28 provided a web link. In other words, 35 per cent of WTO Members have not published a notice of the publications in which draft technical regulations may be found and 83 per cent of WTO Members have not provided online access to such information. These figures illustrate the limited effect that the publication of a notice has had in terms of transparency, even with the Secretariat's efforts to centralise the information.

The Non-exhaustive List of Voluntary Mechanisms and Related Principles of Good Regulatory Practice (GRP) under discussion in the TBT Committee offers further guidance on the publication of a notice.[69] It encourages Members to 'publish a notice of anticipated regulatory activity', for instance by notifying the TBT Committee of the web address where other Members may access information on upcoming regulatory activity. This guidance has only indicative value, however, because the Committee has not yet adopted it. Members may go beyond the requirements set out in the TBT Agreement and choose to submit in-depth forward planning documentation to the WTO Secretariat, sharing information on all planned technical regulations.[70]

The SPS Committee encourages Members to publish measures electronically, as far as possible, to improve the accessibility of information.[71] Publication on the internet is not mandatory, because the TBT Committee recognises that this demands special technical means to which not all WTO Members necessarily have the same access. Hard copies must therefore still be available upon request.[72] Indeed, developing country Members identified as a common problem relating to the publication of a notice 'the lack of specialised publications, and/or to the lack of staff and/or IT resources with which to publish such information'.[73]

---

[69] A first draft of this document was circulated in February 2013 and the latest draft to date was circulated in December 2014.
[70] This is the case for Mexico, which is the only WTO Member to circulate its forward planning tool for technical regulations and standards to all WTO Members. See e.g. WTO, 'Communication from Mexico' (G/TBT/GEN/Add.22, 2016); OECD, *Review of International Regulatory Co-operation of Mexico* (Paris: OECD, 2018), 72.
[71] WTO, 'Recommended Procedures for Implementing the Transparency Obligations'.
[72] WTO, 'Decisions and Recommendations Adopted by the Technical Barriers to Trade Committee since 1 January 1995' (G/TBT/1/Rev.8, 2002).
[73] See WTO, 'A Compilation and Summary of the Responses Received to the Questionnaire for a Survey to Assist Developing Country Members to Identify and Prioritise Their Specific Needs in the TBT Field' (G/TBT/W/186, 14 October 2002), 15.

By using the internet to publish trade measures, WTO Members enrich the effect of publication, which is no longer simply a first-generation 'right-to-know' transparency activity, providing interested parties with basic information, but a third-generation transparency policy, making use of new technologies to make information more easily accessible and user-friendly. This might provide an early opportunity for Members or other stakeholders to submit comments on the draft. However, access to published information remains decentralised – and, as noted, it remains uncommon, requiring that interested parties already be aware of the existence of the website, of a new publication on the website and of the measure's effects for domestic industry.

b Timing the Publication of a Notice The obligation to publish notices aims, first and foremost, at raising awareness among interested parties, but should also leave time for these interested parties to comment on the proposed measures. The notice must therefore be published 'at an early stage'. The TBT Committee has not set out any specific period for publication ahead of adoption of the measure. The appropriate time frame can therefore be determined case by case, as long as it is sufficient for interested parties in other Members to become acquainted with the notice, as is the object and purpose of publication under the SPS and TBT Agreements.

2 Publishing Adopted Regulations

All SPS and TBT regulations that have been adopted must be published promptly 'or otherwise made available'.[74] The requirement for publication of an adopted SPS measure, technical regulation, standard or CAP intervenes at the end of the regulatory process, after notifications have been submitted, any comments have been received and acted upon, and the final measure has entered into force. It is essential in ensuring that there is full transparency throughout the domestic regulatory cycle. This publication obligation can be compared with that which exists under Article X GATT.

As is the case for most transparency obligations under the SPS and TBT Agreements, the scope of the obligation is as inclusive as possible to encourage publication of a wide range of measures. As long as the measure is an adopted regulation, it must be published, and the conditions relating to an existing international standard and the measure's significant effect on trade are no longer in play. Under the SPS Agreement, the

---

[74] Articles 2.11 and 5.8 TBT; Annex B, para. 1, SPS.

three elements that justify publication at this stage are that (a) the measure '[has] been adopted' and (b) the measure is a 'phytosanitary regulation' (namely, a phytosanitary measure such as a law, decree or ordinance) that is (c) 'applicable generally'.[75]

The notions of 'regulation' and 'applicable generally' have already been discussed insofar as they apply to transparency obligations in general. It is worth noting, however, that the notion of 'adopted regulations' does not necessarily mean legally binding regulations. In *Japan – Agricultural Products II*, both the panel and Appellate Body considered that mandatory effect is not a precondition to application of the obligation of publication: 'Nowhere does the wording of this paragraph require such measures to be mandatory or legally enforceable.'[76]

a **Timing the Publication of Adopted Measures** Adopted measures must be published in advance of their entry into force, to give producers in exporting countries time to adapt to the change. The general principle underpinning the publication of adopted regulations is that publication must be prompt.[77] More specifically, the SPS and TBT Agreements require Members to leave a 'reasonable interval' between publication and the entry into force of a measure[78] – which interval is 'normally' considered to be six months under both the SPS and TBT Agreements.[79] This interval may be reduced in either instance, but the reasons that will justify such a reduction are different, which leads to a conclusion that publication functions differently under the two Agreements.

If a new SPS regulation facilitates trade relations and the six-month 'reasonable interval' unnecessarily slows the regulatory process, then that interval can be cut short. Ministers have affirmed that '[t]he entry into force of measures which contribute to the liberalization of trade should not be unnecessarily delayed'.[80] This exception to the 'reasonable interval'

---

[75] This reasoning was applied by the panel in *Japan – Apples* (Panel Report, *Japan – Apples*, §8.109), with regard to the SPS Agreement and, given the exact same language for both Agreements, it may be predicted that similar reasoning would apply for publication of adopted measures under the TBT Agreement.
[76] Panel Report, *Japan – Agricultural Products II*, §8.111.
[77] Annex B, para. 1, SPS; Arts 2.11 and 5.8 TBT.
[78] Annex B, para. 2, SPS; Arts 2.12 and 5.9 TBT.
[79] WTO, 'Implementation-Related Issues and Concerns', Doha WTO Ministerial 2001: Ministerial Declarations and Decisions (CN – WT/MIN(01)/17, 2001).
[80] Ibid., para. 3.2.

between publication and entry into force underlines that the principle of publication under the SPS Agreement aims to contribute to the liberalisation of trade by facilitating better access to information and thereby smoothing trade relations.

A TBT measure may enter into force less than six months after the publication of notice if the longer interval is 'ineffective in fulfilling the legitimate objectives pursued'.[81] The time offered to allow exporting producers to adapt to a new measure is therefore considered less important under the TBT Agreement than the legitimate objective pursued by the new regulation.

b Where to Publish The decentralised character of publication makes it difficult to identify the various sites where adopted regulations will be published in all WTO Members. The list established by the WTO Secretariat is therefore the best resource with which to identify the location of both draft and adopted regulations.

In the context of the TBT Committee's 2018 triennial review, WTO Members reiterated the importance of public access to adopted texts. To make information about adopted texts more systematically and readily available, the Committee agreed to include addenda in the existing notification template or to supply a new addenda notification template and Members pledged to provide the Secretariat with up-to-date information on the websites where adopted final texts could be found. In this respect, the Committee requested the Secretariat to consolidate this information and maintain an up-to-date list of these websites of adopted regulations.[82]

c Targeting the Publication Even in the GATT, the publication obligation stands out as one of the rare provisions that goes beyond inter-governmental relations to the direct benefit of private parties.[83] The Appellate Body has underlined that – given that the publication obligation sets out the principle of transparency, which 'has obviously due process dimensions' – 'Members and other persons affected, or likely to be affected, by governmental measures imposing restraints, requirements

---

[81] Ibid., para. 5.2.
[82] WTO, 'Eighth Triennial Review of the Operation and Implementation', 21.
[83] Petros C. Mavroidis, *The General Agreement on Tariffs and Trade: A Commentary*, Oxford Commentaries on International Law (Oxford/New York: Oxford University Press, 2005).

and other burdens, should have a reasonable opportunity to acquire authentic information about such measures and accordingly to protect and adjust their activities or alternatively to seek modification of such measures'.[84] In other words, the principle of transparency set out in the GATT is inherently related to the objective of ensuring that all interested parties can acquire information about those measures that may affect them.

The SPS Agreement requires that 'interested Members' be able to access information, while the TBT Agreement targets 'interested parties in other Members'. This slight difference in language may have an important consequence for the function of publication under the two Agreements. The consideration of interested parties, beyond merely WTO Members, is nevertheless present in both Agreements. Indeed, both mention the importance of giving producers – particularly those from developing countries – time to adjust to the measure, which highlights the importance of transparency not only for WTO Members but also for private actors.[85]

Publication under the TBT Agreement is Addressed to Interested Parties in Other Members Article 2.9.1 of the TBT Agreement, which requires publication of those trade regulations that are not in accordance with international standards, aims to 'enable interested parties in other Members to become acquainted with [the technical regulation]'. It does not mention other Members, but interested parties *in* other Members. This language does not position other Member governments as the main addressees of the publication of laws, but rather any sub-national entities, whether public or private. While other Members' access to information is not excluded, the publication is to take into account the means by which interested parties in other Members may find information and the manner in which they are most likely to become acquainted with the publication. In this way, the TBT Agreement acknowledges that private parties and other Members may have different ways of finding the necessary information on draft and adopted laws, and that private parties may experience an unfavourable position resulting from information asymmetry.

---

[84] Appellate Body Report, *US – Underwear*, §21.
[85] Annex B, para. 2, SPS; Art. 2.12 TBT.

Publication under the SPS Agreement is Addressed to Other Members Article 7 of the SPS Agreement, which sets out the general principle of transparency, does not specify any addressees of information. This is all the more surprising given that 'notification' and providing information necessarily involve somebody receiving the information, whether or not they go on to do something with it. Further details on the addressees of information under the SPS Agreement are provided for in Annex B, which refers to two different addressees of publication: other Members and producers in exporting Members.

On the one hand, paragraph 1 of Annex B to the SPS Agreement suggests that the information published must be made accessible for 'interested Members'. This is contrary to most other publication measures, in which private parties or Members are also stated as addressees, and it is particularly surprising with regard to the TBT Agreement. Indeed, while the two Agreements share many common traits, the TBT Agreement seems to be addressed mainly to sub-national entities,[86] while the SPS Agreement seems not to require that they be able to acquaint themselves with the measures.

Thus Annex B, paragraph 1, to the SPS Agreement positions the publication obligation as an inter-state commitment. It seems to aim mainly at facilitating the sharing of information between Members and improving their understanding of each other's trade policy environments, ultimately allowing them to adapt to changes in a more timely manner. This publication requirement also allows time for Members to evaluate whether a new regulation has legitimate objectives. Further, Annex B, paragraph 2, requiring a 'reasonable interval' between publication and entry into force, does mention the importance of this delay for the 'producers in exporting Members', adding consideration for private parties – particularly in developing country Members – to the publication obligations.

On the other hand, paragraph 2 of Annex B requires a reasonable interval between the publication and the entry into force of technical regulations 'to allow time for producers in exporting Members, and particularly developing country Members, to adapt their products or methods of production to the requirements of the importing Member'. This wording suggests that the publication must indeed leave time for producers in exporting Members – not only Members, as suggested by paragraph 1 – to adapt to new measures.

---

[86] Article 2.11 TBT: 'interested members *in* other Members' (emphasis added).

The mention of producers 'particularly from developing countries' in the SPS and TBT Agreements accentuates the heavily imbalanced relationship that may exist between Members. This asymmetry is particularly obvious between developed Members and private parties from developing Members, with the latter lacking the financial and institutional means to keep up to date with regulatory developments in all WTO Member countries. The asymmetry is less established between Members and private parties from developed Members, and the focus of both Agreements on producers from developing Members seems to take this difference into account.

B   Targeted Transparency: A Legal Requirement for Centralised Access to Information

By means of the legal obligation to notify to the WTO Secretariat, all WTO Members ensure that information about their draft regulations is centralised within the same repository. Today's electronic tools offer the Secretariat the opportunity to disseminate information on draft regulations more widely, enhancing the effectiveness of this centralised transparency.

1   Notifications: Members' Rights to Access Information

Notification is the key step towards centralising information on Members' trade policies within the WTO. Although we shall see that the notification obligation is still far from fully implemented, the implications of the mechanism are potentially enormous thanks to the centralised access to information they create. Members no longer need to seek out information across the various national publications of their trading partners; instead, they may access it simply through the WTO Secretariat. Furthermore, not only does the WTO Secretariat maintain the information made publicly available, but also it sends the information directly to Members, actively delivering the information in which they may be interested.[87]

Notifications and the related rights to comment or to make enquiries have two important effects in relation to dispute settlement: on the one hand, they facilitate Members' access to and awareness of information, allowing Members to gather the necessary evidence to build a case if relevant; on the other hand, the opportunity to submit comments and the existence of enquiry points empowers Members to enter into dialogue with one another, which gives them an opportunity to prevent their trade concerns from escalating to the level of dispute.

---

[87] Article 10.6 TBT; Annex B, para. 9, SPS.

The basic obligation of notification under the SPS and TBT Agreements is set out in a single article, which sets out the conditions of application in the chapeau, then expands on the scope of the obligation and the timing of the obligation in specific paragraphs.[88]

a   The Content of the Notification Obligation   Both the SPS and TBT Agreements require Members to notify draft regulations in the absence of international standards and when they have a significant effect on trade (as we have already noted). By means of this simple obligation, the Agreements establish the very essence of their transparency framework as being to foster dialogue between Members in an effort to arrive at a regulation that is satisfactory for both the regulating Member, who is (presumably) pursuing a legitimate objective, and the other Members, whose access to the market must not be unnecessarily restricted.

In terms of content, Members are required to share with other Members the 'products to be covered' by the proposed regulation and 'a brief indication of its objective and rationale'.[89] These elements constitute the basic information necessary for other Members or exporters to assess whether or not they might be affected by the measure. The notifications do not include the actual content of the regulations, but the notification informs other Members of a measure that could interest them. If the information contained in the notification does indeed concern the Member or its exporters, the Member may then ask for further information.

Because of the similar scopes of application of the SPS and TBT Agreements, certain measures may fall under both or Members may be unsure which Agreement to apply. The SPS Handbook gives guidance on how to distinguish the two.[90] If the distinction remains too difficult, the Handbook recommends that '[w]hen a regulation contains both SPS or TBT elements, it should be notified according to both the SPS and TBT Agreements, preferably with an indication of which parts of the regulation fall under SPS (e.g., a food safety measure) and which parts fall under the TBT Agreement (e.g., quality or compositional requirements)'.[91]

---

[88] Articles 2.9.2 (for technical regulations), 5.6.5 (for CAPs) and Annex 3, para. L (for standards) TBT; Annex B, para. 5(b), SPS. In addition to this, special provisions determine the conditions for emergency notifications, as we shall see. Cf. Arts 2.10.1 and 5.7.1 TBT; Art. 6 SPS. In analysing the legal obligation, this section will therefore refer to these articles interchangeably unless otherwise specified.

[89] Articles 2.9.2 and 5.6.5 TBT; Annex B, para. 5(b), SPS.

[90] WTO, 'How to Apply the Transparency Provisions of the SPS Agreement'.

[91] Ibid., 12.

The two Committees have then progressively developed more specific requirements on what information to include in the notification. In particular, a model notification format includes several sections that Members are asked to complete.[92]

The TBT format for notifications includes 11 sections, asking for the following details:

(1) the notifying Member;
(2) the agency responsible;
(3) the article notified under;
(4) the products covered;
(5) the title, number of pages and languages of the notified document;
(6) a description of content;
(7) the objective and rationale, including the nature of urgent problems where applicable;
(8) the relevant documents;
(9) the proposed date of adoption and of entry into force;
(10) the final date for comments; and
(11) the source from which the text is available.[93]

The SPS format is slightly more detailed, comprising 13 sections. In addition to the TBT requirements, it requires information on the 'regions or countries likely to be affected, to the extent relevant or practicable' (4) and whether there is a relevant international standard, and if so, which one (8). Section 11 of the SPS format also includes an option to indicate whether a measure is 'trade-facilitating', thus justifying the absence of a period for comments. These criteria include 'tick boxes', encouraging Members to provide an answer rather than to leave the section blank.

b   The Establishment of Notification Authorities   To ensure that notifications are published in practice, the SPS and TBT Agreements provide that WTO Members must designate a 'single central government authority that is responsible for the implementation on the national level of the provisions concerning notification procedures'.[94]

In practice, the same authorities are designated to conduct notifications and to respond to enquiries under both the SPS and the TBT Agreements.

---

[92] WTO, 'Notification Template' (G/SPS/N, undated). www.wto.org/english/tratop_e/sps_e/transparency_toolkit_e.htm; WTO, 'Notification Template' (G/TBT/N, undated). www.wto.org/english/tratop_e/tbt_e/tbt_notifications_e.htm.
[93] WTO, 'Questionnaire on Transparency under the SPS Agreement'.
[94] Article 10.10 TBT; Annex B, para. 10, SPS.

The WTO Secretariat lists all SPS notification authorities separately from enquiry points.[95] The Secretariat does not, however, list any TBT notification authorities.[96]

c **To Whom the Notifications Are Addressed**   According to the SPS and TBT Agreements, the notification must be addressed to 'other Members through the Secretariat'. In addition, the private sector is an important player in relation to notifications: on the one hand, private exporters need to keep up with changing requirements if they are to gain market access in other countries; on the other hand, these same private exporters can offer valuable information to Member States, because they may have a more concrete view of which regulations may impact trade and to what extent.

Other Members through the Secretariat   The specification 'through the Secretariat' is the key element that has allowed for truly effective centralised transparency. Because Members may comment and eventually request amendment of a measure, it is essential that all Members receive the notification.

In practice, the obligation to notify other Members through the WTO Secretariat means that Members send any notification to the Secretariat, which shares it with all other Members.[97]

The Secretariat is responsible for sharing the notifications it receives with all Members and bringing to the attention of developing countries those notifications that may be of particular interest to them. The TBT Agreement also requires the Secretariat to share these notifications with 'interested international standardising and conformity assessment bodies' and the SPS Agreement, with 'interested international organizations'.[98]

Notifications are made to 'other Members' – that is, to *all* Members. However, although Members must have equal access to notifications, not all notifications will affect the trade of all Members. Some notifications may be of interest only to certain Members, in which case it is of particular importance that these Members are made aware of the notifications.

---

[95] http://spsims.wto.org/en/EnquiryPointsNotificationAuthorities/Search.
[96] http://tbtims.wto.org/en/NationalEnquiryPoints/Search.
[97] Cf. Art. 9 SPS and Art. 10.6 TBT, which include similar text, mentioning international standardising and conformity assessment bodies instead of international organisations. The process through which the Secretariat shares the notifications with the Members has evolved as a consequence of new technologies.
[98] Article 10.6 TBT; Annex B, para. 9, SPS.

The SPS Committee encourages Members to identify the countries potentially affected by the proposed regulation in their notifications, thus enabling the Secretariat to alert the Members concerned when a new measure may affect them.[99] The recommended notification procedures include a 'tick box' whereby Members can choose to request the notification of 'all trading partners' or only those specific countries or regions likely to be affected and the tick box makes it less likely that Members will leave the section unanswered. However, Members rarely go into such detail in their regular notification procedures, tending to indicate 'all trading partners' more often than they identify the specific trading partners that may be affected. In the period between September 2017 and September 2018, the WTO Secretariat reports that 15 per cent of regular notifications identified a specific group of countries or a region, while 84 per cent selected the tick box for 'all trading partners'.[100]

In this regard, the Secretariat acknowledges that although such information would be essential for those other Members, it remains difficult for any Member to guess which of the other Members could be affected:

> The comprehension and work of other Members would be facilitated if more specificity were provided by notifying Members on regions or countries likely to be affected. It is understandable, however, that Members may be hesitant to specifically identify potentially affected countries or regions for fear of not accurately assessing who might be affected when submitting notifications.[101]

However, Members do tend to indicate potentially affected Members much more frequently in 'emergency' notifications. In 2018, 90 per cent of emergency notifications identified a specific group of countries or a region – in stark contrast with the 16 per cent who do so in regular notifications.[102]

Emergency situations may well affect more precise regions or specific countries, because an emergency measure may be a response to outbreak of disease with limited geographic impact.[103] Members may also be more

---

[99] WTO, 'Recommended Procedures for Implementing the Transparency Obligations' (G/SPS/7/Rev.3, 2008), 11: 'The geographical regions or countries likely to be affected by the notified regulation should be identified to the extent relevant or practicable. Members are encouraged to be as specific as possible in identifying regions or countries likely to be affected.'

[100] WTO, 'Overview Regarding the Level of Implementation of the Transparency Provisions of the SPS Agreement' (G/SPS/GEN/804/Rev.11, 11 October 2018), 8.

[101] Ibid.

[102] Ibid.

[103] WTO, 'Sanitary and Phytosanitary Measures: E-Learning', February 2014.

willing to notify other Members of potentially trade-restrictive measures when they follow a simplified regulatory process, which is less transparent in certain other aspects.

The recommended notification formats under the TBT Agreement do not provide for the identification of affected Members, because it is less suited to the TBT subject matter. Indeed, neither technical regulations nor CAPs necessarily concern a specific geographic area in the same way as, for example, disease control SPS measures typically do and it is therefore more difficult to advise on who may be affected by technical regulations or CAPs.

Private Exporters and Other Stakeholders   The SPS and TBT Agreements do not mention private stakeholders in the articles on notification. It is important to note, however, that even though they are not explicitly mentioned as potential addressees, private stakeholders have an important interest in receiving information about notifications. In practice, they need to access information on new measures introduced by WTO Members and therefore they may require and receive notifications. The importance that Members attach to export alert systems indicates that there is common agreement on the usefulness of dialogue between Members and the private sector.[104] As will be discussed later in the chapter, interviews with Member delegations to the Committees indicate that well-informed industry groups have access to draft measures even before notifications are made, whereas individual exporters tend to become aware of measures only once the measure has entered into force and they are confronted by the new requirements.

Making notifications of draft measures available to private stakeholders is one of the key features of transparency under the SPS and TBT Agreements, and it represents an important opportunity to tie the domestic regulatory process to the WTO notifications framework. Indeed, the Organisation for Economic Co-operation and Development (OECD) notes that 'compulsory notification of draft regulations to international fora provides potentially an important means by which to alert and draw inputs from foreign stakeholders'.[105] The WTO notification procedure is the most telling example of this. Indeed, by sharing information on draft measures with private stakeholders in advance of their adoption and in

---

[104] Cf. proposal by Canada, discussed later in the chapter, and the support received by other Members in November 2014.
[105] OECD, *OECD Regulatory Policy Outlook 2018*.

opening up an opportunity for comments, even if only through the intermediary of the WTO Member government, these SPS and TBT notification procedures can be embedded into domestic stakeholder consultation processes that aim to gather inputs on regulatory drafts from interested stakeholders.

The language included in BTAs and RTAs is typically more explicit about making private stakeholders the main addressees of notification obligations and thus about embedding opportunities for consultation. For example, even before mentioning the notification obligation, the Comprehensive and Progressive Agreement for Trans-Pacific Partnership (CPTPP) sets out the principle that persons of other parties should be allowed to participate in the rule-making process related to technical regulations: 'Each Party shall allow persons of another Party to participate in the development of technical regulations, standards and conformity assessment procedures by its central government bodies on terms no less favourable than those that it accords to its own persons.'[106]

In the same way, the Comprehensive Economic and Trade Agreement (CETA) between Canada and the European Union requires parties to open their consultation processes to persons of the other party: '... Where a consultation process regarding the development of technical regulations or conformity assessment procedures is open to the public, each Party shall permit persons of the other Party to participate on terms no less favourable than those accorded to its own persons.'[107]

These examples show that there is a possible link between domestic stakeholder engagement processes that are part of the domestic regulatory process and the notifications made of trade agreements. And the language in the WTO SPS and TBT Agreements is sufficiently vague to allow Members to establish this relationship on their own initiative.

d Timing the Notification Obligation The SPS and TBT Agreements provide for an obligation to notify draft measures. It is important that the notification obligation intervenes early enough in the regulatory process that 'amendments can still be introduced and comments taken into account'.[108] However, it is also important that the notification is made late enough in the process that a draft of the complete text of a regulation is available.

---

[106] Article 8.7 CPTPP.
[107] Article 4.6.1 CETA.
[108] Article 2.9.2 TBT; Annex B, para. 5.b, SPS.

The timing of notification is therefore flexible to suit specific national legislative procedures, as long as other WTO Members may comment and these comments may have an influence on the final regulation. The Committees have indicated a minimum period of 60 days for comments.[109] If Members can provide a longer period for comments, such as 90 days, then they are encouraged to do so whenever possible.[110] Members are required to grant extensions of the period for comments whenever practicable, 'in particular with regard to notifications relating to products of particular interest to developing country Members'.[111]

This *ex ante* notification obligation also existed in the Tokyo Round 'Standards Code', but was further specified in the TBT Agreement adopted in 1995. Indeed, Article 2.9.2 adds the new sentence 'such notifications shall take place at an early appropriate stage, when amendments can still be introduced and comments taken into account'. The rationale of transparency is therefore not only that other Members shall be informed but also that an exchange that may result from it: the information disclosed must empower other Members to have a say on trade regulations that affect them.

The Agreements do not require Members to notify their adopted regulations.[112] There is an obligation to ensure that all adopted regulations are published, as we saw earlier, but they do not have to be notified. Indeed, this can be explained by the purpose of notification, which is mainly to foster dialogue about future measures and to allow interested Members to contribute when they see it as necessary to avoid trade barriers. Ideally, such a process would avoid the entry into force of regulations that constitute unnecessary barriers to trade, thus precluding significant costs to interested Members and exporters: the costs of their goods being refused at the border because they do

---

[109] WTO, 'Updating the Decisions and Recommendations Taken by the Tokyo Round Committee on Technical Barriers to Trade Regarding Procedures for Notification and Information Exchange' (G/TBT/W/2/Rev.1, 21 June 1995); WTO, 'Recommended Procedures for Implementing the Transparency Obligations'.

[110] WTO, 'Second Triennial Review of the Operation and Implementation of the Agreement on Technical Barriers to Trade' (G/TBT/9, 13 November 2000); WTO, 'Recommended Procedures for Implementing the Transparency Obligations'.

[111] WTO, 'Procedure to Enhance Transparency of Special and Differential Treatment in Favour of Developing Country Members' (G/SPS/33, 2004), 2.

[112] The draft notification format from 13 June 1980 (TBT/W/9) – at which time, the TBT Agreement included a reference only to certification, not to conformity assessment in general – shows that Contracting Parties considered also obliging the notification of adopted technical regulations and certifications.

not conform with the new legislation; the costs of contesting the legislation – perhaps even of asking the Member to remove the barrier; and, in some cases, the cost of litigation.[113] Notifying adopted measures would not seem to be as useful for the purpose of regulatory dialogue, because changing the measure at this late stage would involve a burdensome legislative process.

e **Following up on the Original Notification** After making regular notifications, Members may then also keep other Members informed of their legislative process and possible changes made to the draft text by means of addenda, corrigenda and revisions.

A follow-up to the original notification is useful to inform interested parties, both to acknowledge the regulatory dialogue that may have taken place before the draft was finalised and to ensure that the trade environment is predictable. Several authors have therefore recommended that the notification obligation be enhanced to encourage further notification of adopted measures, both to allow changes made to be tracked[114] and to clarify the regulatory environment in WTO Member countries. The Committees therefore encourage Members to inform others that the measure notified has been adopted[115] – and if a draft measure has been entirely redrafted, Members are encouraged to use a revision (see below) to inform other Members of this.[116]

In 2014, the TBT Committee adopted new guidelines[117] clarifying the distinction between the different formats and thus 'facilitating the traceability of information pertaining to a given notification (e.g. amendments, availability of the adopted text, entry into force), and avoiding confusion between new notifications and previously notified measures'.[118] Similar guidelines are provided for SPS notifications in the WTO's Recommended Procedures for Implementing Transparency Obligations of the SPS Agreement. When a new notification ('regular notification') has already been submitted, Members may notify additional information related to the notification or the text by means of 'addenda' (e.g. a change in the period for comment, or the adoption,

---

[113] On the costs involved in the pre-litigation phase, see Chad P. Bown, *Self-Enforcing Trade: Developing Countries and WTO Dispute Settlement* (Washington, DC: Brookings Institution Press, 2009).
[114] Wijkström, 'The Third Pillar'.
[115] WTO, 'Recommended Procedures for Implementing the Transparency Obligations'; WTO, 'Fifth Triennial Review of the Operation and Implementation'.
[116] WTO, 'Recommendation on Coherent Use of Notification Formats' (G/TBT/35, 2014).
[117] Ibid.
[118] WTO, 'Decisions and Recommendations Adopted by the Technical Barriers to Trade Committee since 1 January 1995', 22.

publication or entry into force of measure, etc.). They may submit 'corrigenda' to correct minor administrative or clerical errors, and 'revisions' when the text of the measure has been substantially redrafted, opening up a new period for comment. Finally, Members use 'supplements' exclusively to alert others to the availability of unofficial translations of notified measures.[119]

Each of these notification formats is meant to play a specific role in complementing the original notification. However, an uneven understanding of their use may, in certain cases, affect the efficiency of the transparency they facilitate and may result, for example, in the avoidance of periods for comment.[120]

In the 2018 triennial review of the operation and implementation of the TBT Agreement, a number of Members voiced concern about the limitations of notification obligations. The TBT Committee recommended that Members notify adopted final texts of technical regulations and CAPs as addenda to original notifications, to allow Members to track their progress in the regulatory process.[121] To this effect, the Committee also agreed to modify the notifications template for addenda or to develop a new template, 'so as to provide Members with the ability to indicate when the measure entered – or will enter – into force and provide information on where the final text can be obtained, including website address'.[122]

f **Emergency Notifications** Both the SPS and TBT Agreements allow Members to submit notifications more easily and with a shorter period for comments when the measure is a remedy to an urgent problem. Indeed, because the two Agreements protect Members' freedom to pursue certain legitimate objectives, it is in the spirit of the Agreements that they should facilitate Members' adoption of emergency measures when the situation requires it.

The Conditions for an Emergency Procedure to Apply Under the TBT Agreement, the emergency procedures may apply 'where urgent problems of safety, health, environmental protection or national security may

---

[119] WTO, 'Sanitary and Phytosanitary Measures: E-Learning'.
[120] See e.g. this issue noted in a specific trade concern raised against Ecuador: 'Ecuador – Systematic Failure to Publish Notices at an Early Appropriate Stage' (ID 414).
[121] WTO, 'Eighth Triennial Review of the Operation and Implementation', 21.
[122] Ibid.

arise or threaten to arise'.[123] Under the SPS Agreement, these procedures apply 'where urgent problems of health protection arise or threaten to arise'.[124]

Simplified Procedures   Under the emergency circumstances, Members no longer need to publish a notice nor do they need to respect specific timing requirements as for regular notifications.

Members still have to notify, but the language of the two Agreements no longer makes reference to the 'appropriate stage' at which the measures must be notified and instead requires that the notification be made 'immediately'. The SPS Agreement requires that such emergency notifications be notified 'upon adoption' and it leaves all temporal requirements aside, therefore leaving open whether the notification is made before or after adoption.

In addition to still having to notify, Members must continue to provide copies of the text upon request and allow other Members to submit comments.[125]

This emergency notification procedure may, however, be used to circumvent the strict timeline that applies to regular notification procedures – and this has been noted in some STCs.[126]

2   Electronic Tools to Enhance the Effectiveness of Transparency

The enormous wealth of information on domestic measures centralised in the WTO can truly be effective only if it is publicly available for online search. In the early years of the WTO and until quite recently, the Secretariat used to circulate paper copies of notifications.[127] Today, the Secretariat circulates SPS and TBT notifications once a week via e-mail, and publishes them on the information management systems specific to SPS (SPS IMS)[128] and TBT (TBT IMS).[129] Members therefore receive

---

[123] Articles 2.10 and 5.7 TBT.
[124] Annex B, para. 6, SPS.
[125] Articles 2.10.2–2.10.3 TBT; Annex B, para. 6.b–c, SPS.
[126] See e.g. 'Ecuador – Systematic Failure to Publish Notices at an Early Appropriate Stage' (ID 414), 'Ecuador – Cosmetic Products' (ID 417) or 'Ecuador – Certification of Ceramic Tiles' (ID 455).
[127] The exact date on which the Secretariat stopped circulating documents in paper is still to be determined.
[128] http://spsims.wto.org.
[129] http://tbtims.wto.org.

regular updates directly and may also search online at their convenience for the notifications in which they are interested. In addition to the regular e-mails sent to Members with new notifications, SPS[130] and TBT[131] e-mail alert systems have been set up to which anyone may subscribe, reaching beyond WTO Member representatives.

New technologies have increasingly facilitated the sharing of information. In 2012, during the sixth triennial review of implementation of the TBT Agreement, Members insisted on the importance of electronic tools for transparency: 'Members are of the view that an efficient and well-functioning WTO-based IT system that provides a common platform for available information will contribute significantly to an improved implementation of the TBT Agreement's transparency provisions, and in particular those relating to notification.'[132]

In 2015, the TBT Committee delivered a mandate to the Secretariat requiring it to further increase the use of electronic tools – namely:

i. to *encourage* Members in a position to do so to begin using the TBT NSS to facilitate and accelerate the submission and processing of notifications;
ii. to *request* the Secretariat to continue to improve the TBT NSS and TBT IMS in line with the needs of Members;
iii. to *request* the Secretariat to explore the development of an export alert system for TBT notifications, in co-operation with other organizations; and,
iv. to *request* the Secretariat to report back on *d.ii* and *d.iii* above at the Eighth Special Meeting on Procedures for Information Exchange (November 2016); […][133]

This mandate resulted in the launch of 'ePing', an enhanced database for both SPS and TBT measures developed jointly between the WTO, the United Nations Department of Economic and Social Affairs (UNDESA) and the International Trade Centre (ITC).[134] This system was developed particularly with the exporters of least-developed countries (LDCs) in mind: 'The key objective of the project was to improve capacity of LDCs in utilizing the trade-related international support measures to enhance export growth in its priority products by addressing institutional

---

[130] www.wto.org/english/tratop_e/sps_e/sps_mailing_list_e.htm.
[131] www.wto.org/english/tratop_e/tbt_e/tbt_mailing_list_e.htm.
[132] WTO, 'Sixth Triennial Review of the Operation and Implementation of the Agreement on Technical Barriers to Trade under Article 15.4' (G/TBT/32, 2012), para. 17.
[133] WTO, 'Seventh Triennial Review of the Operation and Implementation of the Agreement on Technical Barriers to Trade under Article 15.4' (G/TBT/37, 2015), para. 5.12.d.
[134] www.epingalert.org/en.

constraints in assessing, accessing and sharing information about the availability and use of the measures.'[135] As a result, it allows non-experts to easily search any TBT and SPS measures notified by all WTO Members, to register for tailored e-mail alerts for new notifications and to more easily contact the enquiry points of WTO Members.

This new electronic platform, separate from the WTO SPS and TBT web portals, is a significant improvement on the previous system, which required much more knowledge about the TBT and SPS obligations and about the type of measure searched for. The search engines for SPS and TBT measures were indeed separate, requiring knowledge about the WTO obligations under which measures might fall. The alert systems did not allow for specific e-mail subscriptions, implying subscription either to all notifications or to none. And the web tools comprised an outdated system, making searches difficult and imprecise. The WTO SPS and TBT web portals remain two separate sites with some differences in their search functions, operating in parallel to the ePing portal. Still, the consolidated database of ePing allows the WTO to address the major shortcomings of its portals.

C Collaborative Transparency: Enabling Bilateral and Multilateral Dialogue among WTO Members

In addition to allowing WTO Members the right to be informed and enabling centralised access to information, transparency under the SPS and TBT Agreements is unique in that it makes space for dialogue about the information that Members disclose. This can be seen as 'interactive' transparency, also referred to as 'collaborative', because it results in an exchange about regulations between Members. The basis of this interactive transparency lies in the requirement that Members respond to enquiries and comments (section 1). To allow them to do so, the TBT and SPS Agreements both require that Members designate enquiry points, to facilitate the submission of enquiries by a WTO Member to one single authority and hence to ensure the effectiveness of information sharing (section 2). Against this backdrop, raising STCs in the SPS and TBT Committees has become common practice for discussing individual measures at the multilateral level (section 3).

---

[135] Ibid., 'About us'.

1 Responding to Enquiries and Comments: Transparency that Fosters Dialogue

As a corollary to their obligation to notify regulations, Members have an obligation to respond to enquiries concerning their notifications and to allow other Members the opportunity to comment on them.

a **The Obligation to Respond to Enquiries** Members have an obligation to respond to enquiries about SPS and TBT measures – in particular, with regard to notified measures. Under the SPS Agreement, Members may also be asked about measures that were not necessarily notified, but with which other Members have a concern. The legal provisions in this respect require significant transparency from WTO Members in exposing their domestic regulatory processes to representatives of other Members.

Enquiries about Notified SPS and TBT Measures The TBT Agreement requires that Members provide other Members with 'particulars or copies' of the notified regulation.[136] The SPS Agreement, in turn, requires Members to provide copies of the notified regulation, not specifying anything about 'particulars'.[137] This difference in language seems to call for a more active response by Members on TBT measures, to the extent of offering further details on the regulation if other Members so request. The SPS or TBT Committees provide no further details on this obligation. However, the related requirement that enquiry points respond to 'all reasonable questions' addresses this difference between the two Agreements and calls for substantive answers by both TBT and SPS enquiry points.

The obligation to respond to enquiries is only 'upon request' by other Members. Members are therefore not obliged to attach further details or copies of the legislation to their notification. The TBT Committee did, however, establish the possibility that notifying Members might voluntarily 'provide the WTO Secretariat with an electronic version of the notified draft text (attachment) together with the notification form'.[138]

---

[136] Articles 2.9.3 and 5.6.3 TBT.
[137] Annex B, para. 5.c, SPS.
[138] WTO TBT Committee, 'Attachments to TBT Notifications' (G/TBT/GEN/65, 14 December 2007), para. 2.

Article 2.9.3 of the TBT Agreement refers to 'the proposed technical regulation'.[139] This appears to link enquiries specifically to draft notifications rather than to any regulation already adopted – a point confirmed by the panel in *US – Clove Cigarettes*, which rejected Indonesia's claim that the United States had failed to meet its obligation to respond to Indonesia's enquiry because the enquiry had been made after the US measure had been enacted.

According to the wording of Articles 2.9.3 and 5.6.3 of the TBT Agreement and Annex B, paragraph 5.c, of the SPS Agreement, enquiries are in principle to be answered only when other Members make them. However, the obligations of enquiry points under Article 10 of the TBT Agreement also imply the answering of requests submitted by interested parties in other Members.

Regional trade agreements go a step further in this regard, explicitly providing that enquiry points must respond to queries made not only by other governments but also by the private sector and other stakeholders.[140]

Finally, the obligation to respond to enquiries also includes the requirement to 'identify the parts which in substance deviate from relevant international standards'.[141] Conformity with international standards fosters a presumption of conformity with the WTO Agreements, albeit under slightly different conditions in Article 2.5 of the TBT Agreement and Article 3.2 of the SPS Agreement. In practice, then the obligation to explain the way(s) in which a notified measure is based on international standards mitigates the risk of Members making reference to international standards in bad faith.

Enquiries about Non-notified SPS and TBT Measures Under the SPS Agreement, an additional provision gives Members a right to request further information even when there has been no notification. Indeed, Article 5.8 of the SPS Agreement includes a right to request the rationale underpinning an SPS measure that it considers is or has the potential to be a constraint on its exports:

> When a Member has reason to believe that a specific sanitary or phytosanitary measure introduced or maintained by another Member is constraining, or has the potential to constrain, its exports and the measure is not based

---

[139] Similar language is found in Art. 5.6.3 TBT regarding CAPs ('the proposed procedure'), and Annex B, para. 5.c, SPS ('the proposed regulation').
[140] Iza Lejárraga, 'Multilateralising Regionalism: Strengthening Transparency Disciplines in Trade', OECD Trade Policy Paper No. 152, 26 June 2013.
[141] Article 2.9.2 TBT; Annex B, para. 5.c, SPS.

on the relevant international standards, guidelines or recommendations, or such standards, guidelines or recommendations do not exist, an explanation of the reasons for such sanitary or phytosanitary measure may be requested and shall be provided by the Member maintaining the measure.

As is the case for comments on notifications, the Member maintaining the measure is required to respond to such an enquiry with an explanation. The obligation here is barely different from Annex B, paragraph 5, of the SPS Agreement, but in providing explicitly for a right to raise concerns regarding measures that have not necessarily been notified, it extends the requirement of transparency beyond only those measures about which WTO Members choose to be transparent and allows other Members to actively seek information about undisclosed SPS measures as well.

b   Comments on Notifications   The obligation of notification and the related obligation to take comments into consideration are key components of centralised transparency. They allow all Members to become aware of other Members' domestic drafts, and they encourage Members to be fully open about their measures and to gather insights about their drafts from other Members who may be affected by them. However, any follow-up to the comments remains between the regulating Member and the commenting Member.

Members submit their comments on notifications directly to national enquiry points. Such comments therefore foster a dialogue about the measure, facilitated by the legal requirements under the SPS and TBT Agreements, but in a bilateral context, independent of the WTO.

Even though, in principle, the SPS and TBT Agreements lay the groundwork for a dialogue between WTO Member representatives (i.e. public authorities), in practice the private sector plays an important role in enabling this dialogue. Because companies or industry groups are those most directly affected by trade costs resulting from domestic regulation, they are also the best placed to inform governments about these costs.

The SPS and TBT Obligations to Allow Comments, Discuss Them, Respond to Them and Take Them into Account   Comments on notifications are essential from the perspective of all Members: on the one hand, potentially affected Members may raise their concerns and influence the measure's content to avoid unnecessary barriers to trade; on the other hand, notifications are also an opportunity for the notifying Member to gather comments and to ensure that its measures are consistent with its WTO obligations. In this sense, Members may successfully avoid creating trade barriers thanks to comments or STCs raised by other Members. By avoiding trade barriers and addressing concerns at an early stage, this ultimately may also help prevent disputes from rising.

The SPS and TBT Agreements include the obligations for Members to 'without discrimination allow reasonable time for other Members to make comments in writing, discuss these comments upon request, and take these written comments and the results of the discussions into account'.[142] This provision includes the requirement that notifying Members allow sufficient time not only to submit comments but also to discuss them and to take them into consideration. There is very little data available on the volume of comments on notifications,[143] let alone the replies received by commenting Members and the extent to which the comments were taken into account.[144] Some Members have, however, noted that their comments are very rarely responded to and that this is a systemic issue among developed and developing countries alike.[145] Therefore, regardless of the legal obligation, implementation of the comment requirement is very difficult to monitor.

To encourage implementation, the TBT Committee agreed that the Member receiving comments should 'acknowledge receipt of such comments', explain 'how it will proceed in order to take these comments into account' and 'provide to any Member from which it has received comments, a copy of the corresponding technical regulations or procedures for assessment of conformity as adopted or information that no corresponding technical regulations or procedures for assessment of conformity will be adopted for the time being'.[146] Members were also encouraged to 'share their responses with the TBT Committee'.[147] The TBT Committee reiterated its recommendations to Members several times, urging them to share

---

[142] Article 2.9.4 TBT. Annex B, para. 5(d), SPS is identical, except in requiring these comments to be in writing.

[143] Discussions launched by notifications are in most cases bilateral, between enquiry points of the concerned Member and of the Member adopting the regulation.

[144] Members sometimes inform others of their modifications to legislation, e.g. in response to an STC raised. See e.g. ID 445, in which Mexico informed Chile and the US that it had taken into account all comments in modifying the draft measure on a standard establishing health specifications and health and commercial labelling provisions on alcoholic beverages.

[145] This was noted e.g. by Canada and the EU in discussions on the Private Sector Survey, February 2015. See Appendix B for the survey questions.

[146] WTO, 'Decisions and Recommendations Adopted by the WTO Committee on Technical Barriers to Trade since 1995' (G/TBT/1/Rev.12, 2015), 24.

[147] WTO, 'Third Triennial Review of the Operation and Implementation', para. 26.

with the Committee their comments on draft measures and the related replies[148] – but it seems that, to date, the only Member that publishes the comments it submits is the European Union.[149]

The Private Sector's Role in Submitting Comments on Notifications Notifications often concern private stakeholders, and there is consequently often discussion between private actors and WTO Members on the opportunity to comment on the notification. Prévost notes the usefulness of *ex ante* transparency in this regard, including for private parties: 'Imposing *ex ante* transparency obligations on regulating countries ensures that exporting countries are informed of proposed new or amended SPS measures and that affected foreign traders have the opportunity, through their governments, to raise concerns regarding these proposals and to have these comments taken into account in the regulatory process.'[150]

In a thematic session of the TBT Committee on transparency in June 2014, Members shared their experiences on several issues, including online transparency tools, and the importance of these online tools was reiterated, in particular to facilitate multi-stakeholder dialogue and to collect useful feedback from the private sector. The United States noted, for instance, that 'industry helped determine what questions to ask of other Members regarding notifications',[151] while Kenya identified 'limited feedback from the business community on foreign notifications' as one of its main challenges with regard to TBT transparency.[152]

Discussions relating to a Canadian proposal on an export alert system confirm that there is widespread interest in improving communications with the private sector to gather its views on notifications and then also to provide useful feedback to the notifying Member. The Chilean delegation noted that it was also particularly 'important to bear in mind that public consultations had little effect if the TBT notifications did not reach the interested stakeholders at the right time'.[153] The Swiss delegation saw 'the

---

[148] The latest recommendation was made in 2018: see WTO, 'Eighth Triennial Review of the Operation and Implementation', 21.
[149] http://ec.europa.eu/growth/tools-databases/tbt/en/. See later in this book for trends in EU data.
[150] Marie Denise Prévost, *Balancing Trade and Health in the SPS Agreement: The Development Dimension* (Nijmegen: Wolf Legal, 2009), 785.
[151] WTO, 'Thematic Session of the TBT Committee on Transparency: Moderator's Report' (G/TBT/GEN/167, 17 June 2014), para. 4.
[152] Ibid., para. 3.
[153] WTO TBT Committee, 'Minutes of the Meeting of 5–6 November 2014' (G/TBT/M/64, 5 November 2014), para. 2.285.

instrument proposed by Canada as an inclusive public good, crucial for the adequate functioning of the TBT notification procedures – and at the heart of how to better involve the private sector'.[154]

c   Additional Procedures Specific to the SPS Agreement   The SPS Committee has also adopted specific transparency procedures to reinforce special and differential treatment in favour of developing country Members. These procedures allow developing country Members encountering significant difficulties with a notified measure to request special assistance by means of comments on the notification. In particular:

> In the case of such a request from an exporting developing country Member, the notifying Member would in any discussions examine whether and how the identified problem could best be addressed to take into account the special needs of the interested exporting developing country Member. Resolution of the concern identified could include one of the following, or a combination thereof: (1) a change in the measure to be applied on a MFN [most-favoured nation] basis; (2) the provision of technical assistance to the exporting Member; or (3) the provision of special and differential treatment. Should special and differential treatment be provided, it would apply equally to all developing country Members.[155]

No such requests seem to have been made to date.[156]

2   The Obligation to Establish Enquiry Points

The obligation to establish enquiry points offers a remarkable tool aiming to ensure that Members have efficient access to information to each other's trade policies and to facilitate bilateral dialogue. The function of enquiry points is all the more remarkable in that they offer information reaching beyond the draft measures subject to notification obligations, and they are required to answer not only Members but also other interested parties.

a   Enquiry Points Provide Information on Proposed and Adopted Regulations   The obligation to establish enquiry points was originally established under the Tokyo Round 'Standards Code' (cf. Art. 10.1 et seq.), in virtually identical terms to the TBT and SPS Agreements. The enquiry points provided by both SPS and TBT Agreements have similar

---

[154] Ibid., para. 2.289.
[155] WTO, 'Procedure to Enhance Transparency of Special and Differential Treatment in Favour of Developing Country Members', 2.
[156] Information about this process is not easily accessible to the public. In 2013, the Secretariat circulated a confidential note informing that the process had not yet been used (JOB/TBT/65).

objectives. Under both Agreements, they are meant to offer answers to 'reasonable enquiries' and to provide relevant documents on SPS and TBT regulations.[157] However, the initial text of the Standards Code did not mention the obligation to provide relevant documents. This minor addition in the SPS and TBT Agreements introduces a more tangible aspect to the obligation: evidently, non-compliance with the provision of documents may be more easily demonstrated than non-compliance with an oral response to enquiries.

The TBT Committee considers enquiries to be 'reasonable' when they are limited to certain products or groups of products: '[A]n enquiry should be considered "reasonable" when it is limited to a specific product or group of products, but not when it goes beyond that and refers to an entire business branch or field of regulations, or procedures for assessment of conformity.'[158]

The SPS and TBT Agreements introduce the obligation to respond to enquiries about membership and the participation of the Member, or of relevant bodies within its territory, in international and regional bodies, as well as in bilateral and multilateral agreements and arrangements, and to share the texts of such agreements and arrangements.[159] This additional paragraph – one of the few additions to the text of the Standards Code – extends transparency beyond domestic regulations to include international instruments.

The enquiry points are therefore not meant to be solicited for general enquiries regarding the state of the Member's domestic regulation, broadly speaking, but rather as a tool with which to obtain targeted information on specific issues of concern.

The SPS and TBT enquiry points play an important role in supplementing the information gaps left as a result of the limited scope of notification obligations. Indeed, enquiry points are required to provide relevant documents about 'adopted or proposed' technical regulations, standards or CAPs under the TBT Agreement or SPS regulations.[160] The SPS Transparency Handbook specifies that 'the enquiry point is responsible for answering questions on all existing SPS measures (even those that existed before the WTO and the SPS Agreement came into force)'.[161]

---

[157] For further detail, see Arts 10.1.1–10.1.5 TBT and Annex B, para. 3(a)–(d), SPS.
[158] WTO, 'Updating the Decisions and Recommendations Taken', 13.
[159] Annex B, para. 3.d, SPS; Art. 10.3.3 TBT.
[160] Articles 10.1.1–10.1.3 TBT; Annex B, para. 3.a, SPS.
[161] WTO, 'How to Apply the Transparency Provisions of the SPS Agreement', 8.

Nevertheless, a single failure by an enquiry point to provide information does not in and of itself result in a breach of WTO obligations. The Appellate Body has recently specified that the obligation for enquiry points to provide information is broader than this and that a breach of this obligation can be decided only after 'an examination of all the relevant factors, including the total number of questions received by the enquiry point and the proportion of and the extent to which questions were answered, the nature and scope of the information sought and received, and whether the enquiry point repeatedly failed to respond'.[162]

b Enquiry Points Can Provide Information to Members and Other Interested Parties The major contribution of enquiry points is their openness to enquiries from any individual. This remains an information disclosure mechanism about domestic draft measures or adopted regulations. As such, it does not entail a regulatory dialogue between regulators and interested stakeholders. Nevertheless, it is significant in that it introduces an institutional framework to facilitate information sharing. Mavroidis and Wolfe note the progress that the TBT enquiry point requirement represents for the effectiveness of transparency within the trading system: 'Traders ... do not have to depend on their government ... Inquiry points are the first step towards "single windows" in each Member to reduce the "search costs" of information procurement.'[163]

The Standards Code of the Tokyo Round had already introduced the possibility that 'interested parties' in other countries might require information about regulations. Indeed, Article 10.1 of the Standards Code required the establishment of enquiry points to respond to enquiries from 'interested parties in other parties'.

This wording was retained in the subsequent TBT Agreement and remains in force today. Article 10 of the TBT Agreement acknowledges that the enquiry points are meant to answer questions from both 'other Members and interested parties in other Members'. Information may be requested by any private party interested and, in fact, Koebele notes that, 'in the experience of national enquiry points, the overwhelming

---

[162] Appellate Body Report, *Korea – Radionuclides*, §6.14. In this case, the Appellate Body's decision related to the provisions of Annex B, para. 3, SPS.

[163] Petros C. Mavroidis and Robert Wolfe, 'From Sunshine to a Common Agent: The Evolving Understanding of Transparency in the WTO', RSCAS Research Paper No. PP 2015/01/ Columbia Public Law Research Paper No. 14-461, 25 April 2015, 3. http://papers.ssrn.com/abstract=2569178.

majority of solicitors are private parties, not state actors'.[164] This takes the *effet utile* of publication to a new level, requiring not only that private actors be taken into account in the publication of measures but also that they may actually participate in the dialogue on technical barriers to trade through the enquiry points as their intermediaries. Because of the extensive transparency framework in the TBT Agreement, private parties may even make enquiries about both draft and adopted measures, 'and obtain information without implicating their governments at all (unlike the paradigm for the overwhelming majority of WTO law)'.[165] Private parties are indeed excluded from the rest of the WTO process – in particular with regard to dispute settlement, in which instances they must petition their governments to launch a formal dispute settlement process.[166]

As noted earlier regarding publication, the TBT Agreement includes 'interested parties in other Members' as addressees of information, while the SPS Agreement mentions only other Members. The legal obligation of enquiry points is therefore slightly different under SPS and TBT. In practice, however, it seems that SPS enquiry points function similarly to TBT enquiry points – and in some cases they may even be one and the same authority. In principle, the SPS Handbook on transparency encourages Members to answer all reasonable requests:

> Requests to the enquiry point may come from other countries' enquiry points or originate from other interested parties (such as industry groups) in countries, and from non-Member countries. Although the legal obligation is only to respond to requests from other WTO Members, the enquiry point is encouraged to treat all such enquiries equally, and respond to all reasonable requests for information about the country's SPS measures. It is best to reply directly to whoever makes the request, but to support the enquiry point system, it is recommended to send a copy of replies (and a list of material supplied) to the relevant country's enquiry point.[167]

---

[164] Michael Koebele, 'Article X TBT', in Rüdiger Wolfrum, Peter-Tobias Stoll and Anja Seibert-Fohr, eds, *WTO: Technical Barriers and SPS Measures* (Leiden/Boston, MA: Martinus Nijhoff, 2007), 307–14, 311.

[165] Henrik Horn, Petros C. Mavroidis and Erik N. Wijkström, 'In the Shadow of the DSU: Addressing Specific Trade Concerns in the WTO SPS and TBT Committees – Entwined', *Journal of World Trade* 47, no. 4 (2013): 729–59, fn. 9.

[166] Bernard M. Hoekman and Petros C. Mavroidis, 'WTO Dispute Settlement, Transparency and Surveillance', *World Economy* 23, no. 4 (2000): 527–42.

[167] WTO, 'How to Apply the Transparency Provisions of the SPS Agreement', para. 82.

c **Enquiry Points Bridge the Gap between Regulators and Traders**
Nominated for their overarching vision on the regulations developed in their country, enquiry points have the important role of bridging the gap between trade policy authorities concerned with the trade impacts of regulations and the numerous regulators with mandates as diverse as environmental protection, food security, energy efficiency and consumer protection, to name but a few. This is particularly useful for the implementation of the TBT Agreement, which covers a broader variety of measures.

In this capacity, the enquiry points are meant to ensure that feedback about the likely trade impacts of a draft measure is shared with the correct regulator, thus feeding evidence into the regulatory process.

The authorities designated for the SPS and TBT enquiry points are not from bodies with central oversight or systematically the same. For the SPS Agreement, they are most commonly from the Member's ministry of agriculture, given the specific focus of the SPS Agreement. It is often regulators under the authority of that ministry which develop the measures and the enquiry point is therefore well placed to answer enquiries about them. For the TBT Agreement, the enquiry point is often drawn from units responsible for standardisation or, more broadly, from the ministry responsible for international trade. The TBT enquiry point acts as an intermediary between foreign authorities and/or stakeholders that have a comment or enquiry and the regulators who originated the regulation, standard or CAP at stake.

Today, a large majority of WTO Members have nominated an enquiry point. Of the 164 Member countries, 28 Members have not nominated a TBT enquiry point;[168] 26 developing countries or LDCs have not nominated an SPS enquiry point.[169] This remains a small proportion of the WTO membership. Most WTO Members therefore have the institutional framework within which to receive comments on and enquiries about their draft regulations.

Nonetheless, information about the parties submitting enquiries remains entirely decentralised and enquiries are *de facto* confidential,

---

[168] Namely, Andorra, Angola, Bahamas, Bhutan, Bosnia Herzegovina, Brunei Darussalam, Cabo Verde, Chad, Comoros, Congo, Equatorial Guinea, Ethiopia, Holy See, Iran, Iraq, Lebanese Republic, Libya, Mauritania, São Tomé and Principe, Serbia, Solomon Islands, Somalia, South Sudan, Sudan, Syrian Arab Republic, Timor-Leste, Tonga and Uzbekistan.
[169] Namely, Algeria, Andorra, Azerbaijan, Bahamas, Belarus, Bhutan, Bosnia Herzegovina, Cambodia, Comoros, Equatorial Guinea, Ethiopia, Guinea-Bissau, Holy See, Iran, Iraq, Lebanese Republic, Libya, São Tomé and Principe, Serbia, Somalia, South Sudan, Sudan, Syrian Arab Republic, Timor-Leste, Uzbekistan and Vanuatu.

reserved to each Member's enquiry point. Indeed, the WTO Secretariat does not monitor the resulting dialogue, which remains inherently bilateral. At this stage, then, it is difficult to estimate to what extent enquiry points have made a genuine contribution to improving the transparency of domestic measures.[170]

3 Specific Trade Concerns: A Mechanism of Multilateral Regulatory Dialogue

Specific trade concerns are a unique transparency tool that has emerged from practice, elevating the dialogue promoted by the SPS and TBT Agreements to the multilateral level.

The practice of raising STCs has been in place since the WTO formed the Committees in 1995, but STCs have been increasingly important in Committee discussions since then and the two Committees have consolidated their status progressively.

There is no explicit mention of STCs in the SPS or TBT Agreement, but several articles set out a framework enabling their development (section a). The SPS and TBT Committees formalised the process progressively into what is today a commonplace practice (section b).

a The Text of the Agreements It is under the mandate of the two Committees that Members have developed the mechanism for STCs.[171] It is the consultative function of the TBT Committee that served as its basis, with Article 13.1 of the TBT Agreement providing that the TBT Committee will meet 'for the purpose of affording Members the opportunity of consulting on any matters relating to the operation of this Agreement or the furtherance of its objectives, and shall carry out such responsibilities as assigned to it under this agreement or by the Members'.

Article 12 of the SPS Agreement goes a step further, providing that the Committee shall 'encourage and facilitate ad hoc consultations or negotiations' on SPS 'issues':

---

[170] As rightfully pointed out by Professor Hoekman in his final report on my dissertation, further empirical research on the practical work of enquiry points, the extent to which they are solicited and the parties raising enquiries with them would be invaluable to understand their practical benefits for transparency about SPS and TBT measures.

[171] Horn, Mavroidis, and Wijkström, 'In the Shadow of the DSU'.

1. A Committee on Sanitary and Phytosanitary Measures is hereby established to provide a regular forum for consultations. It shall carry out the functions necessary to implement the provisions of this Agreement and the furtherance of its objectives, in particular with respect to harmonisation. The Committee shall reach its decisions by consensus.
2. The Committee shall encourage and facilitate ad hoc consultations or negotiations among Members on specific sanitary or phytosanitary issues.

In addition to this, the articles on transparency prioritise dialogue between Members on draft measures. They impose not only the obligation to publish and notify draft measures but also the obligation to share requested information on the measure and to respond to Members' comments. The SPS Agreement also gives Members a right to request information on non-notified measures.[172]

The consultative goal of the SPS and TBT Committees, together with the spirit of dialogue encouraged by the articles on transparency, forms the basis for the practice of STCs.

b Evolving Committee Practice

Practice under the GATT During the GATT period, there were no STCs as such. The Secretariat still holds records of certain TBT issues brought to the attention of the Secretariat as affecting trade. These concerns, classified *a posteriori* as 'specific trade concerns', took various forms. In most cases, Members would send reports to the Secretariat to point out the unjustified nature of another Member's measure.[173] In other cases, the Secretariat seemed to take the initiative to keep track of related notifications by various Members that had the potential to create tensions.[174]

As a form of consultations centralised by the WTO, these were 'ancestors' of the current STCs. They show that, even under the GATT, Members did flag certain issues to the Secretariat, calling for an exchange of views with the Member adopting a new regulation through the GATT Secretariat as an intermediary and without resorting to dispute settlement. However, these practices lacked the key feature of STCs as they are known under the WTO in that Members did not raise the issue for public

---

[172] Article 5.8 SPS.
[173] For example, 'The Japanese solid wood products market: profile and outlook', April 1989, or 'The Pinewood Nemtode Threat from Canadian Softwood Exports', October 1987.
[174] In the case of the Chernobyl nuclear incident, the Secretariat assembled notifications (TBT/Notif.86.85, TBT/Notif.86.134, TBT/Notif.161) and a newspaper article on the consequences of the incident. This seemed to be without specific concern raised by any Member, at least in writing.

discussion within the Committees and therefore they did not discuss their concerns in the presence of all other GATT signatories.

Practice under the WTO Under the WTO, the SPS Committee started to discuss STCs under the agenda headings 'Consultations' or 'Implementation of the Agreement – Information from Members'. By October 1997, the SPS Committee had started using an agenda item explicitly named 'Specific Trade Concerns'.[175] The TBT Committee, in turn, had been discussing STCs under the agenda heading 'Statements of Implementation and Administration of the Agreement' since its first meeting in April 1995. The term 'specific trade concern' was first used in the minutes of the TBT Committee meeting of 23 March 2004.[176]

The SPS Committee has since increasingly formalised its practice to ensure better information on the conduct of STCs. One of the main differences between SPS and TBT STCs is that Members are required to notify the status of any STC – that is, whether it has been 'resolved' or 'partially resolved'. Alternatively, the Secretariat lists the status as 'not reported'.[177] Here, the Secretariat plays an important active role, periodically reminding Members of their pending STCs and requiring a declaration of their status. Under the TBT Committee, a similar proposal was made, but Members opposed its adoption, arguing that it would undermine the efficiency of the process, which should remain flexible.

Closely related to the STC practice is a more formalised procedure known as 'good offices of the chair'. The good offices of the SPS chair were developed on the basis of Article 12.2 of the SPS Agreement (set out earlier in the chapter) and the Rules of Procedure for the SPS Committee, which provide that: 'With respect to any matter which has been raised under the Agreement, the Chairperson may, at the request of the Members directly concerned, assist them in dealing with the matter in question. The Chairperson shall normally report to the Committee on the general outcome with respect to the matter in question.'[178]

---

[175] WTO SPS Committee, 'Summary of the Meeting Held on 15–16 October 1997' (G/SPS/R/9, 15 December 1997), 2.
[176] WTO TBT Committee, 'Minutes of the Meeting of 23 March 2004' (G/TBT/M/32, 19 April 2004).
[177] See Horn, Mavroidis and Wijkström, 'In the Shadow of the DSU', for a description of how this practice was progressively introduced in the SPS Committee.
[178] WTO, 'Working Procedures of the Committee on Sanitary and Phytosanitary Measures' (G/SPS/1, 1995), para. 6.

Until 2014, these procedures were not formalised. They were used on three occasions by Members, following similar practices. Once the two parties agree to request the 'good offices', they determine where they will hold the meetings and then present the factual meetings to the chair. The chair presents the Members with options to solve the issue, but the chair's suggestions are not binding. Once the issue is solved, the chair or the Members involved present the results to the Committee.[179]

There have been three instances in which this procedure has been used: in 1997,[180] 1998[181] and 2001.[182] A procedure for the good offices was adopted in 2014,[183] but it has not been used since. This mechanism, which in many ways resembles that of a mediation, has the potential to be an important tool in preventing STCs from escalating into disputes. However, it is hard to assess the procedure before it is put into practice.[184]

The SPS Committee has considered different ways of improving the STC process, in particular with the good offices of the chair. For instance, STCs were the object of considerable discussions during the Second Review of the SPS Agreement. A proposal was made to formalise the consultation process, from the request for information through to the good offices of the chair. The proposal started off with a request for information on the basis of Article 5.8 of the SPS Agreement. This procedure would be used first to exchange documents and then to hold bilateral consultations. Only if the consultations were fruitless would the concerned Members raise an STC. If the concern were to persist after the STC discussions in the Committee, then Members could ask for the good offices of the chair.[185] This 'hierarchisation' of the transparency procedures was not adopted, but further discussions did continue on the good offices of the SPS chair.

---

[179] WTO, 'Ad Hoc Consultations and Resolution of Trade Concerns' (G/SPS/GEN/781, 2007).
[180] In 1997, the request was made by Argentina, Chile, the European Communities, South Africa and Uruguay regarding EC measures relating to citrus canker. See ibid.
[181] In 1998, the United States and Poland requested the good offices of the chair regarding 'restrictions on wheat and oilseeds maintained by Poland'.
[182] In 2001, Canada and Australia requested good offices, but from the Secretariat rather than the chair, regarding India's import restrictions on bovine semen.
[183] WTO, 'Procedure to Encourage and Facilitate the Resolution of Specific Sanitary or Phytosanitary Issues among Members in Accordance with Article 12.2, Decision Adopted by the Committee on 9 July 2014' (G/SPS/61, 2014).
[184] For a recent article on this mediation procedure under the SPS Agreement, see Nohyoung Park and Myung-Hyun Chung, 'Analysis of a New Mediation Procedure under the WTO SPS Agreement', *Journal of World Trade* 50, no. 1 (2016): 93–115.
[185] WTO, 'Ad Hoc Consultations and Resolution of Trade Concerns'.

STCs in Committee Discussions Today Today, STCs represent a very significant proportion of SPS and particularly TBT Committee work. Figures 2.1 and 2.2 illustrate the volume of STCs discussed per Committee

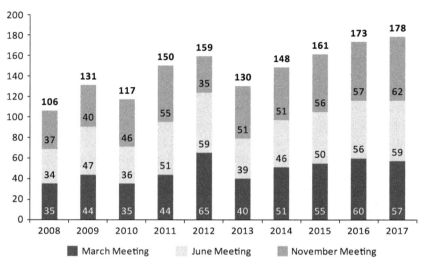

Figure 2.1 STCs discussed per TBT Committee meeting, 2008–2017. Source: WTO, 'Twenty-Third Annual Review of the Implementation and Operation of the TBT Agreement' (G/TBT/40, 12 March 2018), 17.

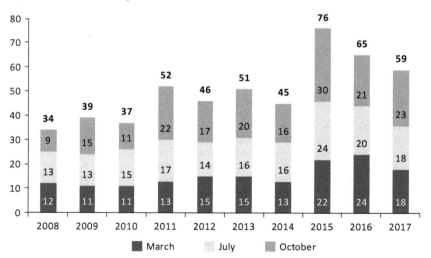

Figure 2.2 STCs discussed per SPS Committee meeting, 2008–2017. Source: SPS IMS, http://spsims.wto.org/.

meeting, including new STCs and STCs previously raised. These figures show that while the number of STCs raised in the TBT Committee has tended to grow quite consistently in the past 10 years, the growth is not as linear as that under the SPS Committee. The number of SPS STCs has remained relatively constant, with a peak in 2015. It is worth noting, however, that the same number of STCs were discussed in the SPS Committee in 2005 as were discussed in 2017.

3

International Regulatory Co-operation under the SPS and TBT Agreements

The legal framework of the WTO Agreements on the Application of Sanitary and Phytosanitary Measures (SPS Agreement, or SPS) and on Technical Barriers to Trade (TBT Agreement, or TBT) is open-ended, leaving Members with leeway to decide the detail of their regulations, under certain conditions, as seen in Chapter 1. To compensate for the uncertainty resulting from their scope, both Agreements set out a number of regulatory transparency provisions that WTO Members must embed into their domestic regulatory processes, requiring them to keep other Members informed of potential measures and eventually to take those Members' points of view into consideration in developing the measure, as seen in Chapter 2. This has resulted in extensive dialogue within the SPS and TBT Committees, demonstrating the potential of these fora to function as platforms for international regulatory co-operation (IRC). Because this IRC is a direct consequence of the transparency provisions and plays an important role in ensuring the implementation of the SPS and TBT Agreements, this chapter will examine the legal principles in the two Agreements that enable such co-operation, as a basis for understanding the dialogue that takes place between WTO Members in the SPS and TBT Committees.[1] As we shall see further later in the book, the co-operation that takes place at the early stages of the domestic regulatory process regarding trade-related measures arguably has the potential to prevent disputes from arising, by allowing Members to better understand each other's regulations and to participate directly in each other's regulatory processes.[2]

---

[1] The implementation of the SPS and TBT Agreements by WTO Members, as viewed through their dialogue in the SPS and TBT Committees, will be further discussed in Part II of this book.

[2] This argument will be further developed in Part III of this book, when we look at regulatory dialogue in the SPS and TBT Committees in practice, and at the disputes that are raised before the WTO Dispute Settlement Body (DSB).

I   What Is International Regulatory Co-operation?

Regulatory heterogeneity is inevitable in a world of sovereign States with different histories, cultures, and political and legal backgrounds. However, these sovereign States face similar – and sometimes common – risks to their welfare. Countries may therefore benefit from co-operating in their regulatory processes not only by learning from each other's regulatory choices but also by developing common approaches to common challenges. An increasing number of trade agreements include regulatory co-operation or 'coherence' chapters, aiming precisely at greater coherence between domestic regulatory regimes, with the objective of facilitating international trade and investment.[3]

Based on this same premise, and acknowledging the cross-border effects of domestic regulations and the specific needs of domestic regulators in a globalised world, the Organisation for Economic Co-operation and Development (OECD) introduced, in its 2012 Recommendation of the Council on Regulatory Policy and Governance, a specific principle on 'international regulatory co-operation' as a key pillar of regulatory policy. In its Principle 12, the OECD therefore recommends that, '[i]n developing regulatory measures, [domestic regulators] give consideration to all relevant international standards and frameworks for co-operation in the same field and, where appropriate, their likely effects on parties outside the jurisdiction'.

The OECD defines IRC as '[a]ny agreement or organisational arrangement, formal or informal, between countries to promote some form of co-operation in the design, monitoring, enforcement, or *ex post* management of regulation'.[4] This definition is very broad and includes within its scope any form of co-operation that takes place between regulators at any stage of the regulatory cycle, from sharing evidence and information at the very early stages of planning and design through to choosing to co-ordinate or recognise mutual approaches to implementing the measure.

---

[3] Andrew Mitchell and Elizabeth Sheargold, 'Regulatory Coherence in Future Free Trade Agreements and the Idea of the Embedded Liberalism Compromise', in Gillian Moon and Lisa Toohey, eds, *Future International Economic Integration: Embedded Liberalism Compromise Revisited* (Cambridge: Cambridge University Press, 2018), 138–9; Alberto Alemanno, 'The Regulatory Cooperation Chapter of the Transatlantic Trade and Investment Partnership: Institutional Structures and Democratic Consequences', SSRN Scholarly Paper, 27 August 2015. http://papers.ssrn.com/abstract=2651091.

[4] OECD, *International Regulatory Co-operation* (Paris: OECD, 2013), 153. www.oecd-ilibrary.org/governance/international-regulatory-co-operation_9789264200463-en.

Not only is regulatory co-operation important to achieving welfare concerns more efficiently, but also it is a key factor contributing to trade liberalisation. Indeed, from the trade perspective, which is the main concern for the WTO, regulatory divergence entails additional costs: the costs of identifying the relevant specifications that are applicable ('information costs'), the costs of complying with them ('specification costs') and the costs of demonstrating that compliance ('conformity assessment costs').[5] Regulatory co-operation helps to reduce these different types of cost by reducing the disparities between regulatory requirements.[6]

The WTO Secretariat has acknowledged the potential that IRC has to liberalise trade, summarising its benefits in the context of the TBT Agreement as follows:

> Regulatory co-operation between Members is, in essence, about reducing *unnecessary* regulatory diversity; it is also about limiting or reducing the costs associated with *necessary* regulatory diversity. Regulatory co-operation is premised on the notion that it is possible to remove unnecessary regulatory diversity and can even improve Member's ability to achieve their legitimate policy objectives. When fruitful, co-operation between Members – in various forms and configurations – can contribute to the reduction of unnecessary barriers to trade, and mitigate the economic impact of necessary barriers.[7]

As such and going beyond the core obligation under the SPS and TBT Agreements of reducing unnecessary barriers to trade, when diverging measures are indeed necessary, IRC can help to limit the costs that result from this regulatory heterogeneity.

Countries have, however, been co-operating in various ways to take into account the range of international trade and policy considerations that may arise in today's regulatory process. This co-operation can be

---

[5] Frank van Tongeren, Véronique Bastien and Martin von Lampe, 'International Regulatory Cooperation: A Trade-Facilitating Mechanism', 15 December 2015. http://e15initiative.org/wp-content/uploads/2015/09/E15-Regulatory-Coherence-van-Tongeren-Bastien-von-Lampe-Final.pdf.

[6] OECD, 'International Regulatory Co-operation and Trade: Understanding the Trade Costs of Regulatory Divergence and the Remedies', 24 May 2017. www.oecd.org/gov/international-regulatory-co-operation-and-trade-9789264275942-en.htm; Bernard Hoekman, ' "Behind-the-Border" Regulatory Policies and Trade Agreements', *East Asian Economic Review* 22, no. 3 (2018): 243–73.

[7] WTO, 'Regulatory Cooperation between Members: Background Note by Secretariat' (G/TBT/W/340, 2011), para. 4, emphasis original.

extremely informal or very formal – or it can fall somewhere in between. The OECD has developed a typology of 11 different approaches:

- harmonisation through supranational institutions;
- specific negotiated agreements;
- formal regulatory co-operation partnerships;
- joint standard-setting through intergovernmental organisations (IGOs);
- trade agreements with regulatory provisions;
- mutual recognition;
- trans-governmental networks of regulators;
- unilateral convergence through good regulatory practices (GRPs);
- recognition and incorporation of international standards;
- soft law principles; and
- dialogue or informal exchange of information.[8]

Revisiting the OECD typology of IRC to adapt it to the WTO context, this chapter will observe how the SPS and TBT Agreements introduce requirements for co-operation throughout Members' regulatory processes. Indeed, of the 11 different approaches identified by the OECD, five are either encouraged or enabled by the WTO SPS and TBT Agreements or Committee practice.[9] On the one hand, both Agreements encourage domestic regulators to engage in regulatory co-operation by means of various procedural obligations – essentially related to transparency, as described in Chapter 2 – and substantive obligations. These include harmonisation, mutual recognition, recognition of international and foreign regulation and standards, and adoption of GRPs. On the other hand, the two Agreements directly enable regulatory co-operation by offering a multilateral forum for regulatory co-operation among all WTO Members. As such, the WTO's SPS and TBT Committees illustrate the important role that IGOs may play in facilitating IRC.[10]

---

[8] OECD, *International Regulatory Co-operation*.
[9] Seven of the 11 IRC approaches can be considered to be relevant to reducing trade costs resulting from regulatory heterogeneity: harmonisation, regulatory provisions in trade agreements, joint rule-making through IGOs, mutual recognition, recognition of international and foreign regulation and standards, adoption of GRPs and dialogue/exchange of information. However, given the highly developed institutional and legal framework of the WTO, IRC will be considered here in relation to only the regulatory provisions in trade agreements, the joint rule-making through IGOs, and the dialogue and exchange of information.
[10] On this, see also OECD/WTO, *Facilitating Trade through Regulatory Co-operation: The Case of the WTO's TBT/SPS Agreements and Committees* (Paris: OECD, 2019). www.oecd.org/gov/facilitating-trade-through-regulatory-co-operation-ad3c655f-en.htm.

Bollyky and Mavroidis argue that the WTO Agreements have an important role to play in fostering IRC.[11] In particular, they point towards three instances of regulatory divergence in which IRC is crucial in reducing the trade costs that result from regulatory divergence: when domestic measures impose duplicative rules or conformity assessment procedures (CAPs); when domestic measures are divergent, but similarly rigorous; or when domestic measures are divergent and rigorous to varying degrees.[12] While recognising that the SPS and TBT Agreements are the WTO agreements that include the most extensive framework to encourage IRC, Bollyky and Mavroidis consider that, 'without a greater mandate and more institutional support, these WTO efforts seem more likely to serve as guidelines for unilateral actions by members'.[13] We look next at how the SPS and TBT Agreements encourage and enable IRC in theory, laying the groundwork for discussions in Part II about the considerable co-operation that does take place in practice between WTO Members.

II International Regulatory Co-operation Encouraged under the SPS and TBT Agreements

This section will present the provisions in the SPS and TBT Agreements that encourage international regulatory co-operation between Members – namely, the obligation to adopt international standards (section A), the provisions regarding recognition (section B), and elements inserting GRPs into Members' domestic regulatory processes (section C).

A Adopting International Standards

According to the OECD IRC typology, harmonisation is the most binding and formal form of IRC. Indeed, it results in an integration of the same set of standards across all governments that are part of the same entity. Benefiting from a supranational institution for the standard-setting process and for centralised enforcement, such institutions also have a better guarantee of compliance. The typical example is the European Union, which develops its own regulations that are integrated as such into the

---

[11] Thomas J. Bollyky and Petros C. Mavroidis, 'Trade, Social Preferences and Regulatory Cooperation: The New WTO-Think', RSCAS Research Paper No. 2016/47, 2 December 2016. https://papers.ssrn.com/sol3/papers.cfm?abstract_id=2879329.
[12] Ibid., 16–17.
[13] Ibid., 19.

domestic law of the EU Member States and are directly enforceable by domestic or European judges.

The SPS and TBT Agreements follow a negative integration approach and therefore do not have such an integrated system. They do not themselves introduce positive obligations to ensure harmonisation nor do they offer centralised adjudication, because only Member States can raise a dispute. However, they do legally mandate both that domestic measures shall be based on international standards whenever they exist and that Members shall participate in international standard-setting bodies in pursuit of harmonisation. According to the logic of the two Agreements, WTO Members should consider whether they might appropriately use an international standard to achieve their domestic policy objectives before they start to develop a unilateral measure.[14]

These obligations under both the SPS and TBT Agreements are an important effort towards reducing regulatory heterogeneity among WTO Members, although they contribute only indirectly to the harmonisation of Members' domestic measures, because the standards referred to are not developed by the WTO, but by other standardising bodies.

From a legal perspective, presenting this as an obligation as opposed to an encouragement or a recommendation shifts the two Agreements towards positive integration, given that its result is to ask Members to follow substantive standards.[15] This is all the more so given that deviation from international standards is allowed only under certain exceptional conditions – that is, when the international standard is inadequate to deal with the domestic policy issue at hand.

1   Harmonisation under the SPS Agreement

The obligation of harmonisation is embedded throughout the SPS Agreement, accompanied by the obligation to base domestic measures on international standards and the caution that deviation from international standards should be exceptional.

---

[14] See e.g. Petros C. Mavroidis, 'Last Mile for Tuna (to a Safe Harbour): What Is the TBT Agreement All About?', *European Journal of International Law* 30, no. 1 (2019): 281.

[15] Howse qualifies the TBT Agreement's approach to international standards, and the Appellate Body's interpretations of it, as a 'new device for creating international legal normativity', virtually transforming voluntary international standards into international legal obligations: Robert Howse, 'A New Device for Creating International Legal Normativity: The WTO Technical Barriers to Trade Agreement and "International Standards" ', in Christian Joerges and Ernst-Ulrich Petersmann, eds, *Constitutionalism, Multilevel Trade Governance and Social Regulation*, Studies in International Trade and Investment Law (Oxford: Hart, 2006), 384.

a **The Objective of Harmonisation**   Recitals 5 and 6 of the Preamble to the SPS Agreement emphasise the importance of international standards and the objective of harmonisation pursued by the Agreement:

> *Recognizing* the important contribution that international standards, guidelines and recommendations can make [to minimise the negative effect on trade of SPS measures];
>
> *Desiring* to further the use of harmonised sanitary and phytosanitary measures between Members, on the basis of international standards, guidelines and recommendations developed by the relevant international organizations, including the Codex Alimentarius Commission, the International Office of Epizootics, and the relevant international and regional organizations operating within the framework of the International Plant Protection Convention, without requiring Members to change their appropriate level of protection of human, animal or plant life or health;
>
> [...]

Because the SPS Agreement explicitly lists three international standard-setting bodies, it comes closer to a model of positive integration than does the TBT Agreement: it requires WTO Members to adopt specific standards and it explicitly pursues the objective of harmonisation. The word 'harmonisation' itself implies a high level of regulatory integration among the WTO Members. Indeed, it is used in the OECD typology of IRC to describe the most integrated mode of IRC. However, the SPS Agreement and the WTO Secretariat assisting in its implementation do not prescribe harmonisation. As the specific obligations related to international standards confirm, harmonisation is merely an objective that WTO Members might pursue in implementing their SPS obligations.

b **The Obligation to Base Domestic Measures on International Standards**   The obligation to base domestic measures on international standards is set out in Article 3.1 of the SPS Agreement, which requires Members to 'base their sanitary or phytosanitary measures on international standards, guidelines or recommendations, where they exist'.

This is a clear requirement to base domestic regulations on international standards. However, this obligation does not result in harmonised regulations among WTO Members, for two main reasons: on the one hand, Members maintain their regulatory autonomy and can decide how to 'base' regulations on international standards; and on the other, the organisations referred to in the SPS Agreement – that is, the World Organisation for Animal Health (OIE), the Codex Alimentarius and the International Plant Protection Convention (IPPC) – are separate from the WTO and develop only voluntary standards.

To look at these in more detail, first, the obligation laid down in Article 3.1 of the SPS Agreement reserves for WTO Members the competence to decide their regulatory objectives and the measure best suited to achieving these objectives. In this sense, WTO Members are required to 'base' their measures on international standards, but not to 'adopt', 'incorporate' or even 'conform with' those standards. The WTO Appellate Body further highlighted the distinction between 'base on' and 'conform with' in *EC – Hormones*, rejecting the panel's earlier interpretation that 'base on' means the same thing as to 'conform to' and thus requires a domestic measure to result in the same level of sanitary protection as the international standard.[16]

This distinction is important because the different ways in which Members 'base' measures on international standards may result in different regulations. Indeed, using an international standard as a basis does not preclude domestic regulators changing certain aspects of that standard to adapt it to their legal framework. In addition, a number of exceptions apply to the obligation, confirming Members' leeway in choosing their regulation, as will be further developed later.

Second, the institutional framework for developing standards is not the responsibility of the WTO; the SPS Agreement refers to international standards developed by other international organisations. These bodies develop voluntary technical standards, which WTO Members are required to adopt only if relevant. The three bodies cited in the SPS Agreement – namely, the OIE, the Codex Alimentarius and the IPPC – do not constitute 'supranational' institutions as understood within the OECD typology, because they do not produce binding measures with direct effect at the domestic level and they do not have the necessary institutional teeth to ensure the enforcement of these standards. However, they can be considered to be international organisations on account of their governance, decision-making and normative power. They enable IRC in relation to their specific subject areas and among their respective constituencies.

c **The Obligation to Participate in Standardising Bodies** In addition to the obligation to base domestic measures on international standards, the SPS Agreement requires Members to play a part in the international

---

[16] Appellate Body Report, *EC – Hormones*, §§166–8.

organisations that develop those international standards that are relevant to sanitary and phytosanitary measures. In so doing, Members must participate in both the development and the 'periodic review of standards, guidelines and recommendations'.[17]

Article 3.4 of the SPS Agreement cites several organisations explicitly and requires that Members '*shall* play a full part' in these organisations – namely, 'the Codex Alimentarius Commission, the International Office of Epizootics, and the international and regional organisations operating within the framework of the International Plant Protection Convention'.

By requiring WTO Members to participate in the standard-setting processes of these organisations, this language establishes a strong relationship between the WTO legal system and these three normative organisations. By involving WTO Members from the outset, from development through to reviews of international standards, the Agreement sets out a favourable framework for the harmonisation of SPS measures among all 164 WTO Members.

While this is a step towards positive integration, 'delegating' the setting of positive standards to other bodies allows the WTO to maintain its negative integration approach. As De Bièvre puts it: '[T]he choice not to elevate the WTO to the locus of standard-setting, but rather to rely on other relevant, specialised agencies, illustrates the imbalance between the strong judicialisation and the weak rule-making arm of the WTO.'[18] Nevertheless, the close relationship between the SPS Agreement and the relevant international standards edges WTO Members towards harmonisation, while leaving Members able to choose whether or not to adopt them.

d   **The Exceptions to the Obligation**   The principles set out in the SPS Agreement regarding international standards encourage IRC in the sense that they prompt WTO Members to co-operate and thus to work towards greater convergence in their regulatory approaches. However, this is only a recommendation, not a mandate, and Members may choose to deviate from international standards. WTO Members are authorised to apply a

---

[17] Article 3.4 SPS.
[18] Dirk De Bièvre, 'Governance in International Trade: Judicialisation and Positive Integration in the WTO', MPI Preprints No. 2004/7, 28 July 2004, 15. https://papers.ssrn.com/sol3/papers.cfm?abstract_id=566501.

higher level of SPS protection than set out under international standards if they consider it to be justified or if such a level is an appropriate response to a risk assessment. Indeed, Article 3.3 of the SPS Agreement provides for measures that result in:

> ... a higher level of sanitary or phytosanitary protection than would be achieved by measures based on the relevant international standards, guidelines or recommendations, if there is a scientific justification, or as a consequence of the level of sanitary or phytosanitary protection a Member determines to be appropriate in accordance with the relevant provisions of paragraphs 1 through 8 of Article 5 ['Assessment of Risk and Determination of the Appropriate Level of Sanitary or Phytosanitary Protection'].

This possibility of deviating from international standards is important to safeguard WTO Members' regulatory autonomy and the spirit of negative integration. At the same time, as we shall see in Chapter 5, such deviation may raise trade costs and therefore lead other Members to raise concerns, seeking to understand why and how the domestic measure differs from the relevant international standard. The scientific justification or risk assessment required under Article 3.3 helps to prevent arbitrary deviations and raising STCs in the SPS Committee is a valuable opportunity to ask questions about those scientific foundations.

2 Harmonisation under the TBT Agreement

The TBT Agreement includes slightly looser references to harmonisation than those in the SPS Agreement. While it also includes an obligation to base domestic measures on international standards, it does not refer explicitly to any international standard-setting bodies nor does it define the attributes of those standards that WTO Members should use. In this sense, the TBT Agreement cannot be seen as introducing positive integration in any way.[19] Nevertheless, the obligations under the TBT Agreement do aim to incentivise Members to adopt international standards, with the aim of achieving regulatory consistency.

The Preamble to the TBT Agreement starts by recognising the importance of international standards in facilitating trade:

> *Recognizing* the important contribution that international standards and conformity assessment systems can make in this regard by improving efficiency of production and facilitating the conduct of international trade.

---

[19] Petros C. Mavroidis, *Trade in Goods* (Oxford: Oxford University Press, 2012).

Desiring therefore to encourage the development of such international standards and conformity assessment systems.

[...]

Recognizing the contribution which international standardization can make to the transfer of technology from developed to developing countries.

The principle established in Article 2.4 of the TBT Agreement is that Members are obliged to base their technical regulations on international standards or relevant parts of them 'when they exist or their completion is imminent'. For their CAPs, Members are required to use relevant guides or recommendations issued by international standardising bodies under these same conditions – that is, when they exist or their completion is imminent.

Under the TBT Agreement, the identification of relevant international standards is not an easy task. For the purposes of the TBT Agreement, international standards are those voluntary standards (as defined in Annex 1 to the Agreement) that have been adopted by international standardisation bodies. However, unlike the SPS Agreement, the TBT Agreement does not explicitly define international standard-setting bodies beyond the very broad terms of Annex 1, paragraph 4 – that is, '[b]ody or system whose membership is open to the relevant bodies of at least all Members'.

To clarify the concept of international standards, the TBT Committee has adopted six principles that should be observed when adopting international standards, guides and recommendations – namely, transparency, openness, impartiality and consensus, effectiveness and relevance, coherence and addressing the concerns of developing countries.[20] The Appellate Body considered this decision to constitute a 'subsequent agreement between the parties regarding the interpretation of the treaty or the application of its provisions', and therefore applied the six principles when seeking, in *US – Tuna II (Mexico)*, to identify whether a body qualified as an international body as understood by Annex 1, paragraph 4, to the TBT Agreement.[21] In broad terms, it may therefore be considered that, for the purpose of the TBT Agreement, international standards are those adopted by bodies following the six principles.

The obligation regarding international standards in the TBT Agreement is, as is that under the SPS Agreement, an obligation to use

---

[20] WTO, 'Second Triennial Review of the Operation and Implementation of the Agreement on Technical Barriers to Trade' (G/TBT/9, 13 November 2000), para. 20 and Annex 4.

[21] Appellate Body Report, *US – Tuna II (Mexico)*, §§372 et seq.

II INTERNATIONAL REGULATORY CO-OPERATION ENCOURAGED

international standards 'as a basis' when developing domestic technical measures. Concretely, and as the Appellate Body suggested in *EC – Hormones*, the requirement is not that the domestic regulation and the international standards should offer an equal level of protection. The wording of the Agreement suggests only that, when regulating, Members base their text on existing international standards; it does not seem to imply that the domestic measure adopted must conform fully with the international standard.[22] However, in interpreting Article 2.4 of the TBT Agreement, the Appellate Body has affirmed that the obligation to base domestic regulations on international standards ensures a very strong relationship between the domestic regulation and the international standard. Indeed, citing the meaning of 'basis of' as used in general language, the Appellate Body considered that the international standard should be treated as the principal constituent – the fundamental principle or theory – of a system of knowledge of the domestic regulation.[23] More specifically, it added that a domestic regulation that *contradicts* an international standard cannot be considered to be 'based on' it.[24] It therefore rejected the argument that a domestic regulation that derived from an international standard to the extent that the Member had considered the standard as a whole and taken on board only elements of it was not sufficiently so to be considered to be 'based on' that standard.[25]

Despite imposing an obligation to use international standards as a basis for national measures, the TBT Agreement – like the SPS Agreement – does acknowledge that there may be good reason for departing from them.[26] Under Article 2.4, it recognises that Members may deviate from international standards when they are 'ineffective or inappropriate means for the fulfilment of the legitimate objectives pursued, for instance because of fundamental climatic or geographic factors or fundamental technological problems'. The same level of scientific justification for deviation is not required as that provided for under the SPS Agreement for SPS measures.

---

[22] See, on this, Joseph H. H. Weiler and Henrik Horn, '*EC – Trade Description of Sardines*: Textualism and Its Discontent', in Henrik Horn and Petros C. Mavroidis, eds, *The American Law Institute Reporters' Studies on WTO Case Law: Legal and Economic Analysis* (Cambridge/New York: Cambridge University Press, 2007), 551–78; Howse, 'A New Device for Creating International Legal Normativity', 384–6.
[23] Appellate Body Report, *EC – Hormones*, §243.
[24] Ibid., §249.
[25] Ibid., §§242–4.
[26] Andrea Barrios Villareal, *International Standardization and the Agreement on Technical Barriers to Trade* (Cambridge: Cambridge University Press, 2018), 111–12.

Finally, like the SPS Agreement, the TBT Agreement requires that Members play a full part in the preparation of standards. Two significant differences appear in this regard, however, in the language of the TBT and SPS Agreements. On the one hand, the TBT article does not specify that Members should participate in the periodic review of the standards, as is the case under the SPS Agreement; on the other hand, the TBT Agreement does not cite any such bodies explicitly. Participation by WTO Members in other organisations is therefore difficult for the WTO to monitor – let alone to enforce.

The competence reserved for WTO Members to decide upon the exact level of consistency between domestic measures and international standards therefore leaves space for differing approaches across WTO Members. An OECD survey confirms that, in practice, few OECD countries have adopted a standardised approach to incorporating international standards.[27] The absence of such an approach may result in different levels of consistency between domestic measures and international standards, precluding the benefits of harmonisation. Transparency about draft measures is therefore the key to understanding the level of consistency among domestic measures and international standards, as well as to clarifying the detail of domestic measures even when they have been based on an international standard.

B The Mutual Recognition of Domestic Requirements

In pursuit of the objective of harmonisation, mutual recognition provides an additional means of delivering convergence among a few Members' domestic technical requirements. Mutual recognition entails a country recognising another country's domestic requirements as equivalent to its own, whether those requirements are set out as regulations, CAPs or standards, and the countries therefore grant automatic market access to each other's compliant products.

'Recognition' can take different forms, including mutual, in which case several countries (but usually two) recognise each other's requirements as equivalent, or unilaterally, whereby one country recognises the requirements of another country as equivalent to its own without such recognition being reciprocated. The recognition can cover rules or standards, or procedures, or the results of conformity assessment. Mutual recognition of rules or standards is the most integrated form of recognition, requiring equivalence of regulatory objectives and resulting in automatic market access of one

---

[27] OECD, *OECD Regulatory Policy Outlook 2018* (Paris: OECD, 2018), 132. www.oecd.org/governance/oecd-regulatory-policy-outlook-2018-9789264303072-en.htm.

country's products in the other regardless of their exporting and importing differences. Mutual recognition of conformity assessment is of more limited effect and mainly involves the conformity assessment bodies of one country assessing conformity with the rules of the other.[28]

Mutual recognition is, however, between only certain Members and usually bilateral, which necessarily leads to a fragmented approach to IRC.

1 The Recognition of Equivalence among International Regulations and Standards

Mutual recognition of 'rules' – that is, technical regulations and standards – is the most ambitious form of mutual recognition, but it is very rare because of the level of proximity in regulatory objectives that it demands. The two main examples are the EU's internal market and the Trans-Tasman Mutual Recognition Arrangement between Australia and New Zealand.[29]

Although such mutual recognition is difficult to achieve, Article 2.7 of the TBT Agreement requires Members to give 'positive consideration to accepting technical regulations of other Members, even if these regulations differ from their own, provided they are satisfied that these regulations adequately fulfil the objectives of their own regulations'. This obligation remains far from enforceable: not only is proving that a Member has not given such *positive consideration* 'extremely difficult, but also, even assuming that Members do give positive consideration to accepting other Members' rules as equivalent, this article does not require that they *actually accept* them.

In Article 4.1 on equivalence, however, the SPS Agreement uses even stronger language, requiring Members to accept each other's SPS measures as equivalent:

> Members shall accept the sanitary or phytosanitary measures of other Members as equivalent, even if these measures differ from their own or from those used by other Members trading in the same product, if the exporting Member objectively demonstrates to the importing Member that its measures achieve the importing Member's appropriate level of sanitary or phytosanitary protection. For this purpose, reasonable access shall be given, upon request, to the importing Member for inspection, testing and other relevant procedures.

---

[28] For a more complete overview of the variety of forms of mutual recognition, see Anabela Correia de Brito, Céline Kauffmann and Jacques Pelkmans, 'The Contribution of Mutual Recognition to International Regulatory Co-operation', OECD Regulatory Policy Working Papers No. 2, 31 August 2016. www.oecd.org/regreform/WP2_Contribution-of-mutual-recognition-to-IRC.pdf.

[29] Correia de Brito and colleagues describe the details of these two systems: ibid., 16.

In addition to this, Article 4.1 encourages Members to enter into consultations 'with the aim of achieving bilateral and multilateral agreements on recognition of the equivalence of specified sanitary or phytosanitary measures'.

2 Mutually Recognising a Conformity Assessment under the TBT Agreement

The TBT Agreement promotes co-operation between Members on the implementation of CAPs. Article 6.1 encourages Members to recognise each other's conformity assessment results, 'provided they are satisfied that those procedures offer an assurance of conformity with applicable technical regulations or standards equivalent to their own procedures'. This is only an encouragement, the provision being modified by the phrase 'whenever possible'. Article 6.1 goes on to give Members discretion over assuring conformity with technical regulations or standards and underlines that 'prior consultations may be necessary in order to arrive at a mutually satisfactory understanding'. In this regard, the TBT Agreement mentions accreditation and mutual recognition agreements (MRAs) as possible means of ensuring confidence in the reliability of conformity assessment results.[30]

The language is very loose and Members are even encouraged not to conclude MRAs, but rather to 'be willing to enter negotiations for the conclusion of agreements'. In the best-case scenario, then, two or three Members – most likely two – will recognise each other's conformity assessment results, but the effects for the multilateral trading system will remain limited.

The TBT Committee cites both MRAs and unilateral recognition of conformity assessment results as ways of facilitating acceptance of the results of CAPs: 'Governments may enter into agreements which will result in the acceptance of the results of conformity assessment originating in the territory of either party. ... A government may unilaterally recognise the results of foreign conformity assessment procedures.'[31]

Members occasionally refer to bilateral MRAs or multilateral MRAs in their specific trade concerns (STCs), both to note a lack of reliance on such MRAs and to recall their benefits in reducing the trade burdens of conformity assessment.[32] However, information about the mutual recognition procedures implemented by Members remains limited. In principle

---

[30] Articles 6.1.1 and 6.3 TBT, respectively.
[31] WTO, 'Second Triennial Review of the Operation and Implementation', Annex 5, 27.
[32] Marianna Karttunen and Devin McDaniels, 'Trade, Testing and Toasters: Conformity Assessment Procedures and the TBT Committee', *Journal of World Trade* 50, no. 5 (2016): 755–92.

trade-facilitating measures, they do not fall under the notification obligation and no specific notification obligation requires that information on MRAs be shared with WTO Members at large. Much as it does for international standards, Article 9 of the TBT Agreement fosters Members' co-operation beyond the WTO: it encourages Members to participate in, become members of, or formulate and adopt international systems for CAPs to facilitate the recognition and acceptance of conformity assessment results, as long as these international systems comply with the provisions of Articles 5 and 6 of the Agreement.

The SPS Agreement includes no separate provision on the recognition of CAPs, although control, inspection and approval procedures may represent significant trade barriers and are the subject of Annex C to the Agreement.

C Good Regulatory Practices

In line with its broad definition of IRC, the OECD includes a variety of approaches within its typology, the common thread being that they promote some form of consistency in cross-border regulations. In this sense, the OECD includes within the scope of IRC those unilateral efforts by domestic regulators that may contribute to better regulatory coherence – namely, GRPs.[33]

Also known as 'better regulation' or 'regulatory quality', among other terms,[34] GRPs cover the substantive and procedural principles that domestic regulators may apply to improve the quality, effectiveness and impact of their regulations. The OECD countries have agreed on a set of recommendations that govern the domestic regulatory cycle and aim to ensure that 'regulations meet public policy objectives and will have a positive impact on the economy and society'.[35] Growing evidence shows that improving regulatory quality can have specific benefits for international

---

[33] OECD, 'International Regulatory Co-operation and Trade', 35.
[34] The terminology used to designate these principles varies according to different fora. In the OECD the terms 'regulatory policy', 'regulatory quality' or 'regulatory reform' are preferred, whereas in the EU 'better regulation', 'smart regulation' or 'regulatory fitness' tend to be used more often. The OECD gathered the varied terminology in OECD, *OECD Regulatory Policy Outlook 2015* (Paris: OECD, 2015). The WTO Secretariat uses 'good regulatory practices', particularly in the discussions of the TBT Committee: see WTO, 'Fifth Triennial Review of the Operation and Implementation of the Agreement on Technical Barriers to Trade under Article 15.4' (G/TBT/26, 2009).
[35] OECD, 'Recommendation of the Council on Regulatory Policy and Governance', 2012, 21. www.oecd.org/gov/regulatory-policy/49990817.pdf.

trade. Indeed, by promoting the transparency of regulations, GRPs help to reduce the information costs for traders, and by improving the quality of regulations, GRPs 'may reduce the likelihood of regulatory duplication, unnecessary regulatory heterogeneity and provide efficient administrative and enforcement procedures', thus also reducing the costs of specification and conformity assessment.[36]

The Agreements do not explicitly provide for GRPs. However, the TBT Committee has recognised their importance to reducing technical barriers to trade by means of 'improved and effective implementation of the substantive obligations of the TBT Agreement'.[37]

It can be argued that the various legal provisions of the SPS Agreement require certain elements of GRP, or 'regulation of regulation'.[38] First, the transparency provisions of the SPS and TBT Agreements, discussed extensively in Chapter 2, are intrinsically useful means of fostering GRPs. In addition, the substantive obligations of both the SPS and TBT Agreements can be seen as calling for the application of GRPs – in particular, the requirements to:

- identify legitimate objectives and avoid unnecessary obstacles to trade;[39]
- select technical regulations based on product requirements rather than design or descriptive characteristics;[40]
- apply the least trade-restrictive alternative;[41]
- base all SPS measures on scientific evidence after conducting a risk assessment;[42] and
- consider the cost-effectiveness of alternative approaches.[43]

Using the WTO Secretariat's figures as a basis, Figure 3.1 adds the substantive obligations of the SPS and TBT Agreements, to underline the phases of the domestic lifecycle in which they fit. This figure shows that the different substantial obligations of both the SPS and the TBT Agreements are to be applied in the early stages of the domestic regulatory cycle.

---

[36] OECD, 'Synthesis Report on Trade and International Regulatory Cooperation' (COM/GOV/TAD(2016)1, 2016).
[37] WTO, 'Fifth Triennial Review of the Operation and Implementation', para. 5.
[38] Joanne Scott, *The WTO Agreement on Sanitary and Phytosanitary Measures*, 44.
[39] Article 2.2 TBT.
[40] Article 2.8 TBT.
[41] Articles 2.2 and 5.6 SPS.
[42] Articles 2.2 and 5.1 SPS.
[43] Article 5.3 SPS.

II INTERNATIONAL REGULATORY CO-OPERATION ENCOURAGED

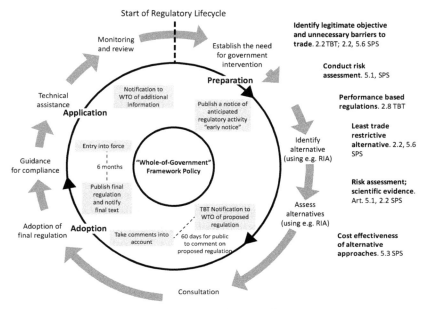

Figure 3.1 Applying GRPs to the lifecycle of TBT and SPS measures.
Source: Author's own, based on WTO, *Technical Barriers to Trade*,
The WTO Agreements Series (Geneva: WTO, 2014), 31.

In this context, the TBT Committee has been discussing since 2009 a set of principles that aim at promoting GRPs among Members when implementing their obligations, labelled a 'Non-exhaustive List of Voluntary Mechanisms and Related Principles of Good Regulatory Practice'.[44] These principles do not introduce new obligations to WTO Members, but rather build on the existing provisions of the TBT Agreement to spell out how they contribute to GRPs. In this context, the list provides a description of the steps that Members should take in preparing, adopting and applying TBT measures, indicating examples of GRPs under each step alongside the relevant TBT Agreement articles. While substance of the principles has been agreed upon, however, the principles have not yet been adopted.[45]

Through their various substantive obligations and encouragements in relation to regulatory co-operation, the SPS and TBT Agreements already provide an important first step towards regulatory convergence between

---

[44] To date, the list remains in draft form and is therefore not publicly available.
[45] Disagreement between Members on the legal disclaimer included in the document blocks its adoption.

Members. However, the obligations remain difficult to follow up – not least because they concern practices that take place outside of the WTO framework, either in other international bodies, or bilaterally or regionally between Members.

III International Regulatory Co-operation Enabled by the SPS and TBT Institutional Framework

As discussed, some provisions and practices require WTO Members not to deliver TBT and SPS measures in isolation, introducing elements of international regulatory co-operation by means of various substantive obligations. Beyond the texts of the WTO Agreements per se, the institutional framework aiming to support their implementation provides a setting in which Members can collaborate multilaterally on their mutual domestic regulatory processes. This institutional framework, together with the specific SPS and TBT legal provisions, makes the SPS and TBT Committees unique platforms for IRC in comparison to other international organisations (section A). At the same time, they follow similar forms of IRC to other international organisations (section B).

A *The WTO SPS and TBT Committees: Unique Platforms for International Regulatory Co-operation*

'Joint standard-setting within international organisations' corresponds to one of the IRC approaches identified by the OECD. Indeed, through their institutional settings and technical expertise, international organisations are an important platform on which countries can collaborate multilaterally in setting international policies and standards, working to align their regulatory approaches.[46]

The WTO is no exception, although it differs considerably from other organisations, especially because of its highly developed legal system and its delivery of third-party adjudication. Indeed, the WTO's central activity is not standard-setting or policy-making, but supporting Members in the operation of the Agreements concluded more than 20 years ago, in 1995. Nevertheless, as we will see, WTO Members have used its TBT

---

[46] The OECD has been working extensively on the role played by international organisations in fostering IRC and provides a comparative analysis of 50 international organisations in this regard: OECD, *International Regulatory Co-operation: The Role of International Organisations* (Paris: OECD, 2016).

and SPS Committees extensively both to develop policy guidance regarding the implementation of the two Agreements and to consult on specific concerns about each other's regulations.

In this sense, while most international organisations are more active in providing their Members with a platform on which to develop international rules or standards – that is, in the upstream stages of the policy cycle – which are then to be adopted at the domestic level, the TBT and SPS Committees serve more as a platform for regulatory co-operation in the downstream phase of the WTO's policy cycle, to ensure the effective implementation of the SPS and TBT Agreements.

However, although the bulk of the IRC in SPS and TBT Committees takes place at the downstream stage of the policy cycle from the perspective of the international norms (i.e. in the implementation phase of the TBT and SPS Agreements), the substantive and procedural obligations of the two Agreements have implications for the development phase of domestic measures. The SPS and TBT Committees therefore provide a platform for the inclusive drafting of domestic measures, allowing Members to contribute to each other's domestic regulatory processes rather than merely monitoring whether resulting measures comply with WTO obligations.

B The Opportunities for Co-operation Throughout the Work of the SPS and TBT Committees

Overall, according to the OECD's analysis of IRC in international organisations, there are nine areas in which international organisations provide an opportunity for their Members to co-operate throughout the regulatory cycle, as illustrated in Figure 3.2.

The WTO SPS and TBT Committees are active in eight of these areas, and notably in both the upstream and downstream activities of the policy cycle.[47] This is rarely the case in other international organisations, which tend to be less active in the downstream activities, in particular enforcement and dispute settlement. Arguably, the coexistence of these different levels of co-operation, from the exchange of information to dispute settlement, ensures continuity of co-operation efforts, which is ultimately conducive to more efficient IRC. In other words, this robust framework for regulatory co-operation among Members creates more opportunities for Members to work together towards effective implementation of their SPS and TBT obligations.

---

[47] The WTO is active in all except crisis management. See OECD, 'International Regulatory Co-operation', 204.

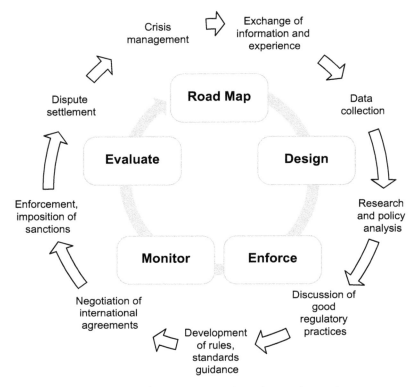

Figure 3.2 Opportunities for co-operation throughout policy cycle.
Source: OECD, *International Regulatory Co-operation* (Paris: OECD, 2013).

Overall, the IRC that takes place under the TBT and SPS Agreements is formal (obligations are binding), multilateral (it goes beyond the usual tendencies for like-minded countries to co-operate at a bilateral or plurilateral level) and comprehensive (geographic coverage is high, and the regulatory functions are upstream and downstream, but the involvement of other stakeholders is low, the policy areas covered are limited to TBT and SPS, and the level of harmonisation is low), and the actors involved are mainly technical experts, often with scientific expertise.[48]

---

[48] Petros C. Mavroidis and Erik N. Wijkström, 'Moving out of the Shadows: Bringing Transparency to Standards and Regulations in the WTO's TBT Committee', in Tracey Epps and Michael J. Trebilcock, eds, *Research Handbook on the WTO* (Cheltenham: Edward Elgar, 2013), 204–37.

1 Regulatory Co-operation in the Upstream Activities of the Policy Cycle

The majority of international organisations are active in the upstream activities of the policy cycle, exchanging information, collecting data and developing international policies or legal instruments under their mandate. While the WTO does conduct such activities, all of them are exclusively focused on supporting Members in their implementation of the SPS and TBT Agreements.

a Exchanging Information Information exchange is one of the core activities of both the SPS and TBT Committees, essential to helping Members to implement the Agreements and to share their experiences. Information is exchanged not only about implementation of the Agreements but also on international standards adopted in other bodies.[49]

The triennial reviews of operation and implementation of the TBT Agreement are required under the TBT Agreement as a means of continuously adapting the legal framework. Within these reviews, Members exchange information and issue a set of recommendations that define the Committee's programme of work for the subsequent years.[50]

b Data Collection and Policy Analysis Although research and policy analysis is less frequent in the WTO, largely because the organisation is Member-driven, the Secretariat does regularly collect data on the implementation of both the SPS and the TBT Agreements.

In particular, the Secretariat conducts annual reviews of implementation of the TBT Agreement and triennial reviews accounting for Members' implementation of the two Agreements.

The Secretariat essentially relies on Members to provide information and has no active role in researching independent data.[51] Although the data is published with minimum analysis, the comparative perspective that the Secretariat offers does facilitate insights on present and/or persisting trends in Members' implementation practices.[52]

---

[49] For further information on information exchange in Committees, see Mavroidis and Wijkström, 'Moving out of the Shadows'; Scott, *Cooperative Regulation in the WTO*.

[50] The seven triennial reviews that have been adopted to date can be found at G/TBT/5, G/TBT/9, G/TBT/13, G/TBT/19, G/TBT/26, G/TBT/32 and G/TBT/37.

[51] The Trade Policy Review Body (TPRB) has a more active role in this regard, because the Secretariat may use other sources in the preparation of its Member reviews.

[52] See e.g. the most recent review of implementation of the TBT Agreement, at G/TBT/38/Rev.1.

c **Discussing GRPs** The TBT Committee has been discussing the conduct of Members in relation to GRPs. As mentioned earlier in the chapter, the TBT Committee has been actively developing a set of voluntary principles that aim to help domestic regulators to apply GRPs when preparing, adopting and implementing TBT measures.

The SPS Committee has also been raising the issue of GRPs in its meetings since 2005. Mexico submitted a proposal to establish GRP guidelines to help Members to ensure their compliance with SPS obligations before the adoption of new measures. However, as was the case in the TBT Committee, this proposal was not pursued.[53]

d **Developing Rules, Standards and Guidance** The SPS and TBT Committees develop recommendations, decisions and principles, focusing either on procedural issues of Committee practice or on facilitating Members' implementation of the two Agreements. All Committee rules are adopted by consensus.

Wijkström notes that, by 'delving into the nitty gritty of implementation, delegations have turned the Committee into a laboratory for multilateral regulatory co-operation that is quite effectively (up to now) generating material that is both relevant and of practical use. This has lent dynamism to the treaty texts ... .'[54]

Among the rules developed by the TBT Committee are rules of procedure applicable to the Committee itself,[55] as well as a decision for the development of international standards, guides and recommendations,[56] frequently referred to by international standardising bodies.[57]

---

[53] Regarding Mexico's proposal, see G/SPS/W/166. The Committee merely recommended that Members 'provide information regarding their experiences in the use of the guidelines developed by the Committee with respect to transparency, equivalence, recognition of pest- or disease-free areas, and the avoidance of arbitrary or unjustifiable distinctions in levels of protection': see WTO, 'Review of the Operation and Implementation of the SPS Agreement' (G/SPS/53, 3 May 2010), 29.

[54] Erik Wijkström, 'The Third Pillar: Behind the Scenes, WTO Committee Work Delivers', *E15 Initiative*, 15 December 2015, 3.

[55] WTO TBT Committee, 'Minutes of the Meeting Held on 21 April 1995' (G/TBT/M/1, 28 June 1995).

[56] WTO, 'Second Triennial Review of the Operation and Implementation', Annex 4.

[57] Indeed, several standard-setting organisations apply the six principles established by the TBT Committee to qualify their standards as 'international standards' under the TBT Agreement and thereby to encourage further compliance with them.

In addition to its own rules of procedure,[58] the SPS Committee has adopted various decisions or guidelines to help Members to fulfil their obligations under the SPS Agreement, for instance regarding consistency[59] or transparency.[60]

The WTO's Appellate Body recently held that the decisions adopted in the TBT Committee were to be considered to be a 'subsequent Agreement between the parties regarding the interpretation of the treaty or the application of its provisions', within the meaning of Article 31(3)(a) of the Vienna Convention on the Law of Treaties.[61] Although specifying that the extent to which Committee decisions would inform the interpretation of the TBT Agreement in a specific instance had to be decided case by case, the Appellate Body reinforced the legal effect of Committee decisions, and it has been argued that this has contributed to the difficulties currently faced by both the SPS and TBT Committees in adopting new decisions.[62]

e **Negotiating International Agreements** In addition to implementing existing Agreements, providing the platform for treaty negotiations among WTO Members continues to be an important function of the WTO Secretariat. The most recently adopted agreement at time of writing, concluded in November 2013, was the Trade Facilitation Agreement (TFA).[63] Negotiations continue in a number of areas, including non-agricultural market access (NAMA) and trade in agricultural products. Some discussions on TBT were held in the context of the NAMA negotiations.[64]

---

[58] More generally, the SPS Committee's rules of procedure are included in the following documents: Rules of Procedure for Meetings of the Committee on SPS Measures (G/L/170, 1997); Rules of Procedure for Sessions of the Ministerial Conference and Meetings of the General Council (W/T/L/161, 1996); and Working Procedures of the Committee (G/SPS/1, 1995).

[59] WTO, 'Guidelines to Further the Practical Implementation of Article 5.5' (G/SPS/15, 2000).

[60] WTO, 'Recommended Procedures for Implementing the Transparency Obligations of the SPS Agreement (Article 7)' (G/SPS/7/Rev.3, 2008).

[61] Appellate Body Report, *US – Tuna II (Mexico)*, §§370–2.

[62] As mentioned earlier, the TBT Committee faces political barriers to its adoption of voluntary guidelines on GRP. The SPS Committee has been struggling to adopt a common definition on private standards. For further details on this, see Petros C. Mavroidis and Robert Wolfe, 'Private Standards and the WTO: Reclusive No More', RSCAS Research Paper No. 2016/17, 2016. https://cadmus.eui.eu/bitstream/handle/1814/40384/RSCAS_2016_17.pdf?sequence=1.

[63] www.wto.org/english/tratop_e/tradfa_e/tradfa_e.htm.

[64] TN/MA/W/103/Rev. 3/Add. 1 and Corr. 1, 21 April 2011.

2 Regulatory Co-operation in the Downstream Activities of the Policy Cycle

The SPS and TBT Committees, as part of the WTO institutional framework, benefit from the enforcement and dispute settlement mechanisms that apply to all WTO subject matter. In addition, the two Committees are particularly active in enabling dialogue with Members on the implementation of their obligations.

a Monitoring Implementation

Monitoring the Process of Harmonisation   The SPS Committee is explicitly required to monitor the process of international harmonisation and to co-ordinate with the relevant organisations in this regard.[65] The SPS Committee therefore adopted a harmonisation procedure in 1997, aiming:

> ... [t]o identify where there is a major impact on trade resulting from the non-use of those international standards, guidelines or recommendations and to determine the reasons for the non-use of the standard, guideline or recommendation concerned. Moreover, it should also help to identify, for the benefit of the relevant international organizations, where a standard, guideline or recommendation was needed or was not appropriate for its purpose and use.[66]

Revised in 2004,[67] the procedure generally allows Members to raise in the Committee issues they identify as being related to international standards, either because other Members have not applied relevant standards or because there is an area in which there is no relevant standard. It provides in particular for the Committee to invite relevant standard-setting bodies to provide information and that the Secretariat should prepare annual reports on the results of monitoring the process.

The limited impact of this monitoring has, however, been noted and criticised on the basis of its limited use by Members. Indeed, practice shows that Members prefer to raise issues regarding the implementation of standards as STCs rather than under the special procedure relating to international standards.[68]

---

[65] Article 3.5 SPS.
[66] WTO, 'Procedure to Monitor the Process of International Harmonization' (G/SPS/11, 1997), 1.
[67] WTO, 'Revision of the Procedure to Monitor the Process of International Harmonization: Decision of the Committee' (G/SPS/11/Rev.1, 2004).
[68] WTO, 'Procedure to Monitor the Use of International Standards: Proposal by Argentina' (G/SPS/W/255, 2010). See also OECD/WTO, *Facilitating Trade through Regulatory Co-operation*, 80.

Discussing STCs The STC procedure, which was described in Chapter 2 and which will be the subject of considerable discussion throughout the rest of the book, is a remarkable IRC process.[69] It provides a unique platform for co-operation in the downstream phase of the policy cycle of the TBT and SPS Agreements, ensuring that Members can spontaneously monitor the implementation of the two Agreements in at least two main ways.[70] On the one hand, concerned Members may request that regulating Members modify their domestic measures to bring them in line with legal obligations under the WTO Agreements. The concerned Members therefore serve as a 'watchdog', monitoring implementation, and they also provide information to the regulating Member on the cross-border effects of their measures and of possible alternatives. On the other hand, the regulating Member may point out, in response to an STC, the insufficient compliance of the concerned Member with its requirements and thus encourage the concerned Member to align its practice to gain market access.

The impetus of this mechanism of regulatory co-operation towards regulatory convergence is all the stronger given that it stems from a legal obligation to notify and discuss bilaterally draft measures at a time when changes can still be made. The policy dialogue therefore takes place in the early stages of the domestic policy cycle and the multilateral consultations between WTO Members that may be the result can clearly contribute to improving the quality of the domestic measure in question.

Monitoring by the Trade Policy Review Mechanism Beyond the SPS and TBT Committees, the WTO encourages implementation of all WTO agreements through the Trade Policy Review Mechanism (TPRM). The TPRM was specifically established to achieve greater transparency and thereby greater adherence among Members to all WTO obligations. More specifically:

> The purpose of the TPRM is to contribute to improved adherence by all Members to rules, disciplines and commitments made under the Multilateral Trade Agreements and, where applicable, the Plurilateral Trade Agreements, and hence to the smoother functioning of the multilateral trading system, by achieving greater transparency in, and understanding of, the trade policies and practices of Members.[71]

---

[69] This aspect of STCs will be developed further in Part II.
[70] Scott notes that, '[i]n practice, the raising of a specific trade concern will imply oversight not only of the Member complained about, but also of the complaining Member. ... Accountability in this multilateral setting is two-way': Scott, *The WTO Agreement on Sanitary and Phytosanitary Measures*, 56.
[71] Annex III, para. A(i), WTO.

The Trade Policy Review Body (TPRB) periodically reviews Members' policies, basing its report on inputs by the reviewed Member and by the Secretariat. This monitoring helps to ensure enforcement, although the frequency of the trade policy reviews (TPRs) has been criticised. Indeed, the frequency of monitoring varies according to Members' impact on the multilateral trading system, 'defined in terms of their share of world trade in a representative period'.[72] The major trading Members (including the EU) are subject to TPRs every two years, the 16 Members with the next biggest share of world trade, every four years, and other Members are, in principle, reviewed every six years. To a certain extent, this can be seen as benefiting developing countries in terms of the information they gain on their developed trading partners' policy environment.[73] However, when considering the logic of transparency as implied under the SPS and TBT Agreements, transparency about domestic regulations should be beneficial not only for other countries but also for the regulating country itself. Indeed, transparency mechanisms – and, in this case, an in-depth peer review – can provide feedback and institutional learning that helps to shape domestic regulatory frameworks to better fit WTO requirements. In this sense, developing countries would benefit from more regular TPRs.[74]

The information disclosed in TPRs remains highly descriptive and general, raising questions about the usefulness of the information, in particular for developing countries.[75] More recently, Kende has also concluded that while the TPRM generally functions as a successful mechanism for peer review in comparison with those of other international organisations, the TPRs themselves lack an analytical perspective, being of insufficient depth to support countries in their reform efforts.[76] The reviews are designed to ensure overall adherence, but not so much to generate information useful for the conduct of trade. Indeed, '[b]ecause TPRs do not typically explain to an exporting firm (or someone seeking to assist that firm) why it has suffered a reduction in foreign market access that might be WTO-inconsistent, they do not provide the smoking gun'.[77]

---

[72] See Art. C(ii) TPRM.
[73] Bernard M. Hoekman and Petros C. Mavroidis, 'WTO Dispute Settlement, Transparency and Surveillance', *World Economy* 23, no. 4 (2000): 533.
[74] Petros C. Mavroidis, *The Regulation of International Trade, Vol. 1: GATT* (Cambridge, MA/London: MIT Press, 2016), 694.
[75] Arunabha Ghosh, 'Developing Countries in the WTO Trade Policy Review Mechanism', *World Trade Review* 9, no. 3 (2010): 419–55.
[76] Mathias Kende, *The Trade Policy Review Mechanism: A Critical Analysis*, International Economic Law (Oxford: Oxford University Press, 2018).
[77] Chad P. Bown, *Self-Enforcing Trade: Developing Countries and WTO Dispute Settlement* (Washington, DC: Brookings Institution Press, 2009), 219.

b Dispute Settlement According to the OECD report, the final stage of IRC in international organisations' policy-making cycle is dispute settlement. The WTO's Dispute Settlement Body (DSB) acts as an important enforcement tool for both the SPS and TBT Agreements, underlining the binding nature of their obligations and ultimately enhancing the effectiveness of IRC, which can therefore be said to take place 'under the shadow of the formal dispute settlement system'.[78] Indeed, arguably, the STC discussions that take place in the TBT and SPS Committees are all the more efficient precisely *because* they operate in that shadow: 'The raising of a specific trade concern is viewed by Members as a way of turning up the political heat, without necessitating costly and acrimonious recourse to the "courts". But still, if resolution is not forthcoming, that option remains.'[79]

The SPS and TBT Committees of the WTO are a unique example of an international organisation that enables IRC throughout the entire policy cycle. In the upstream phase of international policy-making, both Committees enable the exchange of information, collect data and develop certain rules. In the downstream phase, both Committees enable enforcement through the discussion of STCs, which plays an important role in ensuring that Members meet their SPS and TBT obligations, as will be further developed in Part II. Finally, the SPS and TBT obligations are subject to compulsory dispute settlement, acting as an important guarantee that the Agreements will be enforced.

While the SPS and TBT Committees' development of new policy instruments is much more limited than in other international organisations, it is well integrated into the domestic policy cycles of its Members by means of both substantive and procedural obligations. As a result, the regulatory co-operation between WTO Members takes place not only regarding multilateral rules applied equally to all Members but also on each Members' regulations specifically, early on in the domestic policy cycle.

---

[78] Joanne Scott, *The WTO Agreement on Sanitary and Phytosanitary Measures: A Commentary*, Oxford Commentaries on the GATT/WTO Agreements (Oxford: Oxford University Press, 2009), 58.

[79] Ibid.

The WTO Secretariat underlines that regulatory co-operation is a tool intended to prevent disputes by addressing trade frictions between regulators before a measure enters into force:

> A common feature across all forms and degrees of regulatory co-operation is that it is a forward-looking process, aimed at the early identification of potential regulatory frictions. In this way, potential unnecessary regulatory diversities can be avoided before they become entrenched in national legislation and specific measures affecting trade. Once a specific measure has entered into force, it is often 'too late'. Effective co-operation should function as a means of pre-empting trade concerns that arise between Members – concerns that might arise informally at a bilateral level, formally at the TBT Committee, or even in a dispute settlement context.[80]

---

[80] WTO, 'Regulatory Cooperation between Members: Background Note by Secretariat', para. 7.

Conclusion of Part I

Domestic regulations cannot – and should not – be eliminated in the same way as tariffs have been. In many cases, regulatory heterogeneity is justified by specific domestic needs, and the SPS and TBT Agreements grant WTO Members the competence to determine their preferred regulations, subject to certain conditions.

However, in some cases, regulatory divergence may create unnecessary trade costs. These costs may be the result of domestic regulators working in isolation, without sufficient consideration for the international environment.[1] The negotiators of the Tokyo Round 'Standards Code' and later of the SPS and TBT Agreements set out principles that WTO Members should consider before adopting unilateral measures and throughout the rule-making cycle, aiming to rationalise regulatory interventions and reduce the undue costs of regulatory divergence. WTO Members retain the regulatory autonomy to adopt the measure they consider most appropriate to fulfilling their policy objective, but the drafters included a wide range of transparency obligations that complement the core SPS and TBT provisions. They aim to improve Members' ability to anticipate and understand domestic regulations, and to ensure that domestic SPS and TBT measures are developed inclusively, allowing for comments from WTO Members. Coupled with opportunities within the WTO system for international regulatory co-operation, these transparency obligations allow WTO Members to exchange ideas on draft measures before they are adopted and to work together towards effective implementation of the SPS and TBT Agreements.

These transparency obligations have been increasingly implemented in the past two decades or more, strikingly more frequently than similar obligations under other agreements. Part II will describe the extent to which WTO Members use the transparency mechanisms, as enabled by

---

[1] OECD/WTO, *Facilitating Trade through Regulatory Co-operation: The Case of the WTO's TBT/SPS Agreements and Committees* (Paris: OECD, 2019), 9. www.oecd.org/gov/facilitating-trade-through-regulatory-co-operation-ad3c655f-en.htm.

the WTO Secretariat, to fulfil the three objectives of making regulations known and publicly available, allowing other Members – in particular developing countries – to adapt to newly adopted measures and opening space for dialogue throughout the regulatory process. Part II will therefore explore how these objectives help Members to implement their wider SPS and TBT obligations, and ultimately help Members to avoid disputes.

PART II

Transparency as a Substitute for Dispute Settlement

The Most Effective Compliance Tool in the WTO?

There are potentially as many approaches to regulation as there are countries. We saw in Part I that the legal framework in the WTO Agreements on the Application of Sanitary and Phytosanitary Measures (SPS Agreement, or SPS) and on Technical Barriers to Trade (TBT Agreement, or TBT) is open-ended, leaving plenty of space for different domestic approaches among Members. The transparency provisions of the two Agreements are therefore an essential tool because they allow for predictability within this regulatory heterogeneity and, thanks to the dialogue they enable, help Members to avoid inconsistencies in newly drafted measures.

Part II will present the uses that Members make of the transparency tools set out in the SPS and TBT Agreements, to demonstrate that transparency can be – and is – a substitute for the dispute settlement procedure, both by preventing conflicts and by managing conflicts before they escalate into disputes.

The *ex ante* transparency set up under the two Agreements helps Members to prevent conflicts by ensuring that they can access information about each other's policies and by encouraging co-operative rule-making. Indeed, both the Member implementing its transparency obligations and all the other Members potentially affected by the domestic measure may use transparency to co-operatively work towards mutually beneficial compliance with their common obligations. While the other Members will use the transparency provisions to gather information about the domestic measures of a country to which their companies may be willing to export, the regulating Member will use transparency to obtain feedback on the cross-border effects of its measure. Ultimately, transparency ensures that Members implement both the SPS and TBT Agreements more effectively and helps them to preclude disputes arising.

If trade frictions do occur, however, the opportunity for bilateral and multilateral dialogue offered within the SPS and TBT frameworks allows Members to manage those frictions informally. Whether the measure is still in draft or already adopted, other Members may choose to flag their concerns to the regulating Member and they may do so within the SPS and TBT Committees. While little evidence exists on bilateral dialogue between Members, the multilateral discussions that take place in the Committees are a valuable source of insight into the sorts of issues that create tensions between Members in relation to the Agreements and into the sort of exchanges that take place between Members on these issues.

As a structure in which to explore the various functions of transparency, all of which result ultimately in the prevention and management of conflicts, this book will use the metaphor of a pyramid that starts with a purely factual disagreement and escalates to the point of formal dispute. Indeed, many authors have used a pyramid to illustrate this type of issue precisely because its volume reflects the disparity between the high number of interactions that have the potential to cause a dispute and the far fewer disputes that are finally tried before the highest appellate court of a legal system.

Initially used in the domestic 'dispute' literature,[1] the 'pyramid' of disputes can be described as starting with a baseline of transactions that then transform progressively to become disputes. The first stage of the transformation is referred to as 'grievance' – that is, the point at which a person, group or organisation believes 'it is entitled to a resource which someone else may grant or deny'.[2] Depending on various factors, the affected party may decide to act upon the grievance by directly contacting the person or group they consider responsible. This is referred to as the 'claiming' stage, in which a party communicates 'a sense of entitlement to the party perceived as responsible'.[3] At this stage, the other party may respond to the claim by accepting responsibility and offering compensation, or it may reject the claim or offer only weak compensation. If the accused party accepts responsibility and offers compensation, the issue escalates no further and is considered solved. If the accused party rejects the claim or offers only inadequate compensation, however, the affected party may decide to dispute the claim. This 'disputing' stage

---

[1] This wide literature draws attention to the stages leading to dispute settlement before the court phase was developed under the direction of Mauro Cappelletti, initiated as the 'Florence Access to Justice Project'. An overview of this research project can be found in Mauro Cappelletti and Bryant Garth, 'Access to Justice: The Newest Wave in the Worldwide Movement to Make Rights Effective', *Buffalo Law Review* 27, no. 2 (1978): 181–292.
[2] Richard E. Miller and Austin Sarat, 'Grievances, Claims, and Disputes: Assessing the Adversary Culture', *Law & Society Review* 15, no. 3/4 (1980): 527.
[3] David W. Neubauer and Stephen S. Meinhold, *Judicial Process: Law, Courts, and Politics in the United States* (Boston, MA: Cengage Learning, 2012), 292.

does not yet mean that a formal court case has been filed. Indeed, at this stage, the affected party is likely to attempt other less costly and burdensome means of settling the dispute.[4] If these still do not deliver satisfaction, the affected party may decide to hire a lawyer. Lawyers can be considered 'a critical part of the disputing pyramid, serving as intermediaries (or gatekeepers) between clients and the legal system'.[5] Finally, it is only after all of these stages have proved unsuccessful that the affected party will resort to filing a lawsuit, with the help of the lawyer.

This pyramid describes the pre-litigation stages of civil lawsuits at the domestic level well – although, of course, by simplifying them considerably. The same stages can be seen in the WTO, *mutatis mutandis*, although the efforts necessary to identify the appropriate claims can prove more complex, as we will see in Part III. Indeed, particularly when dealing with domestic measures such as those covered by the SPS and TBT Agreements, it is not easy to define a domestic measure as illegal given the open-ended character of the obligations. Identifying what specific claim to make may therefore prove difficult.[6] A similar succession of events may nevertheless be observed in the WTO context. Figure P2.1 illustrates the 'disputing pyramid', as imagined at the domestic and the WTO levels. The pyramid underlines the contrast between the wide range of interactions between Members that may affect trade and those very few cases that end up before a review tribunal, at the 'tip' of the pyramid.

More specifically, as shown in Figure P2.2, the WTO disputing pyramid ranges from domestic measures affecting trade that may create tensions and give rise to bilateral consultations, through those being brought for discussion in the Committee as specific trade concerns (STCs), those becoming the subject of formal requests for consultations and those brought before a WTO panel, to those few cases submitted to the WTO's Appellate Body for review.[7] Wolfe argues that 'most of the real action in

---

[4] Ibid.
[5] Ibid.
[6] Part III will be dedicated to the difficulties of fulfilling the various steps of the pyramid and managing to file a formal dispute regarding SPS and TBT measures.
[7] Petros C. Mavroidis and Robert Wolfe, 'From Sunshine to a Common Agent: The Evolving Understanding of Transparency in the WTO', RSCAS Research Paper No. PP 2015/01/ Columbia Public Law Research Paper No. 14-461, 25 April 2015. http://papers.ssrn.com/abstract=2569178; Petros C. Mavroidis and Erik N. Wijkström, *Moving out of the Shadows: Bringing Transparency to Standards and Regulations in the WTO's TBT Committee*, Research Handbooks on the WTO (Cheltenham: Edward Elgar, 2013), 204–37.

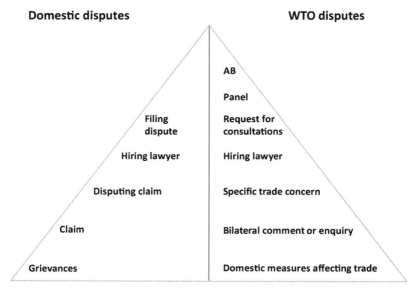

Figure P2.1 Disputing pyramid.

holding Members accountable for their obligations is lower down towards the base [of the pyramid]'.[8] This pyramid is an illustration of transparency as the 'antechamber' of dispute settlement.[9]

There is little evidence with which to define the exact proportions of the pyramid in the WTO context. The number of domestic measures affecting trade is impossible to quantify, even if only within the framework of the SPS and TBT Agreements. Indeed, it is likely that not all SPS and TBT measures affecting trade are notified, and the notifications that are submitted do not take into account measures already in place. In addition, no data is available on the comments and enquiries made directly to Members on their domestic measures or simply of bilateral contact that

---

[8] Robert Wolfe, 'Letting the Sun Shine in at the WTO: How Transparency Brings the Trading System to Life', Staff Working Paper No. ERSD-2013-03, 22 November 2013, 24. http://papers.ssrn.com/sol3/Delivery.cfm?abstractid=2229741. Wolfe bases his argument on a similar theory established in American public law scholarship and developed, in particular, by Hart and Sacks, which they described as the great pyramid of legal order: Henry Melvin Hart, Albert Martin Sacks, William N. Eskridge and Philip P. Frickey, *The Legal Process: Basic Problems in the Making and Application of Law* (Westbury, CT: Foundation Press, 1994).

[9] This expression was used by Henrik Horn, Petros C. Mavroidis and Erik N. Wijkström, 'In the Shadow of the DSU: Addressing Specific Trade Concerns in the WTO SPS and TBT Committees – Entwined', *Journal of World Trade* 47, no. 4 (2013): 729–59.

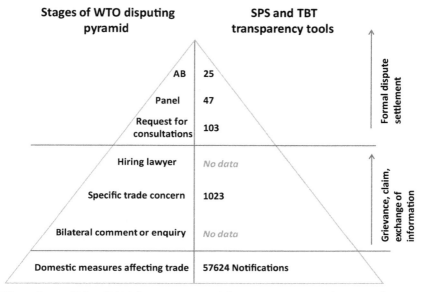

Figure P2.2 SPS and TBT disputing pyramid, from transparency to dispute settlement, 1995–2018.[10]

takes place between Members. Notifications, STCs and requests for consultations, panel reports and Appellate Body reports do, however, give an indication of the order of magnitude that distinguishes the informal interactions between Members that escalate to disputes in very few cases.

This part will describe the contents of the foundational layers of the pyramid in the WTO context. Focusing on an overview of notifications, comments on notifications and STCs, it will present the high volume of dialogue that takes place thanks to transparency at the basis of the disputing pyramid, and discuss how SPS and TBT transparency plays a role in managing conflicts. As Wolfe notes: 'In between the informal base and the highly formal tip of the pyramid, we find a variety of forms of conflict management.'[11] Indeed, arguably, the information sharing and regulatory co-operation that takes place as a result of the TBT and SPS transparency mechanisms act as filters at each level of the pyramid, reducing the reasons for raising a formal dispute, as shown in Figure P2.2.

---

[10] An equivalent 'inverted pyramid' is used in various presentations by the WTO Secretariat, and can also be found in Mavroidis and Wijkström, 'Moving out of the Shadows'. The figure reproduced here uses the model produced by the Secretariat, with additional language for clarity.
[11] Wolfe, 'Letting the Sun Shine in at the WTO', 24.

Chapter 4 will illustrate the information that is made available to WTO Members through transparency in the SPS and TBT context – that is, the 'supply side' of information. This will show that the SPS and TBT Agreements allow Members to obtain a considerable volume of information on each other's domestic measures, thus improving the overall predictability of the trading system with regard to domestic requirements for trade in goods. The high volume of information about SPS and TBT measures shows that Members are making substantive use of the transparency tools. Data remains limited, however, on whether the information to which they have access matches their information needs. The main indication in this regard, the STC discussions, suggests that Members still have a high demand for further information, including about measures that have not been notified, and therefore that the overall level of disclosure of SPS and TBT measures remains insufficient.

Chapter 5 will examine what Members search for when using the transparency mechanisms, focusing more on the 'demand side' of transparency and identifying the characteristics of the 'conflicts' that arise between Members. Through an overview of the STCs that get resolved, this chapter will also suggest a number of areas in which transparency is particularly effective in resolving concerns between Members and in which it can therefore be considered a sufficient compliance mechanism.

The same disputing pyramid will serve as a basis for our developments in Part III, in which we shall see how transparency may help Members to 'climb' the pyramid by ensuring that they have equal access to the WTO dispute settlement system.

4

The Steps in the WTO Disputing Pyramid

From Domestic Measures to Disputes

The transparency mechanisms set out in the WTO Agreements on the Application of Sanitary and Phytosanitary Measures (SPS Agreement, or SPS) and on Technical Barriers to Trade (TBT Agreement, or TBT) provide for an essential centralised source of information. Via the WTO Secretariat, Members can access the information on other Members' regulations that results from notifications of draft regulations submitted to the Secretariat and the open dialogue that takes place regarding draft or adopted regulations within the SPS and TBT Committees.

This centralised information is accessible to all WTO Members equally. The implications are significant, because Members no longer need to search the various national publications of their trading partners; instead, the WTO Secretariat informs WTO Members of measures that may have a significant effect on trade by means of regular alerts about new notifications and triannual meetings, at which specific trade concerns (STCs) may be raised. Thanks to the availability of electronic resources, not only does the WTO Secretariat maintain the information available, but also it delivers the information directly to Members, more easily bringing to their attention the information in which they may be interested.

This chapter presents the successive levels of transparency within the WTO SPS and TBT frameworks as they impact on the 'disputing pyramid', including the different forms of transparency that offer opportunities for Members to gather information and engage in dialogue, and it explains how these different levels interact to form a comprehensive system of transparency of domestic regulations with significant effect on trade. The chapter first offers an overview of Members' practices regarding notifications, which appear at the base of the pyramid and represent the first and most comprehensive source of information on SPS and TBT measures to date (section I). Moving up the pyramid, the chapter then looks at the information and understanding that Members acquire through regulatory dialogue, whether bilateral or multilateral (section II). Finally, the chapter gives an account of the role that the private sector plays in generating information behind the scenes, even if it has no formal voice in the WTO Committees (section III). Ultimately, the chapter demonstrates that while there is a substantial volume of information available, it is not yet comprehensive information about domestic SPS and TBT frameworks.

I   The Base of the Pyramid: Centralised Access to the Measures of All WTO Members

Notifications are the crucial first step towards certainty and equal access to information about domestic measures among all WTO Members. Thanks to the high volumes of notifications centralised by the WTO Secretariat and made available on its online platform, access to information on regulatory frameworks throughout the world is significantly better now than it once was (section A). Nevertheless, some factors point towards today's notification practices remaining inadequate: some barriers remain to Members notifying systematically and WTO Members have raised many concerns regarding those measures that have not been notified (section B). Little evidence exists on the actual use made of notifications, but the EU receives comments on around a quarter of its notifications, from countries at all levels of development. That this evidence is available only for the EU means, however, that it is to be treated cautiously (section C).

A   Members' Notification Practices: High Levels of Engagement with SPS and TBT Transparency

The number of notifications under the SPS and TBT Agreements is significantly higher than under any other WTO agreement.[1] One of the explanations may simply be that Members adopt more SPS and TBT measures than other types of domestic regulatory measure, such as those concerning government procurement services, agriculture, antidumping, State trading enterprises, etc. Indeed, technical regulations, conformity assessment procedures (CAPs) and standards, as well as SPS regulations, may span a broad range of very specific measures, which may therefore result in a large volume of notifications. Another explanation may be the different forms of notification obligation that exist under the

---

[1] As noted earlier, SPS and TBT notifications represent almost 90 per cent of total notifications submitted to the WTO.

different agreements. Indeed, there are necessarily far fewer 'one time only' notifications – presumably one per country – and some prescribe annual notification requirements rather than ad hoc notification requirements that apply whenever a new measure is adopted.[2] Finally, under certain agreements, WTO Members seem cautious about the potential for notifications to be self-incriminatory. Wolfe presents a list of six factors that might explain why WTO Members do not notify, ranging from bureaucratic incapacity to lack of trust and co-ordination between trade negotiators and other government officials.[3]

Whatever the reason for the high number of notifications made under the SPS and TBT Agreements, it is undeniable that WTO Members do make an active effort to give each other access to their draft regulations, even though the ease of that access may be uneven among Members. The WTO Secretariat complements these efforts with significant support, aiming to lessen that disparity.

1 Does an Increase in Notifications Mean an Increase in Transparency?

The growing number of notifications means generally that more information on draft measures is available. In terms of transparency, notifications serve a double purpose: on the one hand, they inform the entire WTO membership and any interested stakeholders of changes to a Member's regulatory environment; on the other hand, notification to the WTO launches a period for comment, thus opening up the opportunity for bilateral regulatory co-operation.

The practices of WTO Members since 1995 have improved transparency from both points of view. The overall volume of both SPS and TBT notifications has indeed grown considerably since 1995, showing that WTO Members are generally more engaged in ensuring the transparency of their domestic regulations (see Figures 4.1 and 4.2). However, it is important to keep in mind that the number of notifications is not

---

[2] For an overview of the different notification obligations that exist throughout WTO agreements falling under the remit of the Council on Trade in Goods, see WTO, 'Updating the Listing of Notification Obligations and the Compliance Therewith as Set Out in Annex III of the Report of the Working Group on Notification Obligations and Procedures' (G/L/223/Rev.26, 13 March 2019).

[3] Robert Wolfe, 'Letting the Sun Shine in at the WTO: How Transparency Brings the Trading System to Life', Staff Working Paper No. ERSD-2013-03, 22 November 2013, 19. http://papers.ssrn.com/sol3/Delivery.cfm?abstractid=2229741.

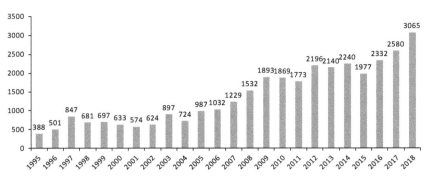

Figure 4.1 Total TBT notifications, 1995–2018.[4] Source: TBT IMS, http://tbtims.wto.org.

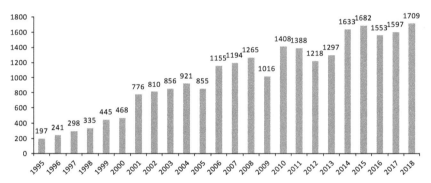

Figure 4.2 Total SPS notifications, 1995–2018.[5] Source: SPS IMS, http://spsims.wto.org/.

necessarily proof of the level of transparency. A country may submit fewer notifications simply because it is introducing fewer draft measures and hence fewer notifications should not be assumed to mean that a country is withholding information.

Despite generally increasing transparency about draft measures as a result of an increasing volume of notifications, transparency remains much more limited when it comes to following up on the notification – in particular, when adopting the final text. In a perfectly functioning system of regulatory transparency, all regular notifications would be followed up appropriately. Sharing any modifications to original notifications, in the

---

[4] The number above the columns represents the total number of notifications, including regular notifications, revisions, addenda and corrigenda.
[5] As above.

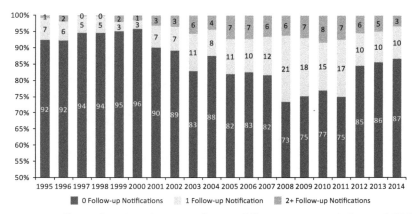

Figure 4.3 Share of TBT notifications subject to follow-up, 1995–2015. Source: WTO, 'Twentieth Annual Review of the Implementation and Operation of the TBT Agreement' (G/TBT/36, 23 February 2015).

forms of addenda and corrigenda, keeps the membership informed as a measure evolves ahead of its adoption. Because addenda and corrigenda do not usually open a new comment period, their role is mainly informative. The proportion of such follow-up notifications on amending original TBT notifications indicates that transparency about a regulation's evolution has risen slightly since 1995, but it remains low (see Figure 4.3). Indeed, only roughly 13 per cent of notifications are followed up with addenda and corrigenda.

Revisions – which notify substantial redrafting of the original and, unlike addenda and corrigenda, do open a new comment period – can be seen as a sign of a fruitful exchange on the initial draft. These remain very rare, however, with less than 2 per cent of notifications followed up with revisions.[6]

2 Members' Engagement in Transparency by Development Status

The increase of SPS and TBT notifications is largely accounted for by the increasing volume of notifications submitted by developing countries. Indeed, as shown in Figure 4.4, developed Members have fairly consistently notified a total of around 300 TBT measures per year in the past 20 years, whereas developing countries have dramatically increased their submissions from a total of 75 in 1995 to 1,145 in 2015. This is excluding

---

[6] WTO, 'Twenty-First Annual Review of the Implementation and Operation of the TBT Agreement' (G/TBT/38, 2016).

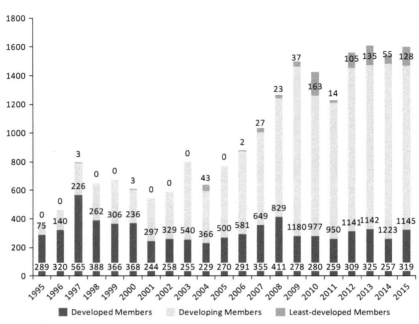

Figure 4.4 TBT notifications, by development status, 1995–2015. Source: TBT IMS, http://tbtims.wto.org.

notifications by the least-developed countries (LDCs), whose notifications remain marginal compared to those of the rest of the membership, but which have also grown significantly, from no notifications at all almost consistently between 1995 and 2003 to as many as 128 notifications in 2015. Strikingly, developing country notifications, including those submitted by LDCs, represented 80 per cent of all TBT notifications in 2015.

Developing countries also submit notifications to the SPS Committee more frequently than others, accounting for a significant share in the increase of notifications since 1995. Indeed, that share has consistently been higher than 50 per cent since 2007. However, the number of LDC-submitted SPS notifications remains fewer than 20 in total to date (see Figure 4.5).

3 The Opportunity to Make Comments on Notifications

An important corollary to the notification obligation is the period allowed for other WTO Members to make comments on the draft text. Members increasingly comply with the 60-day comment period recommended by the TBT Committee, as shown in Figure 4.6. While no similar data is available

I   THE BASE OF THE PYRAMID

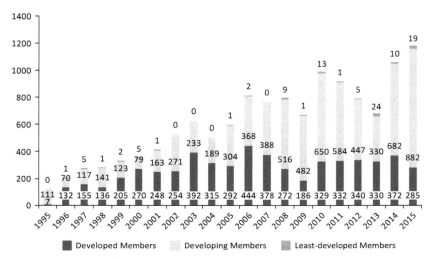

Figure 4.5 SPS notifications, by development status, 1995–2015. Source: SPS IMS, http://spsims.wto.org/.

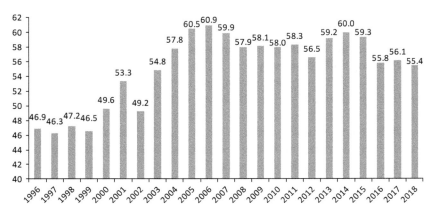

Figure 4.6 Average time period left for comments after TBT notifications by Members, 1996–2018. Source: WTO, 'Twenty-Fourth Annual Review of the Implementation and Operation of the TBT Agreement' (G/TBT/42, 25 February 2019), 14.

for the SPS Committee at this stage, the WTO Secretariat has reported that Members generally tend to leave more than 55 days for comments. However, it is striking that while in 2014 Members did leave an average of 60 days as recommended, there has been a downward trend since then, reaching an average of 55.4 days in 2018. This demonstrates that practice is not yet fully established in terms of the period allowed for comments.

4 The Role of the Secretariat in Ensuring Availability by Means of Electronic Tools

The major benefit of notifications in comparison with publication is that they are centralised courtesy of the WTO Secretariat. As a multilateral organisation, the WTO therefore ensures the dissemination of the notifications to all WTO Members and plays a crucial role in ensuring the effectiveness of regulatory transparency. The Secretariat's added value has become even more overt now that electronic tools support the transparency framework. Members can now submit notifications through an electronic Notification Submission System (NSS) and can access new notifications through alert mechanisms. Moreover, the ePing project – a joint effort between the WTO Secretariat, the International Trade Centre (ITC) and the United Nations Department of Economic and Social Affairs (UNDESA) – allows for delivery of alerts tailored by product for SPS and TBT notifications together (or separately).

a Facilitating Notification Submission through the Electronic Notification Submission System The NSS, launched in 2011 for SPS[7] and 2013 for TBT,[8] is a voluntary system aiming 'to foster more expedient processing and circulation of notifications by the Secretariat'.[9] The Secretariat noted that its benefits were already visible in 2014: 'Online submission has facilitated the submission and processing of notifications, leading to more rapid circulation and increasing the time available to Members to submit comments on notifications of interest.'[10]

---

[7] WTO SPS Committee, 'Summary of the Meeting of 30 June–1 July 2011' (G/SPS/R/63, 12 September 2011).

[8] WTO TBT Committee, 'Minutes of the Meeting of 30–31 October 2013' (G/TBT/M/61, 5 February 2014).

[9] WTO, 'Decisions and Recommendations Adopted by the WTO Committee on Technical Barriers to Trade Since 1995' (G/TBT/1/Rev.12, 2015), 22.

[10] WTO, 'Twentieth Annual Review of the Implementation and Operation of the TBT Agreement' (G/TBT/36, 23 February 2015), 10.

In 2014, in the first year of its implementation for TBT notifications, 23 Members submitted a total of 779 notifications via the NSS, corresponding to 35 per cent of total notifications. On the SPS side, 32 Members submitted their notifications via the NSS.[11] The proportion of TBT notifications submitted electronically doubled in the tool's first four years of existence, with 70 per cent of all TBT notifications submitted using the NSS in 2018.[12]

Members at all levels of development use the NSS to submit both SPS and TBT notifications, as illustrated for TBT measures in Table 4.1.[13]

The significant use of the NSS by certain developing countries (e.g. Brazil, Kenya, Rwanda, South Africa and Uganda) demonstrates their active involvement in the effective implementation of their WTO obligations. Of course, these figures do not prove that they have notified all the measures they should have or that the notifications submitted comply correctly with their obligations. They do, however, show the countries' willingness to comply with their obligations under the TBT Agreement and to do so by the most efficient means possible.

Those Members who do not notify online indicated, in a survey regarding SPS notifications, that this is mainly because of 'unreliable internet connection, internal regulatory procedures that do not allow for the possibility of notifying online, and the lack of awareness of the possibility to do so'.[14]

Overall, the increasing use of the electronic system in its first few years of existence, together with the varying levels of development among those Members using it, suggests that the NSS is likely to substantively improve notifications in coming years.

b Disseminating Information through E-mail Alerts and an Online Database As noted earlier, the WTO Secretariat has played an important role in disseminating information via electronic tools. In this sense, while the TBT and SPS Information Management Systems

---

[11] WTO, 'Analysis of the Replies to the Questionnaire on Transparency under the SPS Agreement' (G/SPS/GEN/1402, 20 March 2015).

[12] WTO, 'Twenty-Fourth Annual Review of the Implementation and Operation of the TBT Agreement' (G/TBT/42, 25 February 2019), 17.

[13] For SPS, the pilot countries that first started using the NSS were Belize, Chile, Costa Rica, the European Union, the Netherlands and New Zealand: WTO SPS Committee, 'Summary of the Meeting of 30 June–1 July 2011'.

[14] WTO, 'Analysis of the Replies to the Questionnaire on Transparency', 4–5.

Table 4.1 *Members submitting notifications through TBT NSS, 2014–2015*

Member	2014	2015
United States	176	280
Brazil	120	111
European Union	87	78
Canada	61	49
Israel	50	15
Kenya	37	12
Korea	35	71
Indonesia	32	17
Rwanda	30	0
South Africa	29	27
Japan	26	37
Uganda	19	100
Chile	17	0
Turkey	17	13
United Arab Emirates	15	25
Malaysia	10	12
Czech Republic	5	33
Georgia	5	0
Ireland	2	0
Sweden	2	2
Ukraine	2	10
Germany	1	N/A
United Kingdom	1	4
China	0	78
Chinese Taipei	0	32
Thailand	0	15
Switzerland	0	7
India	0	2
Zambia	0	2
Bolivia	0	1
Denmark	0	1
TOTAL	779	1,034

Source: WTO, 'Twentieth Annual Review of the Implementation and Operation of the TBT Agreement' (G/TBT/36, 23 February 2015), 11; WTO, 'Twenty-First Annual Review of the Implementation and Operation of the TBT Agreement' (G/TBT/38/Rev.1, 24 March 2016), 11.

(TBT IMS and SPS IMS, respectively) have already provided electronic access to all notifications and STCs, the new ePing system described in Chapter 2 allows any interested party to subscribe to e-mail alerts. This is a crucial step forward in terms of sharing the information that is centralised by the WTO Secretariat. The Secretariat has organised and delivered several training activities as part of its general technical assistance to developing countries, to help all WTO members to share the benefits of ePing.[15] This is, of course, useful to ensure that the information 'supply side' functions well. However, the main question in practice remains to what extent the private sector – in particular SMEs, which are not usually active in WTO discussions and in commenting on notifications – will make use of ePing. The WTO Secretariat reports that, by 31 December 2018, 5,569 users had registered for ePing notifications from 175 countries and territories, half of whom were from government and the other half from the private sector, non-governmental organisations (NGOs), academia, etc.[16] This demonstrates that the tool has indeed been accepted as a useful means of accessing information about draft regulations – but further research into the specific users and the notifications accessed would be necessary to confirm that ePing has truly managed to reach users other than the usual parties already making use of the WTO's notification tools.

B The Shortcomings of the Notifications System

Although notifications have the potential to inform all WTO Members about each other's domestic measures and their potential impacts, a number of factors still indicate that there are deficiencies in information they provide.

On the supply side of information, Members still face difficulties in notifying correctly and sufficiently (section 1). On the demand side of information, a number of STCs indicate that there are, in fact, domestic measures with potentially negative trade impact that are not notified at all (section 2).

1 Remaining Practical Difficulties in Notifying

The submission of effective notifications requires capacity and resources. Although developing countries are now relatively active notifiers, there remains among Members an uneven level of implementation of the notification obligations.

---

[15] WTO, 'Twenty-Third Annual Review of the Implementation and Operation of the TBT Agreement' (G/TBT/40, 12 March 2018), 13.
[16] WTO, 'Twenty-Fourth Annual Review of the Implementation and Operation', 18.

a **Practical Difficulties Involving Resource Constraints** In 2002, the TBT Committee asked the Secretariat to report back on responses provided by developing country Members to a questionnaire on the difficulties they encountered in implementing the TBT Agreement. Sixty-nine per cent of respondents identified 'Infrastructure and capacity building in relation to the transparency provisions of the Agreement' as an issue calling for specific technical assistance.[17] More specifically on notifications, Members cited issues such as lack of co-ordination between regulators and notification authorities, 'Lack of human resources as well as hardware and software equipment to facilitate the effective operation of notification authorities' and 'Lack of financial means to obtain the IT capacity'. Nearly two decades later, these problems seem to persist for some countries, although the rise in notifications among developing countries since then indicates that many have managed to address them successfully. Indeed, while in 2002 developing country Members submitted only 350 notifications, in 2018 developing and emerging economies submitted 2,501 notifications, corresponding to 57 per cent of total notifications.[18]

This undoubtedly represents an important improvement in developing countries' capacity.[19] Nevertheless, this represents notifications in 2018 from only 59 of 83 developing and emerging economies.[20]

Beyond the general lack of infrastructure, interviews conducted in 2014–2015 with several TBT delegations from developing, least-developed and developed countries showed that dialogue with the private sector is one of the key remaining issues with the potential to level the playing field for Members hoping to benefit from transparency mechanisms.[21]

---

[17] WTO, 'An Analysis of the Priorities Identified by Developing Country Members in Their Responses to the Questionnaire for a Survey to Assist Developing Country Members to Identify and Prioritise Their Specific Needs in the TBT Field' (G/TBT/W/193, 2003), 2. This was the second most-cited issue calling for technical assistance or co-operation, after the need 'to improve the knowledge, to disseminate and raise awareness of the Agreement, including to build up local capacity and human resources on TBT issues' (73 per cent): ibid.

[18] WTO, 'Twenty-Fourth Annual Review of the Implementation and Operation', 11.

[19] Other factors may explain this increase in notifications, such as more countries adhering to the Organisation or more TBT measures being adopted. Further analysis will illuminate these other factors, but it is safe to say that such a significant rise in notifications by developing countries does demonstrate an increase in capacity.

[20] WTO, 'Twenty-Fourth Annual Review of the Implementation and Operation', 11.

[21] These interviews were conducted by Marianna Karttunen. Results will be discussed later in the book.

In 2014, the SPS Committee asked the WTO Secretariat to develop a questionnaire that would allow Members to identify the difficulties they encountered in implementing their transparency obligations – that is, areas in which progress may be made.[22] Developing countries were the most responsive (56 per cent of total respondents), followed by LDCs (23 per cent) and developed countries (20 per cent).[23] The survey exposed the main difficulties Members encounter when submitting a notification as relating to qualifying the domestic measure using international criteria. The most frequently selected were:

- 'Identifying whether the notified SPS regulation conforms to an international standard';
- 'Identifying relevant Harmonized System (HS) Codes';
- 'Identifying whether the notified SPS regulation is trade-facilitating';
- 'Choosing the appropriate type of notification (regular, emergency, addendum, revision, etc.)'; and
- 'Identifying the relevant international standard'.[24]

We can conclude that Members generally lack sufficient capacity to fully comply with their notification obligations and related format requirements (i.e. to provide the detailed content required). From the perspective of the information seekers, this is a barrier to their ability to access the relevant information to determine whether or not notified measures might affect their trade. Indeed, if the notifying Member has difficulty identifying whether the SPS regulation conforms to international standards, it is unlikely that the detail it supplies – if any – will be sufficient to inform the foreign observer. This therefore undermines the systematic effectiveness of the notification system. Likewise, if the notifying Member does not identify the relevant HS code, exporters may not be alerted of changes in regulations that affect their products, thus undermining the positive effects of the notification altogether. And if the notifying Member uses the wrong type of notification, this may deprive other Members of the opportunity to make comments and to raise their concerns.

---

[22] WTO, 'Questionnaire on Transparency under the SPS Agreement' (G/SPS/GEN/1382, 2 February 2015).
[23] The results of this document can be found in WTO, 'Analysis of the Replies to the Questionnaire on Transparency'.
[24] Ibid., 4.

b Political Difficulties Relating to Sensitive Information Notification may also be difficult from a political point of view, because proposed new measures on sensitive issues might encounter considerable opposition – especially because information about the measure is distributed beyond the domestic level to foreign governments and stakeholders. This is particularly true under agreements in which notification implies a self-incrimination, such as the Agreement on Subsidies and Countervailing Measures (ASCM).[25]

Indeed, as Mavroidis notes:

> A government typically looks good when it adopts a measure against the ozone layer, but not so good when it favours one segment of society (and in extreme cases, one particular economic operator) over another, since (at least in democratic society) its popularity increases when it provides and safeguards public goods and decreases when it cherry picks beneficiaries.[26]

It is possible that politically sensitive SPS and TBT measures also fail to be notified, though no evidence exists to confirm what volume of SPS and TBT measures this might involve.

2 Remaining Information Gaps in Notifications

In the SPS and TBT framework, notifications are submitted directly by the WTO Member adopting the measure. Unlike other WTO agreements, the SPS and TBT Agreements do not give other Members a right of 'reverse notification'.[27] There is therefore in principle no information held about measures that are *not* notified and the WTO Secretariat does not have the mandate to actively search for such information. However, a closer look at the STCs allows us to gather some evidence about non-notified measures, showing generally that, in both the SPS and TBT contexts, there are indeed some SPS and TBT measures that are not notified to the WTO, but which affect trade with other Members in some way.

As shown in Figure 4.7, this is particularly true of the SPS Committee, in which more STCs since 2010 have been raised about non-notified measures than about notified measures. As such, SPS STCs have a key role in informing Members about domestic measures: all WTO Members have

---

[25] See esp. Robert Wolfe and Terry Collins-Williams, 'Transparency as a Trade Policy Tool: The WTO's Cloudy Windows', *World Trade Review* 9, no. 4 (2010): 551–81; Wolfe, 'Letting the Sun Shine in at the WTO'.

[26] Petros C. Mavroidis, *Trade in Goods* (Oxford: Oxford University Press, 2012), 817.

[27] See e.g. Art. 12.8 Safeguards Agreement, Art. 25.10 of the Agreement on Subsidies and Countervailing Measures, Art. 18.7 of the Agriculture Agreement or Art. III.5 of the General Agreement on Trade in Services.

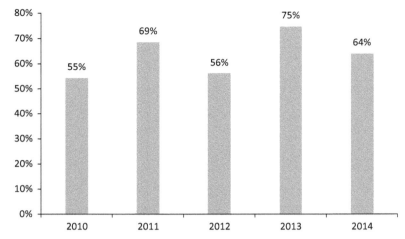

Figure 4.7 Share of SPS STCs raised against non-notified measures, 2010–2014.[28]
Source: Author's own based on SPS minutes, SPS IMS, http://spsims.wto.org/.

access to information about the measure and the effects it has or may have on the concerned Member.

Figure 4.8 shows that a considerable number of STCs have been raised against non-notified TBT measures since 1995, although fewer than in the SPS Committee.

The figures for TBT STCs dating back to 1995 show that there is no trend across time for TBT STCs raised against notified or non-notified measures. In the early years of the WTO, between 1995 and 1997, STCs were raised very frequently against non-notified measures, no doubt reflecting the lower levels of notifications at that time. A decline in the number of STCs raised regarding non-notified measures was already apparent in 1998–1999, when STCs were largely raised against notified measures, and the proportion of STCs regarding non-notified measures has been low on average since then. In 2015, the share of STCs regarding non-notified measures rose for the first time since 2000 (to 51 per cent).

Conformity assessment procedures offer a striking example of a TBT area in which notifications are poor – many are submitted under the wrong article – whereas STCs are high. Between 2010 and 2014, of 102 STCs that raised issues concerning CAPs, only 19 had been notified correctly under

---

[28] The data available regarding SPS STCs and related notifications is less complete than that available for TBT STCs, because the WTO Secretariat does not gather the information. Further research is necessary to complete this data to beyond this limited time frame.

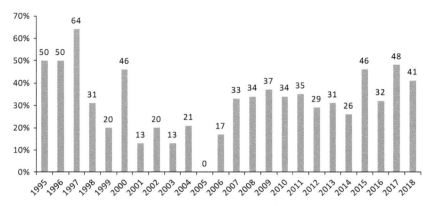

Figure 4.8 Share of TBT STCs raised against non-notified measures, 1995–2018.
Source: Author's own based on WTO, 'Twenty-Fourth Annual Review of the Implementation and Operation of the TBT Agreement' (G/TBT/42, 25 February 2019).[29]

Article 5.6 of the TBT Agreement.[30] Submitting a notification under the wrong article or otherwise in error reduces the mechanism's effectiveness, particularly when WTO Members or industry representatives have requested alerts about specific types of notification.

Interestingly, STCs regarding non-notified measures are most commonly raised against the G2, followed by the BRICS countries (i.e. Brazil, Russia, India, China and South Africa). This is more or less in line with the general figures on country groups maintaining STCs (see Figures 4.9 and 4.10), and can be explained by the fact that larger economies also tend to have more trade relations and their measures therefore tend to affect other countries more than do those of smaller economies that trade less.

Nevertheless, this is telling in terms of the use of notifications. This trend suggests that the largest trading countries – that is, the G2 and the BRICS – do not notify all of their measures that may raise concern. It is possible that the notification authorities are not aware of all of the measures with an effect on trade adopted throughout their government by different regulators and which should therefore be notified. It is also possible that the restrictive notification obligations exclude from notification many

---

[29] Although this document lists STCs related to notified measures.
[30] Of these 102 CAP STCs, 47 had been notified under Art. 2 TBT exclusively, which requires Members to notify technical regulations; 39 had not been notified at all.

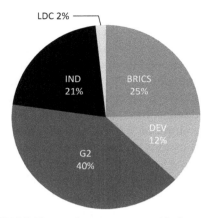

Figure 4.9 Share of SPS STCs raised against non-notified measures by country group, 2010–2014. Source: Author's own, based on SPS Committee minutes, SPS IMS, http://spsims.wto.org/.

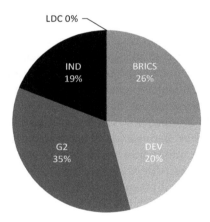

Figure 4.10 Share of TBT STCs raised against non-notified measures by country group, 2010–2014. Source: Author's own, based on TBT Committee minutes, TBT IMS, http://tbtims.wto.org.

measures that affect trade. In particular, it can be difficult to determine what is a 'significant' effect on trade and the absence of a precise methodology with which to do so leaves some leeway for Members to decide whether or not to notify. Finally, it may also be that Members choose not to notify certain measures in bad faith – but no explicit evidence exists about active choices not to notify and hence this remains hypothetical.

Those non-notified measures that were the cause of concerns were not necessarily subject to the notification obligation. In some cases, the measure may have been based on an international standard and hence non-notification was justified, or the effect on trade may not have been *significant* as required under the TBT and SPS Agreements. It may even be that a WTO Member raises a concern in the TBT Committee even though the measure does not fall within the scope of the TBT Agreement.

The considerable volume of SPS STCs raised on non-notified measures underlines that notifications are not the primary source of information of WTO Members on SPS and TBT measures: the multilateral and public setting of the WTO Committees is an essential complement to ensure transparency about domestic regulations. At the same time, these figures on STCs regarding non-notified measures underline the dual nature of STCs, which serve as a mechanism both to question notifications and to raise awareness on non-notified measures.

C The Use Made of Notifications by Other Members or Stakeholders

Notification to the WTO is in itself a tremendous step forward for ensuring the availability and centralisation of information within the WTO, and it has the potential to foster highly inclusive regulatory dialogue at the early stages of the regulatory process. However, the question remains to what extent this information can be used effectively.

It is impossible to estimate how many notifications each WTO Member reads and uses, not least because Members may not themselves have such data. Indeed, once the information on draft regulations is disclosed, foreign exporters might integrate it directly, preparing for the change in requirements without even consulting with their government and hence leaving no trail.

The only quantifiable indication of the usefulness of notifications for the purpose of regulatory dialogue is the comments made on notifications. Such information is not available for the majority of WTO Members; only the European Union (EU) regularly publishes the comments it makes on notifications and the comments it has received from other Members on its own notifications.[31] Although the comments disclosed may not be comprehensive, they can still be used for indicative purposes.[32]

---

[31] http://ec.europa.eu/growth/tools-databases/tbt/en/search/.
[32] It is likely that not all comments are disclosed. Indeed, there is a discrepancy between the general statistics published by the EU Commission on comments received and on the comments available.

According to this data, between 2010 and 2014 the EU received comments on 88 of its 370 regular notifications (24 per cent).[33] A majority of these received comments from only one country (59 of the 88 notifications), 21 received comments from two countries and only 8 received comments from three or more countries.

Only a handful of countries made comments on the EU's notifications during the five years of the sample, as presented in Table 4.2. Strikingly, China was the most active Member, submitting 43 comments, while the United States sat in second place with 25 comments. Other Members commenting included nine developing countries and eight industrialised countries, as well as one LDC (Uganda).

Overall, these figures indicate that comments on EU notifications remain relatively low. We might therefore predict even fewer comments on notifications by other WTO Members with fewer trading partners and lower stakes than the EU. Nevertheless, that the comments were submitted by countries at all levels of development, albeit with different frequencies, signals the perceived usefulness of notifications in informing Members about new regulations whether or not the regulating and commenting countries have other means for bilateral dialogue. Furthermore, as we shall see next, comments on notifications remain significantly more commonplace than STCs raised in the Committees.

II From Centralised Information to Regulatory Dialogue

The provisions of the SPS and TBT Agreements provide essentially for *bilateral* regulatory dialogue. The notification obligation creates centralised access to information, and the obligation to take comments into account enables a bilateral dialogue between Members, facilitated by the requirement to establish enquiry points in all WTO Members. In addition, in practice, Members increasingly co-operate at the multilateral level within the SPS and TBT Committees, by means of the mechanism of STCs, at which we looked in the last section. This regulatory dialogue within the Committees allows the WTO to 'multilateralise' the benefits of bilateral regulatory dialogue. Indeed, not only may several Members raise STCs at the same time,

---

[33] The data is available only for regular notifications, whether the comment was made on the regular notification or for a subsequent amendment.

Table 4.2 *Countries submitting comments on EU notifications, 2010–2014*

WTO Member	Number of Comments
China	43
US	25
Colombia	9
Australia	8
Japan	8
Korea	7
Canada	6
Norway	4
New Zealand	3
Switzerland	3
India	2
Paraguay	2
Argentina	2
Chile	1
Thailand	1
Uganda	1
Chinese Taipei	1
Peru	1
Mauritius	1
Malaysia	1
Malawi	1

Source: http://ec.europa.eu/growth/tool-databases/tbt/en/search/.

but also the discussions are held in Committee meetings that are attended by all Committee Members. As such, all WTO Members can learn from the discussions held among other Members and decide to join in if appropriate.

A   From Notifications to STCs: The WTO Framework Supporting Centralised Dialogue

In many cases, STCs may be triggered by notifications, which effectively launch consultations. As Mavroidis and Wijkström note, 'the number of STCs raised in the Committee has, over time, been strongly correlated

II   FROM CENTRALISED INFORMATION TO REGULATORY DIALOGUE   157

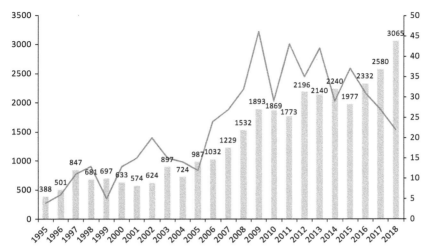

Figure 4.11   Trends in TBT notifications and STCs, 1995–2018. Source: TBT IMS, http://tbtims.wto.org.

with the number of TBT notifications, suggesting that the latter have served as a source of information behind the STCs'.[34] This is true when looking generally at notifications and at the STCs discussed in the TBT Committee – the level at which the WTO Secretariat assesses them.[35] It is less true when comparing overall notifications with new STCs raised in both the SPS and TBT Committees, as shown in Figures 4.11 and 4.12. In addition, as we saw in the last section the volume of STCs raised in relation to non-notified measures tempers the observation. While it is likely that notifications trigger a certain number of concerns and that the mechanism of notifications facilitates an important opportunity for regulatory dialogue, it seems that the correlation between rising numbers of notifications and of STCs is more indicative of an increase in transparency and dialogue than it is evidence that notifications trigger STCs.

Overall, although notifications are an important source, they are not the main source of information on measures raising concerns. The number of STCs raised against non-notified measures confirms that many Members find out about domestic regulations through other means, perhaps through their own monitoring activity or alerts raised by the private sector, as will be discussed later.

---

[34] Petros C. Mavroidis and Erik N. Wijkström, 'Moving out of the Shadows', 204–37.
[35] WTO, 'Twenty-Fourth Annual Review of the Implementation and Operation', 29.

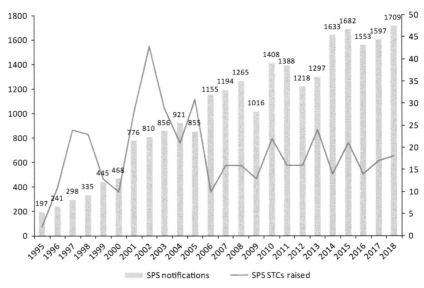

Figure 4.12 Trends in SPS notifications and STCs, 1995–2018. Source: SPS IMS, http://spsims.wto.org.

B Specific Trade Concerns: A Source of Information Raising Awareness of Measures

A Member raising an STC in a Committee meeting raises awareness among all WTO Members not only of the existence of a specific measure and of whether it was notified or not but also of its potential effects. As such, STCs allow Members to 'cross-notify', or 'reverse-notify' measures proposed by other Members even though no such obligation formally exists under the TBT and SPS Agreements. The mechanism of STCs therefore positions Members as the guardians of transparency, informing the entire membership when a regulating Member has not done so itself.

As we have seen, the proportion of all TBT STCs that relate to non-notified measures has not risen, suggesting that TBT STCs are raised consistently in relation to both notified and non-notified measures. However, Figure 4.13 does show an increase in the absolute number of TBT STCs raised regarding non-notified measures. This suggests that TBT STCs do indeed serve as a tool to raise awareness about measures, complementing the notification process in enhancing the transparency of TBT measures in general.

In the SPS Committee, STCs are raised regarding non-notified measures much more frequently. Although data for SPS STCs is available for only

II FROM CENTRALISED INFORMATION TO REGULATORY DIALOGUE 159

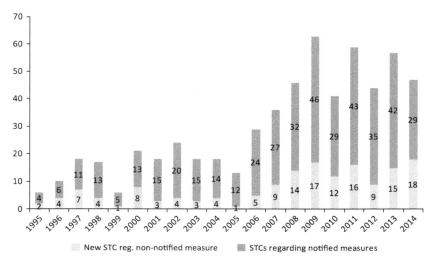

Figure 4.13 Number of TBT STCs relating to non-notified measures. Source: Author's own based on TBT IMS, http://tbtims.wto.org.

2010–2014, the trend differs from that of TBT STCs: in the SPS Committee, the number of SPS STCs regarding non-notified measures is always higher than the number of SPS STCs regarding notified measures. This is consistent with the types of STC raised, which commonly relate to practical impediments to trade rather than to potentially burdensome draft measures, as is more the case in the TBT Committee (see Figure 4.14).

Beyond improving awareness, the comments that they can make on notifications and the STCs that they can raise in the SPS and TBT Committees offer Members an opportunity to request further information on measures so that they can better understand the proposed requirements. However, understanding the impact or likely impact of a measure on trade is more difficult for those governments that do not directly import and export goods, and hence they must engage in regulatory dialogue with both foreign peers and the private sector.

C The Role of Regulatory Dialogue in Improving Understanding of a Measure

When Members are in doubt about other Members' draft or actual regulations, they may make enquiries related to notifications – as well as non-notified measures under Article 5.8 of the SPS Agreement – and they may

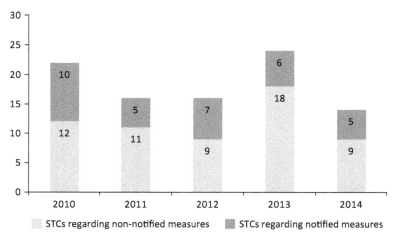

Figure 4.14 Number of SPS STCs relating to non-notified measures.
Source: Author's own based on SPS IMS, http://spsims.wto.org.

seek further information, as well as copies of the measures. This is an important complement to the information that is disclosed through notifications, which remains limited.

In addition and particularly when the regulating Member has not responded to bilateral requests, STCs can be used as a tool to obtain information. Indeed, the public nature of the fora in which STC discussions take place provides a strong incentive for the Member maintaining the measure to respond to the original request.

Requests for information are a significant reason for raising concerns in the TBT Committee: most TBT STCs request clarification or further information (80 per cent of all TBT STCs in the period examined) or note a lack of transparency in the regulating Member's practice (47 per cent).[36] Figure 4.15 illustrates the significance of these concerns in relation to other issues raised. This confirms that the mechanism of STCs is used not only to flag issues of concern to other Members but also to trigger discussion

---

[36] These figures have been calculated based on data from TBT IMS for the period of 2010–2014. The TBT IMS describes systematically the issues that are raised in each STC under a section headed 'Issues Raised'. To the extent that the categories are the same, this has been completed using Committee minutes. The figures differ to a certain extent from data disclosed by the Secretariat because of additional categories included. The SPS IMS does not list the issues raised in the same way as does the TBT IMS, so SPS STCs were not used for this dataset.

II FROM CENTRALISED INFORMATION TO REGULATORY DIALOGUE 161

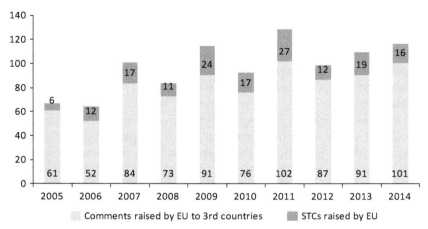

Figure 4.15 Number of EU comments on notifications and STCs raised, 2003–2014.[37] Source: http://ec.europa.eu/growth/tools-databases/tbt/en/.

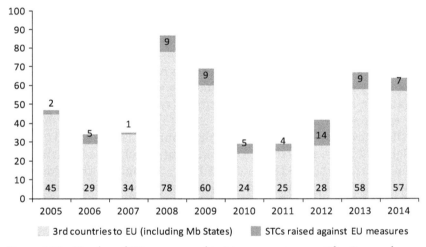

Figure 4.16 Number of EU measures subject to comments on notifications and to STCs, 2003–2014. Source: http://ec.europa.eu/growth/tools-databases/tbt/en/.

of the content and scope of the measure and the status of the domestic regulatory process.[38] Requests for information or clarification are less frequently mentioned in SPS STCs, as illustrated in Figure 4.16, with only 25 per cent of SPS STCs between 2010 and 2014 citing this as their subject.

[37] Information on the EU database has been available only since 2003.
[38] For further details on the content of STCs related to requests for information and clarification, see Chapter 5.

D   From Comments on Notifications to STCs: Taking a Concern to the Multilateral Level

The ability to comment on notifications is the first level of actual dialogue that the transparency provisions of the SPS and TBT Agreements enable. While comments are not centralised by the WTO, the information on which the comments are based – the notifications – is, and the obligation to respond to the comments and to take the results of discussions into consideration is a legal obligation embedded in both the SPS and TBT Agreements. Thus the bilateral dialogue that takes place is still a matter of concern to the WTO. However, very little information is available on the extent to which Members submit comments on each other's notifications in practice. Indeed, most data on comments on notifications remains confidential, reserved for the notifying Member and the commenting Member. This confidentiality may benefit the regulating Member, giving it the opportunity to respond informally and in due course without having to justify its position before the entire membership in Committee meetings. Although less likely, the commenting Member may favour confidentiality lest the trade concern bring to light privileged business information. Finally, comments may be kept confidential merely because of the practical burden that publishing all of them would impose on a Member: sending a bilateral e-mail to a contact point remains easy, whereas hosting a public website on which all comments on notifications are published and easily accessible requires considerable resources. This practical obstacle might be addressed by the WTO Secretariat, which already has an electronic portal – the SPS IMS and TBT IMS – through which all Members and the general public could easily access the comments, just as they currently do notifications and STCs.

In this author's survey in 2014 of Member delegations to the TBT Committee, few shared figures on the number of comments they had made or received on notifications. One large emerging Member estimated that it had made comments on 10–15 per cent of all TBT notifications; another raised around 10 comments per year, most of them originating in comments previously made by other Members. Smaller developing Members mentioned that they made comments very rarely, if ever. Some developed Members found it difficult to estimate the number of comments because, upon receiving a notification, it encourages dialogue with a wide array of stakeholders from both public and private sectors.

Members did underline the importance of comments on notifications. They appreciated not only the opportunity to comment on and stall the adoption of other Members' trade-restrictive measures but also the benefits of receiving comments in terms of improving their own policies. Two large developing countries, for instance, insisted that this mechanism helped them to improve their regulations and bring them in line with their WTO obligations, allowing them to demonstrate to other agencies that they had paid attention to their trading partners.

One large developed country noted, however, that it frequently did not receive replies to the comments that it submitted on other Members' notifications and that this was true of Members at all levels of development.

The EU is the only WTO Member to make all comments on TBT notifications that it makes and receives publicly available.[39] This information gives some indication of the number of comments it has made on notifications compared with the number of STCs it has raised.[40]

In practice, the EU raises very few STCs in comparison with the number of comments it makes on notifications, thus highlighting the likelihood that commenting is the stage at which a large proportion of issues are resolved. Between 2005 and 2014, the EU raised 161 STCs and made 818 comments on notifications. Other Members made 438 comments on EU notifications and raised only 65 STCs against EU measures.[41] Figures 4.15 and 4.16 (see above) give an idea of the distribution of comments on notifications and STCs annually over the period.

Overall, although the data remains very limited, the EU figures clearly indicate that comments on notifications are a more frequently used method of regulatory co-operation than STCs.

To some extent, the number of STC discussions in SPS and TBT Committees allows us to estimate the significance of bilateral meetings that take place at the margins of multilateral STCs. As shown in Figures 4.17 and 4.18, STCs are almost always accompanied by bilateral discussions. Indeed, Members frequently make reference to either comments on notifications or other bilateral contacts with the regulating Member.

---

[39] See http://ec.europa.eu/growth/tools-databases/tbt/en/. Unfortunately, similar information is not available for SPS.

[40] Given that the European Union is the most active Member in raising STCs, the information is particularly from the perspective of a Member that has mastered the TBT transparency mechanisms. The practice with regards to comments on notifications may be different in Members at other levels of development.

[41] Including 44 measures of EU Member States: http://ec.europa.eu/growth/tools-databases/tbt/en/.

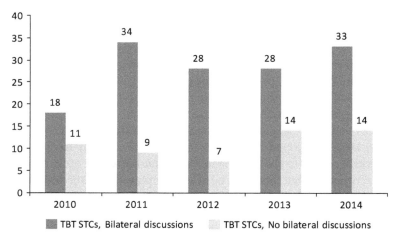

Figure 4.17 TBT STCs and bilateral discussions. Source: Author's own based on TBT IMS, http://tbtims.wto.org.

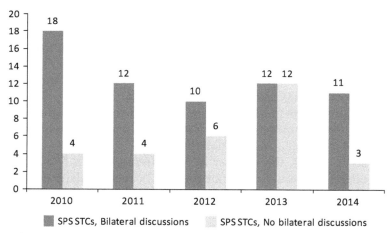

Figure 4.18 SPS STCs and bilateral discussions. Source: Author's own based on SPS IMS, http://spsims.wto.org.

In the interviews with Member delegations to the TBT Committee at which we looked earlier, Members indicated that STCs are commonly raised to gather further information on a measure (particularly in the absence of a response to bilateral comments), to bring a controversial measure into the spotlight or even to support like-minded Members in raising their own concerns. One developed country noted that it also raised STCs regarding measures that could be WTO-inconsistent even though its own exports were not significantly affected. Several Members agreed that they raised STCs only after trying to solve issues bilaterally through comments sent to enquiry points or discussions in the margins of the Committee meetings, positioning raising STCs as another action that might yet allow them to avoid formal dispute settlement.[42]

There is, however, insufficient information publicly available on the content of bilateral dialogue, in particular of comments on notifications, and of STCs to support a conclusion that fewer STCs than comments on notifications is a sign that STCs raise or escalate the same issues that were raised in comments. Further research could focus on comparing the substantive issues raised in EU comments and in EU STCs to explore the relationship between these differing mechanisms for regulatory dialogue.

After examining the practices that lead Members from notifications to STCs, Chapter 5 will seek to identify the issues that are discussed in STCs and hence the function played by this invaluable tool for transparency and dialogue, even when Members have only imperfect information.

The transparency mechanisms in place under the SPS and TBT Agreements raise Members' awareness of each other's measures, and increasing engagement among Members demonstrates that the information available is also expanding. However, evidence suggests that not all measures that affect trade and which are not based on an international standard are notified; in these instances, Members use other means of obtaining information. The regulatory dialogue triggered by STCs that takes place in the Committees provides Members with additional information on the impacts of measures and non-notified measures, and the private sector informs Member governments when a national industry is particularly affected. However, the information gathered through STCs is not systematic and dialogue with the private sector depends on a well-established relationship with domestic industries. We can conclude, therefore, that while treaty-based transparency (notifications) delivers a guarantee of transparency for all but is not equally implemented, the transparency developed in practice has much promise but is plagued by barriers.

---

[42] For example China, Russia and Canada.

III Behind the Scenes: The Private Sector's Role in Measuring the Impacts of Domestic Regulations

To understand the impact of a measure, Members inevitably need to make some sort of contact with the companies involved in the conduct of international trade. While such dialogue may be formal or less formal – which explains both why there is only incomplete data in this regard and why Members' levels of awareness about other Members' regulations differ – the discussions in the TBT and SPS Committees offer some indication of the number of STCs raised after exchanges between Members and the private sector.

This section is largely based on the results of interviews that this author conducted with Member delegations to the TBT Committee in 2014–2015[43] and related Committee discussions.[44] These interviews aimed to elicit insight into the concrete reasons behind WTO Members' uneven use of TBT transparency mechanisms, from commenting on other Members' notifications to raising STCs in the TBT Committee. A wide variety of factors may be at play, spanning a lack of human capital, inadequate financial resources, institutional shortcomings, cultural differences, and a lack of awareness and understanding of their benefits. Concerns raised in the TBT Committee suggest, however, that the level of dialogue between a Member government and the private sector is the key factor predicting the Member's level of use of transparency mechanisms.

A The Role of the Private Sector in the Trading System

Overall, the interviews offered evidence that the private sector is essential in a Member's evaluation of the effects of trading partners' measures on domestic exports and in helping Members to monitor their rights under the WTO Agreements. As we will discuss further shortly, half of those interviewed affirmed that the private sector plays an important role in raising awareness about the trade effect of other Members' measures. Similarly, 7 of the 11 Member delegations interviewed confirmed that the STCs they raised most often originated in private sector concerns.

---

[43] For interview questions, see Appendix B. The Members that replied to this survey include Brazil, Canada, Chile, China, European Union, India, Peru, Russia, South Africa, Trinidad and Tobago, and Uganda.

[44] In addition, this section takes into account presentations made by Kenya, the United States and Ukraine during a thematic session of the TBT Committee on transparency (WTO, 'Thematic Session of the TBT Committee on Transparency: Moderator's Report', G/TBT/GEN/167, 17 June 2014).

However, the interviews also confirmed that the level of dialogue between Member and private sector is currently uneven, depending on elements such as, on the one hand, whether the human resources in government (particularly any TBT experts) are able to effectively communicate with the private sector and, on the other hand, the capacity of the private sector itself to understand the impact of TBT measures.

Because the private sector plays an important role in raising governments' awareness of the trade effects of foreign regulations, Members who have difficulty eliciting feedback from the private sector tend to be less aware of those measures that may impact their trade. This results in a weaker capacity to comment on other Members' draft measures and to raise STCs in the TBT Committee. Ultimately, as we will discuss further, this barrier to participation in the transparency framework is an important factor contributing to unequal access to formal dispute settlement: without fluid dialogue with the private sector, governments have less evidence on which to base an assessment of the opportunity costs of launching a formal dispute.

B   Specific Trade Concerns Citing the Private Sector

There is no quantitative evidence of how many WTO Members consult with industry before making comment on a notification or before raising an STC. This can be partly explained by the often informal character of the dialogue that takes place with the private sector on a case-by-case basis. In addition, because the decision to comment or raise a concern remains its prerogative, the Member government may not keep track of the private sector representatives who originally informed it of the measure.

Some STCs do, however, make explicit reference to dialogue with the private sector prior to the Committee meeting. This offers an indication – likely to be an under-estimation – of the number of foreign regulations that Members become aware of through private sector intervention.

There is a large discrepancy between SPS and TBT STCs in this regard. A significant share of TBT STCs contain references to the private sector: between 2010 and 2014, 126 of 196 TBT STCs (65 per cent) made reference to preliminary dialogue with the private sector. For SPS STCs, the figure is only 22 per cent.

It might also be noted that LDCs started raising STCs in the TBT Committee only in 2009 and that all eight of these concerned tobacco measures. This might be an indication that LDCs have sufficient information on and awareness of trade-restrictive effects on their domestic exports mainly because of the support of tobacco industry representatives.

When mentioning private interests in the TBT Committee, a Member may explicitly convey the concern of the private sector or offer that concern as evidence of an obstacle to trade. Some Members explicitly state that the private sector has brought to their attention the burdensome and/or costly character of new requirements. India, for example, noted in a concern regarding a certification process relating to medical devices that its 'traders found this certification process time consuming and expensive, reportedly costing more than USD 20,000, with an approval timeframe of as long as four years'.[45]

Members may also simply recall comments made by industry representatives to the regulating Member. The United States, for example, mentioned that 'US industry had voiced concerns with this proposed measure: on its mandatory nature; stringent requirements for the critical nutrients; and, the large number of products that could have to bear front-of-pack (FOP) icons and undergo relabelling'.[46]

Without explicitly reporting industry concerns, Members may simply give voice to the additional burdens that producers would face as a result of the measure in question. For example, the EU noted that it 'was particularly concerned about the possible negative impact that some of the proposed labelling obligations would have on EU economic operators, which would have to redesign their labels for the Brazilian market only'.[47]

Finally, in various cases, Members call for an opportunity for not only WTO Members but also industry representatives to comment on a measure: 'Transparency in [the] medical devices issue has been a recurring concern of [the] regulated community in China, in particular the US industry. It put unnecessary burden on these industries, depriving them of the ability to provide full well-reasoned comments in China's regulatory system.'[48]

---

[45] 'Brazil – Higher Risk Medical Devices Good Manufacturing Practice (GMP) Certification' (ID 429), para. 3.18.
[46] 'Korea – Proposed SAR Values or EMF Exposure in Cell Phones' (ID 371, G/TBT/M/59), para. 2.26.
[47] 'Brazil – Alcoholic Beverages' (ID 263, G/TBT/M/50), para. 27.
[48] 'China – China Food and Drug Administration (CFDA) EMC Enforcement Notice for Medical Devices of 19 December 2012' (ID 387), para. 3.33.

C Assessing the Impact of Notifications

Some Members noted that the private sector informed them of the trade-restrictive effects of a measure before the measure's entry into force. This is particularly the case for larger countries, both developing and developed. Certain respondents explained that industry often spotted measures before the notification, but tried to solve the issue independently before contacting the government authorities.

In most cases, however, the private sector becomes fully aware of the impact of new measures on trade only once the measure has already entered into force, largely because the time frame for commenting may be too short for the relevant representatives to become aware of the notification, to understand it and to submit their comments to their own authorities in time for the Member then to comment accordingly on the other Member's measure. In addition, it is only once the measure is enforced that the private sector becomes aware of its actual costs and implications for trade. Individual companies in smaller developing countries may therefore play a common role in raising STCs on adopted measures rather than in commenting on draft measures.

D Initiatives Addressing STCs

All Members responding to the survey acknowledged that the private sector played an important role in their decision to raise STCs in the TBT Committee. While they remained vague about the figures, all mentioned that the private sector was the origin of 'most', if not all, of the STCs they had raised. Only one country said that 'not many' STCs originated within the private sector.

Overall, it seems that developed country Members or larger developing country Members tend to benefit from regular contact with the private sector that brings to their attention the trade-restrictiveness of a measure either when it is notified or even before. Smaller developing countries, however, noted that their industry actors became aware of new measures and their trade impacts only once the measures were implemented and the trade effects were real.

E Drafting STCs

The drafting of STCs does not, in principle, require legal counsel: the Committees' work is more like peer review, and that work is rather more technical and pragmatic than legal. However, interviews with Member delegations to the TBT Committee confirmed that larger Members sometimes ask for legal counsel when drafting their STCs, because of the complexity of the matter and the potential violation of the TBT Agreement that they are trying to prove. That counsel may come from private law firms that the Member itself contracts,[49] academic groups or the law firms of affected private companies. One large developed Member indicated that it has many lawyers involved at many different stages. In particular, specific lawyers from the enquiry point carry out an independent analysis of notifications received and collect inputs from different departments.

Smaller developing Members tend to draft STCs on their own, except when supported by specific industries in the case of an issue of serious concern to them. These Members do not refer to private legal counsel because of the high cost this represents for a matter that is not yet in formal dispute settlement. Some may show their results to their in-house lawyers, but in smaller Members expertise in TBT matters is mainly in the hands of TBT experts and counsel from general legal divisions may not be of much help.

F Forms of Collaboration with the Private Sector

The provision of information from the private sector to government representatives implies the existence of some sort of relationship between the two. The survey showed that government representatives engage in exchange with their domestic industry in formalised or less formalised ways.[50] Overall, most interviewed Members send regular e-mail updates to their exporters on trade partners' notifications.

1 Existing Processes for Co-operating with the Private Sector

Most interviewed countries have in place procedures whereby they alert their exporters to new measures notified by WTO Members. Typically, it is the TBT enquiry point that identifies the measures that could affect

---

[49] The role of the ACWL is important for smaller developing countries, which do sometimes ask for advice on notified measures to help them to draft a comment and an STC if necessary.

[50] Of 21 contacted, 11 Members responded to the survey: Brazil, Canada, Chile, China, European Union, India, Peru, Russia, South Africa, Trinidad and Tobago, and Uganda. Nine of these are developing countries, including all of the BRICS. Canada and the EU were the only developed countries to answer the survey. This section also takes into account presentations made by Kenya, the United States and Ukraine during a thematic session of the TBT Committee on transparency (WTO, 'Thematic Session of the TBT Committee on Transparency').

the national exports. In some cases, the enquiry point translates the texts and sends e-mail alerts to the relevant industry representatives. Larger Members also hold regular meetings with private sector representatives regarding measures notified by other Member countries. These meetings may take the form of regular information sessions, in which particularly interested parties participate. During these meetings, if the effects of the measure are significant to the Member's exports, the private sector representatives and technical experts might jointly draft a comment, which the TBT notification authority will then send to the notifying Member.

The regular meetings can also mirror TBT Committee meetings with various different stakeholders, usually three times a year. Describing such practice, one large developed country explained that, prior to all of its mirror Committee meetings, it contacts all of its embassies, consulates and trade offices around the world, its local constituencies, and domestic and foreign trade associations based in its territory to find out if they have any feedback on WTO-incompatible trade-restrictive measures. Certain larger developing Members have also set up similar systems, with subscriber-based e-mail alerts for new notifications and three stakeholder meetings a year in advance of TBT Committee meetings.

The EU has an extremely efficient online database that gathers all TBT notifications and related comments – an initiative that is particularly aimed at providing information to businesses, but which is publicly accessible.[51] This database also permits anyone to subscribe to e-mail alerts for notifications and any related documents. Independent of this, the EU authorities meet frequently with industry representatives, for example through the 'market access advisory committee', to discuss issues including technical barriers to trade. This therefore gives all parties the opportunity to obtain information on measures affecting EU exports.

The United States has an export alert system with 'nearly 3,000 subscribers and [it has] enabled them to obtain full text notifications, learn about deadlines for comments and to submit comments on notifications'.[52]

Ukraine has been issuing, with the support of the Swedish Board of Trade, ' "business-oriented" "free-of-charge" publications, providing information on new TBT/SPS notifications, TBT/SPS proposed measures, and relevant topics in TBT/SPS Committee meetings'.[53] Although this has not yet resulted

---

[51] http://ec.europa.eu/growth/tools-databases/tbt/en/.
[52] During the thematic session of the TBT Committee on transparency (WTO, 'Thematic Session of the TBT Committee on Transparency'), para. 4.
[53] Ibid., para. 2.

in a formal dialogue, it has led to a more active business sector and increased questions sent to Ukraine's enquiry point.

Despite Member governments systematically sharing with the private sector information on other Members' notifications, they are not necessarily reaping useful information in return. In particular, developing Members noted that the majority of their industry actors rarely reply to information received. One large developing country regretted the limited feedback from the business community on foreign notifications, even though it has set up an e-mail export alert system.

Developing Members explained that this weak response was likely a result of the technical language used in notifications and, more generally, a lack of understanding within the private sector of the notified measure. This is also sometimes linked to language barriers, because not all exporters have proficient knowledge of one of the WTO's official working languages. In addition, while notifications are made available in all three WTO languages, the measures themselves are rarely translated, making it all the more difficult to understand the details.

2   Who in the Private Sector Is the Main Counterpart?

In most cases, it is large trade associations or federations (the case for most interviewed Members) and sometimes lobby groups who are in contact with the government about TBT measures. These may be national or international bodies. Sectoral international organisations, such as the World Wine Trade Group for wine exporters or the West Indies Rum and Spirits Producers' Association (WIRSPA) for rum exporters in the West Indies, may raise awareness about non-notified measures and encourage their Member governments to comment on drafts or to raise STCs. This explains why Members' levels of awareness of their trading partners' trade policies are very different across different sectors, depending largely on each industry's level of involvement.

In particular cases, big exporting companies may also be in contact with the government directly, although it is less likely to be the case in smaller developing countries. The US delegation mentioned the involvement of law firms, and of testing and calibrating organisations.[54]

Its role in improving governments' understanding of each other's regulations and their possible impacts on trade means that the private sector is instrumental in drawing out the benefits of transparency within

---

[54] Ibid., para. 4.

the WTO: they can help governments to estimate the impact of measures notified to the WTO and to identify what measures justify the raising of an STC. Nevertheless, the private sector has no formal role within the WTO, and each Member determines the shape and scope of its cooperation with the private sector according to its own legal and institutional context and capacity. As such, and as confirmed by the interviews and Committee discussions described in this chapter, Members benefit very unevenly from private sector inputs.

The transparency framework spans all WTO Members. Notifications allow them to share information about regulatory drafts, making them known and publicly available, and leaving time for Members and interested stakeholders to adapt to the upcoming regulations. Nevertheless, STC discussions suggest that a number of measures with a significant effect on trade fail to be notified. The right to send bilateral comments on notifications via enquiry points and to raise STCs in the multilateral setting of SPS and TBT Committees opens up space for essential dialogue throughout what becomes an inclusive regulatory process. This grants WTO Members an opportunity to flag measures that do or may raise trade costs significantly and which are or may be inconsistent with WTO obligations. In the next chapter, we will look at the specifics of this dialogue, and at how Members use the tools of the SPS and TBT transparency framework to prevent disputes from arising.

5

The Content of the WTO Disputing Pyramid

What Do Members Need to Know to Prevent Disputes from Arising?

An important effect of specific trade concerns (STCs) is that they allow WTO Members to gather information about each other's domestic regulations. The STCs allow them not only to clarify the information that is already available but also, and perhaps more significantly, to engage in more substantive exchanges through which they come to understand the measures and on which they can base constructive feedback in line with the WTO obligations. This chapter will describe the variety of issues about which Members raise concerns in the Committees established under the WTO Agreements on the Application of Sanitary and Phytosanitary Measures (SPS Agreement, or SPS) and on Technical Barriers to Trade (TBT Agreement, or TBT). In this way, we will explore the 'demand side' of information and demonstrate that, in practice, the functions of STCs under the two Agreements are threefold: Members active in the STC discussions are either seeking further information or clarification of a measure, or they may intend to influence draft regulations by feeding into another Member's regulatory process, or they may be trying to overcome a problem they face in implementing the measure. These functions may overlap within the same STC.

Overall, these three functions contribute to a better understanding among WTO Members of each other's regulatory frameworks and the mutual dialogue that supports evidence-based rule-making in a globalised context. By fulfilling these functions and in combination with the transparency mechanisms that appear lower in the 'disputing pyramid' (that is, publication, notifications and comments), STCs allow WTO Members to engage in technical dialogue about domestic regulations, against the backdrop of the SPS and TBT Agreements, without having their discussion having legal consequences. Indeed, it is important to underline that STCs are not legal claims; rather, they are 'concerns', meaning that they reflect 'a cause of anxiety or worry'[1] to the Members raising them in the

---

[1] Angus Stevenson, ed., *Oxford Dictionary of English*, 3rd edn (Oxford: Oxford University Press, 2010), 'concern'.

Committees. We shall see that, in many cases, Members frame these concerns as questions, asking whether their understanding of the measure at stake is correct rather than alleging that the measure is inconsistent with WTO obligations.

This chapter will therefore explore the STC process under the broad framework of the SPS and TBT Agreements as an informal dialogue that aims to work towards improved implementation. As such, transparency at this level can be seen as shaping Members' behaviours without requiring new agreements or the enforcement of existing ones.[2] In the context of the SPS and TBT Committees, this dialogue is essential in allowing Members to manage trade frictions regarding domestic measures and to prevent those frictions from escalating into formal disputes, and hence STCs can be seen as a substitute for dispute settlement.

I   The Trend Underlying STCs: Understanding Domestic Regulation among WTO Members

Analysis of SPS and TBT STCs over five years, between 2010 and 2014, suggests that very similar concerns are raised in the two Committees. Although there were more than double the total number of TBT STCs in that time (196 TBT STCs versus 93 SPS STCs), the frequency with which various issues were raised is comparable, as illustrated in Figures 5.1 and 5.2.

Overall, the issues that feature most frequently are those related to the rationale or scientific justification of a measure, its necessity or its conformity with international standards, with some variations between the two Committees that may be explained by the differences between the Agreements. Transparency concerns,[3] flagging inconsistency with publication or notification obligations, are also commonly raised, together with concerns relating to the opportunity to comment on domestic draft measures and the need for a 'reasonable interval' for traders to adapt to new requirements. Discrimination is less frequently raised than necessity-related concerns – and this is particularly true of SPS STCs. Finally,

---

[2] Robert Wolfe, private communication with the author.
[3] For the purpose of this part, which aims to underline the different objectives fulfilled by SPS and TBT transparency, the provisions that fall under the general scope of 'transparency obligations' as presented in Part I have been subdivided into those that imply a disclosure of information (by means of notification and publication), those that open the opportunity for regulatory dialogue (via comments on notifications) and those that guarantee traders time to adapt to new requirements (by providing for a reasonable interval between adoption and implementation).

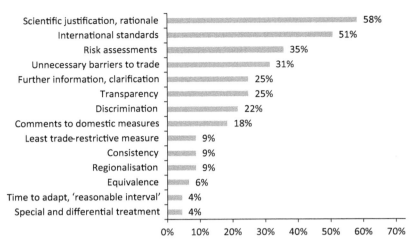

Figure 5.1 Types of issue raised in SPS STCs, as share of total SPS STCs, 2010–2014. Source: SPS Committee minutes, SPS IMS, http://spsims.wto.org/.

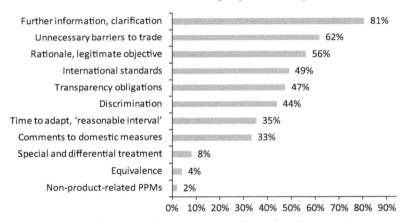

Figure 5.2 Types of issue raised in TBT STCs, as share of total TBT STCs, 2010–2014. Source: TBT Committee minutes, TBT IMS, http://tbtims.wto.org.

issues that are highly specific to the SPS or TBT Agreement, such as consistency, regionalisation or non-product-related processes and production methods (PPMs), come up less often, as does special and differential treatment.

As will be presented further in depth later in this chapter, the STCs raised combine procedural issues with substantive concerns. In Figures 5.1 and 5.2, transparency, further information and clarification, and time to adapt can be considered to be procedural, whereas the rest can

I THE TREND UNDERLYING STCs

be considered more substantive. Whether procedural or substantive, STCs are always about domestic regulations – draft or adopted – which have or may have a significant effect on trade. This essence is the reason why both procedural and substantive questions result in a form of regulatory co-operation. Indeed, as noted in Chapter 3, all forms of co-operation between Members that contributes to regulatory coherence may be defined as international regulatory co-operation (IRC). Concerns as procedural as those asking for an extension of the delay before implementation, calling for a notification to the WTO Secretariat or even merely asking about the date of entry into force all involve authorities from one country commenting on the domestic drafts or measures of another country that have the potential to influence their own measures. As such, the raising of concerns feeds international considerations into domestic rule-making and thus helps to promote regulatory coherence among WTO Members. Further research could indicate the extent to which the divide between procedural and substantive concerns may be related to the measures' effects on trade and the co-operation that takes place in the Committees.

Looking beyond their subject matter, STCs may be raised at different stages of the domestic policy cycle. Both SPS and TBT STCs address actual and potential trade barriers, each aiming to modify the measure so that it is less trade-restrictive. While discussion of potential trade barriers contributes to the drafting of a measure, discussion of actual trade barriers aims to remove a provision from an existing regulation. On this point, the STCs raised in the SPS and TBT Committees differ considerably, as shown in Figure 5.3. In the SPS Committee, STCs are most often raised because the concerned Member has encountered actual trade barriers, whereas in the TBT Committee, STCs are most often used to obtain further information and generally relate to prospective effects on trade. This may be because the subject matter covered by the SPS Agreement requires urgent action to prevent not only high trade costs but also the spread of animal or plant diseases.

In addition, STC discussions are generally highly technical: other than in some exceptional cases in which Member country delegations are particularly outspoken against another Member's regulation, STCs tend to seek a concrete response to a concrete concern. This, as we shall see in Part III, helps to explain the success of STCs as the 'antechamber' of dispute settlement.[4]

---

[4] Henrik Horn, Petros C. Mavroidis and Erik N. Wijkström, 'In the Shadow of the DSU: Addressing Specific Trade Concerns in the WTO SPS and TBT Committees – Entwined', *Journal of World Trade* 47, no. 4 (2013): 729–59.

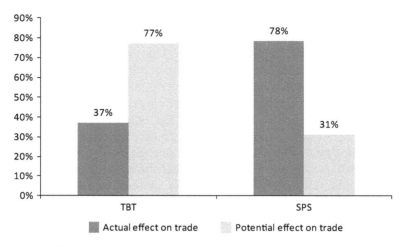

Figure 5.3 STCs about actual or potential trade effects. Source: Author's own based on SPS Committee minutes, SPS IMS, http://spsims.wto.org/, and TBT Committee minutes, TBT IMS, http://tbtims.wto.org.

II The Broader Content of STCs: Transparency, Regulatory Co-operation and Practical Impediments to Trade

The issues raised in STCs can be broadly divided among three objectives: transparency (section A), contribution to regulatory processes (section B) and addressing a practical impediment to trade (section C). These three categories underline the general uses made of the mechanism of STCs. Some concerns may pursue more than one of the objectives at once.

A Transparency, Information and Clarification

Transparency is itself one of the functions pursued by STCs. This covers concerns requesting further information on a measure and those taking issue with the measure's alleged non-compliance with the transparency obligations under the SPS and TBT Agreements.

1 Requests for Information: A Clarification

Specific trade concerns are an essential source of information thanks to the direct contact that concerned Members have with the regulating Member and the latter's incentive to provide information in response to concerns raised in the presence of the entire WTO membership. Members therefore use the mechanism of STCs to submit requests for information or to draw attention to a lack of transparency in the regulating Member's regulatory process. The former is, however, far more commonplace in the TBT Committee than it is in the SPS Committee.

In the TBT Committee, 'further information, clarification' is overwhelmingly the issue most frequently raised in STCs. According to WTO Secretariat data, it was an objective specified in 67 per cent of all TBT STCs raised between 1995 and 2015.[5] In the sample period 2010–2014, this share goes up to 81 per cent of TBT STCs.[6] These figures clearly demonstrate that the TBT Committee is perceived as an effective forum for the exchanging and obtaining of information.

Requests for information submitted through TBT STCs complement the information provided in notifications. This is particularly important because of the wide variety of different institutional systems and regulatory cultures among Members.

The type of information requested within STCs demonstrates why dialogue is essential if Members are to understand their trading partners' regulatory processes and cultures, and why STCs may involve procedural and substantive issues. Indeed, information required may be both procedural, seeking information on the status of a draft measure, and substantive, seeking further clarification on the scope of application or the specific requirements it establishes.

a **Requesting an Update on the Status of a Draft Measure** Information about the regulatory process may help Members to evaluate the leeway that they have to introduce changes to the draft before its adoption and the opportunities that remain to gather additional inputs from governments or other stakeholders. For instance, concerned with the European Union (EU) proposal regarding country-of-origin labelling (COOL) of certain products from third countries, 'the US representative asked for updated information on the status of this proposal in the European Parliament, and on the process by which the European Union would request input from Members and other stakeholders. He also asked for more information about when the European Council would consider the measure.'[7]

---

[5] This data comes from WTO, 'Twenty-First Annual Review of the Implementation and Operation of the TBT Agreement' (G/TBT/38, 2016), 19.

[6] According to the TBT IMS and TBT Committee minutes, 158 of the 196 TBT STCs raised between 2010 and 2014 included requests for further information or clarification.

[7] 'EU – Proposal for a Council Regulation on the Indication of the Country of Origin of Certain Products Imported from Third Countries' (SEC(2005)1657, TBT ID 285, G/TBT/M/52), para. 58.

In addition, additional information about the status of a draft measure makes upcoming regulatory changes easier to anticipate, thus complementing the predictability facilitated by notification of the draft. Indeed, while the TBT and SPS Agreements require draft measures to be notified, adopted measures need only be published. For instance, regarding India's proposed Order on electronics and information technology goods, the United States 'expressed confusion as to whether the Order was a proposed or final measure, given that the published measure included an entry into force timeframe and did not specify a final or revised measure being issued before then'.[8]

Such requests for an update on the status of the measure within the regulatory process also pin down more precise information on the way in which the measure will be implemented. Another boost to predictability among the concerned Member and the entire membership, this information will then also be accessible to any stakeholder either through its Member government or as published in the Committee meeting minutes.

b Requesting Clarification of Scope or Requirements Like the requests for procedural information, requests for clarification of the scope or of the measure's requirements aim to fill in the gaps in an inadequate description given in the notification or otherwise made available, aiming in particular at uncovering whether a measure may impact a Member's trade with the regulating country. For example, Indonesia, as a major producer of palm oil, required information from the EU on its measure regarding the labelling of vegetable oils and it asked the EU to 'clarify whether the term vegetable oil therein applied to palm oil only or also to rape seed oil'.[9]

Clarification of a measure's requirements can explore concrete issues, aiming to expose its true implications and possible costs. This reflects the technical nature of STCs, seeking genuine clarification for traders and a clearer picture of whether the measure is consistent with the Member's WTO obligations. For instance, concerned with a draft French measure containing labelling requirements for recyclable products, the United States asked for 'clarification about at what point in the supply chain the labels could be affixed: in the country of origin or in a bonded warehouse?

---

[8] 'India – Electronics and Information Technology Goods (Requirements for Compulsory Registration) Order, 2012' (TBT ID 367), para. 2.4.
[9] G/TBT/M/64/Rev.1, para. 2.59.

The US also asked for clarification on where the logo was required to be placed and how large the logo was required to be.'[10]

In the SPS context, similar requests for information also arise. This was the case regarding a US measure that India wanted to understand better, in terms of both process and scope:

> The representative of India expressed the need to understand the proposed legislation. Indian industry had questions regarding the duration of the registration process, whether it was modelled on international standards, whether foreign government and sector associations would be notified before or after a food facility was inspected, and how the fast-track process for registration would work. Once it had a better understanding of this process, India would seek further clarification.[11]

In some cases, Members go beyond asking that information be given to them directly to request that the requirements of a measure be clarified within the measure itself. For instance, when the EU argued that Ukraine's draft technical regulation on the labelling of foodstuff contained unclear requirements that might be discriminatory, it 'requested that Ukraine authorities review and clarify requirements for mandatory origin labelling, since as currently formulated, the requirements seemed to apply only to imported products'.[12]

These examples of STCs show that requests for information or clarification allow a concerned Member government not only to improve its understanding of the measure but also to share its concerns and to inform the regulating Member of the potential barriers that the draft measure creates as it stands.

2 Lack of Transparency in a Draft Measure

Beyond asking for information, Members also frequently flag the lack of transparency of regulating Members – namely, a failure to disclose draft measures, whether through publication or notification.[13]

---

[10] 'France – Recycling Triman Mark: "Draft Decree on a common set of symbols informing the consumer about recyclable products subject to a system of extended producer responsibility associated with waste sorting instructions" ' (TBT ID 420, G/TBT/M/62), para. 2.53.
[11] 'US 2009 Food Safety Enhancement Act' (SPS ID 299, G/SPS/R/59), para. 22.
[12] 'Ukraine – Draft Technical Regulation on the Labelling of Foodstuff' (TBT ID 293, G/TBT/M/53), para. 83.
[13] The other requirements that fall under 'transparency obligations' are reflected in other sections because of their differing functions, e.g. predictability for the obligation of providing a reasonable delay or opening regulatory dialogue for comments on notifications.

Compliance with the transparency obligations is difficult to enforce through dispute settlement. Indeed, regulatory transparency is not an end in itself; rather, it is the mechanism that informs all Members and traders about measures that might have a negative impact on trade. As such, the burdensome process of adjudicating simply because a measure does not comply with transparency obligations seems by itself disproportionate – and all the more so given that the remedies are unlikely to be satisfactory.

The multilateral, yet informal, context of Committee meetings can therefore be a more apt route through which to flag a lack of compliance with transparency obligations and encourage Members to comply, without escalating the issue to full dispute procedure. The TBT STCs reflect this, given that 47 per cent of those concerns raised in the period examined cited lack of transparency as an issue. This is, however, much less true of SPS STCs, which mention transparency in only 25 per cent of cases.

In some cases, Members examine the full regulatory process and raise concerns about the absence of transparency at various stages. For example, raising concerns about a Chinese measure on food additives, the United States took the opportunity to remind China of its transparency obligations – namely, both publication and notification:

> Procedurally, this measure was not published in draft form, thereby preventing interested stakeholders from submitting their comments. The measure claimed to have two objectives, namely ensuring food quality (a TBT issue) and food safety (an SPS issue). Nevertheless, the measure was not notified to either the TBT or SPS Committee, despite the fact that the measure appeared to have taken effect less than six weeks after it was announced by China.[14]

Among the transparency obligations discussed in STCs, the obligation of notification is cited in STCs most frequently. Publication is rarely mentioned, possibly because adopted measures are more often already published and because lack of notification has more direct implications for traders. Five TBT concerns during the period examined cited the issue of publication, whereas 61 TBT STCs mentioned the obligation of notification. In the SPS Committee, no concerns raised during the period examined mentioned publication, while 19 SPS concerns cited a lack of notification or inappropriate notification.

---

[14] 'China – Specification for Import and Export of Food Additives Inspection, Quarantine and Supervision (2011 No. 52) – Disclosure of Formulas for Imported Food Additives' (TBT ID 326, G/TBT/M/55), para. 34.

II THE BROADER CONTENT OF STCs

A Member might raise a failure to notify, reminding the regulating Member of its legal obligation under the Agreement, as did Canada when concerned with a Russian measure: 'The representative of Canada expressed disappointment that this measure, as required by Articles 2.9 of the TBT Agreement, had not been notified to the TBT Committee.'[15] This can be an opportunity for the regulating Member to explain the reason for not notifying the measure, such as its limited effect on trade or the early stage of the draft. In this case, in response to Canada's concern, Russia indicated that it had not notified because the measure at stake did not introduce new requirements.

Beyond individual measures that have not been notified, Members use STCs as an opportunity to underline some other Members' systemic failures to notify. This sort of STC goes beyond one particular measure that creates a trade barrier to reflect a more long-standing concern and, importantly, to encourage the regulating Member to reconsider its practices and make the necessary institutional changes.

For instance, in relation to Indonesia's lack of notification of new mandatory labelling requirements, the EU – supported on this point by the United States – 'drew Indonesia's attention to the fact that this was already the third occurrence in a short period of time that legislation containing important requirements affecting a large number of goods had not been notified to the TBT Committee. The representative of the European Union regretted this omission.'[16] In this particular case, Indonesia took note of this concern and notified the measure a month after the STC was raised – a positive step that the EU acknowledged at the next meeting.[17]

A similar concern was raised by Canada, the EU, Costa Rica, Brazil, Chile and the United States regarding Ecuador's systematic failures to notify: 'While Canada recognised that occasional lapses could occur for any Member, systemic late notifications were of concern. Since October 2013, there had been 41 notifications from Ecuador, 18 of which had been notified well after the relevant measures had entered into force.'[18]

---

[15] 'Russia – Federal Service for Market Regulation (FSR) – New Provisions for the Mandatory Notification of Liquor Products' (TBT ID 412, G/TBT/M/62), para. 2.17.

[16] 'Indonesia – Labelling Regulations (Ministry of Trade Regulation 62/2009 and 22/2010)' (TBT ID 279, G/TBT/M/52), para. 26.

[17] The Indonesian notification can be found at G/TBT/N/IDN/47. However, the notification was made even though the measure had already entered into force. The EU noted this at the subsequent meeting, but did not represent the central issue in the STC, which was discussed at five TBT Committee meetings.

[18] 'Ecuador – Systematic Failure to Publish Notices at an Early Appropriate Stage' (TBT ID 414), G/TBT/M/62, para. 2.21.

In response, Ecuador explained that it was undergoing significant domestic reforms and that, in this context, 'there were weaknesses both in the regulations themselves, but also of a more institutional nature'.[19] Ecuador indicated that it was working to improve its notification processes and took Members' comments into account.

In addition to failures to notify, Members also note when a notification has been submitted to the wrong Committee or in the wrong format. Indeed, incorrect notification may prevent the information from reaching the interested parties: if the notification is submitted to the wrong Committee, the wrong delegations will be informed and they may not be qualified to estimate the legality or effects of the measure. Notifications made to the import licensing committee or to the SPS or TBT Committees are therefore sometimes raised in the SPS and TBT Committees, when relevant, asking for notification to the right Committee.[20] Such STCs draw the attention of all relevant delegations to the measures wrongfully notified, whether or not the concern is then followed up with the correct notification.

The use of the wrong notification format may also deprive Members of the opportunity to comment on the notification. This would be the case for notifications of new measures making changes, but notified by way of addenda, or measures notified as emergency notifications in circumstances that are not urgent.

In this sense, pursuing its previous concern regarding Ecuador's failures to notify, Canada raised the further concern that when Ecuador did notify, it used the emergency format:

> Although [failure to notify] was troubling in itself, given that Members' right to comment had been violated, Canada was more troubled by Ecuador's decision to invoke Articles 2.10 and 5.7 (urgency). In Canada's view, changes to rules concerning cosmetics, french fries, energy efficiency and surface tension agents did not qualify as 'urgent problems of safety, health, environmental protection or national security'. This was a misapplication of a key provision of the TBT Agreement, which diluted the meaning and intent of the emergency provisions.[21]

In this same concern, the EU underlined the negative effects that the wrongful emergency notification had had for its exports: 'The adoption

---

[19] Ibid., para. 2.26.
[20] See e.g. 'Indonesia – Permits on Horticultural Products' (SPS ID 343); 'France – Ban on Bisphenol A' (SPS ID 346); 'Malaysia – Draft Protocol for Halal Meat and Poultry Production' (TBT ID 317).
[21] 'Ecuador – Systematic Failure to Publish Notices at an Early Appropriate Stage' (TBT ID 414), G/TBT/M/52, para. 2.21.

of this technical regulation under the emergency procedure had caused a total block of cosmetic exports from the EU to Ecuador.'[22]

The timing of notification is an important attribute to guarantee that comments may still be made and that the draft may still be amended accordingly. In this sense, Members often underline the importance of complying with notification obligations at an appropriately early stage in the regulatory process for the purpose of taking other Members' comments into account:

> While the decree had been under development for some time, and was now in its 14th draft, it was still not notified to the WTO. Australia recalled that the notification of proposed measures at an early appropriate stage, together with an indication of their objective and rationale, was essential so as to allow comments to be taken into account and amendments to be introduced, before the proposed measures entered into force. Australia therefore urged Vietnam to notify Decree 40 to the WTO so that concerns could be taken into account when finalising the final version of the measure.[23]

Finally, even when notifying, Members need to take into account the addressees of information, providing sufficient time for them to process the volume of information disclosed. Indeed, overloading Members and concerned stakeholders with notifications, especially when those notifications are not accompanied by sufficient details and time for comments, may deprive the notifications of their *effet utile*. Such a case was flagged in the SPS Committee regarding China's numerous notifications regarding food safety: 'China had submitted almost 100 SPS notifications on food additives in a few days, providing only a 15 days deadline for comments. None of the notifications included references to the original text.'[24]

China replied to this concern by explaining that the notifications concerned texts that had been based on international standards and therefore had minimal trade effects, and the concern was no longer pursued in Committee discussions.[25]

B Contribution to Domestic Regulatory Processes

By enabling inputs into WTO Members' domestic regulatory processes and fostering dialogue on the quality of draft regulations, STCs may

---

[22] Ibid.
[23] 'Viet Nam – Regulations Relating to Liquor Production and Trading' (TBT ID 349, G/TBT/M/57), para. 36.
[24] 'China's SPS Notification Practices' (SPS ID 296, G/SPS/R/59), para. 15.
[25] Ibid., para. 16.

promote regulatory consistency between concerned and regulating Members. On the one hand, the concerned Member can share their experience and regulatory preferences with the regulating Member at a time when the measure can still be modified, eventually driving a change in the draft measure; on the other hand, STCs provide the regulating Member with feedback on their domestic measure, which may give insights into alternatives or different scientific evidence that it might consider, or simply into the costs the measure imposes beyond its own borders. Indeed, domestic regulatory impact assessments (RIAs) do not necessarily provide sufficient information on the cross-border effects of a measure. This function of the STC is therefore crucial for both regulating and concerned Members as a tool for regulatory co-operation.

The STCs raised show that there is demand for a multilateral forum in which Members can co-operate on their domestic processes to reduce regulatory barriers to trade. Indeed, STCs offer the multilateral complement to regulatory dialogue that the TBT and SPS Agreements require at the bilateral level: the presence of all Members and of the Secretariat delivers incentives to the regulating Member, encouraging it to respond to comments. Given the public and multilateral setting in which STCs are raised, the information that a concerned Member gains is shared with the entire WTO membership, who become spectators of, if not participants in, the regulatory dialogue. Regardless of the passive role of the WTO Secretariat, the Committee setting within the WTO framework means that the regulatory co-operation that takes place in this context remains focused on ensuring the effective implementation of the SPS and TBT Agreements.

Members consequently raise concerns that are either procedural in nature, because Members have been deprived of the opportunity to make comments and therefore to contribute to the other Member's regulatory process (section 1), or more substantive, initiating a form of regulatory co-operation within the SPS and TBT Committees (section 2).

1   A Timely Opportunity to Discuss and Influence Measures

Certain STCs are more procedural in nature and request the regulating Member to grant more time either for bilateral discussions – because the time for comments is considered insufficient – or before the measure enters into force. In the latter case, the concerned Member acknowledges the barriers that a measure will create and asks the regulating Member to adapt its regulatory agenda accordingly.

a **Concerns Involving the Opportunity to Comment**   The first level of regulatory co-operation enabled under the SPS and TBT Agreements is the opportunity to comment on notifications.[26] As mentioned earlier, this obligation grants Members the right to comment on draft regulations but also imposes on the regulating Member the obligation to discuss these comments and to take the comments and results of the discussions into account.

This remains a bilateral dialogue between WTO Members and is not centralised by the WTO Secretariat. It is therefore difficult to monitor or even to assist in the implementation of these obligations. In this context, it is up to Members themselves to flag failures to respond to their comments. The STCs provide them with an opportunity to do so without escalating the issue to the level of formal legal complaint before the WTO's Dispute Settlement Body (DSB). In the period examined, 33 per cent of TBT STCs raised issues related to comments on notifications, compared with 18 per cent of SPS STCs.

Whereas timely notifications, centralised via the WTO Secretariat, raise Members' awareness that a new draft regulation is in preparation, the time left for comments after notification and before adoption allows Members to contribute to each other's domestic regulatory processes. This, as previously mentioned, is important in reducing regulatory heterogeneity and the barriers to trade that may result. Therefore, when Members have not notified or have notified without allowing sufficient opportunity for comments, other Members may request such by raising an STC – presumably after the regulating Member has refused bilateral demands.

For instance, the United States, concerned with an EU measure that prohibited the use and sale of seeds treated with certain plant protection products, asked for the comment period to be extended: 'The European Union had provided an unusually short comment period of only 11 days. Given the complexity of this technical measure, the United States asked the European Union to extend the comment period to the recommended 60-days, to allow trading partners to review and provide comments.'[27]

Even where a period for comment is provided, however, responses may not be sent in writing to the commenting Members. In this case again, Members will use the Committees to obtain an answer. For example, in a concern raised about Russian provisions for notification of liquor products,

---

[26] Articles 2.9.4 and 5.6.4 TBT; Annex B, para. 5(d), SPS.
[27] 'EU – Prohibition of Use and Sale of Treated Seeds' (SPS ID 350), para. 3.57.

Canada regretted before the TBT Committee that Russia had not replied to the concerns that Canada initially voiced bilaterally – that 'the letter Canada had sent to Russia on 1 October 2013 expressing these concerns had still not been replied to'.[28] As a consequence of the STC, Russia provided a detailed response in the Committee and Canada did not reiterate its concern.

Finally, in addition to the questions relating to opportunity to comment or response to comments made, Members also expect their comments to be taken into consideration when the regulating Member finalises the measure in question. For instance, in the SPS Committee, Panama noted that a recent notification by Costa Rica on the maximum residual limits (MRLs) for the medication of live animals was in fact already in place. In this context, 'Panama asked Costa Rica to explain how it had provided for a reasonable period of time for Members to make comments; how those comments were taken into account; and how its trading partners had been informed about the content of the Directive'.[29]

Costa Rica replied that it had notified only for transparency purposes, because the measure was based on an international standard. As a result, it argued that it did not need to provide a comment period.[30]

India was more adamant that Chinese Taipei take into account its comments on a measure posing new requirements regarding roasted and powdered coffee: 'Chinese Taipei's requirements would adversely affect India's growing exports of coffee. India urged Chinese Taipei's competent authority to take into consideration India's comments when finalising the measure on tolerances of mycotoxins in foods.'[31]

Other Members joined India in raising concerns and Chinese Taipei ended up modifying the measure in accordance with the comments received. The EU reported the concern resolved.[32]

The India–Chinese Taipei STC illustrates the complementarity between bilateral comments on draft measures and multilateral dialogue aiming to influence a domestic regulator to select a less-restrictive alternative measure. In both the SPS and TBT Committees, Members raise substantive concerns as a way of participating in the regulating Members' domestic rule-making.

---

[28] 'Russia – Federal Service for Market Regulation (FSR) – New Provisions for the Mandatory Notification of Liquor Products' (TBT ID 412, G/TBT/M/62), paras 2.17–2.18.
[29] 'Costa Rica – MRLs for Veterinary Medicines in Live Animals' (SPS ID 349), para. 3.55.
[30] Ibid., para. 3.56.
[31] 'Chinese Taipei – MRLs for Roasted and Powdered Coffee' (SPS ID 334, G/SPS/R/67), paras 20–23.
[32] Ibid., paras 20 et seq.

b Concerns with Time to Adapt When Members foresee considerable costs and delays in adapting to a new foreign measure, they request a delay before the measure's entry into force under the 'transparency' obligations set out in Articles 2.12 and 5.9 of the TBT Agreement and Annex B, paragraph 2, to the SPS Agreement, which provide that a 'reasonable interval' must be left between publication and entry into force. The concerns raised in the Committees relate to the 'reasonable' character of the interval. They represent 35 per cent of all TBT STCs during the period examined, but only 4 per cent of the SPS STCs.

The lack of sufficient time to adapt can be directly related to the absence of transparency around the measure. In the US concern about China's new provision on the General Administration of Quality Supervision, Inspection and Quarantine (AQSIQ), the United States noted that the lack of publication and notification meant that 'China did not grant sufficient adaptation time to importers before the specification entered into force'.[33]

The 'reasonable interval' is generally defined as no less than six months.[34] Members sometimes raise STCs because the proposed delay is much shorter than six months and others, because their traders need more time.

The EU requested a six-month implementation period for Korea's measure establishing a new self-certification procedure for motor vehicles. Learning about an implementation measure that had been published and entered into force on the same day, the EU asked Korea to 'suspend [the measure's] application until Members have had an opportunity to provide comments, which should be taken into account. It also requested Korea to provide a reasonable period – of at least six months – between the publication of [the measure] and their entry into force.'[35] In response, Korea granted a three-month grace period for manufacturers to adapt.[36]

---

[33] 'China – Specification for Import and Export of Food Additives Inspection, Quarantine and Supervision (2011 No. 52) – Disclosure of Formulas for Imported Food Additives' (TBT ID 326, G/TBT/M/55), para. 34.

[34] WTO, 'Implementation-Related Issues and Concerns', Doha WTO Ministerial 2001: Ministerial Declarations and Decisions (CN – WT/MIN(01)/17, 2001).

[35] 'Korea – Draft Amendment of Ordinance and Regulation of Motor Vehicle Control Act' (IMS ID 376, G/TBT/M/59), para. 2.57.

[36] Ibid., para. 2.58.

Some Members ask for considerably more time because of specific circumstances. For instance, in their concern regarding an EU regulation on cadmium in cocoa, Ecuador and some other countries supporting its concern asked the EU to extend the implementation date. Without providing particular justifications why, they 'requested that, if the new measure were adopted, the European Union allow a transition period of at least five years, to permit producers to adapt to the measures'.[37] Taking note of this concern, the EU confirmed that a 'reasonable transition period would be provided'.[38]

Japan further justified its request that India postpone the entry into force of its new Order on electronics and information technology goods:

> The representative of Japan requested that India postpone the enforcement date of the Electronics and Information Technology Goods (Requirements for Compulsory Registration) Order 2012. He noted that Article 3 of the Order prohibited manufacturing, storing for sale, importing, selling or distributing products which did not conform to the Order after the enforcement date of 3 April 2013, which was six months from the date of publication in the Official Gazette. However, Japanese industry estimated that it would take more than nine months to comply with all requirements in the Order. He additionally noted a lack of testing laboratory capacity in relation to the Order; India had designated only four testing laboratories, all of which were located in India. For these reasons, the representative requested that India postpone entry into force to 12 months from the date of publication in the Official Gazette, at the earliest.[39]

India provided for a seven-month adaptation period after publication of the measure. Because the concern persisted over six meetings and was raised by six Members altogether, India then postponed implementation of the measure until 1 June 2016.[40]

2 Questioning the Necessity of a Measure

As we saw in Part I, the SPS and TBT Agreements both set out a requirement that domestic regulations be effective in achieving policy objectives: simply put, they must not be more trade-restrictive than necessary.

---

[37] 'EU Regulations on Cadmium in Cocoa' (SPS ID 325, G/SPS/R/67), para. 141.
[38] Ibid., para. 142.
[39] 'India – Electronics and Information Technology Goods (Requirements for Compulsory Registration) Order' (ID 367, G/TBT/M/59, 2012), para. 2.2.
[40] Ibid. See also G/TBT/M/68, para. 2.128.

The 'necessity' of a measure is relative to the objective pursued and to the scientific evidence on which it is based. Unavoidably, the objectives and methodological approaches of the 164 Members of the WTO vary, resulting in additional costs of access to each market.

Being able to discuss the 'necessity' of domestic measures at a draft stage compensates for the WTO's negative integration approach: while Members remain free to choose their policy measures, they do have to take comments into account. This may help to align domestic policies or reduce the burdens that might result from regulatory divergence. Transparency is therefore particularly key to the implementation of the obligation to adopt measures that do not create unnecessary barriers to trade.

The variety of obligations specific to both Agreements is reflected in the SPS STC discussions.

Articles 2.2 and 5.1.2 of the TBT Agreement set out that Members shall not adopt technical regulations and conformity assessment procedures (CAPs), respectively, that are more trade-restrictive than necessary to fulfil a legitimate objective, taking into account the risks of non-fulfilment. Article 2.2 of the SPS Agreement provides that Members shall ensure that their SPS measures are applied only to the extent necessary to protect human, animal or plant life or health, based on scientific principles.

The general requirement of 'necessity' is raised in STCs in both Committees, although much more significantly in the TBT Committee. Sixty-two per cent of all TBT STCs in the period examined raised the issue of necessity of the domestic regulation, compared with only 31 per cent of SPS STCs. These STCs related only to unnecessary barriers to trade. Those that raise the issue of the rationale for the measure, be it the legitimate objective pursued by the measure (TBT) or the scientific basis for the measure (SPS), are also brought before the Committee frequently and can therefore be distinguished.

That fewer 'necessity' concerns are raised in the SPS Committee can be explained by the distinction between 'necessity' concerns and concerns regarding the scientific evidence justifying the measure. When concerns relate to both in combination, as they are set out in Article 2.2 of the SPS Agreement, they account for 65 per cent of all SPS STCs. Combining the figures for STCs raised in relation to necessity and those raised in relation to legitimate objectives in the TBT Committee gives a total of 76 per cent of TBT STCs.

Members concerned with the necessity of a measure tend to raise the issue from one of two positions: they may ask about the rationale of the measure or they may flag the costs of complying with the proposed requirements.

Those who raise it from another perspective tend to request that the regulating Member explain the proportionality of the measure at stake to the risk.

Discussions about 'necessity' demonstrate the co-operative efforts that Members go to in pursuit of a mutually satisfactory measure. Indeed, while a Member raising an STC about a measure essentially focuses on lowering its trade-restrictiveness and the regulating State may have various reasons for choosing that specific measure, the SPS and TBT framework limits the Member's ability to adopt the measure. The measure must be in pursuit of a legitimate objective or based on scientific evidence, and hence the playing field is levelled within the regulatory discussions and a certain level of regulatory quality is guaranteed.

a   **The Rationale behind the Measure**   The rationale underpinning a certain policy option is key to deciding whether a measure is justified, in line with the SPS and TBT Agreements. Under the TBT Agreement, the criterion used to determine necessity is pursuit of a 'legitimate objective', whereas under the SPS Agreement, it is scientific evidence.

Legitimate Objective   To determine whether a measure is necessary to fulfil a certain objective, Members ask the regulating State to share further details about the causality between the chosen policy option and the pursued objective. This was clearly raised, for instance, by New Zealand. Concerned about Italy's draft regulation on the labelling of dairy products, New Zealand:

> ... encouraged Italy to explain the causal link made in the draft legislation between banning the use of protein in cheese-making and preventing fraud in the dairy industry. In the absence of such evidence, it was New Zealand's view that the proposed ban did not appear to be in line with Article 2.2 of the TBT Agreement. The representative of New Zealand also questioned whether the measure adopted by Italy was the least trade-restrictive measure that could be chosen to fulfil its objective.[41]

When regulating in pursuit of a specific legitimate objective, concerned Members also question whether the measure is proportionate to the risk it aims to remedy.

---

[41] 'Italy – Dairy Products' (TBT ID 261, G/TBT/M/50), para. 15. In March 2011, after discussing the STC in four meetings, the European Commission informed the Committee that discussions between the Commission and Italian authorities were ongoing and therefore remained an internal procedure. The STC was no longer raised after that.

In addition, while the TBT Agreement does not require scientific evidence to justify the necessity of a measure, some Members do advance scientific evidence and risk assessments to argue *against* a particular policy. In particular, Israel argued that an EU measure that resulted in withdrawal of a plant protection product was not justified because scientific data precluded a risk from exposure to the product:

> Israel was aware of the EU's legitimate concerns regarding the protection of human health and the environment. However, Israel was of the view that the proposed exclusion could not be justified based on the available scientific information since the confirmatory data proved there was no risk. Israel stressed the following points: (i) that it considered the proposed measure as an 'unnecessary obstacle to international trade' under Article 2.2 of the TBT Agreement; (ii) that the available scientific information within the context of an EU risk assessment process established that no risk existed to human health and that the environmental risk was limited and controllable and therefore there was no scientific justification to exclude *Sulcotrione* from the list of approved active substances in Europe ...[42]

Scientific Rationale The scientific rationale behind an SPS measure is the issue most raised before the SPS Committee, cited in 58 per cent of SPS STCs during the period examined. Such STCs allow Members to ask the regulating Member for further explanation of the scientific evidence on which the measure was based or to argue that the evidence used is insufficient or wrong. While the concerns raised at the Committee level reveal the main issues around scientific evidence, further discussions and regulatory co-operation at the bilateral level are more likely to lead to a mutually acceptable solution.

For instance, Paraguay raised a concern regarding Japan's MRLs for pesticides in sesame, claiming that they were not based on scientific evidence. The discussions over the course of three SPS Committee meetings demonstrated a co-operative effort between the concerned and regulating Members to identify the relevant scientific data:

> Paraguay reiterated its concerns over Japan's application of MRLs to sesame and maintained that uniform limits were inconsistent with the SPS Agreement since they were not based on scientific principles and were maintained without sufficient scientific evidence. ... Paraguay understood that under Japanese regulations, the uniform tolerance limit for pesticides not listed in such table was of 0.01 mg/kg, however, Japan allowed higher

---

[42] 'Israel – Warning Regulations on Alcoholic Beverages' (TBT ID 364, G/TBT/M/58), para. 2.5.

tolerance limits for other imports, such as sunflower seed, rapeseed, and other oilseeds. Paraguay believed that the limits were arbitrary and inconsistent with the concept of appropriate level of protection, as higher limits existed for routinely consumed products such as rice and spinach.[43]

Given that Japan did not use the pesticide in question in its sesame production, it applied a uniform level for import tolerance. It 'requested Paraguay to submit scientific data, including residue trial data, so that the necessary scientific assessments could be carried out'.[44] While the concern was not explicitly notified as resolved, it has not been raised in the SPS Committee since October 2013, indicating that bilateral consultations between Japan and the concerned Members allowed the parties to progress the issue.

The EU raised a concern about an import ban imposed by Russia without scientific evidence. In this case, Russia argued that there was scientific evidence and a risk assessment justifying the measure:

> In October 2012, the European Union raised a concern regarding measures taken by Russia to ban imports of live non-breeding pigs and ruminants from the whole EU territory and breeding pigs from part of the European Union due to alleged Brucella findings. Russia had not provided scientific evidence to justify the ban, nor information on the proportionality of the measure nor the negative effects the ban sought to limit. Russia had identified only two cases of concern related to live animals, which the European Union deemed insufficient to provide justification for the complete ban.[45]

While Russia maintained that the measure was justified, it declared itself to be 'ready for further dialogue with the European Union'.[46] Because the measure was not raised again in the Committee, it is likely that the two Members pursued discussions bilaterally.

Risk Assessment   Whether a measure is proportionate to a risk is discussed in the TBT Committee under 'necessity', as noted earlier. However, the SPS Agreement includes a specific article requiring Members to base their SPS measures on risk assessments, which requirement is to be read

---

[43] 'Paraguay – Japan's MRLs Applied to Sesame' (SPS ID 321, G/SPS/R/73), para. 3.49. See also Paraguay's written submission at G/SPS/GEN/1091.
[44] 'Paraguay – Japan's MRLs Applied to Sesame' (SPS ID 321, G/SPS/R/73), para. 3.51.
[45] 'Russian Federation – Import Ban on Live Animals from the EU' (SPS ID 338, G/SPS/R/69), para. 15.
[46] Ibid., para. 16.

together with that for scientific evidence. It is thus discussed separately in the SPS Committee and was cited in 35 per cent of SPS STCs during the period examined.

Assessment of the risks to human, animal or plant life or health allows a regulating Member to identify proportionate policy responses to specific issues. In this sense, risk assessments may provide evidence that a measure is necessary or non-discriminatory.

The EU considered the lack of a risk assessment to be evidence of the unnecessary nature of the Russian import ban on live animals: 'Russia had not provided a risk assessment warranting a total ban on imports, and the European Union asked Russia to lift the import ban on live breeding and non-breeding pigs.'[47]

Risk assessment can also be used to demonstrate the absence of discriminatory intent. This was the case, for instance, in a concern raised by the United States regarding a Philippine measure. Concerned about temperature requirements throughout the supply chain that were applied only to frozen and chilled meat, primarily imported, and not applied to fresh meat, the United States asked the Philippines to demonstrate its lack of discriminatory intent by sharing its risk assessment: 'The traceability, packaging and labelling requirements in both AO 22 and the new draft Administrative Order imposed additional burdens on the marketing and sale of frozen meat and meat products in the Philippines, yet there was apparently no risk assessment to support the adoption of these measures.'[48]

While a risk assessment allows a Member to justify a measure, that measure must still be proportionate to the risk evaluated. In this sense, while the Philippines responded that the measure was based on a US Department of Agriculture (USDA) risk assessment, the United States considered it to be disproportionate to the conclusions of that assessment:

> The United States noted that the measures, which the Philippines said were based in part on a USDA risk assessment, needed to be proportional to the risks identified in that risk assessment. The management tools and decisions by the Philippines went far beyond what was identified in the risk assessment, and the United States requested that the Philippines provide additional scientific evidence to justify its measures.[49]

The dialogue that took place in this STC helped both the concerned and regulating Members to understand the basis of the measure at stake and

---

[47] Ibid., para. 15.
[48] 'Philippines – Restrictions on Imported Fresh Meat' (SPS ID 320, G/SPS/R/63), para. 25.
[49] Ibid., para. 29.

then the best measure to be applied in light of the existing risk assessment. Members noted that they had engaged in 'constructive discussions' bilaterally[50] and the concern was not raised again in the Committee after October 2011.

Questions about Regulatory Impact Assessments and Other Good Regulatory Practices Finally, while good regulatory practices (GRPs) and RIAs more specifically are not legal obligations under the SPS or TBT Agreements, some concerns still ask regulating Members to observe GRPs or to provide information about the RIA performed.

For instance, the EU, raising a concern about China's Decree on the Application and Acceptance of Administrative Licensing for Cosmetics, urged China to adhere to GRPs: '[China's] delegation urged the SFDA [State Food and Drug Administration] to adhere to principles of good regulatory practice – for example, through a thorough regulatory impact assessment and public consultation, as well as notification of TBT-related measures to the TBT Committee while measures were still in draft stage, and comments could still be taken into account.'[51]

The United States, raising concern about the EU's proposal for categorisation of compounds as endocrine disruptors, asked that the EU share its impact assessment:

> The United States noted that the European Union planned to publish a road map outlining different options and a preliminary impact assessment in its process to assess, classify and regulate endocrine disruptors. The United States urged the European Union to swiftly notify the roadmap, any future proposals and the draft impact assessment, and to take into account comments from Members. The United States requested that the European Union explain its endocrine disruptor assessment program, particularly the timing for public consultations, as well as the timeframe for notifications and the manner in which Members' comments would be taken into consideration.[52]

These concerns about GRPs and RIAs show that Members use the STC mechanism to obtain evidence and potentially to encourage regulating Members to build further evidence before adopting a measure, even though such evidence is not a legal requirement.

---

[50] See 'US – Default MRLs, Limits of Determination or Limits of Quantification on Basmati Rice' (SPS ID 328, G/SPS/R/64), para. 76.
[51] 'China – Provisions for the Administration of Cosmetics Application Acceptance' (TBT ID 296, G/TBT/M/53), para. 103.
[52] 'EU – Revised Proposal for Categorization of Compounds as Endocrine Disruptors' (SPS ID 382, G/SPS/R/74), para. 4.3.

b   Measures No More Restrictive Than Necessary   While, on the one hand, the 'necessity' obligation under both SPS and TBT Agreements requires that the measure achieves a legitimate objective or is based on scientific evidence, on the other hand, the transparency obligation requires the measure be no more *restrictive* than necessary. In this regard, Members raising concerns in the SPS and TBT Committees may mention the additional burdens and costs that a measure imposes or flag the risk of duplicative requirements.

Significant Costs of Compliance   Members may explicitly refer to the extra burden and costs that a domestic measure imposes on producers. For example, India voiced concerns about the excessive cost that Italy's requirements on compulsory labelling of textile, leather and footwear products would entail: 'In particular, he was concerned that these criteria would be difficult to meet for an industry that relied on global and multiple sourcing. The cost of compliance for exporters from developing countries in particular, could make this labelling scheme more trade-restrictive than necessary to fulfil its legitimate objectives.'[53]

The extra burdens may be a result of the CAPs necessary to comply with the domestic measure. For example, India voiced concerns about the cost and time frame for Brazil's Good Manufacturing Practices (GMP) certification scheme for medical devices. India said that the measure:

> ... requires health products considered as having a 'higher risk' to present a certificate at the time of their registration proving compliance with Brazil's Good Manufacturing Practices (GMP certificate). [India] noted that ANVISA [the Brazilian Health Regulatory Agency] would be responsible for issuing these GMP certificates on the basis of inspections conducted by ANVISA at the production facilities.... India's traders found this certification process time consuming and expensive, reportedly costing more than USD 20,000, with an approval timeframe of as long as four years. India asked Brazil to explain why such a process should not be considered more trade-restrictive than necessary under the TBT Agreement's applicable disciplines.[54]

---

[53] 'Italy – Law on "Provisions Concerning the Marketing of Textile, Leather and Footwear Products" ' (TBT ID 272, G/TBT/M/52), para. 3.

[54] 'Brazil – Higher Risk Medical Devices Good Manufacturing Practice (GMP) Certification' (ID 429, G/TBT/M/63), para. 3.18.

Within the SPS Committee, the EU considered Malaysia's procedures for approval of foreign abattoirs to be burdensome: 'The process of approval for foreign abattoirs was unnecessarily lengthy and burdensome, and applications for approval were often not addressed by the Malaysian Department of Veterinary Service. In addition, EU exporters were confronted with a non-automatic import permit system which was unnecessarily lengthy and burdensome, and not transparent.'[55]

Delays in the performance of CAPs, including because of limited domestic quality control infrastructure, have been highlighted as potential unnecessary barriers to trade. For example, regarding Brazil's mandatory certification requirements for the security of electronic appliances, Mexico:

> ... was concerned about the excessive and unjustified cost imposed on Mexico's export industries by mandatory compliance ... [and] ... asked what considerations led Brazil to demand mandatory certification and use of the seal of conformity for these products. [Mexico] also sought information on the deadlines and timeframes required to obtain these certifications, and whether the necessary infrastructure existed in order not to create unnecessary barriers to trade through delays.[56]

Duplication A specific concern that is raised in relation to CAPs is what Members perceive to be unnecessary duplication of procedures.[57] Members have highlighted different forms of duplication, such as the need to perform the same or similar procedures more than once to get market access, the requirement for several overlapping certificates throughout the supply chain, when in-country testing is required in addition to existing testing already performed by internationally accredited laboratories under international systems, duplication between national and regional CAPs, and the general rejection of foreign CAPs.

For example, concerning procedures for energy-efficiency labelling of appliances under the US Energy Star Programme, Korea highlighted potential unnecessary barriers to trade resulting from the duplication of CAPs:

---

[55] 'Malaysia – Import Restrictions on Pork and Pork Products' (SPS ID 323).
[56] 'Brazil – Disposition (Portaria) n° 371, 29 December 2009 and Annex; INMETRO Approves Conformity Assessment Requirements for Security of Electronic Appliances' (ID 299, G/TBT/M/53), paras 120–4.
[57] These developments come from Marianna Karttunen and Devin McDaniels, 'Trade, Testing and Toasters: Conformity Assessment Procedures and the TBT Committee', *Journal of World Trade* 50, no. 5 (2016): 755–92.

The representative of Korea raised concerns regarding US draft requirements for accreditation bodies and testing laboratories in the Energy Star Program. It was Korea's belief that the additional requirement imposed by the US Environmental Protection Agency (EPA) was duplicative and unnecessary. The representative of Korea urged the United States to reconsider by allowing for the designation of accreditation bodies for Energy Star without an additional process involving ILAC/MRA accreditation bodies.[58]

Duplication can also arise between national and regional CAPs. For example, the United States mentioned the possibility of duplication between Saudi Arabia's certificate of conformity for toys and the Gulf Co-operation Council (GCC) Gulf Conformity Mark (or G-Mark) applied at the regional level:

> [T]he US had some concerns with respect to the lack of uniformity in transparency in the development of regional technical regulations and with the duplication of conformity assessment procedures – both regional and national being applied by some GCC members.... The US also expressed hope that any work at the GCC level would result in requirements that would be implemented in a consistent manner at the national level and that products would be mandated to test conformity with only one set of requirements.[59]

3 International Standards

Members cited international standards in 49 per cent of the TBT STCs and 51 per cent of the SPS STCs that they raised during the period examined. In line with the provisions of Articles 2.4 or 5.4 of the TBT Agreement and Article 3 of the SPS Agreement, Members use STC discussions to explore the relationship between a specific measure and relevant international standards, to better identify the rationale should other Members deviate from those standards or to encourage their implementation.[60]

---

[58] 'US – Conditions and Criteria for Recognition of Accreditation Bodies & Laboratories for the Energy Star Program' (ID 268, G/TBT/M/51), para. 21.

[59] 'Kingdom of Saudi Arabia – Certificate of Conformity (not notified) and GSO Marking Requirements for Toys' (TBT ID 435, G/TBT/M/63), paras 3.37–3.38.

[60] Wijkström and McDaniels underline three types of discussion that take place within the TBT Committee in relation to international standards: the concerned Member may challenge the regulating Member about a deviation from a standard (a 'challenge'); the regulating Member may cite an international standard to demonstrate presumed consistency with the TBT Agreement (a 'defence'); or the absence of international standard may be observed ('No (obvious) standard'). See Erik N. Wijkström and Devin McDaniels, 'Improving Regulatory Governance: International Standards and the WTO TBT Agreement', *Journal of World Trade* 47, no. 5 (2013): 1013–46.

Members sometimes take the opportunity to gather, in TBT Committee discussions, information about the relationship (and degree of alignment) between a given Member's CAP and international standards. Consider the example of the testing requirements under China's draft standard for carpets, in relation to which the EU 'sought clarification whether ISO 6347 had been adopted in its full integrity, without modification, or if certain aspects had been modified'.[61]

Members also question the reasons for departing from an international standard. In particular, Members identify what they perceive as specific deviations from relevant international standards in other Members' CAPs. For example, while voicing concern about Korea's certification procedure for thin-film solar panels, the United States:

> ... pointed out that while the Korean standard appeared to be based on the international standard IEC 61646, which also dealt with thin-film solar panels, the Korean standard only applied to one type of solar panel, amorphous silicon type thin-film solar panels, excluding other types of thin-film solar panels. He explained that as a result, other leading solar panels ... could not be tested or certified under the Korean standard and thus were not able to gain the necessary certification to be placed on the Korean market.[62]

Finally, Members may be more adamant in directly requesting that Members comply with a certain standard. For example, the EU noted the Dominican Republic's deviation from Codex Alimentarius and required the Republic to remedy that: '[T]he EU called for the draft regulation to be aligned with the Codex Alimentarius. At present the draft did not allow the use of processing aids, and it prohibited the use of sweeteners for some beverages, both of which were permitted under Codex.'[63]

Another example is a concern raised by Argentina regarding a ruling of the European Court of Justice (ECJ), which it considered to be contrary to international standards: 'Argentina stated that on 6 September 2011, the [ECJ] had adopted a new interpretation of the scope of EC Regulation No. 1829/2003, considering pollen derived from GM crops as an ingredient of honey and not a natural component. This was in conflict with the Codex standard for honey.'[64]

---

[61] 'China – National Standard of the People's Republic of China, Direction for Use and Labels for Carpets' (ID 280, G/TBT/M/52), para. 31.

[62] 'Korea – KS C IEC61646:2007 Standard for Thin-Film Solar Panels' (IMS ID 271, G/TBT/M/51), paras 33–4.

[63] 'Dominican Republic – Draft of the Technical Regulation "Categorization of Alcoholic Beverages" ' (TBT ID 333, G/TBT/M/56), para. 10.

[64] 'EU – EU Court of Justice Ruling Regarding Pollen Derived from GMOs' (SPS ID 327, G/SPS/R/71), para. 4.38.

At the second SPS meeting in which the STC was raised, the EU informed the Committee that a new directive was in progress that would address the concern: 'According to this proposal, pollen would be considered as a natural constituent of honey and, as such, would not need to be mentioned in the list of ingredients.'[65] The issue was no longer raised before the Committee.

The SPS Agreement additionally provides for a specific procedure that calls upon relevant international organisations or their subsidiary bodies to examine specific matters with respect to a particular standard. Members raising concerns about deviation from an international standard may take advantage of this opportunity to elicit feedback directly from the relevant international organisation. For example, India raised a concern about an import alert measure issued by the US Food and Drug Administration (FDA) because of the presence of a fungicide (tricyclazole), resulting in the detention of a shipment of basmati rice from India. India was worried because the measure resulted in huge losses to the exporter and it alleged that the residue limit for tricyclazole imposed under the US measure did not take into account the objective of minimising trade effects as required under Article 5.4 of the SPS Agreement. India therefore urged the Committee to invite the Codex Alimentarius Commission to examine the scientific basis of the US measure, because it argued that no international standards existed in relation to the issue. However, the chair of the SPS Committee informed India that the Committee had to decide by consensus whether or not to invite the Codex to intervene on this matter. The United States informed the Committee that the FDA was working with Indian authorities and rice export associations to address the issue. The concern has not been raised since July 2012.

4 Discrimination

The SPS Agreement prohibits arbitrary or unjustifiable discrimination between Members in identical or similar conditions. In other words, discrimination may be justified, in some circumstances, if the Members in question are subject to different 'conditions'. The TBT Agreement sets out, in Article 2.1, an obligation to accord 'treatment no less favourable than that accorded to like products of national origin and to like products originating in any other country'. As we saw in Part I, the WTO's Appellate Body has specified that a less favourable treatment may be justified if there is a 'legitimate regulatory distinction'.[66] Therefore, even

---

[65] Ibid.
[66] Appellate Body Report, *US – Clove Cigarettes*, §174.

though the prohibition of discrimination seems clearer than that of creating 'unnecessary barriers to trade', the regulating Member may be able to explain a difference of treatment.

In this sense, discrimination is an issue mentioned in discussions in the TBT and SPS Committees less frequently than necessity, international standards and transparency. Nevertheless, it was raised in 44 per cent of TBT STCs and 22 per cent of SPS STCs during the period examined.

In such cases, the concerned Member primarily questions the rationale behind what appears to be a differing treatment of foreign and domestic products. For instance, in the US STC taking issue with the Philippines' measure regarding meat products, the United States noted that:

> It was not clear why the prescribed cold chain requirement for frozen, chilled meat and chilled meat products, which are primarily imported, was not being equally applied to fresh meat. ... There seemed to be no scientific justification for this requirement, which appeared to discriminate against imports, and which undermined the food safety advantages of frozen meat.[67]

There are also STCs in which Members do not directly claim that a measure is discriminatory, but rather ask the regulating Member for further details on the measure, so that they can estimate whether there is a difference in the treatment of domestic and foreign exporters and whether this difference is discriminatory.

The EU asked Korea whether it had conducted an impact assessment for its measure on reducing carbon dioxide emissions and increasing motor vehicle fuel efficiency, and whether it had further details on the impacts it may have on foreign producers:

> Could Korea provide indications, in percentage points, as to the emission cuts to which imported car makers would be subject to on average, as compared to those required of domestic car makers? Her delegation estimated that EU carmakers would be subject to emission cuts more than double those applicable to domestic car makers. ... [W]hat measures were Korean authorities considering to take into account for the specific situation facing foreign car makers in Korea, so as to avoid negative impacts on imports?[68]

In another concern, the United States asked Viet Nam whether the same procedures applied to foreign and domestic producers: '[The US delegation] asked for confirmation whether any quality control procedures

---

[67] 'Philippines – Restrictions on Imported Fresh Meat' (SPS ID 320, G/SPS/R/63), para. 25.
[68] 'Korea – Automobile Standards of the Efficiency of Average Energy Consumption and Allowable Emission of Greenhouse Gases' (TBT ID 281, G/TBT/M/52), para. 37.

implemented were also applied to domestic producers and if that was the case, what mechanism was used to ensure that local producers undertake the same or comparable procedures.'[69]

Finally, Members also make reference in the SPS Committee under Article 5.5 of the SPS Agreement to inconsistent levels of protection under one measure compared with that under other domestic measures. India explicitly raised such a concern regarding a US import ban on an Indian shipment. Indeed, in the STC regarding the import ban on basmati rice because of the presence of the fungicide tricyclazole, India noted that 'Article 5.5 was not respected as the FDA permitted MRLs of Tricyclazole in rice bran, rice hulls and rice polishings of up to 30 ppm'.[70]

5 The Special Needs of Developing Countries

The SPS and TBT Agreements both recognise the particular challenges that developing countries may encounter when implementing their obligations. They therefore include articles on technical assistance, whereby Members 'agree to facilitate the provision of technical assistance to other Members'[71] or commit to 'advise other Members' and grant technical assistance,[72] and on special and differential treatment.[73]

The special needs of developing countries are seldom raised in STCs. It is an issue that might usefully be discussed in STCs highlighting negative trade impacts that a regulating Member may not have considered. However, only 4 per cent of STCs raised in the SPS Committee and 8 per cent in the TBT Committee raise the special needs of developing countries.

Developing countries tend to use STCs to underline the significant impact that they predict a given measure will have on their economy. Several developing countries typically join the concern to amplify it. This was the case, for instance, in a concern that Ecuador raised regarding the EU's regulation considering modifying the maximum level of cadmium in cocoa and cocoa products. While Ecuador cited issues such as its scientific rationale and consistency with international standards, it also mentioned the special needs

---

[69] 'Viet Nam – Conformity Assessment Procedures for Alcohol, Cosmetics, and Mobile Phones (Notice Regarding the Import of Alcohol, Cosmetics and Mobile Phones, No.: 197/TB-BCT (6 May 2011) and Ministry of Finance No.: 4629/BTC-TCHQ on the Importation of Spirits and Cosmetics (7 April 2011)' (ID 316, G/TBT/M/54), para. 125.

[70] 'US – Default MRLs, Limits of Determination or Limits of Quantification on Basmati Rice' (SPS ID 328, G/SPS/R/64), para. 47.

[71] Article 9 SPS.

[72] Article 11 TBT.

[73] Article 10 SPS; Art. 12 TBT.

of developing countries in the third meeting of the Committee discussing the STC. On this occasion, several other developing countries supported its point: 'Cameroon, Colombia, Cuba, Dominican Republic, Jamaica, Mexico, Nicaragua, Peru and Venezuela supported the concern by Ecuador, further noting that the EU measure would adversely affect the small and subsistence farmers and producers of cocoa in developing countries.'[74]

The issue is also raised systematically in STCs concerning tobacco products, amplifying the high reliance of developing economies on tobacco. For instance, in its written statement accompanying an STC against a proposed EU Directive on the manufacture, presentation and sale of tobacco and related products, Cuba underlined the effects the measure would have on developing economies, drawing attention:

> ... to the Resolution on Tobacco that was approved by the ACP [African, Caribbean and Pacific] Council of Ministers at its 97th Session on 5 June, in which this group of countries urged the EU to take into consideration the implications of its proposal for small, vulnerable and under-developed producing and exporting economies and invited it to reconsider its proposal, taking into account that it is more restrictive to trade than necessary to achieve its legitimate policy objectives. We hope that the voice of such an important group will be properly taken into account.[75]

Developed countries may also raise concerns about the effect that certain measures may have on developing countries. Although such concerns are uncommon, Japan cited that effect in relation to Korea's draft measure restricting the use of certain materials in PVC flooring material, wallpaper and toys: 'Japan was of the view that restrictions on cheap and useful PVC products could have a significant trade impact on many developing countries in the world.'[76]

These concerns demonstrate that flagging the effects a measure may have on developing countries can be an additional argument that supports concerns about the trade effects of a measure. It can also be the basis of a developing country's request for special provisions to mitigate the negative effects that it may experience. In this regard, Mexico questioned whether a US measure would take into account issues pertaining to the special needs of developing countries: '[The Mexican delegation]

---

[74] 'EU – Regulations on Cadmium in Cocoa' (SPS ID 325, G/TBT/R/69), paras 36–7.
[75] 'EU – Tobacco Products, Nicotine-Containing Products and Herbal Products for Smoking – Packaging for Retail Sale of Any of the Aforementioned Products' (TBT ID 377, G/TBT/W/365), para. 14.
[76] 'Korea – PVC Flooring Material and Wallpaper and Paper Linoleum, and Toys' (TBT ID 302, G/TBT/M/53), para. 135.

inquired whether the United States envisaged including within the law's implementation provisions aspects pertaining to special and differential treatment and technical assistance for developing countries.'[77]

C Addressing a Practical Impediment to Trade

Finally, a significant number of STCs address existing barriers to trade. In such cases, a conflict between the concerned Member and regulating Member already exists, but its discussion remains at the informal stage. The actual barriers to trade were discussed in the majority of SPS concerns (78 per cent), but far fewer TBT concerns (36 per cent), during the period examined (see Figure 5.3).

Among these concerns, some may raise complete import bans on certain products or restrictions to imports, while others simply flag the high costs that exporters are experiencing. In such cases, the concerned Members use STCs as a medium through which to entirely eliminate the barrier to trade.

A concern raised in the Committee supports efforts usually held bilaterally to re-establish trade between the concerned and regulating Member. For instance, India, in an STC about an import ban to the EU of mangoes and four of its vegetables, noted the situation in the Committee and expressed its willingness to find a solution:

> In July 2014, India noted that, as of 1 May 2014, the European Union had banned the import of mangoes and four other vegetables from India, on the grounds of the increasing number of interceptions of harmful pests and organisms in the consignments exported to the European Union. India had held discussions with the European Union to share information on the various control measures which it had taken to address this issue. The EU ban had been imposed prior to the consideration of the outcome of several alternative methods for treating mangoes, such as hot water treatments or irradiation. As a result, the entire mango crop destined for the EU market could not be exported. An EU technical team would visit India in September 2014 to inspect the various facilities and India welcomed an early solution to this concern.[78]

After reiterating discussions held in the Committee, the Dominican Republic voiced its concern over a similar situation it was also facing with

---

[77] 'United States – Food Safety Modernization (FSMA) Public Law 111–353' (TBT ID 300, G/TBT/M/53), para. 129.
[78] 'EU – Ban on Mangoes and Certain Vegetables from India' (SPS ID 374, G/SPS/R/75), para. 4.7.

the EU.[79] The STC was discussed at four meetings, but the EU maintained until the end that while the general import ban had been lifted, it continued to intercept harmful organisms in shipments from India, explaining its prohibition of imports.[80]

The STC may also allow a Member to request the application of a specific interim measure, particularly for products already imported into the market. South Africa, for instance, raised a concern regarding import restrictions on fresh fruits resulting from Thailand's Plant Quarantine Act, which prohibited imports of certain fresh produce until a pest risk analysis (PRA) had been completed. Thailand had in place an interim provision allowing the entry of those products that had already been imported to Thailand before the prohibition came into force, but South Africa had not managed to benefit from this arrangement: 'South Africa urged Thailand to apply the interim arrangement to its exports, and to conclude the PRA so that trade in the affected products could resume.'[81] Because the concern persisted for a year, Thailand suggested that the national plant protection organisations of both countries 'engage directly to find a mutually satisfactory solution to the issue'.[82] The issue was not raised again thereafter.

Beyond actual import bans, concerned Members may flag their difficulties in implementing measures, asking that the Committee take into account their specific situations. South Africa, for instance, noted that complying with an EU draft implementing regulation on the labelling and presentation of certain wine sector products was practically impossible for producers from the Southern Hemisphere:

> The 30 June 2012 deadline was problematic for South African producers because the 2012 wine harvest had already been completed in the southern hemisphere and labelling had already commenced. Furthermore, consignments of wine could take over a month to ship from South Africa to Europe. Without guidance and clarity on the labelling for individual EU member states, it would be difficult for exporters to comply with the current deadline. ... South Africa, therefore, requested the postponement of the implementation date for the labelling regulation of at least six months to allow a reasonable chance of compliance by South African exporters.[83]

[79] See G/SPS/R/79, para. 3.48.
[80] See G/SPS/R/81, para. 3.55.
[81] 'Thailand – Restrictions on Table Grapes, Apples and Pears' (SPS ID 326, G/SPS/R/64), para. 42.
[82] See G/SPS/R/69, para. 44.
[83] 'EU – Draft Implementing Regulations amending Regulation (EC) No. 607/2009 laying down detailed rules for the application of Council Regulation (EC) No. 479/2008 as regards protected designations of origin and geographical indications, traditional terms, labelling and presentation of certain wine sector products' (ID 345, G/TBT/M/57), para. 3.

This concern has persisted for four years and has been raised in no fewer than 21 Committee meetings by South Africa, New Zealand, Australia, Argentina, Brazil, Canada and the United States.

While this particular concern has not been solved, the reiteration by several Members of those concerns about practical impediments to trade may be seen as a useful means of putting pressure on the regulating Member to address the barrier.

Discussions between WTO Members in the context of STCs amplify the regulatory co-operation that takes place within the SPS and TBT Committees as a result of the transparency framework under the Agreements. Thanks to information shared in notifications or the sharing of information that was not notified, Members potentially affected by other Members' domestic measures are able to request further detail on domestic draft measures, suggest changes in legislation to mitigate the potential effects on trade or request urgent action to remove a barrier.

The content of these discussions is very much shaped by the subject matter of the SPS and TBT Committees – that is, TBT and SPS measures. Indeed, given the WTO's negative integration approach, Members retain their prerogative to adopt whatever measure they consider to be appropriate. And yet both Agreements use relatively vague provisions to ensure that trade effects are not excessive. Transparency is essential to pinning down the detail of such provisions and helping Members to arrive at balanced measures that fulfil domestic policy objectives without creating unnecessary barriers to trade.

The obligations set out in the SPS and TBT Agreements are the legal framework on which WTO Members rely when discussing STCs, even though these discussions have no legal consequence for WTO adjudicators. Indeed, the regulatory co-operation that takes place in the Committees remains limited to the obligations of transparency, necessity, international standards or non-discrimination. It is, however, a potent form of regulatory co-operation allowing WTO Members to enhance the implementation of the Agreements.

III When Is Transparency Enough? Those Cases that Do not Escalate to Formal Dispute Settlement

In the last section, we saw how the STC mechanism is largely used to seek clarification and transparency in relation to domestic regulations, to contribute to domestic regulatory procedures and to address practical impediments to trade. For which of these issues are STCs useful in and of themselves? In other words, when is transparency – as facilitated by

STCs – enough to solve trade frictions between countries without the need for formal dispute settlement?

The STC mechanism proves particularly effective in solving issues about those practical impediments to trade, or procedural questions or points of clarification, that are not perceived as so costly that they justify formal dispute settlement. Indeed, the majority of officially resolved SPS STCs are about such issues, whereas these are much less central in formal disputes. This is true of STCs officially declared as resolved in the SPS Committee or presumed resolved because of limited discussions in Committees.

The chair of the SPS Committee sends annual questionnaires encouraging Members to inform the Committee of STCs that have been 'solved'. Delegations to the SPS Committee therefore make declarations about officially resolved STCs, whereas a similar declaration procedure does not exist in the TBT Committee. There is therefore some indication of what types of SPS issue the mechanism of STC discussions helps to resolve (section A).

Overall, however, the number of officially 'solved' STCs remains very low. Limiting any examination of the efficiency of the mechanism to these explicitly resolved STCs would be to overly simplify matters. Indeed, some concerns are never reported as resolved, yet are raised only once or twice in the SPS and TBT Committees. When such STCs are not raised for several years after their first instance, it is safe to assume that the issue has been solved (section B).

A SPS STCs Explicitly Notified as 'Resolved': Addressing Procedural Questions and Practical Impediments to Trade

Resolved STCs are a valuable testament to the flexibility of WTO Members, who adapt to their trading partners' concerns to prevent regulations from imposing unnecessary costs. In total, between 1995 and 2018, 167 SPS STCs were reported as resolved, corresponding to around 37 per cent of the 452 STCs raised in the SPS Committee during that period. These resolved concerns were discussed very few times: on average, these 167 SPS STCs were each discussed 1.6 times (i.e. at no more than two Committee meetings).

Taking a closer look at STCs raised for the first time between 2010 and 2018, only 20 of 162 STCs were officially reported as resolved (around 12 per cent).[84] Certain of these concerns may be resolved, but not yet reported as such.

Some of these concerns relate to import bans or other concrete barriers to market access. In these cases, lifting the ban or eliminating the barrier

---

[84] In addition to STCs reported resolved, 33 STCs were reported as 'partially resolved'.

is an easy way of responding to the concern, if another mutually acceptable solution can be found. However, in some cases, the STCs relate to provisions under draft regulations that result in high trade costs. In such cases, the resolved STCs evidence that Members are willing to modify their regulations to mitigate their effect. Finally, it is worth mentioning that STCs get resolved regardless of the power dynamics and do not reflect large trading nations imposing their views on smaller nations.

1 Resolving Practical Impediments to Trade

The majority of concerns that get resolved are about concrete and ongoing barriers to trade. Indeed, 19 of the 20 SPS STCs reported resolved were about practical impediments to trade – that is, about trade barriers already having an effect. One explanation for this is that if the regulating Member eliminates the barrier, then in principle the concerned Member should be satisfied. This is confirmed by the typical length of time it takes to resolve a concern: between 2010 and 2018, STCs were reported resolved on average after being discussed in the SPS Committee no more than once – and sometimes not at all. This confirms that resolved STCs were mostly about pressing issues that Members make a particular effort to resolve in parallel to the Committee discussions, so that they make progress more quickly.

Typically, progress of this sort may be made when exporters are facing particularly burdensome procedures at the border, without sufficient justification. This was the case, for example, in relation to a concern raised by Nigeria regarding Mexican verification procedures for the import of hibiscus flowers. Nigeria reported burdensome and costly verification procedures in Mexico, and stated that it was prepared to request the 'good offices of the chair' if Mexico ignored its concern.[85] Mexico explained that it had changed its requirements because 14 shipments of hibiscus flowers had been accompanied by false SPS certificates. The delays that Nigeria was experiencing were because it was now necessary for Mexico to review and validate all such certificates. Ultimately, however, Mexico and Nigeria were able to resolve the issue bilaterally, both in the margins of the SPS Committee meetings and directly between their governments. Mexico confirmed that the two countries had 'exchanged documentation and had decided to improve communication and coordination at the national level, [and to] set up contact points'.[86] In March 2016, one year after it had initially raised the concern, Nigeria confirmed that the issue had indeed been resolved with Mexico.

---

[85] See G/SPS/R/81, paras 3.48–3.50.
[86] Ibid., para. 3.50.

In some cases, concerns may also be declared resolved because the domestic regulation has been modified, particularly when the concern relates to a draft regulation, for example one that has been notified to the WTO before its adoption. In that case, the STC-led discussion provides Members with an opportunity to comment on the draft and work towards a mutually acceptable final text.

This was the case with one concern raised by India and the EU against Chinese Taipei, which concern was reported resolved when the measure was still in draft form.[87] In this case, there were no actual effects on trade, but the draft was open for comments and could therefore still be amended to reflect other Members' concerns. The EU reported that the concern was resolved because Chinese Taipei notified a modified draft that took India's and the EU's comments into account.

The draft regulation established an MRL for a certain toxin (ochratoxin A) that is produced by mould in coffee. Chinese Taipei explained that the climate within its territory promoted the growth of mould in coffee, justifying a higher MRL. It confirmed that it had based the measure on a local background survey and a risk assessment. However, India, supported by the EU, alleged that the MRL was arbitrary, was not based on scientific evidence and differed from the relevant Codex standard.

In September 2012, two months after the concern was first raised before the SPS Committee, Chinese Taipei submitted a new notification, in which the measure had been amended to align MRLs with the recommendations of the EU and India. Chinese Taipei confirmed that the measure had entered into force at the end of August that year.

2 Resolved STCs: Raising Questions about International Standards, Scientific Justification and Control, Inspections and Approval Procedures

It has been noted that the majority of resolved STCs are about practical impediments to trade (19 of the 20 resolved between 2010 and 2018). The issues that get raised in these concerns are mostly about specific questions regarding international standards (60 per cent of the 20 SPS STCs resolved between 2010 and 2018), about the scientific justification of a measure (40 per cent) or about control, inspections and approval procedures (40 per cent). This aligns closely with the issues that are most

---

[87] 'Chinese Taipei – MRLs for Roasted and Powdered Coffee' (SPS IMS 334).

frequently raised in the SPS STCs in general, as shown in Figure 5.1. In other words, it seems that the issues most frequently raised in STCs are also those most likely to be resolved.

Those STCs that related to necessity, discrimination and risk assessment, however, were much less frequently resolved (15 per cent of those relating to necessity and 20 per cent for discrimination). These are also issues less frequently raised in SPS STCs in general, confirming the above conclusion.

As a consequence, risk assessment and discrimination are those issues most likely to be escalated to formal dispute.

3 Resolving Concerns Regarding Large or Small Trading Nations Alike

It is difficult to establish a clear pattern of the trading status of the countries resolving concerns because so few concerns have been resolved, particularly between 2010 and 2018. To some extent, we might conclude that the range of Members who have been satisfied as a result of the 20 STCs resolved over that period is indicative that resolution does not depend on larger economies imposing pressure on smaller ones. Indeed, on the contrary, the concerns that were resolved were almost indifferently raised by BRICS (Brazil, Russia, India, China and South Africa), industrialised and developing countries, with only three concerns raised by G2 countries (all by the EU).

For instance, bilateral discussions and an additional discussion within the SPS Committee resulted in resolution of a concern raised by Costa Rica against the United States. In March 2010, Costa Rica raised a concern regarding a US regulation that restricted imports of ornamental plants taller than 18 inches.[88] To export certain plants – namely, Dracaena marginata – to the United States without restrictions, Costa Rica conducted risk assessments. In addition, at the request of the United States, the two countries had set up a clean stock programme to reduce the volume of surveillance and inspections, and thus to limit the interceptions of Dracaena at the border. This programme had concluded its work in December 2008. Nevertheless, Costa Rica continued to experience restrictions for more than a year thereafter. In response to Costa Rica's concern, the United States explained in Committee discussions that it had been waiting for a progress report from Costa Rica before it

---

[88] 'United States – Prohibition of Ornamental Plants Larger than 18 Inches' (ID SPS 292).

could finalise the science-based review process. Costa Rica reported the concern resolved in July 2012, thanks to the United States' publication of a modified regulation.

Other examples of resolved STCs raised by smaller trading nations against their larger trading partners include Sri Lanka's concern regarding an EU measure[89] and Namibia's concern against South Africa.[90]

B STCs Assumed to Have Been Resolved Because of Short Discussions and Long Periods of Inactivity

The STCs declared as 'resolved' are most commonly discussed only once or twice within the Committees. Nevertheless, in both the SPS and TBT Committees, a large number of STCs that are raised no more than twice are not raised again in the next four years, even though no information exists on their resolution. This is the case for 261 of the 454 total TBT STCs raised between 1995 and 2014, and 234 of the 380 total SPS STCs.[91]

In the TBT Committee, STCs seem to be more easily resolved either when their subject matter is about only transparency or they relate to a potential trade barrier. Narrowing the period examined to 2010–2014,[92] 104 TBT STCs of the 196 (53 per cent) were discussed no more than twice. Of these resolved concerns, the majority of issues raised related to transparency (84 per cent) or the potential trade effects of a measure (76 per cent). Discussions about necessity or scientific rationale or legitimate interest were raised in around half of these presumably resolved STCs,[93] whereas issues about discrimination or actual implementation were not as easily resolved.[94] In other words, necessity and discrimination – which presumably may leave more scope for interpretation – require more extensive consultation.

---

[89] 'Sri Lanka – Restrictions on Cinnamon' (ID SPS 231).
[90] 'South Africa's Revised Veterinary Health Certificates for the Import of Cattle, Sheep and Goats from Botswana, Lesotho, Namibia and Swaziland' (ID SPS 404).
[91] For SPS STCs, this excludes the SPS STCs officially declared resolved or partially resolved.
[92] This shorter time span is used because detailed data was gathered as part of this author's PhD research for both SPS and TBT STCs between 2010 and 2014. In addition, if we are to assume that an STC is resolved, it is safer to focus on STCs that were discussed a few years ago, because more recent STCs may yet be raised again.
[93] Of the presumably resolved STCs, 50 per cent asked about the necessity of a measure and 49 per cent questioned the rationale or the legitimate interest behind a measure.
[94] Of the presumably resolved STCs, 32 per cent raised concerns about discrimination; 34 per cent were about actual implementation issues.

III WHEN IS TRANSPARENCY ENOUGH? 213

A notable share of SPS STCs seem to be resolved, whether officially declared such or not. Between 2010 and 2014, 48 of 92 SPS STCs (beyond those already declared resolved or partially resolved) were raised only once or twice. If we combine the figures of STCs officially declared as resolved and those discussed no more than twice, we can assume that 64 STCs of all STCs raised between 2010 and 2014 were resolved (70 per cent). These figures also appear to confirm that SPS STCs tend to be resolved when they are about practical impediments to trade, the scientific basis of the measure, international standards or control, inspections and approval procedures.

Overall, the STCs reported or assumed to have been resolved confirm that Committee discussions have undeniable potential to resolve trade frictions. This is especially true of SPS STCs concerning practical impediments to trade and of TBT STCs relating to transparency or potential barriers to trade. Looking only at 'minor' STCs that are discussed in the Committee no more than twice, 57 per cent of TBT STCs and 70 per cent of SPS STCs can be considered to be resolved. Beyond these, it is highly likely that many other STCs that are discussed in more than two Committee meetings have also been resolved, even though there is no official declaration as such. Indeed, focusing on 'serious' STCs raised in three or more meetings, Mavroidis and Wijkström find that 88 per cent of SPS STCs and 53 per cent of TBT STCs can be considered resolved.[95] It is important to note, however, that all of these figures are only estimations – and they are likely to be under-estimations.

---

[95] Horn, Mavroidis and Wijkström, 'In the Shadow of the DSU', 28–9.

Conclusion of Part II

Part II offered an overview of how WTO Members use the SPS and TBT transparency tools, and how these constitute the very basic levels of the SPS and TBT 'disputing pyramid'. The notifications centralised by the WTO are generally an important source of the information of which WTO Members – including a number of developing countries – make extensive use, but specific trade concerns (STCs) are still needed alongside these notifications if Members are to obtain further insights on the impacts of measures and in instances of non-notified measures. The 'cross-notification' that raising STCs in the SPS and TBT Committees grants to Members allows them to perform a monitoring role, ensuring that the measures of their trading partners are consistent with their WTO obligations. Scott refers to this as 'mutual accountability through mutual oversight'.[1] The technical and informal quality of the discussions in Committee largely allow this oversight to be non-confrontational, and this allows Members to co-operate towards mutually acceptable implementation of the SPS and TBT Agreements.

The presence of the private sector in the background to STCs underlines the concrete nature of the discussions. While the private sector does not have a formal role in the WTO negotiations or in dispute settlement, its role seems to be more openly acknowledged in TBT Committee discussions because of the undeniable source of information they represent regarding barriers to trade. This role is, however, still uneven among Members and this may partly explain the uneven use that Members make of STCs themselves.

Members extensively use the regulatory co-operation enabled by the transparency framework to obtain further information on each other's measures, to try to influence each other's domestic policies and, eventually, to address an existing trade effect. Those STCs officially declared as

---

[1] Joanne Scott, *The WTO Agreement on Sanitary and Phytosanitary Measures*, 46.

resolved confirm that STC discussions are particularly useful to address practical impediments to trade in the SPS Committee and to respond to transparency concerns or to prevent potential barriers to trade in the TBT Committee. Still, evidence on the resolution of the STCs remains unsatisfactory, because Members tend to under-report the outcomes of their discussions. Nevertheless, while only some issues are officially resolved, the scarcity of STCs that escalate to formal dispute confirms the usefulness of this mechanism as a means of managing conflicts between Members.

Even though an STC does not result in the change of a domestic regulation and in the 'resolution' of a dispute, it is important to recall that simply allowing WTO Members the opportunity to contribute to each other's regulatory processes in a transparent and multilateral setting is in itself a unique development in building an evidence basis for regulations, whatever the outcome of the regulatory process. Indeed, gathering inputs from foreign trading partners allows Members to build awareness about the likely unintended impacts of their measures beyond the border – although what the regulating Member ultimately decides to do with this information remains its prerogative.

The final part will move on to examine those cases that end up in formal dispute settlement. The fact that the majority of disputes are raised first in STCs confirms that there is a complementary relationship between transparency and dispute settlement. In this respect, Part III will explore the potential roles that transparency may play to equalise access to dispute settlement among all WTO Members.

PART III

Transparency as a Complement to Dispute Settlement

Information and Dialogue towards a Mutually Acceptable Solution

The formal dispute settlement system is a much better-known mechanism with which to solve trade conflicts than transparency. It is used frequently by WTO Members to obtain third-party adjudication over significant trade disputes and it is often referred to as the 'jewel' in the WTO's 'crown'. As in any judicial system, the tensions that are eventually raised before the WTO's Dispute Settlement Body (DSB) emerge well before a formal complaint is made before the adjudicator. We have seen in previous chapters that the transparency framework under the WTO Agreements on the Application of Sanitary and Phytosanitary Measures (SPS Agreement, or SPS) and on Technical Barriers to Trade (TBT Agreement, or TBT) is very comprehensive, and that WTO Members use it to resolve trade tensions and, to some extent, as a substitute for formal dispute settlement. However, in some cases, the tensions require intervention. Part III shows that, even in these cases, transparency remains an essential 'complement' to dispute settlement, often used in addition to, before, in parallel with or after dispute proceedings have terminated. Indeed, the SPS and TBT transparency mechanisms facilitate access to information and foster dialogue, thus allowing all WTO Members to learn more about the domestic contexts, both factual and legislative, behind trade frictions. This is all the more essential under the SPS and TBT Agreements, which allow Members to establish their own regulatory objectives while setting out requirements to 'rationalise' the development of the measures adopted to achieve these objectives, in the form of specific obligations of non-discrimination, necessity, scientific evidence and regulatory co-operation.

To illustrate the dynamics between transparency and dispute settlement, Chapter 6 will examine the sequence from transparency to dispute settlement and the general trends in the use of specific trade concerns

(STCs) or formal disputes. In so doing, it will highlight the distinguishing features of transparency and dispute settlement, and summarise their complementary roles.

Chapter 7 will present the factors generally perceived in existing literature to explain why some WTO Members have recourse to adjudication and, more specifically, why others do not. This will point towards the difficulty of accessing WTO dispute settlement, particularly for Members with fewer resources, and it will highlight the strong incentive that all WTO Members have to try to avoid dispute settlement as far as possible. On the basis of these factors, Chapter 8 will then consider how the transparency mechanisms under the SPS and TBT Agreements can address these specific challenges in accessing dispute settlement.

Finally, Chapter 9 will review to what extent the current transparency framework might yet be enhanced to ensure that transparency both complements and can be a substitute for dispute settlement, to the benefit of the entire WTO Membership.

6

Transparency and Disputes

Where Is the Difference?

Part II demonstrated the extent to which transparency is an effective non-judicial tool with which to ensure compliance with WTO obligations. We saw that Members do indeed manage to address the majority of their concerns within the transparency framework, either bilaterally or in the Committees. Of the issues raised as specific trade concerns (STCs), only 3 per cent end up at the tip of the 'disputing pyramid' – that is, brought before the WTO's Appellate Body. This chapter compares those frictions that escalate into full-blown disputes with those issues that get resolved within the transparency framework. It demonstrates that the two fora are complementary, used most commonly one after the other or in parallel. This is true of all requests for consultations that mention the WTO Agreements on the Application of Sanitary and Phytosanitary Measures (SPS Agreement, or SPS) and on Technical Barriers to Trade (TBT Agreement, or TBT), and it is all the more so when the main subject matter of the dispute is either of those Agreements. Generally speaking, STCs serve as a forum for dialogue that aims to reach a common understanding of WTO-compliant measures, whereas formal disputes are raised when agreement cannot be reached, and allow Members to seek a clear and authoritative interpretation from a third party. All country groups tend to participate in both fora, while developing countries are most active in trying to solve an issue through an STC before pursuing dispute settlement. Overall, by means of an empirical study of Members' activities in practice, this chapter confirms the importance of regulatory co-operation to the effective implementation of the SPS and TBT Agreements.

After summarising the trends in the use of STCs and of requests for consultations (section I), the chapter goes into more depth on those disputes that centre on SPS and TBT claims to highlight the significance of transparency mechanisms within them (section II). In general, the chapter demonstrates that the majority of SPS and TBT disputes are also tackled within the SPS and TBT Committees as STCs, either first or in parallel, confirming that the STC mechanism is systematically complementary to dispute settlement – especially when disputes centre substantively on SPS and TBT issues.

I From STCs to Requests for Consultations: A Systematic Sequence?

The general trends in SPS and TBT STCs and disputes show that there is, overall, a tendency towards STC dialogue before or in parallel to dispute proceedings, confirming a complementary role between transparency and dispute settlement (section A). There are some differences between the two fora in terms of the issues that are raised (section B), and while most developed countries tend to be most active in both contexts, there is still a tendency – particularly among developing countries – to try to solve issues first in an STC before submitting a formal request for consultations (section C).

A General Trends in SPS and TBT STCs and Disputes

A close look at the disputes that are raised before the WTO's Dispute Settlement Body (DSB) confirms that STCs are used frequently, if not systematically, to solve trade frictions in a less formal setting. The STCs raised in the SPS Committee tend to complement requests for consultations more commonly than do those raised regarding TBT matters (section 1). The issues raised are also slightly different depending on whether they are raised as STCs or requests for consultation, illustrating that STCs facilitate dialogue towards a common understanding of WTO-compliant measures, whereas formal disputes are raised when agreement cannot be reached and Members need a clear and authoritative interpretation from a third party (section 2).

1 Committee Discussions Preceding a Majority of SPS Disputes

Members affected by another country's SPS measures tend to seek a solution in the SPS Committee rather than raise a formal dispute, confirming the complementary role of the SPS STC mechanism in relation to formal dispute settlement. Of 48 disputes raising SPS issues, 31 were first raised as STCs in the SPS Committee (i.e. 65 per cent). Of these same 48 disputes, only 12 were about measures that had been notified, 8 of which were notifications submitted before the request for consultation.

I FROM STCs TO REQUESTS FOR CONSULTATIONS

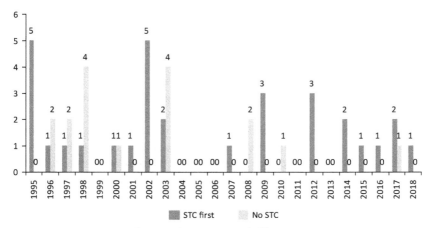

Figure 6.1 SPS requests for consultations preceded by STCs, 1995–2018.
Source: www.wto.org/english/tratop_e/dispu_e/dispu_agreements_index_e.htm.

This trend has been true since the very establishment of the SPS Committee. Figure 6.1 shows that, in 1995, Members had already started to raise SPS STCs before making any request for consultations.

In fact, even the first disputes and STCs raised in the early years of the WTO itself confirm the complementarity between transparency and dispute settlement, both of which are used in parallel by the same countries to address the same issues. Indeed, five requests for consultations were submitted that first year, all of which were discussed in the Committee as well:

- Korea – Measures Concerning the Testing and Inspection of Agricultural Products (DS3);
- Korea – Measures Concerning the Shelf-Life of Products (DS5);
- Australia – Measures Affecting Importation of Salmon (DS18);
- Korea – Measures Concerning Bottled Water (DS20); and
- Australia – Measures Affecting the Importation of Salmonids (DS21).

The three disputes raised regarding Korean measures did not end up in formal dispute settlement; they seem to have been solved at some point between the Committee discussions and the consultations. Indeed, the minutes of the Committee confirm that the two fora played a complementary role, preventing the dispute from escalating to the next level of the disputing pyramid – that is, being brought before a panel. This is particularly true of the two disputes between the United States and Korea, relating to inspections and testing methods (DS3),[1] and the government-mandated shelf life of certain products (DS5).[2] In Committee discussions parallel to the STC, Korea noted that the disputes were caused by 'ambiguities and lack of clear guidance'[3] in the implementation of the SPS Agreement. In particular, Korea informed the other WTO Members and WTO Secretariat that these issues were being discussed in the context of the consultations, but that the consultations had not been successful in solving some of the ambiguities, such as which were the relevant international standards or which country's approach was appropriate, given a range of different practices among different Members. Finally, Korea concluded that it was the 'task of the committee to shed light on such aspects in the implementation of the Agreement'.[4] The parties to the disputes reported, in July 1995 and April 1996, that they had found a mutually agreed solution, but both matters continued to be discussed in the SPS Committee both as STCs and bilaterally. Ultimately, the United States reported the two concerns resolved in 2001.

The other two requests for consultations submitted in 1995 related to Australian measures. These two disputes, raised by the United States and Canada against Australian measures affecting the importing of salmonids, resulted in the establishment of a panel. The STC in this dispute was raised after the request for consultation was made,[5] confirming a willingness among Members to discuss the matter in parallel to formal consultations, in the presence of the WTO Secretariat and of all other WTO Members. The discussions in the Committee illustrated how difficult Canada, the United States and Australia found it to agree on an appropriate level of protection from diseases.[6] Ultimately, this dispute escalated to the very tip of the disputing pyramid, resulting in a hearing before the Appellate Body report between Canada and Australia, with the United States intervening as a third party. While there had been less discussion in the Committee than in the Korean cases, the concern remained pending before both the Committee and the DSB until Australia adopted an amendment to its

---

[1] The related STC was 'Korea – Import Clearance Measures and Practices' (SPS IMS 2).
[2] The related STC was 'Korea – Shelf-Life Requirements' (SPS IMS 1).
[3] WTO SPS Committee, 'Summary of the Meeting Held on 26–27 June 1995' (G/SPS/R/2, 18 July 1995), para. 40.
[4] Ibid.
[5] 'Australia – Ban on Salmon Imports' (SPS IMS 8).
[6] See WTO SPS Committee, 'Summary of the Meeting Held on 8–9 October 1996' (G/SPS/R/6, 14 November 1996), paras 13 et seq.; WTO SPS Committee, 'Summary of the Meeting of 19–20 March 1997' (G/SPS/R/7, 29 April 1997), paras 58 et seq.

quarantine policies on fresh, chilled and frozen salmonids in May 2000. After it introduced this new measure, both Canada and the United States notified the DSB that they and Australia had reached a mutually satisfactory solution, and that the concern raised in the SPS Committee was resolved.[7]

Between 2009 and 2018, of 15 SPS disputes raised, only one request for consultation was made citing the SPS Agreement without an STC having first been raised in the SPS Committee – namely, Ukraine – Measures Relating to Trade in Goods and Services (DS525) – and neither was this dispute raised in the TBT Committee, making it one of the rare examples in which transparency was not used at all to complement dispute settlement. Nevertheless, this one exception is not enough to invalidate the general trend in SPS disputes: the STC mechanism is used not only in a large number of cases to resolve issues before they escalate into formal disputes but also almost systematically in parallel with dispute settlement even when formal disputes are raised.

2 TBT Committee Discussions Increasingly Complementing Dispute Settlement, Although not Systematically

In the context of TBT disputes, significantly more requests for consultations are raised without first being raised as STCs than is the case for SPS disputes. In total, 60 per cent of requests for consultations are made without first discussing the same matter in the TBT Committee or discussing it in parallel. This was particularly true in the first years of the WTO, likely because the STC mechanism was used in the TBT Committee only infrequently at that time. Indeed, until 1997, the 14 first requests for consultations were made without first being raised as STCs, as illustrated in Figure 6.2. Unlike the systematic approach taken towards SPS disputes, practice in relation to TBT matters has evolved only slowly towards a more consistent use of transparency to complement dispute settlement.

Between 2009 and 2018, however, the trend leaned more consistently towards transparency mechanisms. Of 17 requests for consultations made in relation to TBT claims, only 5 were not raised first or at the same time in the TBT Committee. These five disputes (which will be discussed more in depth later in the chapter) suggest that there are still some issues that Members do not even try to discuss in the extra-judicial STC space. Those 12 requests for consultations that were accompanied by transparency mechanisms do, however, confirm a broader steer away from relying only on formal dispute settlements to resolve conflicts.

---

[7] WTO, 'Australia – Measures Affecting the Importation of Salmonids: Notification of Mutually Agreed Solution' (WT/DS21/10, 1 November 2000).

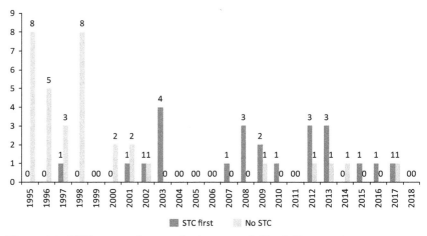

Figure 6.2 TBT requests for consultations preceded by STCs, 1995–2018.
Source: Author's own based on www.wto.org/english/tratop_e/dispu_e/dispu_agreements_index_e.htm.

B Issues Raised in STCs and Disputes

The issues raised within the transparency framework by means of STCs are not systematically the same as those that are commonly raised in dispute settlement, as illustrated in Figures 6.3 and 6.4. This suggests that the two different fora have different purposes and may be used in different circumstances. Nevertheless, a common trait persists between the two: STCs are used systematically to raise issues about a measure's consistency with core obligations under the SPS and TBT Agreements that require further information and which may be solved through a better understanding of mutual perspectives. This is particularly the case regarding SPS and TBT obligations requiring transparency, necessity or a scientific justification, and TBT obligations regarding international standards. Formal disputes tend to be raised for issues requiring clarification from a third party. This is the case, for instance, regarding risk assessment – an issue that is raised in the majority of SPS disputes, yet far less frequently in STCs.

However, the approaches taken in relation to SPS and TBT issues differ considerably. On the one hand, TBT STCs grant the Committee a more active role in most issues, and unnecessary barriers to trade, international standards, transparency, discrimination and a reasonable interval to adapt are all raised more frequently in the TBT Committee than

I   FROM STCS TO REQUESTS FOR CONSULTATIONS   225

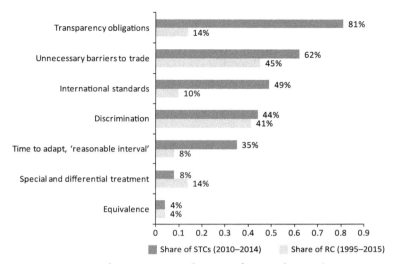

Figure 6.3 Issues raised in TBT STCs and requests for consultations.[8]
Source: Author's own based on TBT Committee minutes, TBT IMS, http://tbtims.wto.org, and www.wto.org/english/tratop_e/dispu_e/dispu_agreements_index_e.htm.

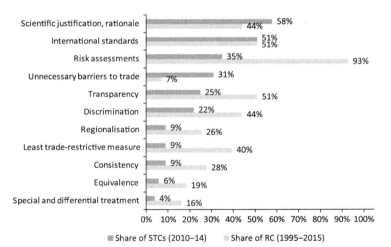

Figure 6.4 Issues raised in SPS STCs and requests for consultations. Source: Author's own based on SPS Committee minutes, SPS IMS, http://spsims.wto.org/, and www.wto.org/english/tratop_e/dispu_e/dispu_agreements_index_e.htm.

[8] The data on the issues raised in STCs has been adapted to make it comparable with the data available on requests for consultations. It therefore differs slightly from that presented in Part II: the transparency obligations in this figure include concerns related to all obligations under Arts 2.9–2.11 TBT.

in requests for consultations. As Figure 6.3 shows, the only issue more frequently raised in TBT requests for consultations than in STCs is special and differential treatment. On the other hand, SPS STCs are used less often to compensate for issues that are not raised in requests for consultations. Indeed, the majority of issues are raised more frequently in requests for consultations than in STCs (see Figure 6.4).

The core obligations of the TBT Agreement are all raised in a substantial number of STCs. On the one hand, this may be because of the 'fuzziness' of these obligations – that is, the difficulty in establishing their legality – and the importance of dialogue between Members to identify whether or not measures are consistent with obligations under the Agreement. In such a situation, it may be more apt to make use of a transparent dialogue, in the presence of other WTO Members, than to resort to dispute settlement, which has an uncertain outcome. This can typically be the case for international standards, which are discussed in a high proportion of STCs (62 per cent), whereas they are raised only in 10 per cent of TBT requests for consultations. Indeed, as seen in Part I, the language on international standards in the TBT Agreement is particularly open-ended, including in the scope of the Agreement neither a specific definition nor explicit reference to international standardising bodies. It is therefore a legal principle under which the absence of clear-cut obligation calls for dialogue rather than third-party adjudication. Indeed, Part II shows that STCs related to international standards tend to examine the relationship between a specific measure and relevant international standards, aiming to better identify the rationale behind other Members' deviations from international standards or to encourage their implementation. Solutions to such concerns may be achieved through STC dialogue and hence these instances do not necessarily call for authoritative interpretation by a third-party adjudicator.

On the other hand, TBT STCs serve as a more appropriate tool to achieve timely reactions to a trade concern that has immediate consequences, but which does not have a substantive economic impact. In particular, while 14 per cent of TBT requests for consultations include claims related to transparency obligations, a massive 81 per cent of TBT STCs relate to transparency. A reasonable interval for traders to adapt to new requirements is mentioned in 35 per cent of STCs, whereas it is raised in only 8 per cent of TBT requests for consultations. An alleged breach of transparency obligations or requiring a 'reasonable interval' to adapt to a new regulation may receive more rapid and adequate attention if raised as an STC, the remedial action required typically being notification of the measure or a delay to its entry into force. Dispute settlement, which may entail a lengthy process,[9] is disproportionate to the goals in such 'minor' cases. Nevertheless, we shall see that, in some cases, such as when breaches of transparency are systematic and enduring, then there is more reason to escalate them to the level of dispute.[10]

Surprisingly, STCs and requests for consultations are used slightly differently in the SPS Committee. Like TBT STCs, STCs are used at least as often as, if not more often than, formal disputes for SPS issues that require further information and which may be solved through a better understanding of mutual perspectives. This is certainly the case where the scientific justification, rationale or necessity of a measure is in question. Indeed, as we have seen, raising concerns on such issues is key to deciding whether or not the measure is justified under the SPS Agreement. A concern may therefore be raised to obtain from the regulating Member further information to better explain the rationale or the necessity of a measure – and the explanation may be sufficient to resolve the matter.

However, the specific differences emerging in relation to those core obligations are unique to the SPS Agreement. Broadly speaking, SPS requests for consultations are more detailed than SPS STCs, covering more issues than are raised in STCs. As mentioned in Part II, SPS STCs are commonly used to solve practical issues with implementation – that is, issues that Members have encountered when implementing other Members' SPS measures; SPS disputes, however, are more commonly raised for complex issues that require clarification from a third party. The most striking issue raised more commonly in dispute settlement than in SPS STCs is risk assessment – an issue raised in 93 per cent of requests for consultations, yet only 35 per cent of STCs. Risk assessment is a core principle of the SPS Agreement, ensuring that domestic regulations are based on science rather than arbitrarily conceived. At the same time, as we saw in Part I, while the SPS Agreement

---

[9] Horn, Johanesson and Mavroidis calculated the average lengths of each stage of the WTO dispute settlement proceedings for cases between 1995 to 2010. They found that the average length of delay for consultations was 164.6 days (5.5 months) and the average for panel proceedings was 444.9 days (14.7 months) – far longer than the statutory deadlines of 60 days and 180 days, respectively: See Henrik Horn, Louise Johannesson and Petros C. Mavroidis, 'The WTO Dispute Settlement System 1995-2010: Some Descriptive Statistics', IFN Working Paper No. 891, 16 November 2011, 44. www.ifn.se/wfiles/wp/wp891.pdf.

[10] See e.g. Russia – Measures Concerning the Importation and Transit of Certain Ukrainian Products (DS532).

introduced a reliance on scientific evidence to rationalise regulatory interventions, Members still only vaguely understand what 'sufficient' scientific evidence is under the terms of the SPS Agreement – and that means that an adjudicator must clarify the provision. The volume of cases brought to dispute proceedings to seek interpretation of the provisions on risk assessment confirms that Members perceive the WTO dispute settlement system to be better suited to solving such issues than are bilateral or STC-driven discussions. The majority of other SPS core principles – namely, least trade-restrictive measure, consistency, regionalisation and equivalence – are also the substance of considerably more requests for consultations than STCs, confirming that WTO Members generally prefer to seek the WTO adjudicator's interpretation of these principles and their specific meaning in the SPS context.

C Participating Members

The differences among Members' use of transparency mechanisms and dispute settlement also highlight the distinctions and the dynamics between the two.

Again, the different practices between the SPS and TBT Committees are striking. Focusing merely on STCs, developing countries seem to employ SPS STCs to avoid dispute settlement, whereas developed countries (both the G2 and IND) most actively use TBT STCs and developing countries (DEV) participate mostly in support of STCs raised by other Members.

However, the benefits of STCs in comparison to dispute settlement emerge more clearly when examining the path from one to the other. Indeed, in both SPS and TBT Committees, developing countries tend to try to solve issues through STCs before escalating an issue to dispute settlement. For SPS measures, this is a general trend for most country groups; for TBT measures, the G2 stands apart, submitting most of its disputes directly to the DSB. The most intuitive explanation for this is that STCs offer developing countries a less burdensome way of resolving an issue than dispute settlement. Developed countries, however, may have the resources to gather the necessary evidence and better capacities to build a legal case to support immediate escalation of an issue to formal dispute. In addition, developed countries may also have other alternative fora in which to solve their frictions, such as in the context of bilateral trade agreements.

In exploring the number and ways in which Members participate in STCs and requests for consultations, we can accurately reflect the number of countries that take the initiative by raising a 'bilateral' concern with the

1 FROM STCs TO REQUESTS FOR CONSULTATIONS

regulating Member.[11] Unlike previous literature on country participation in STCs, we will distinguish Members *launching* a concern from Members *supporting* a concern.[12] By distinguishing between Members in this way, we can explore additional detail in which Members play a more active role in initiating a dialogue and which benefit from the STCs that others launch.

Members launching a concern can be defined as those that demonstrate substantial concern with the STC from the first Committee meeting at which it is discussed. This implies that the launching Member has taken the initiative and asked the WTO Secretariat to put an item on the agenda of the meeting. In other words, to raise such a concern, the Member must have gathered information about the measure and its potential effects, either by means of a notification or through its own independent research.

The WTO Secretariat distinguishes between 'launching' and 'supporting' Members for SPS STCs in its SPS Information Management System (IMS), but it does not make the same distinction for TBT STCs. In this book, then, we distinguish between the two based on the substance of TBT Committee meeting minutes. For this same reason, the period examined in relation to STCs is limited to 2010–2014.[13] Nevertheless, given the higher volume of STCs than of disputes, the five-year time frame helps to give us a broad idea of countries' practice in these Committees.

For requests for consultations, the time period examined is 1995–2018, to reflect all requests for consultations made in relation to SPS and TBT claims since the WTO's establishment.

1 Members Active in SPS STCs and Disputes

There were 225 bilateral STCs raised in the SPS Committee between 2010 and 2014. Of these, 104 were raised by Members launching the concern and 121 by supporting Members.[14] Further details are summarised in Tables 6.1 and 6.2.

Contrary to the dispute settlement system, in which they are overwhelmingly the most active groups in both submitting and defending

---

[11] This is consistent with previous literature regarding WTO dispute settlement: Henrik Horn, Petros C. Mavroidis and Håkan Nordström, 'Is the Use of the WTO Dispute Settlement System Biased?', in Petros C. Mavroidis and Alan O. Sykes, eds, *The WTO and International Trade Law/Dispute Settlement* (Cheltenham: Edward Elgar, 2005), 454–86; Henrik Horn, Louise Johannesson and Petros C. Mavroidis, 'The WTO Dispute Settlement System 1995–2010: Some Descriptive Statistics', *Journal of World Trade* 45, no. 6 (2011): 1107–38.

[12] Sofia Boza and Felipe Fernández, 'Development Level and WTO Member Participation in Specific Trade Concerns (STCs) and Disputes on SPS/TBT', SECO/WTI Working Paper No. 2014/17, 16 June 2014. https://papers.ssrn.com/sol3/papers.cfm?abstract_id=2618535.

[13] For the sake of comparison, the same time frame was adopted for both SPS and TBT STCs.

[14] The WTO Secretariat distinguishes between 'launching' and 'supporting' Members in SPS IMS. The Secretariat's classification was used in this regard.

Table 6.1 *Participation in SPS STCs, 2010–2014*[15]

Country Group	Launching STC	%	Supporting STC	%	Total Concerns	%	Maintaining the Measure	%
BRICS	37	36	12	10	49	22	37	17
DEV	22	21	54	45	76	34	25	11
G2	25	24	18	15	44	20	100	45
IND	19	18	33	28	52	23	58	26
LDC	1	1	3	3	4	2	1	0
'Certain Members'[16]	0	0	0	0	0	0	3	1
TOTAL	104	100	120	100	225	100	224	100

Source: Based on SPS Committee minutes, SPS IMS, http://spsims.wto.org/.

[15] This data is based on 'bilateral' SPS STCs, i.e. counting each Member launching or supporting a concern as raising an individual STC against the regulating Member. Percentages are rounded.
[16] In a few particular cases, SPS STCs are launched against 'certain Members' without clearly identifying which ones.

Table 6.2 *Participation in SPS requests for consultations, 1995–2018*[17]

Country Group	Complainant	%	Respondent	%
BRICS	5	10	5	10
DEV	10	21	3	6
G2	16	33	18	38
IND	17	35	22	46
LDC	0	0	0	0
TOTAL	48	100	48	100

Source: Based on classification www.wto.org/english/tratop_e/dispu_e/dispu_agreements_index_e.htm.

requests for consultations, the G2 and IND countries are much less dominant in raising or supporting SPS STCs. Indeed, in the period examined, the total engagement of Members at different levels of development is relatively even: with the exclusion of least-developed countries (LDCs), which are completely absent from SPS STCs as they are from dispute settlement, the other four country groups are quite similarly active, all participating in more than 20 per cent of SPS STCs.

The BRICS (Brazil, Russia, India, China and South Africa) are the most active in launching SPS STCs (36 per cent), whereas the developing countries are most active in supporting such concerns (45 per cent). The country group most active in both launching and supporting concerns are developing countries, with a total of 34 per cent of bilateral SPS STCs. Developing countries are, however, the least active country group (with the exclusion of the LDCs) in raising requests for consultations. While the LDCs are wholly absent from formal disputes, they have participated in both launching and supporting STCs, albeit very scarcely. Only one SPS STC was raised in the period by an LDC – by Senegal against the United States, in relation to a US import ban on tomatoes affecting Senegal.[18]

The European Union (EU) and the United States (i.e. the G2) are most commonly the subject of concerns, responding to 45 per cent of all SPS STCs in the period examined.

---

[17] This data presents Members launching and responding to a request for consultation with an SPS claim between 1995 and 2018. The data does not take into account third parties to the disputes. Percentages are rounded.

[18] 'United States – Restrictions on Tomatoes' (ID 339), raised in the SPS Committee on 18 October 2012.

Looking more closely at requests for consultations relating to SPS claims, it is striking to compare which country groups first raised an STC and which did not. The overwhelming majority of both the G2 and developing Members pursue an STC before raising a request for consultations.[19] For emerging and industrialised economies, however, that same majority is marginal, probably because of the heterogeneity of these country groups.[20]

2 Members Active in TBT STCs and Disputes

The country groups raising concerns in the TBT Committee differ slightly from those raising concerns in the SPS Committee, with developed countries most commonly launching concerns and requests for consultations in the TBT space. Indeed, in the TBT Committee, developed countries – both G2 and IND – are much more active than developing countries in launching concerns (the G2 and IND together launching 75 per cent of TBT STCs). In addition, it is notable that the EU and the United States raise the most concerns against Members outside the G2. This contrasts with the requests for consultations that the two make, which are commonly within the G2, suggesting that while these two members do have concerns with other Members' measures, they choose not to escalate them to the level of formal disputes.

The general figure for developing countries supporting TBT STCs reaches 31 per cent of TBT STCs, but their total appearances in the STCs – that is, their role in both launching and supporting STCs – still remain below those of both G2 and IND.

In the TBT Committee, LDCs have participated in more STCs than in the SPS Committee, with a total of 13 appearances both as launching and supporting Members. All of these instances relate to tobacco products.[21]

---

[19] This is especially true of developing countries, for whom 8 out of 10 requests for consultations were first raised as STCs. For G2 Members, 11 out of 16 requests for consultations were raised in the SPS Committee.

[20] The BRICS countries submitted 5 SPS requests for consultations, 3 of which were also raised in STCs; industrialised countries submitted 17 SPS requests for consultations, 9 of which were also raised in STCs.

[21] These 13 appearances make reference to bilateral STCs, therefore counting as separate STCs all concerns that are raised by several Members at once. These STCs are: 'Brazil – Draft Resolution No. 112, 29 November 2010; Maximum Levels of Tar, Nicotine and Carbon Monoxide Permitted on Tobacco Products and Prohibition of Additives' (ID 288); 'Australia – Tobacco Plain Packaging Bill 2011' (ID 304); 'New Zealand – Proposal to Introduce Plain Packaging of Tobacco Products in New Zealand' (ID 361); 'European Union – Tobacco Products, Nicotine Containing Products and Herbal Products for Smoking; Packaging for Retail Sale of Any of the Aforementioned Products' (ID 377); 'United Kingdom – Proposal to Introduce Plain Packaging of Tobacco Products' (ID 424); 'France – Proposal to Introduce Plain Packaging of Tobacco Products' (ID 441).

They did not, however, submit any requests for consultations, even though some of them intervened in the cases as third parties (Tables 6.3 and 6.4).[22]

Despite the less active role of developing countries in launching STCs – in comparison with other country groups – that role is still noteworthy in that, as they are in the SPS Committee, developing Members are very consistent in launching STCs in complement to dispute settlement procedures, either before or after submitting a request for consultations. Indeed, of the 11 requests for consultations made by developing Members, 8 were also discussed as STCs in the TBT Committee. Meanwhile, G2 countries behave quite differently in the TBT Committee compared with the SPS Committee, with only 2 of their 14 requests for consultations making claims that had also been discussed in TBT STCs.

The general trends in country groups offer a broad overview of the uses countries at different levels of development make of STCs and formal dispute mechanisms. Nevertheless, the heterogeneity of the groups – in particular DEV and IND – makes it difficult to draw clear conclusions. Indeed, the activity of a country group is likely to be promoted by a few well-organised Members within it. The next section aims to give insight into specific country practices, with a focus on a selection of SPS and TBT disputes.

II SPS and TBT Requests for Consultations: An Overview of Transparency Steps

Of a total of 102 SPS and TBT requests for consultations, 57 were also discussed in STCs. While this is only just over half, the figure may be skewed by the fact that the actual disputes may include only 'minor' SPS and TBT claims. If this is the case, Members may not have felt the need to raise the issue within the SPS or TBT Committees. However, it is difficult to determine whether a claim is 'major' or 'minor' in requests for consultations. Indeed, there is no access to the content of the confidential discussions that take place between the parties to requests for consultations; their arguments are made public only if the dispute goes on to be heard

---

[22] For example Malawi was a third party in Australia – Certain Measures Concerning Trademarks, Geographical Indications and Other Plain Packaging Requirements Applicable to Tobacco Products and Packaging (DS467); both Malawi and Zambia participated as third parties in Australia – Certain Measures Concerning Trademarks, Geographical Indications and Other Plain Packaging Requirements Applicable to Tobacco Products and Packaging (DS435) and Australia – Certain Measures Concerning Trademarks and Other Plain Packaging Requirements Applicable to Tobacco Products and Packaging (DS434).

Table 6.3 *Participation in TBT STCs, 2010–2014*

Country Group	Launching STC	%	Supporting STC	%	Total Appearances	%	Members Maintaining the Measure	%
BRICS	36	10	21	11	57	10	125	23
DEV	48	13	57	31	105	19	144	26
G2	145	41	29	16	174	32	147	27
IND	122	34	73	39	195	36	128	24
LDC	7	2	6	3	13	2	0	0
TOTAL	358	100	186	100	544	100	544	100

Source: Based on TBT Committee minutes, series G/TBT/M/, TBT IMS, http://tbtims.wto.org.

Table 6.4 *Participation in TBT requests for consultations, 1995–2018*

Country Group	Complainant	%	Respondent	%
BRICS	6	11	4	7
DEV	11	20	5	9
G2	14	26	31	57
IND	23	43	14	26
LDC	0	0	0	0
TOTAL	54	100	54	100

Source: Based on www.wto.org/english/tratop_e/dispu_e/dispu_agreements_index_e.htm.

before a panel or the Appellate Body, which is not always the case. This section therefore focuses on those disputes in which SPS or TBT measures were the major subject matter of disputes discussed before panels and the Appellate Body.

Tables 6.5 and 6.6 list these disputes, together with the related transparency dialogue that took place around them. These cases show that a significant majority of these major SPS and TBT disputes were raised both in STCs and in dispute settlement proceedings, confirming that, for the specific subject matter of SPS and TBT, the transparency framework and dispute settlement process are genuinely complementary (section A). The factor common to those disputes that are raised only in dispute settlement appears to be that there are issues of implementation relating to WTO agreements other than the SPS or TBT Agreements (section B).

A 'Major' SPS and TBT Disputes: Systematically Complemented by Transparency?

Among those disputes that can be said to include 'major' SPS or TBT claims, it is striking that a majority were also discussed either first or in parallel in the SPS and TBT Committees. This is true of disputes initiated by Members at different levels of development, with no apparent pattern and hence no apparent systematic practice. For example, the United States and Canada both raised concerns on numerous occasions before

Table 6.5 *WTO disputes with major SPS claims*

Dispute	Respondent	Complainant(s)	Dispute (request for consultations)	STC	Notification
Australia – Salmon	Australia	United States	5 October 1995	× 2 1996–1997	14 September 1995
EC – Hormones	European Union	Canada, United States	26 January 1996	No	No
Japan – Agricultural Products II	Japan	United States	7 April 1997	× 3 1996–2001	No
Japan – Apples	Japan	United States	1 March 2002	× 4 2001–2002	No
EC – Approval and Marketing of Biotech Products	European Union	Argentina, Canada, United States	13 May 2003	× 9 (TBT Committee) 2001–2004	30 August 2001
Australia – Apples	Australia	New Zealand	31 August 2007	× 7 2005–2007	No

Korea – Bovine Meat	Korea	Canada	9 April 2009	×1 2007	No
US – Poultry	United States	China	17 April 2009	×8 2007–2010	No
India – Agricultural Products	India	United States	6 March 2012	×17 2004–2011	11 October 2011
US – Animals	United States	Argentina	30 August 2012	×3 2011–2012	No
Russia – Pigs	Russia	European Union	8 April 2014	×1 2014	23 October 2014
Korea – Radionuclides	Korea	Japan	21 May 2015	×5 2013–2015	No

Source: Based on http://spsims.wto.org/ and www.wto.org/english/tratop_e/dispu_e/dispu_status_e.htm.

Table 6.6 *WTO disputes with major TBT claims*

Dispute	Respondent	Complainant	Dispute (request for consultations)	STC	Notification
EC – Sardines	European Union	Peru	2 March 2001	× 2 March–July 2003	10 March 2003
US – Tuna II	United States	Mexico	24 October 2008	× 5 February–November 2000	10 January 2000
US – COOL	United States	Canada	1 December 2008	× 9 2000–2009	23 October 2002
EC – Seal Products	European Union	Canada	5 November 2009	× 15 (3 ≠ STCs) 2006–2010	Belgium: 8 March 2003 Netherlands: 9 March 2006 Germany: 28 February 2008 EC: 11 February 2009

US – Clove Cigarettes	United States	Indonesia	7 April 2010	×1 November 2009	None
Australia – Plain Packaging	Australia	Ukraine, Honduras, Dominican Republic, Cuba	13 March 2012 (Ukraine) 4 April 2012 (Honduras) 18 July 2012 (Dominican Republic) 3 May 2013 (Cuba)	×4 2011–2012	8 April 2011
Indonesia – Chicken	Indonesia	Brazil	16 October 2014	×1 November 2013	0
Russia – Railway Equipment	Russian Federation	Ukraine	21 October 2015	×2	0

Source: Based on http://tbtims.wto.org and www.wto.org/english/tratop_e/dispu_e/dispu_status_e.htm.

raising several disputes,[23] but they each also initiated a dispute with the EU without raising the issue as an STC at all.[24]

Nevertheless, given that there is a common trend to raise STCs before, in parallel with or after SPS and TBT dispute settlement proceedings, it seems safe to conclude that STCs are used to address substantive issues. The few examples available to date confirm that climbing the disputing pyramid is not a linear process: in some cases, STCs are raised in parallel or even after the disputes, and notifications may be prompted by requests for consultations or by panel or Appellate Body reports. Overall, the chronology of STCs and disputes suggests that STCs are used both as a 'substitute' for dispute settlement – that is, to allow Members to manage conflicts and preclude disputes from arising – and as a 'complement' to dispute settlement, either in parallel to the dispute proceedings or afterwards.

Evidence of trade conflicts that have progressed through the entire 'disputing pyramid' remains scarce. Indeed, the information and dialogue that is exchanged before STCs are raised is very limited. Notifications offer a small hint of the information that may be made available at an early stage, which may open a bilateral dialogue, but there is almost no information publicly available on the dialogue in which the parties may have engaged between submitting the notification and raising the STC. In addition, in the SPS and TBT disputes at which we look in this section, only a few have their origins in a notification: 3 of 12 SPS disputes and 5 of 8 TBT disputes. Among these, the notifications were not always made before the request for consultations; indeed, some notifications actually seem to have been prompted by the formal dispute. Similarly, STCs are not always raised before the dispute consultations start.

Nevertheless, a closer look at some of these disputes and the various steps within the transparency framework that Members took before or concurrently with the formal dispute proceedings shows how closely interlinked transparency and dispute settlement are in the fields of SPS and TBT.

The *Russia – Pigs (EU)* dispute is a telling example of a dispute that went through all stages of the 'disputing pyramid', although not in chronological order. It shows in particular an issue that was already perceived as contentious within the Committee discussion, which was immediately followed by a request for consultation. The notifications, in this case, seem to have been influenced by the Committee discussions or dispute consultations rather than to have introduced information about the dispute.

---

[23] *India – Agricultural Products*; *Japan – Apples*; *US – COOL*; *EC – Seal Products*.
[24] *EC – Hormones*, at which we look further later.

The 'conflict' between the EU and Russia on this matter was first flagged in the WTO context as an STC in the SPS Committee in March 2014. The EU presented its concern that Russia had taken a measure to ban imports from the entire EU territory because of a finding of African swine fever (ASF) in two EU Member States, Lithuania and Poland. The EU considered this measure to be disproportionate, more trade-restrictive than necessary and discriminatory, not least because there was contrary evidence indicating that ASF had spread to Lithuania and Poland from Russia, where ASF was already widespread. Russia replied in the Committee that it had already informed its trading partners of the actions it had taken to prevent and eradicate ASF, that it had imposed a temporary restriction on live pigs and pig products from countries that had notified the disease outbreak to the World Organisation for Animal Health (OIE), and that the EU should comply with requirements for veterinary certificates on which it and Russia had already agreed. The discussion was not progressed in the SPS Committee and, a month after the first Committee discussion took place, the EU submitted a request for consultations with Russia. A few months later, Russia submitted several emergency notifications regarding the ban of products, in particular products from Lithuania.[25] The dispute resulted in hearings before a panel and then the Appellate Body, which touched upon the same issues raised in the original STC. After the Appellate Body circulated its report on 23 February 2017, Russia submitted a notification confirming the abolition of its restrictions on imports of live pigs.

Another example of a dispute going through all phases of the 'disputing pyramid', this time in parallel, is the *Australia – Plain Packaging* dispute. This dispute, which comprised several different requests for consultations with Australia from Ukraine, Honduras, Dominican Republic and Cuba, offers several interesting insights into the different stages of the 'disputing pyramid'. Particularly detailed STC discussions reveal many things about the conduct of the dialogue between the complainants and Australia, which were not limited to the STC discussions per se. The TBT Committee discussions were accompanied by written statements deepening the arguments of all concerned Members, statements were made in another WTO forum – the WTO's Trade-Related Aspects of Intellectual Property Rights (TRIPS) Council – and Members explicitly mention the private sector's role in highlighting the measure's effects.

---

[25] G/SPS/N/RUS/48; G/SPS/N/RUS/48/Add.1; G/SPS/N/RUS/48/Add.2.

Chronologically, the disputing pyramid started as might be expected, with Australia submitting a notification on 8 April 2011.[26] The notification contained a description of its draft Tobacco Plain Packaging Bill 2011, a copy of the Bill and an announcement for upcoming consultations, scheduled for the second half of 2011. This notification was shortly followed by Ukraine's request for consultations with Australia, in which Ukraine provided a detailed account of all provisions of the Bill that it considered unlawful, alleging in particular that the Tobacco Plain Packaging Bill was inconsistent with Article 2.2 of the TBT Agreement because it constituted an unnecessary obstacle to trade and was more trade-restrictive than necessary to achieve the stated health objectives. Ukraine made the same argument in the subsequent TBT Committee meeting that took place in June 2011, noting that industry actors had drawn its attention to the potential effects of the measure. Ukraine also noted that it had made a statement in the TRIPS Council to voice its concerns about inconsistencies with that Agreement. After this discussion in the TBT Committee, Honduras, the Dominican Republic and Cuba followed Ukraine's lead, submitting requests for consultations in April 2012, July 2012 and May 2013, respectively. The first dispute that was launched (i.e. that launched by Ukraine) did not result in panel hearings; instead, Ukraine and Australia notified their willingness to find a mutually agreed solution in May 2015. However, the three other disputes were consolidated and brought before a panel, which circulated its report in June 2018.

Finally, the relationship between transparency and dispute settlement not only is chronologically flexible but also may allow the Member some choice over the Committee in which to discuss the issue. The dispute *EC – Approval, Marketing of Biotech Products*, for example, in which Argentina, Canada and the United States raised concerns about EU measures, kicked off with a TBT notification and discussions in the TBT Committee spanning nine meetings between 2001 and 2004.[27] Members were concerned about EC-wide measures controlling genetically modified organisms (GMOs). Canada, the United States and Argentina each submitted a request for consultations in May 2003, after two years of TBT Committee discussions, in which they alleged violations of the 1994 General Agreement on Tariffs and Trade (GATT 1994) and of both the

[26] G/TBT/N/AUS/67.
[27] TBT ID 58. In addition, numerous other TBT STCs also raised the EU's approach to GMOs. See esp. European Communities – Amendment to the Directive on the Deliberate Release of GMOs (TBT ID 16); European Communities – Compulsory Indication of the Labelling of Certain Foodstuffs Produced from GMOs (TBT ID 17); European Communities – Novel Foods Regulations (TBT ID 18).

SPS and TBT Agreements. The dispute resulted in an extremely complex panel report of more than 1,000 pages, covering a variety of legal issues under the three Agreements. The panel's findings went well beyond the initial discussions in the TBT Committee and resulted, in particular, in important conclusions with regard to the SPS Agreement.[28] The STC mechanism being flexible and informal, there is nothing that ties the discussions taking place in the Committee to the substance of the dispute. It is therefore all the more important to remember that discussions in the Committee may help to solve certain issues in such a way that they no longer need to be addressed in a dispute.

B Disputes that Emerged 'Out of Nowhere': Any Common Traits?

While Members of the WTO raising a dispute tend also to have tried addressing the issue in an STC, as we have seen, of the 102 requests for consultations with SPS and TBT claims, 45 raised issues that were not discussed in the Committees (i.e. slightly less than half). Disputes over SPS subject matter tend to be more frequently discussed in the Committee than are TBT disputes. Only 17 of 48 SPS disputes had not been raised in an SPS STC, whereas 28 of 54 TBT disputes had not been discussed in an STC. These figures seem surprisingly high, calling into question the systematic relationship between the transparency framework and disputes. However, it seems that this may be largely because the scope of disputes reaches well beyond the remits of the SPS and TBT Committees. Indeed, as described in the previous section, the majority of 'major' SPS and TBT requests for consultations were also discussed in the Committees. Only one of the 'major' disputes listed in Tables 6.5 and 6.6 was not directly discussed in an STC, and we shall see that this can be explained by extensive parallel discussions in other fora and in related STCs.

It is likely that those disputes that are not raised in STCs do not contain substantive SPS or TBT arguments, and therefore are less suited to the technical discussions taking place in the two Committees. Indeed, a majority include substantive claims rooted in other agreements and make only a general reference to provisions under the SPS Agreement. For example, in *Ukraine – Measures Relating to Trade in Goods and Services* (DS525), Russia raised concerns against a general import ban imposed by Ukraine

---

[28] For a detailed account of the panel's findings, see Robert Howse and Henrik Horn, 'European Communities – Measures Affecting the Approval and Marketing of Biotech Products', *World Trade Review* 8, no. 1 (2009): 49–83.

on a broad range of Russian goods, ranging from food products (especially meat, dairy, fish, confectionery, tea and potato products, such as crisps, etc.), through spirits and beer, cigarettes, railway and tram track equipment, diesel-electric locomotives, octanol, potash chloride, detergents, certain agricultural chemicals and certain plant products. Russia therefore included detailed claims in the request for consultations spanning the General Agreement on Trade in Services (GATS), the TBT Agreement, the Protocol of Accession, the Agreement establishing the WTO, the GATT and the Import Licensing Agreement.[29] While there were also a number of SPS claims and a few TBT claims,[30] it seems that a mere discussion in the SPS and TBT Committees would not have been sufficiently comprehensive to cover all of Russia's concerns.

In some cases, an STC is raised in the one Committee even though the legal dispute ends up focusing more on issues that ought to be discussed in the other. For example, the request for consultations in *United States – Measures Affecting the Production and Sale of Clove Cigarettes* (DS406) mentions Articles 2, 5 and 7 of the SPS Agreement without going into further detail, but specifies the provisions of the TBT Agreement that seem to be at stake – namely, Article 2.[31] This dispute was not discussed in the SPS Committee, but was raised as an STC in the TBT Committee,[32] five months before the request for consultation was submitted.

Of the 20 'major' SPS and TBT disputes listed in Tables 6.5 and 6.6, only one was never discussed in either Committee: *EC – Hormones*. This single dispute highlights the limits of the STC mechanism – and arguably, to a certain extent, also those of dispute settlement – in achieving a mutually acceptable solution for WTO Members. It confirms that, in some cases, the approaches of sovereign States are too different to be reconciled, whether through co-operation or through third-party adjudication.[33] Nevertheless, the fact that only one dispute has been an exception

---

[29] 'Ukraine – Measures Relating to Trade in Goods and Services, Request for Consultations by the Russian Federation' (WT/DS525/1, 1 June 2017).

[30] Citing Arts 2, 3, 5, 7 and 8 and Annex C SPS, and Arts 2, 4 and 5 TBT.

[31] Especially Arts 2.1, 2.2 and 2.4 TBT.

[32] 'United States – Ban on Clove Cigarettes' (ID 257).

[33] On a similar dispute with regard to subject matter and legal questions, Shaffer and Pollack study the significant number of different fora in which bilateral, multilateral and formal disputes took place between the United States in the context of the 'EU EC – Approval, Marketing of Biotech Products' dispute. Noting that, despite these lengthy discussions, the parties still ended up with an unsatisfactory solution for both, they conclude that it is a case of 'when co-operation fails': Mark A. Pollack and Gregory C. Shaffer, *When Cooperation Fails* (Oxford: Oxford University Press, 2009).

to the general practice of resorting to STCs before or in parallel with disputes with major SPS or TBT claims confirms that all Members facing a trade conflict perceive STCs as an important tool.

EC – Hormones concerned the highly politically charged issue of foodstuffs destined for human consumption and reflects the complexity of the WTO adjudicator's role in reconciling the WTO's original mandate with public health considerations. It is the result of diametrically opposed cultural and scientific approaches, pitting the EU's traditional precautious approach to risk on the one side and the innovative approaches to agriculture in the Americas (particularly in the United States and Canada) on the other. However, it is clear that not all 'politically charged' disputes are excluded from Committee discussions. Typically telling examples of highly political and sensitive issues include *EC – Seal Products, Australia – Plain Packaging* and *EC – Approval, Marketing of Biotech Products*, all of which were discussed in depth in STCs.[34] It seems, then, that other circumstances may explain the absence of specific STCs preceding these disputes in the SPS Committee.

First of all, the *EC – Hormones* dispute emerged quite early on in the establishment of the WTO.[35] Although the STC mechanism already existed and had been well used in the SPS Committee in particular since its very first meetings, it is possible that, for such a politically charged trade dispute, the Members involved did not see the value added in holding discussions in the multilateral setting provided by the SPS Committee. In addition, after the dispute was first raised in requests for consultations submitted in January and July 1996, there were innumerable discussions in both the SPS and TBT Committees about various hormone-related import requirements imposed, in particular, by the EU. In the event, the parties – the United States, Canada and the EU – had the opportunity to exchange in other fora in more depth, making the resort to WTO Committees less important.[36]

Members' recourse to STCs and dispute settlement confirms that transparency can be complementary to dispute settlement. It allows WTO Members to work together towards mutually acceptable solutions

---

[34] 'European Communities – Seal Products' (ID 222); 'Germany – Ban on Seal Products' (ID 188); 'Belgium and The Netherlands – Seal Products' (ID 112); 'Australia – Tobacco Plain Packaging Bill 2011' (ID 304).
[35] The requests for consultations were made in July 1996 (*EC – Hormones*) and in May 2003 (*EC – Approval, Marketing of Biotech Products*).
[36] Pollack and Shaffer, *When Cooperation Fails*.

that comply with the SPS and TBT Agreements. It also grants all WTO Members, and developing countries in particular, a route through which to try and resolve conflicts without the costs of dispute settlement. When conflicts persist, however, WTO Members do need to turn to the DSB for an authoritative interpretation of the Agreements.

The 'disputing pyramid' reflects well the volume of notifications, comments on notifications and STCs that exist in the pre-litigation stages, and which contrast with the far fewer issues that end up in requests for consultations or brought before a WTO panel or the Appellate Body. However, the evidence presented in this chapter is evidence that the pyramid should not be seen as mandating a chronological sequence from notification to dispute settlement. The reality is more complex. In some cases, STC discussions prompt notifications; in some cases, panel or Appellate Body reports prompt notifications; in some cases, there is no notification at all.

Nevertheless, a chronological sequence from the base of the pyramid to its tip would be the optimal sequence for a fully transparent system in which all Members have equal access to the same information. When the sequence follows this pathway, simply put: all trading partners are able to access information; all trading partners are able to engage in dialogue; and all trading partners are able to manage tensions and prevent disputes from arising. The following chapters will discuss the pre-litigation phases in more depth and the role that transparency mechanisms may play in levelling the playing field – that is, equalising Members' access to adjudication.

7

Climbing the WTO Disputing Pyramid

The Challenges Leading up to Disputes

The formal WTO dispute settlement system plays a crucial role in ensuring effective compliance with WTO obligations. Indeed, the risk of a dispute and retaliation threatens high costs that may offset any gains a Member may make by avoiding their obligations.[1] As we have seen, disputes are consequently usually a Member's last resort. The dispute settlement system is a costly and burdensome process that may be worthwhile only in instances of high trade losses.[2] It is arguably in the best interests of any country, whatever its level of development, to avoid disputes, because of the resources that disputes demand, their political implications and their uncertain results, which may not be favourable to the complainant.

Nevertheless, the over-representation of developed countries as complainants in WTO disputes suggests that bringing a case before the adjudicator remains more difficult for some countries than for others. Indeed, the majority of disputes across all WTO agreements are brought by a subset of WTO Members: it has been reported that, in 2014, only 22 per cent had ever been one of the main parties to a case before the Appellate Body.[3] In the specific areas covered under the WTO Agreements on the Application of Sanitary and Phytosanitary Measures (SPS Agreement, or SPS) and on Technical Barriers to Trade (TBT Agreement, or TBT), only 37 of the 164 WTO Members (i.e. 23 per cent) had been either a respondent or a complainant in an SPS or TBT dispute.

---

[1] Bernard M. Hoekman and Michel M. Kostecki, *The Political Economy of the World Trading System: The WTO and Beyond* (Oxford: Oxford University Press, 2009).

[2] Bown explains the costs of resorting to dispute settlement based on the costs of implementing each step in the extended litigation process: Chad Bown, *Self-Enforcing Trade: Developing Countries and WTO Dispute Settlement* (Washington, DC: Brookings Institution Press, 2009).

[3] Joost Pauwelyn and Weiwei Zhang, 'Busier than Ever? A Data-Driven Assessment and Forecast of WTO Caseload', *Journal of International Economic Law* 21, no. 3 (2018): 3; Joost Pauwelyn, 'Minority Rules: Precedent and Participation before the WTO Appellate Body', in Laura Nielsen and Henrik Palmer Olsen, eds, *Establishing Judicial Authority in International Economic Law* (Cambridge: Cambridge University Press, 2016), 139.

Transparency can be seen as a useful tool to level the playing field, insofar as it allows Members to gather in-depth information about other Members' domestic measures and to attempt to resolve disputes through technical dialogue.

To understand the ways in which transparency might equalise access to dispute settlement, we shall first look at the process that leads from a Member's adoption of a domestic measure to its challenge by another Member before the WTO Dispute Settlement Body (DSB). Building on the existing literature and evidence, this chapter offers an overview of the factors that allow countries to adjudicate in the WTO and, perhaps more importantly, those factors that act as barriers.

In terms of the 'disputing pyramid' in general, a grievance leads to a decision to sue – that is, a disagreement on the facts is transformed into a formal dispute. Alongside Bown and Hoekman's description of the 'pre-litigation' phase,[4] this sequential transformation is useful in helping us to identify the steps that precondition Members' access to adjudication.

Two major stages can be distinguished in WTO adjudication, in which different types of challenge may be raised.[5] On the one hand, the 'upstream' stage starts with identifying a negative effect, researching its consistency with WTO obligations, estimating the economic benefits of eliminating the WTO-inconsistent measure and convincing a government to take the case forward to adjudication. This process is generally referred to as the 'pre-litigation' phase.[6] On the other hand, the 'downstream' stage starts when the adjudication process is launched and it corresponds to various phases of proceedings before a panel or the WTO's Appellate Body. In the 'extended litigation process', it corresponds to the 'litigation' and 'post-litigation' phases, in which countries develop and prosecute the legal case, calculate the costs of retaliation and generate public and/or political support for elimination of the measure.[7]

This chapter focuses on the 'upstream' stage of dispute settlement – that is, the 'pre-litigation' stage. Arguably, the greatest role played by the transparency mechanisms that we have examined is when the Member is

---

[4] Chad P. Bown and Bernard M. Hoekman, 'WTO Dispute Settlement and the Missing Developing Country Cases: Engaging the Private Sector', *Journal of International Economic Law* 8, no. 4 (2005): 861–90.

[5] Bernard M. Hoekman and Petros C. Mavroidis, 'WTO Dispute Settlement, Transparency and Surveillance', *World Economy* 23, no. 4 (2000): 527–42.

[6] Bown and Hoekman, 'WTO Dispute Settlement and the Missing Developing Country Cases'.

[7] This description is based on ibid.

deciding whether or not to pursue adjudication and then when it is building its case. Once countries have entered into adjudication, their resources – essentially their access to adequate legal representation and impartial procedures – will remain imbalanced.[8] However, because the study of transparency and regulatory co-operation leads us to focus on non-judicial compliance tools within the WTO, we will consider here the stages that precondition a Member's access to dispute settlement. Indeed, paying attention to access for all at these earlier stages helps to ensure the effectiveness of rights and obligations within the WTO for all of its Members, and hence also allows them to contribute equally to ensuring compliance with WTO agreements.

This leads us to underline an important caveat. Adjudication is not an end in itself and, as noted earlier, transparency is a more efficient and less costly way of ensuring compliance with the SPS and TBT Agreements. However, it is true that when a Member considers its rights to be violated, it should be as easily able to access justice as is any other Member. Our approach will therefore focus on the 'access to justice' of all WTO Members. In line with literature on social justice in internal law, we will argue that 'justice' in the multilateral trading system *'presupposes* effective access'.[9]

Access to justice can be defined as 'the ability to avail oneself of the various institutions, governmental and non-governmental, judicial and non-judicial, in which a claimant might pursue justice'.[10]

Access to justice *in the WTO* implies being able to fulfil the necessary steps in the pre-litigation process to gather sufficient evidence on a domestic measure with which to evaluate the opportunity costs of litigating and to try to address the issue through alternative means, and then – if the alternative means fail – to raise a formal dispute.

In this sense, three general factors explain WTO Members' access to WTO adjudication: Members are likely to bring disputes whenever they have the information and the resources, and they lack alternative fora in which to solve the conflict. Although the existing literature does not

---

[8] Hoekman and Mavroidis, 'WTO Dispute Settlement, Transparency and Surveillance'.
[9] Mauro Cappelletti and Bryant Garth, 'Access to Justice: The Newest Wave in the Worldwide Movement to Make Rights Effective', *Buffalo Law Review* 27, no. 2 (1978): 182, emphasis original. Although literature from the domestic level provides a useful theoretical framework for reflections on access to justice in the WTO, the WTO legal system has specific features that will be underlined throughout this chapter.
[10] Marc Galanter, 'Access to Justice in a World of Expanding Social Capability', *Fordham Urban Law Journal* 37, no. 1 (2010): 115–16.

necessarily name these three categories and there is no chronological sequence from one to the next, it is obvious that information and resource factors in particular may be pivotal throughout the process and that, in reality, the distinction between each factor is not clear-cut. For this reason, this chapter will focus on these various 'factors', rather than on the linear logic of the 'disputing pyramid'.

I Information about WTO-Inconsistent Measures

The first precondition to a Member bringing a dispute before the WTO is that it must be aware of the measure that is causing it harm. In the early domestic 'dispute' literature, this was termed the 'naming' stage,[11] involving recognising and identifying an injury, which then turns into a 'grievance'.

In the WTO context, before raising a dispute, a Member must be able to identify the trade barrier, connect it to another WTO Member's measure, evaluate that measure's inconsistency with WTO obligations and estimate the benefits that might emit from litigating. Mavroidis notes that: 'Knowledge about the facts is at any rate the necessary first step towards establishing (un)lawful behaviour.'[12] Bown and Hoekman describe this, within their extended litigation process, as 'step 1: Identify the foreign WTO-inconsistent policy'.[13] In the SPS and TBT context, gathering information about the measure may prove to be particularly difficult, both in terms of identifying the measure and determining its inconsistency with WTO obligations. The private sector is an essential source of information for governments at this stage and therefore an efficient ongoing dialogue with the private sector is an important determinant of which countries will choose to litigate.

A Better Capacity to Detect Deviations

Larger trading partners have more sources of information and better capacity to detect deviations from WTO obligations. This is closely linked with a country's human and capital resources, which capacity has been found to be a factor predicting a country's likelihood to seek adjudication.

---

[11] William L. F. Felstiner, Richard L. Abel and Austin Sarat, 'Emergence and Transformation of Disputes: Naming, Blaming, Claiming ...', *Law & Society Review* 15, no. 3–4 (1980–81): 631–54.
[12] Petros C. Mavroidis, *Trade in Goods* (Oxford: Oxford University Press, 2012), 816.
[13] Bown and Hoekman, 'WTO Dispute Settlement and the Missing Developing Country Cases', 869.

I INFORMATION ABOUT WTO-INCONSISTENT MEASURES   251

Countries with many trading partners have an advantage because they have invested abroad and developed sources of information within their trading partners, in the form of exporting firms or trade diplomacy.[14] Horn, Mavroidis and Nordström note that 'large trade administrations in the world devote considerable resources to screen the trade policies of other countries, and maintain well-oiled routines for handling complaints by the export industry'.[15] Beyond the monitoring efforts that countries may make unilaterally thanks to their own infrastructure and human resources, larger traders may also benefit from information that foreign private or diplomatic contacts may share with them.

B *The Difficulty of Identifying the SPS and TBT Measures at the Source of the Trade Effect*

Identifying the domestic measure responsible for a trade effect might not be easy, sometimes simply because of the wide range of domestic measures in all WTO Members that could potentially affect trade, and sometimes because of the difficulty in establishing causality between the measure and the effects on trade. Bown underlines that disputes about behind-the-border measures in the WTO are the most illustrative of imbalanced access between developed and developing countries.[16] He describes such measures as having 'low observability' and notes that, between 1995 and 2008, developing countries raised disputes about such measures considerably less frequently than did developed countries.[17] Among such measures, Bown includes subsidies, other domestic regulations, such as those relating to intellectual property rights, and export restrictions. The SPS and TBT measures that are the focus of this book fall under this last category, and the requests for consultations raised between 1995 and 2015 citing such issues also demonstrate the dominance of industrialised countries versus developing countries under the two Agreements (cf. Tables 6.2 and 6.4).

In addition, establishing causality between the trade effect and a domestic measure may be particularly difficult when WTO legal violations happen at the same time as a natural shock. In such cases,

---

[14] Bernard M. Hoekman and Petros C. Mavroidis, *The World Trade Organization: Law, Economics, and Politics*, 2nd edn (New York: Routledge, 2016).
[15] Henrik Horn, Petros C. Mavroidis and Håkan Nordström, 'Is the Use of the WTO Dispute Settlement System Biased?', CEPR Discussion Paper No. 2340, December 1999, 14. https://cepr.org/active/publications/discussion_papers/dp.php?dpno=2340.
[16] Bown, *Self-Enforcing Trade*, 78–9.
[17] Ibid., 79.

adjudication regarding the WTO legal violation may not be worth pursuing, 'because correction of the legal violation will not restore the lost market access'.[18]

C Obtaining Relevant Information from the Private Sector

As a main actor within the trading system, the private sector – whether represented by industry groups or private companies – is best placed to notify governments about the effects that another Member's domestic measures may be having on trade because it is the first to be affected.

Shaffer proposes that wealthier and better organised representatives of the private sector work closely in the 'shadow' of government-to-government WTO litigation to promote their own commercial interests and to pursue adjudication.[19] Bown and Hoekman further suggest that the private sector – which they define as including firms, industry associations, lawyers and consultants – plays a role throughout the WTO dispute settlement process, and in particular in the pre-litigation phase, conducting the 'economic and legal research necessary to convince its government officials of the legal merits and economic benefits to pursuing a case'.[20] Bown further argues that '[f]irms that can cover the cost of engaging in the WTO's extended litigation process to protect their market access interests are the ones that can enforce the agreement'.[21]

These arguments underline the importance for WTO Members of having an open and ongoing dialogue with their private sector players, to ensure that they share with their government information about potential disputes. However, there may be several obstacles in the way of such dialogue: cultural and institutional tradition may mean that it is poor; the private sector itself may lack the resources with which to obtain information; and it may lack the incentive to raise awareness of an issue because it anticipates that its government is unlikely to seek adjudication.

There are high costs to the private sector in obtaining information about foreign measures that affect it and the potential legal actions that

---

[18] Ibid., 210.
[19] Gregory C. Shaffer, *Defending Interests: Public–Private Partnerships in WTO Litigation* (Washington, DC: Brookings Institution Press, 2003).
[20] Bown and Hoekman, 'WTO Dispute Settlement and the Missing Developing Country Cases', 869. Bown and Hoekman also argue that the private sector plays a role in two additional phases: private actors may go on to petition their governments to raise disputes through formal means; and they may help to encourage the foreign Member to comply when the DSU authorises retaliatory measures: ibid.
[21] Bown, *Self-Enforcing Trade*, 109.

might be taken against them in WTO dispute settlement. Among these, Bown identifies the costs of research into the legal, economic and political background to the measure, affecting its market access and whether or not it is WTO-inconsistent.[22] This is partnered with the costs of engaging policy-makers, which might involve the costs of affected companies organising politically, the costs of expanding evidence on a measure's trade effects across a larger sample of industry representatives or the costs of obtaining access to policy-makers.

Finally, Hoekman and Mavroidis have noted that governments may decide not to pursue a case, for instance for fear of counter-claims or because they fear retaliatory consequences in non-trade areas.[23] In the light of these possiblities, the private sector may decide that it is not worth informing its government of the problem – and hence the government may never become aware of the effect on its industry of a problematic measure and the matter will remain outside the WTO framework.

II The Resources Required to Access Adjudication

A WTO Member's resources may influence its adjudication behaviour in many ways and this has been the subject of significant empirical research. The next section will present the existing evidence said to explain the predominance of large traders in the dispute settlement system. The main arguments are based on the number of disputes that affect larger traders with more trading partners but also on a large trader's legal capacity to identify WTO-inconsistent measures and to argue a case before the WTO.

The general resources of a country are commonly represented by its gross domestic product (GDP), and the human and institutional resources it can draw on to evaluate the legality of the measure under WTO obligations, as well as when developing a legal strategy.

A A Country's Overall Resources

Like access to information, empirical studies have shown that not only do larger traders have more opportunity to detect WTO-inconsistent behaviour, but also – because they have more diversified export portfolios, spanning a range of products and partners, and a larger volume of

---

[22] Ibid., 112–13.
[23] Hoekman and Mavroidis, 'WTO Dispute Settlement, Transparency and Surveillance'.

trade – they engage in more disputes.[24] At the other extreme are the least-developed countries (LDCs), which have both low export volumes and low levels of GDP, and therefore might be said to have little investment in litigation.[25]

The general resources of the country are all the more relevant as predictors of adjudication in that the economic gains to be made from bringing a case are relatively limited. With the remedies few, the incentives for countries with limited resources to invest in adjudication are low.[26] At the domestic level, it has also been observed that recourse to adjudication varies according to the institutionalisation of remedy systems.[27]

B   Members' Relative Resources

Regardless of the absolute resources that a Member may have, its resources relative to those of its trading partners may also precondition its decision to bring a case against them. On the one hand, if a country experiencing negative trade effects because of a potentially WTO-inconsistent measure is dependent on the regulating Member for development aid, this dependency means it is less likely to bring the case before the WTO.[28] On the other hand, if the regulating Member is not likely to retaliate, then the Member is more likely to challenge its WTO-inconsistent measures.[29]

This being said, while evidence indicates that a country's resources do influence its adjudication behaviour, evidence does not support 'power' arguments, according to which powerful traders exploit the system to maintain the power balance in their favour and weaker traders do not adjudicate because they fear taking on a powerful trading partner. Horn, Mavroidis and Nordström have found that the largest traders, which are most active in disputes, do not use the system disproportionately against

---

[24] Horn, Mavroidis and Nordström, 'Is the Use of the WTO Dispute Settlement System Biased?'.

[25] Joseph Francois, Henrik Horn and Niklas Kaunitz, 'Trading Profiles and Developing Country Participation in the WTO Dispute Settlement System', IFN Working Paper No. 730, 12 January 2010. https://papers.ssrn.com/sol3/papers.cfm?abstract_id=1534766.

[26] Hoekman and Mavroidis, 'WTO Dispute Settlement, Transparency and Surveillance'.

[27] Richard E. Miller and Austin Sarat, 'Grievances, Claims, and Disputes: Assessing the Adversary Culture', *Law & Society Review* 15, no. 3/4 (1980): 525–66.

[28] Francois, Horn and Kaunitz, 'Trading Profiles and Developing Country Participation'.

[29] Bruce A. Blonigen and Chad P. Bown, 'Antidumping and Retaliation Threats', NBER Working Paper No. 8576, November 2001. www.nber.org/papers/w8576; Chad Bown, 'Trade Disputes and the Implementation of Protection under the GATT: An Empirical Assessment', *Journal of International Economics* 62, no. 2 (2004): 263–94.

Table 7.1 *Complainants and respondents in SPS requests for consultations, 1995–2018*[30]

Country group	G2	IND	BRICS	DEV	LDC	TOTAL
BRICS	2	2	0	1	0	5
DEV	4	4	1	1	0	10
G2	4	8	4	0	0	16
IND	0	8	8	1	0	17
LDC	0	0	0	0	0	0
TOTAL	10	22	13	3	0	48

Source: Based on www.wto.org/english/tratop_e/dispu_e/dispu_status_e.htm.

Table 7.2 *Complainants and respondents in TBT requests for consultations, 1995–2018*[31]

Country group	G2	IND	BRICS	DEV	LDC	TOTAL
BRICS	2	2	0	2	0	6
DEV	8	3	0	0	0	11
G2	6	5	1	2	0	14
IND	15	4	3	1	0	23
LDC	0	0	0	0	0	0
TOTAL	31	14	4	5	0	54

Source: Based on www.wto.org/english/tratop_e/dispu_e/dispu_status_e.htm.

weaker traders.[32] This is confirmed by a look at the requests for consultations launched between 1995 and 2014, citing SPS and TBT Agreements, as shown in Tables 7.1 and 7.2.

Guzman and Simmons also challenge the power argument from the developing-country perspective, proving that while capacity constraints

---
[30] The columns in Table 7.1 reflect country groups as complainants and the rows, country groups as respondents.
[31] The columns in Table 7.2 reflect country groups as complainants and the rows, country groups as respondents.
[32] Horn, Mavroidis and Nordström, 'Is the Use of the WTO Dispute Settlement System Biased?'.

do limit smaller traders' adjudication practices, power balances do not, because when these countries do initiate a dispute, they tend to be challenging larger traders: 'Limitations on a government's capacity to litigate seem to be more important than the fear of political or economic retribution. Controlling for many alternative explanations, we find that poorer complainants have tended to focus on the big targets, strategy that is consistent with a tight capacity constraint rather than fear of retaliation.'[33]

C Members' Legal Capacity

Literature has underlined that a Member's legal capacity – albeit a result of its resources – more accurately determines that country's likelihood to adjudicate than does the absolute volume of resources the country has. In other words, a country's general wealth is important only because it helps to ensure that its administration has the necessary capacity to evaluate the measures adopted by its trading partners.

The initial assumptions that tie large traders to higher legal capacity were made by linking gross national product (GNP) per capita or number of delegates per WTO delegation to the complainants in WTO disputes,[34] or were based on the World Bank Government Efficiency, Regulatory Quality, and the Rule of Law Index.[35] Busch, Reinhardt and Shaffer conducted a survey asking all WTO delegations about 'professional staff, bureaucratic organisation at home, bureaucratic organisation in Geneva, experience handling general WTO matters, and involvement in WTO litigation'.[36] A telling result of this survey was that '67% of respondents chose ... legal capacity-oriented factors to explain why they intervened as a third party instead of filing their own complaint', those factors including the high cost of litigation, lack of private sector support and training for future disputes.[37] Overall, the qualitative and quantitative data they gathered allowed these authors to better reflect the reasons for variations among the relative legal capacities of developed and developing countries,

---

[33] Andrew T. Guzman and Beth A. Simmons, 'Power Plays and Capacity Constraints: The Selection of Defendants in World Trade Organization Disputes', *The Journal of Legal Studies* 34, no. 2 (2005): 591.

[34] Horn, Mavroidis and Nordström, 'Is the Use of the WTO Dispute Settlement System Biased?'.

[35] Francois, Horn and Kaunitz, 'Trading Profiles and Developing Country Participation'.

[36] Marc L. Busch, Eric Reinhardt and Gregory Shaffer, 'Does Legal Capacity Matter? A Survey of WTO Members', *World Trade Review* 8, no. 4 (2009): 560.

[37] Ibid., 567.

and to ground in more solid evidence the suggestion that legal capacity is indeed the main constraint preventing developing countries from accessing WTO dispute settlement.

At the domestic level, some evidence suggests that educational level and/or legal contacts is a more important determinant than income level in predicting grievances.[38] A similar argument is made in the WTO context, contrasting the per capita income of countries with the comparatively high level of education of the trade administration. In this sense, Members with lower levels of per capita income may still adjudicate frequently thanks to educated bureaucracy. Horn, Mavroidis and Nordström identified India as a Member with low levels of income per capita, but a 'comparatively well educated bureaucracy'.[39] While this may be true of WTO dispute settlement in general, however, this is less clearly reflected in the SPS and TBT context. For example, the BRICS countries (Brazil, Russia, India, China and South Africa) have been found to submit fewer requests for consultations citing the SPS or TBT Agreements. Arguably, this might be because, under the SPS and TBT Agreements, the information factor outweighs legal capacity because of the 'low observability' of the measures at stake.

If they invest in adjudication once, developing countries can acquire the legal capacity that allows them to do so again. At the domestic level, Galanter introduced the theory that 'repeat players' (i.e. larger entities with higher resources) have less to lose from the costs of litigation and that interests developed over the long run are more advantageous than 'one-shot' procedures, the costs of which can be prohibitively high relative to the potential remedies.[40] In this context, Galanter argues that repeat players enjoy economies of scale. Davis and Blodgett Bermeo apply this same logic to the WTO context and demonstrate empirically that developing countries, having participated at least once in WTO adjudication, whether as complainants or defendants, are more likely to have acquired the necessary legal capacity to become 'repeat players' and to adjudicate again.[41] However, they note that '[p]rior experience, either through

---

[38] Miller and Sarat, 'Grievances, Claims, and Disputes'.
[39] Henrik Horn, Petros C. Mavroidis and Håkan Nordström, 'Is the Use of the WTO Dispute Settlement System Biased?', in Petros C. Mavroidis and Alan O. Sykes, eds, *The WTO and International Trade Law/Dispute Settlement* (Cheltenham: Edward Elgar, 2005), 15.
[40] Marc Galanter, 'Why the "Haves" Come out Ahead: Speculations on the Limits of Legal Change', *Law and Society Review* 9, no. 1 (1974): 95–160.
[41] Christina L. Davis and Sarah Blodgett Bermeo, 'Who Files? Developing Country Participation in GATT/WTO Adjudication', *The Journal of Politics* 71, no. 3 (2009): 1033–49.

initiation or as a defendant, does not appear to have any significant effect on the likelihood of initiating'.[42] Indeed, the information and start-up costs involved in the launch of a new dispute may act as less of a barrier for developed countries, since their overall resource capacity is higher.

Busch and colleagues conclude that, because they found legal capacity to be the most predictive factor limiting developing countries' access to WTO dispute settlement, the increasing legalisation of the WTO system, including of the dispute settlement system, and the increasingly complex case law pose 'asymmetric challenges for developing countries, perhaps allaying some concerns over the distribution of economic power, but raising new ones over the distribution of legal capacity'.[43] Indeed, the preparation of a legal case challenging an SPS or TBT measure may be particularly difficult in light of the burden of proof that is required of the complainant.

The burden of proof that lies with the complainant may be particularly difficult to establish with regard to certain aspects of the TBT and SPS Agreements. Indeed, while it is the general rule in the WTO – as in most legal systems – that the burden of proof lies with the party that brings the case,[44] the Appellate Body has interpreted the burden of proof on the complainant under the SPS and TBT Agreements quite extensively, requiring complainants to deliver evidence of what they consider to be the regulating Members' rationale in adopting its domestic measure.[45]

For example, under the SPS Agreement, the Appellate Body ruled in *EC – Hormones* that a complainant alleging a regulating Member's deviation from its obligation to apply international standards cannot rely only on this deviation being an 'exception'. Indeed, the Appellate Body considered that a Member may establish a *prima facie* case based on information obtained from the regulating Member by transparency mechanisms[46] – in particular, the possibility under Article 5.8 of the SPS Agreement of asking the regulating Member to explain why it is adopting an SPS measure. The Appellate Body added that imposing the burden of proof on the regulating Member because it chose to apply an exception would end up amounting to imposing a 'penalty' on the regulating Member.

---

[42] Ibid., 1046.
[43] Busch, Reinhardt and Shaffer, 'Does Legal Capacity Matter?', 577.
[44] Appellate Body Report, *US – Wool Shirts and Blouses*, §16; David Palmeter and Petros C. Mavroidis, *Dispute Settlement in the World Trade Organization: Practice and Procedure*, 2nd edn (Cambridge: Cambridge University Press, 2004), 59.
[45] See Chapter 1.
[46] Appellate Body Report, *EC – Hormones*, §102.

In the TBT jurisprudence, the Appellate Body has considered that the complainant carries the burden of proving that a certain international standard is 'ineffective or inappropriate' to fulfil a legitimate objective of a measure.[47] In *EC – Sardines*, the panel had held that the burden fell on the regulating Member to prove that the international standard was inappropriate and ineffective to fulfil its legitimate objective – namely, because it is the regulating Member itself that makes this assertion and the complainant is not in a position to 'spell out' its legitimate objective, and because the appropriateness of the standard 'may extend to considerations which are proper to the Member adopting or applying a technical regulation'.[48] The Appellate Body reversed the panel's decision, explaining that the complainant had sufficient opportunity to obtain information about the regulating Member's rationale under the transparency obligations set out in the TBT Agreement and as a consequence of the transparency exercised between the parties ahead of the panel proceedings. The Appellate Body pointed in particular towards Members' obligation, under Article 2.4 of the Agreement, to respond to questions about the justification of their technical regulations and to the requirement for enquiry points, under Article 10.1.

However, the empirical data presented in Part II shows that the very number of specific trade concerns (STCs) in which Members question the rationale or legitimate objective of a domestic measure proves it is an issue that they find it hard to evaluate. Following the logic of the Appellate Body regarding the burden of proof, Members who have raised STCs should have the information necessary to carrying the burden of proof before a panel. However, this logic is based on the premise that there has been a bilateral contact and that the regulating Member has offered a response in good faith. Even assuming that the one Member asked the other to share its rationale through bilateral means, nothing guarantees that the regulating Member will deliver a complete answer – and, indeed, the number of STCs raised in the Committees on the rationale of domestic measures indicates that sufficient answers were *not* provided at the bilateral level.[49]

---

[47] Appellate Body Report, *EC – Sardines*, §282.
[48] Panel Report, *EC – Sardines*, §§7.50–7.51.
[49] Peru made this same argument in *EC – Sardines*, but the Appellate Body rejected it, saying at §278: 'We must assume that Members of the WTO will abide by their treaty obligations in good faith, as required by the principle of *pacta sunt servanda* articulated in Article 26 of the Vienna Convention. And, always in dispute settlement, every Member of the WTO must assume the good faith of every other Member.'

Finally, the Appellate Body held in *EC – Sardines* that:

> ... the dispute settlement process itself also provides opportunities for the complainant to obtain the necessary information to build a case. Information can be exchanged during the consultation phase, and additional information may well become available during the panel phase itself. On previous occasions, we have stated that the arguments of a party 'are set out and progressively clarified in the first written submissions, the rebuttal submissions and the first and second panel meetings with the parties', and that '[t]here is no requirement in the DSU [Dispute Settlement Understanding] or in GATT [General Agreement on Tariffs and Trade] practice for arguments on all claims relating to the matter referred to the DSB to be set out in a complaining party's first written submission to the panel'. Thus, it would not be necessary for the complainant to have all the necessary information about the technical regulation before commencing an action under the DSU. A complainant could collect information before and during the early stages of the panel proceedings and, on the basis of that information, develop arguments relating to the objectives or to the appropriateness that may be put forward during subsequent phases of the proceedings.[50]

Acknowledging that parties may not need to have all information when raising a dispute seems in theory to support the fact that any Member may raise disputes. However, this same opportunity may in fact have the opposite effect in practice, by preventing Members from predicting a case's judicial merits before they launch the adjudication process. Such jurisprudence seems excessively burdensome on WTO Members and may deter them from bringing an SPS and TBT case because they may feel that they lack sufficient evidence.

III   The Lack of Alternative Fora in which to Address Trade Frictions

The availability or otherwise of alternative fora in which a Member may address trade frictions does not constitute a precondition to accessing dispute settlement, but rather a useful means of reaching a negotiated agreement and thereby obtaining enforcement without adjudication. It is nevertheless included in this discussion because it arguably represents an important distinction between Members in terms of their behaviour in accessing WTO justice.

Because formal dispute settlement is costly, both politically and economically, all countries have an interest in not going down that route. The WTO's Dispute Settlement Understanding (DSU) itself insists that

---

[50] Appellate Body Report, *EC – Sardines*, §280.

it is preferable that parties try to find a mutually acceptable solution: '... A solution mutually acceptable to the parties to a dispute and consistent with the covered agreements is clearly to be preferred. ...'[51]

Members therefore try to reach an agreement through other less politically or economically costly means, be it informal bilateral consultations or within other fora that provide less burdensome procedures than the WTO. As a result, resort to adjudication is likely to be had only when a Member cannot access another forum or when consultations in other fora have failed. Indeed, the existing literature and empirical data suggests not only that Members have unequal access to alternative fora but also that, even when they do dispose of the same alternative fora for extra-judicial negotiations, they do not have the same success rates in settling the conflict before it escalates to dispute.

A Informal Dialogue

It is likely that Members will already have established bilateral contact before they raise requests for consultations[52] and the figures on STCs confirm that a high proportion of requests for consultations are made only after the issues were raised as STCs.[53]

Empirical evidence on these informal consultations is sporadic and can be illustrated with only a few examples. In their first study aiming to estimate the bias within WTO dispute settlement, Horn, Mavroidis and Nordström acknowledged that – as at the domestic level, where out-of-court settlements are very common – WTO disputes also are likely to be preceded or accompanied by informal consultations: 'In many cases, informal bilateral consultations may resolve the issue without need for formal adjudication.'[54] They regret, however, that '[i]t is not clear how often such informal bilateral consultations take place, nor do we know the success rate of such consultations, and the extent to which this rate systematically varies across countries'.[55] In the absence of such evidence and for the purposes of their statistical model, they therefore assume that all countries have the same success rate in their informal consultations.

---

[51] Article 3.7 DSU.
[52] Palmeter and Mavroidis, *Dispute Settlement in the World Trade Organization*.
[53] See Part II.
[54] Horn, Mavroidis and Nordström, 'Is the Use of the WTO Dispute Settlement System Biased?', 20.
[55] Ibid.

Pollack and Shaffer studied the extensive co-operation efforts between the European Union (EU) and the United States about genetically modified organisms (GMOs) before these were brought before the WTO DSB.[56] Davis further points out that the same countries, in challenging relatively similar measures and within the same time frame, may choose to tackle the issues in diplomatic meetings or with WTO adjudication.[57] She looks at the numerous bilateral meetings between the United States and Japan about Japan's bans on imports of fresh potatoes, in parallel to formal disputes that the United States also raised against Japan, but regarding apples.[58] Although evidence is scarce, it seems that the pursuit of adjudication does not prevent Members from continuing with informal dialogue – and indeed this may be the case in most disputes.

B Preferential Trade Agreements

Increased trends towards the 'regionalisation' of trade law and a move away from multilateral fora for trade negotiations have sparked a movement in terms of dispute settlement. Recent research estimates the impact that setting out dispute settlement procedures in bilateral or regional preferential trade agreements (PTAs) may have on dispute settlement in the WTO.

The existence of – or even negotiations towards – PTAs may offer alternative fora to trading partners in two senses. On the one hand, they may provide for an alternative forum for dialogue and exchange of information, allowing for the informal resolution of trade frictions before they amount to disputes; on the other hand, the PTA may have dispute resolution provisions that are different from those offered within the WTO DSB.

Mavroidis and Sapir have found that the EU and the United States litigate very rarely with their PTA partners before the WTO.[59] Strikingly, the number of disputes with a country fell significantly when the EU or the US had concluded a PTA with that country. In addition, Mavroidis

---

[56] Mark A. Pollack and Gregory C. Shaffer, *When Cooperation Fails* (Oxford: Oxford University Press, 2009).

[57] Christina L. Davis, *Why Adjudicate? Enforcing Trade Rules in the WTO* (Princeton, NJ: Princeton University Press, 2012), 16–17.

[58] The disputes to which Davis makes reference are *Japan – Agricultural Products II* and *Japan – Apples*.

[59] Petros C. Mavroidis and André Sapir, 'Dial PTAs for Peace: The Influence of Preferential Trade Agreements on Litigation between Trading Partners', *Journal of World Trade* 49, no. 3 (2015): 351–72.

III THE LACK OF ALTERNATIVE FORA

and Sapir have found that even the launch of PTA negotiations reduces the likelihood of disputes. Indeed, they underline that the United States has not entered disputes with the EU since the launch of Transatlantic Trade and Investment Partnership (TTIP) negotiations and has entered a dispute with only one negotiating party to the Trans-Pacific Partnership (TPP) (i.e. Viet Nam), and they point to similar data for the EU.[60]

However, their data shows that there is no forum diversion – that is, parties are not seeking PTA dispute settlement *instead of* WTO dispute settlement.[61] Rather, it seems that PTAs reduce the likelihood of disputes altogether. As a result, it seems that it is more the forum for exchange of information and technical and diplomatic negotiations that facilitates dispute prevention than it is any different dispute settlement procedure. Indeed, Mavroidis and Sapir conclude that the PTAs – which are mostly about regulatory issues[62] – serve as an additional level of transparency allowing PTA parties to 'solve most past disputes between the partners and to anticipate many future disputes'.[63] Indeed, while transparency in the WTO helps to prevent disputes between WTO Members, as we saw in Part II, PTAs provide an additional means of doing the same between trade partners outside of the WTO framework: 'Transparency can work as substitute for litigation, and increased transparency across PTA partners is a plausible contributing factor explaining why the amount of litigation across PTA partners has steadily decreased.'[64]

Focusing on PTAs concluded by the EU, Melillo confirms that the committees established under PTAs foster dialogue and allow partners to find technical solutions to disputed issues, in the same way as do the WTO SPS and TBT Committees.[65]

Davis posits that there are two principle reasons why alternative fora may not be sufficient and WTO adjudication may be pursued – that is, because the Members need third-party interpretation or a clarification of WTO agreements, or because the concerned Member is seeking authorisation for retaliation.[66]

---

[60] Ibid.
[61] Ibid., 357.
[62] Henrik Horn, Petros C. Mavroidis and André Sapir, 'Beyond the WTO? An Anatomy of EU and US Preferential Trade Agreements', *The World Economy* 33, no. 11 (2010): 1565–88.
[63] Mavroidis and Sapir, 'Dial PTAs for Peace', 360.
[64] Ibid.
[65] Margherita Melillo, 'Informal Dispute Resolution in Preferential Trade Agreements', *Journal of World Trade* 53, no. 1 (2019): 95–127.
[66] Davis, *Why Adjudicate?*.

C Requests for Consultation

Requests for consultations are the first stage in launching a formal dispute. Nevertheless, the Appellate Body sees them as a forum for gathering further information, as we saw in the case law explored earlier.

According to the DSU, the first stage in launching adjudication in the WTO is a request for 'consultations' between the complainant and the respondent, during which Members must aim to solve their issue: 'In the course of consultations in accordance with the provisions of a covered agreement, before resorting to further action under this Understanding, Members should attempt to obtain satisfactory adjustment of the matter.'[67]

This stage is therefore still a non-judicial stage, during which neither the WTO Secretariat nor a panel nor the Appellate Body intervenes, and the discussions will be 'without prejudice to the rights of any Member in any further proceedings'.[68] It aims to 'enable the parties [to] gather correct and relevant information, for [the] purposes of assisting them in arriving at a mutually agreed solution, or failing which, to assist them in presenting accurate information to the panel'.[69] A Member may therefore still learn more about the other Member's measure and strengthen its argument even if the two do not reach agreement.

Although informal dialogue is, in theory, open to any WTO Member and is not necessarily particularly costly, Busch and Reinhardt demonstrate that developing countries are less successful in settling negotiations in the consultations phase, and hence they find that Members' resources determine their level of success in settling disputes prior to panel proceedings.[70]

Although requests for consultations remain a discussion phase in the absence of an adjudicator, we still consider it to be the first step in WTO adjudication. Indeed, a request for consultations implies identifying the measure at issue and indicating the legal basis of the complaint.[71] In practice, therefore, when a Member is formally requesting consultations, it should already have gathered sufficient evidence to support its case before a panel.

---

[67] Article 4.5 DSU.
[68] Article 4.6 DSU.
[69] Panel Report, *Korea – Alcoholic Beverages*, §10.23.
[70] Marc L. Busch and Eric Reinhardt, 'Three's a Crowd: Third Parties and WTO Dispute Settlement', *World Politics* 58, no. 3 (2006): 446–77.
[71] Article 4.4 DSU.

8

Access to the WTO Disputing Pyramid

The 'Transparency Staircase'

Using the framework exposed in Chapter 7, this chapter presents how the transparency mechanisms under the WTO Agreements on the Application of Sanitary and Phytosanitary Measures (SPS Agreement, or SPS) and on Technical Barriers to Trade (TBT Agreement, or TBT) described in Parts I and II serve to deliver a number of the factors that WTO Members need if they are to access adjudication. It will, however, underline the disparity that remains, suggesting some explanations for Members' unequal access to dispute settlement.

The proposition that transparency can help to equalise access to WTO adjudication is not new.[1] This section will draw on these other authors' arguments and expand them with evidence of SPS and TBT transparency practices, to propose that the WTO transparency system is already helping to improve access to adjudication to a certain extent. In addition, it will advocate in favour of improving the existing transparency mechanisms within the WTO, which are arguably better suited to equalising litigation opportunities for Members than would be parallel mechanisms outside the WTO. Bown argues that the WTO transparency framework is essentially useful for Members to trigger one another's self-enforcement. According to him, 'while the WTO itself does not provide information to allow exporters to self-enforce their trading interests, the WTO has created an infrastructure for others to use by developing and disseminating information needed to trigger members' self-enforcement of their access to foreign markets'.[2] The following section will demonstrate that, in fact, the framework has the potential to be an even more effective tool to support self-enforcement of the SPS and TBT Agreements than it is today, providing Members with

---

[1] See e.g. Bernard M. Hoekman and Petros C. Mavroidis, 'WTO Dispute Settlement, Transparency and Surveillance', *World Economy* 23, no. 4 (2000): 527–42; Chad P. Bown, *Self-Enforcing Trade: Developing Countries and WTO Dispute Settlement* (Washington, DC: Brookings Institution Press, 2009).

[2] Bown, *Self-Enforcing Trade*, 215.

information about other Members' regulations (section I), bridging the gaps caused by resource disparities (section II) and offering alternative fora for negotiations about trade frictions (section III).

I Information about Other Members' Regulations

As noted in the last chapter, Members need information if they are to raise a dispute: an affected Member needs to identify the trade barrier, recognise that it stems from another WTO Member's measure, evaluate its consistency or otherwise with WTO obligations and estimate the benefits that might be associated with litigation (i.e. the benefits of eliminating the barrier) versus the economic and political costs of dispute settlement proceedings. In other words, to be able to follow the different steps of the 'extended litigation process' that Bown and Hoekman describe,[3] Members need several levels of information:

- *knowledge* of a measure – that is, the ability to find the information;
- *awareness* of the measure – that is, the ability to identify which are the important trade measures among the high volume notified by other Members;
- *understanding* of the information and of its impact – that is, on the one hand, an understanding of the requirements of the domestic legislation and, on the other, the ability to predict when it may have an impact on trade; and
- the ability to *use* the information – that is, once Members have the information, they need to know how to act upon it, perhaps by contacting the regulating Member.

To some extent, these information needs may be fulfilled by WTO transparency mechanisms (section A) and an improved dialogue with the private sector (section B), which may also take place within the WTO framework.

A SPS and TBT Transparency to Improve Information Imbalances

Table 8.1 maps these information needs, connecting them with the SPS and TBT transparency mechanisms that might help a Member to address them and the stages in the pre-litigation phase to which they correspond.

---

[3] Chad P. Bown and Bernard M. Hoekman, 'WTO Dispute Settlement and the Missing Developing Country Cases: Engaging the Private Sector', *Journal of International Economic Law* 8, no. 4 (2005): 861–90.

Table 8.1 *SPS and TBT transparency mechanisms in response to information needed in the pre-litigation phase*

Information Need	Stages in Pre-Litigation Phase	TBT/SPS Transparency Mechanisms
Knowledge of a measure	Identify trade barrier	Publication of adopted measures
Awareness of the measure		Notification of draft
Understanding of content of the measure	Assess scale and scope	Response to enquiries on notification
Understanding of the measure's (potential) impact		Internal process, esp. dialogue with private sector; facilitated by electronic tools
Use of information: reaction to the measure	Input into foreign policy-making process	Comment on notification; STCs
	Negotiate settlement	STCs; bilateral meetings in the margins of STCs

The first stage of information – having *knowledge* of a measure – implies only very summary information on a measure, reflecting the relatively weak effects of publication in terms of informing Members and preventing disputes. Indeed, publication allows only a decentralised form of transparency, requiring interested parties to seek out new measures in national legal publications. In terms of improving Members' access to dispute settlement, simple knowledge of a measure has very limited effects.

Members gain better *awareness* of each other's policies through notifications, which are centralised by the WTO Secretariat in a common database and shared with all Members via e-mail. These notifications are intended to deliver to Members all the relevant information on the sector and products that a measure concerns. Notifications are therefore a tool with which Members can identify any new measure that may represent a trade barrier. In addition, the common practice in the SPS and TBT Committees of raising specific trade concerns (STCs) regarding non-notified measures complements the information gaps left by those Members that fail to comply with the notification requirement. As a result, even when measures are not notified, Members obtain information in STC discussions.

Understanding the measure, so as to be able to assess its scale and scope, has two components. On the one hand, it involves understanding the content of the measure – which implies making sense of other Members' legislation, which might be very technical or only briefly summarised in English (with no translation of the original text). To help in this regard, the SPS and TBT Agreements require that Members provide copies of the proposed text,[4] and both Committees have recommended that Members provide translations of the draft texts whenever possible. On the other hand, Members need to assess the scale and scope of the measure in both legal terms (i.e. its consistency with WTO obligations) and economic terms (i.e. its effects on trade). The possibility of requesting further information, commenting on notifications and raising STCs allows Members to reach such an understanding.

While the obligations to respond to enquiries and to take comments into account are legal obligations, it remains difficult to monitor the extent to which regulating Members have respected these obligations. In addition, the possibility of raising an STC, while not a legal obligation, provides an effective route through which to better understand the measure. As we saw in Part II, Members raise concerns in the SPS and TBT Committees for exactly this reason. The pressure of the multilateral setting and the presence of the WTO Secretariat act as useful incentives encouraging the regulating Member to respond. Importantly, the information requested and obtained in the Committee setting benefits not only the concerned Member but also the entire WTO membership. As a result, STC discussions allow Members to obtain invaluable information on the potential trade effects of measures.

Finally, the last level of information needed in the pre-litigation phase is to empower Members to *use* the information they have acquired on the measure. Indeed, if it has acquired an adequate level of information through the 'transparency staircase', a Member may choose to approach the regulating Member. It may make comments on the notified text, which in practice go through national authorities and in most cases remain purely bilateral.[5]

---

[4] Annex B, para. 5.c, SPS; Art. 2.9.3 TBT.
[5] Only the European Union systematically discloses all the comments on notifications that it makes and receives.

I INFORMATION ABOUT OTHER MEMBERS' REGULATIONS 269

It may also raise a concern within the SPS or TBT Committee, thus also informing the entire membership of the issue arising and perhaps gathering the support of other countries with similar concerns.

This access to information that the WTO guarantees its Members is essential not only to prevent disputes, as we saw in Part II, but also to allow Members to raise disputes if they have failed to resolve the conflict within the transparency framework. In this case, all the transparency mechanisms will have been essential in ensuring that the concerned Member understands the measure and has the information on which to base a formal dispute.

B The Role of the Private Sector in the Chain of Information

The SPS and TBT transparency obligations require disclosure of information on trade regulations to the public more widely and notifications to be made publicly available to anyone. Transparency centralised by the WTO therefore opens up space for other stakeholders to react to WTO Members' draft measures if they have sufficient incentive to do so.

To ensure the effectiveness of the WTO transparency system to the benefit of all WTO Members, it seems important for the WTO Secretariat to provide equal access for domestic private sectors from all of the WTO Member countries (section 1). This is also in line with the SPS and TBT Agreements, which aim at sharing information not only among WTO Members, but also with 'interested parties'.[6] However, to date, Members' practices remain uneven when it comes to exchanging with the private sector (section 2).

1   The Importance of Involving the Private Sector in Transparency

The WTO remains an intergovernmental organisation (IGO) – a key strength that allows it to avoid capture by certain interest groups. The potential political and economic consequences of an intergovernmental dispute are such that governments accept some trade-offs to benefit the nation as a whole.[7] There are therefore several non-trade considerations that might enter into play and issues arising may be filtered in the light of these.

---

[6] See Chapter 2.
[7] Bernard M. Hoekman and Michel M. Kostecki, *The Political Economy of the World Trading System: The WTO and Beyond* (Oxford: Oxford University Press, 2009).

However, this filter is less important at the level of transparency. Indeed, the Committee level represents technical discussions between Members and should therefore deliver necessary information to the Member's government, precisely to allow it to make a more informed decision on adjudication. The political and strategic stakes and necessary resources are less high for a State raising an STC versus raising a dispute, and the Member may therefore choose to raise concerns to solve issues of even minor importance.

The minutes of the SPS and TBT Committee meetings attest to the fact that the private sector is an essential bystander in the co-operation that takes place between regulators and trade negotiators in this context. A private sector actor may be highly motivated to contact its government because of the effects that it is experiencing directly – that is, because its products are being retained at the border, for instance, or because it has to adapt its stock to specific requirements of the importing market.

Therefore, while there are some disincentives for the private sector to generate information for disputes,[8] this is much less true at the level of STCs. While generating information about the potential benefits of adjudication might be a disproportionately costly process in comparison to the likely gains, gathering information on concrete trade barriers at the simple 'transparency' phase is relatively easy and cost-free, and the gains that actors may make from ensuring early regulatory co-operation between governments are presumably higher.

In this sense, the private sector plays an essential role in general throughout the entire pre-litigation process, as Bown and Hoekman mention,[9] but also more specifically in raising Members' awareness about new measures and drawing attention to their true impact.

Nevertheless, the private sector remains a bystander more commonly than an actor in this process, because, as in formal dispute settlement, the final decision of whether or not to raise an STC belongs to the Member State. As a result, dialogue with the private sector remains essentially an internal affair.[10]

---

[8] This was especially noted by Bernard Hoekman and Petros Mavroidis, 'Enforcing Multilateral Commitments: Dispute Settlement and Developing Countries', Working Paper, 14 September 1999. www.iatp.org/sites/default/files/Enforcing_Multilateral_Commitments_Dispute_Set.htm; Bown, *Self-Enforcing Trade*.

[9] Bown and Hoekman, 'WTO Dispute Settlement and the Missing Developing Country Cases'.

[10] Hoekman and Kostecki, *The Political Economy of the World Trading System*.

I   INFORMATION ABOUT OTHER MEMBERS' REGULATIONS   271

2   Uneven Information Obtained from Private Sector

At the time of writing, Members' practices remain uneven when it comes to formalising public–private co-operation.[11] Developed Members have very formalised systems of alerting their private sector to new notifications and tend to hold regular meetings with industry representatives to discuss the impacts of new measures on the domestic economy. This allows both parties to become aware of the potential trade effects of notified measures, to make comments on notifications within the 60-day comment period and, eventually, to raise an STC if the issue persists or is of sufficient importance.

Large developing Members have similar co-operation systems with the private sector. However, smaller developing Members and the least-developed countries (LDCs) have less regular contact with the private sector. Although some may have established mechanisms to inform their industries of new notifications, responses from industry tend to be rare. It is only in cases in which major economic interests are at stake that industry representatives may contact LDC governments, asking them to act upon proposed measures.[12] There are, however, certain major exporting sectors that may be particularly active in smaller developing countries and which may therefore play a more active role.[13]

Either way, it seems important that the private sector communicates with national authorities bilaterally and not through the WTO, to ensure that WTO Members maintain their prerogative to decide on the adequate balance between legitimate policy objectives and the necessity of trade restrictions. Indeed, it is key that, after their dialogue with the private sector, governments may still consider the private sector's concerns to be too restrictive in relation to what the Member considers a legitimate objective.

Members have increasingly been discussing the issue of improving dialogue with the private sector with the help of e-mail alert systems informing industry actors of new SPS or TBT notifications made to the WTO Secretariat. The new ePing system described in Chapter 2 may help to achieve this goal, as soon as developing countries become sufficiently aware of its potential.

---

[11] For further details on this, see Part II.
[12] This was the case in particular regarding plain packaging measures adopted by certain countries. Tobacco industry representatives encouraged LDCs to raise STCs and even assisted in their drafting.
[13] For instance, in the context of the interviews with TBT delegates, Trinidad and Tobago explained that it has a very active International Rhum Organisation (RISPA), which was likely to be at the origin of both STCs (a guess that could not be confirmed because the Member delegate had arrived in post only recently).

II Resources

The resource disparity between WTO Members is a reality that is unlikely to change any time soon. However, by reducing information gaps in the pre-litigation phase, the WTO transparency mechanisms place Members on a more equal footing when it comes to building a case.

Among the consequences of resource disparities, differing legal capacity is seen as a crucial distinction preconditioning WTO Members' access to justice. Although transparency does not help to improve legal capacity, it can improve Members' understanding of the obligations and allow them to gather evidence about the regulating Member's measure.

The discussions in Committees may help Members to better evaluate what constitutes a violation of the SPS and TBT Agreements. Indeed, given the negative integration approach taken under both Agreements, the obligations remain vague and hence it is difficult to estimate the extent to which Members comply with them. Transparency may help Members get more acquainted with the institutional system, and to distinguish what might be 'necessary' trade restrictions from what might constitute violations of the SPS and TBT obligations. This is all the more so given that, in some cases, countries enlist the help of private law firms or the Advisory Centre on WTO Law (ACWL) in drafting their STCs.[14] In such a situation, therefore, a Member may acquire more knowledge and understanding about the measure, potentially reducing the costs of repeat litigation.

In addition, the possibility of gathering further information from regulating Members by means of bilateral enquiries and STCs can help concerned Members to build the evidence necessary to bring a case of WTO-inconsistency before the adjudicator. In particular, the WTO's transparency obligations can help Members to better understand each other's measures and therefore to build better cases. The Appellate Body advanced this argument to justify its imposition on the complainant of the burden of proving the rationale of a measure or its departure from international standards[15] – a decision that can be criticised on the basis that it ignores some Members' failure to comply with transparency obligations. However, if notifications and responses to comments were effectively implemented, they would indeed improve Members' opportunities to

---

[14] This was confirmed by the interviews with TBT delegates. It seems particularly apparent in the written submissions of countries raising concerns over tobacco-related measures.
[15] *EC – Hormones*; *EC – Sardines*.

gather the necessary evidence to prove a case alleging that a regulating Member is in violation of its WTO obligations.

III Alternative Fora and Negotiating Capacity

The opportunity to resolve conflicts in another forum and thus avoid adjudication is valuable, helping Members to avoid the burdensome costs of WTO dispute settlement. As we saw in Chapter 7, some Members have access to privileged fora under their bilateral or regional preferential trade agreements (PTAs). The SPS and TBT transparency tools offer the same opportunities to all Members to manage conflicts before they escalate to disputes. The bilateral comments sent to Members via their enquiry points and in STCs offer WTO Members alternative fora in which to discuss their concerns and avoid dispute settlement. As such, being accessible to all Members, they provide an important opportunity to resolve the issue without resorting to adjudication. In this sense, each step of the 'disputing pyramid' is just as useful for helping Members to gather the information necessary if they are to bring disputes before the WTO. This further underlines the importance of *all* Members having the ability to raise concerns in Committees, to ensure that they have equal opportunities to enforce their rights under the SPS and TBT Agreements.

This is particularly true of conflicts affecting small trade volumes and thus not justifying a formal dispute. Recognising that certain disputes involving smaller traders might pertain to small trade volumes for which the efforts to pursue WTO adjudication would be disproportionately high, Hoekman and Mavroidis propose the introduction of 'light' procedures for 'small' cases.[16] These might indeed involve lower costs in the course of the proceedings – but the costs of gathering information and unequal legal capacity to build the case would remain barriers to access. As a result, the most relevant forum with which to address such 'small' cases appears to be the STC raised in one of the Committees – a conclusion confirmed in particular by the many TBT STCs that cite transparency obligations or request for more time to adapt to new regulatory requirements.

---

[16] Bernard M. Hoekman and Petros C. Mavroidis, 'WTO Dispute Settlement, Transparency and Surveillance', 536.

9

Is the Current Interaction between Transparency and Dispute Settlement the Best It Can Be?

Transparency has the potential to facilitate trade by making domestic market access requirements more predictable and by improving convergence among those requirements by means of more co-operative rule-making. When tensions arise, transparency mechanisms facilitate dialogue, allowing trading partners to address those tensions informally. Transparency can therefore largely function as a substitute for dispute settlement, offering parties a more cost-effective route to resolution than resorting to third-party adjudication. Transparency can also complement dispute settlement, insofar as it allows trading partners to gain useful information about measures that they may decide to challenge in disputes. There is, however, room for improvement in the WTO's transparency framework in both regards: the WTO might improve the availability of information and it might support its Members when they engage in regulatory co-operation.

Based on what we have seen of the potential effects of the transparency framework under the WTO Agreements on the Application of Sanitary and Phytosanitary Measures (SPS Agreement, or SPS) and on Technical Barriers to Trade (TBT Agreement, or TBT) and its limitations, this final chapter will examine the main ways in which the WTO might improve the system.

These recommendations focus on what WTO Members, on the one hand, and the WTO Secretariat, on the other, can do to improve the effectiveness of transparency, ultimately aiming to enhance the day-to-day implementation of the SPS and TBT Agreements, to prevent disputes or to facilitate more effective disputes if they prove to be unavoidable. While the existing rules and institutions are already being used as a way of working co-operatively towards effective implementation, there remains much untapped potential, and there is scope for a far more effective transparency framework that will support the development of WTO-consistent measures, the reduction of unnecessary regulatory divergences and trade frictions, and ultimately the widening of access to WTO adjudication if needed. For these purposes, it is important that the WTO work to level the playing field across all of its Members, ensuring that they have equal access to and make equal use of the transparency tools, and that they can leverage the institutional knowledge and capacities held within the WTO Secretariat.

Attempting to achieve these aims by amending or adding to the text of the Agreements would be ill-advised. Not only would the necessary multilateral negotiations be difficult, but also the imbalance of power and resources among Members is such that this type of exercise might simply perpetuate the inequalities that it seeks to solve.[1]

At the same time, while external initiatives are key to increasing the effectiveness of the WTO's transparency framework,[2] these recommendations will make them a priority. An independent assessment always adds value, offering a more accurate and objective critical view of domestic policies. However, for the purposes of implementing WTO obligations, it is essential that transparency is first and foremost reinforced from within the WTO. The texts of both SPS and TBT Agreements already set out the necessary framework for in-depth transparency about domestic regulations and, as shown throughout this book, WTO Members are already making significant use of these tools.

The WTO Secretariat therefore has an essential role to play in bridging information gaps between Members and in supporting Members who are presently failing to notify.[3] As the primary depositary of the information

---

[1] Galanter argues that unequal levels of participation in rule-making are at the root of unequal access to and success in adjudication: Marc Galanter, 'Why the "Haves" Come out Ahead: Speculations on the Limits of Legal Change', *Law and Society Review* 9, no. 1 (1974): 95–160.

[2] See e.g. Bernard M. Hoekman and Petros C. Mavroidis, 'WTO Dispute Settlement, Transparency and Surveillance', *World Economy* 23, no. 4 (2000): 527–42; Chad P. Bown and Bernard M. Hoekman, 'WTO Dispute Settlement and the Missing Developing Country Cases: Engaging the Private Sector', *Journal of International Economic Law* 8, no. 4 (2005): 861–90. In this vein, the Global Trade Alert (GTA) was created to provide information on State measures that may affect trading partners' commercial interests: Simon J. Evenett, 'Global Trade Alert: Motivation and Launch', *World Trade Review* 8, no. 4 (2009): 607–9. The GTA is an independent group of analysts who monitor the domestic measures adopted particularly in response to the economic crisis. For more on this mechanism, see Robert Wolfe, 'Protectionism and Multilateral Accountability during the Great Recession: Drawing Inferences from Dogs not Barking', *Journal of World Trade* 46, no. 4 (2012): 777–814.

[3] Petros C. Mavroidis and Robert Wolfe, 'From Sunshine to a Common Agent. The Evolving Understanding of Transparency in the WTO', RSCAS Research Paper No. PP 2015/01/Columbia Public Law Research Paper No. 14-461, 25 April 2015, 4–5. http://papers.ssrn.com/abstract=2569178.

that Members provide to the WTO, the Secretariat is best placed to identify areas in which this information is insufficient and in which it is not benefiting *all* Members. Indeed, it might play the role of a common agent, 'collecting, aggregating and disseminating trade policy intelligence'.[4] In various ways, other international organisations can contribute to the WTO Secretariat's role – not least those international standardising bodies whose mandate is closely linked to the subject matter of the SPS and TBT Agreements. These organisations, which often develop only voluntary standards, benefit from the incentives set out within both the SPS and TBT Agreements encouraging WTO Members to adopt international standards. Indeed, as seen in Part I, given that domestic measures are presumed to be necessary when they conform to such standards, there is significant incentive for WTO Members to implement these otherwise voluntary instruments.

Ultimately, the recommendations set out in this chapter aim to ensure that all Members implement and therefore reap the potential benefits of transparency to the same extent. Wolfe and Mavroidis note that '[t]ransparency obligations aim to equalise conditions of procuring information across all trading nations and their traders, assuming of course fair play by all'.[5] Equal conditions to information are indeed important to reduce power asymmetries not only between WTO Members but also between the domestic private actors that may have defensive interests in raising a WTO dispute.

Momentum is currently high to reinforce transparency within the WTO. While the organisation's dispute settlement and negotiation functions have been weakened by a political stalemate,[6] transparency is nevertheless seen as an important pillar of the regular work that plays an important role in ensuring the effective operation and implementation of WTO agreements. With this in mind, a group of 'like-minded WTO Members'[7] made a commitment at a ministerial meeting in Ottawa not only to strengthen the WTO dispute settlement system, to reinvigorate the negotiating function of the WTO, but also to 'strengthen the

[4] Ibid.
[5] Ibid.
[6] See esp. Joint Communiqué of the Ottawa Ministerial on WTO Reform, noting 'difficulties to achieve outcomes under the negotiating pillar', and the group's deep concern that 'continued vacancies in the Appellate Body present a risk to the WTO system as a whole': WTO, 'Joint Communiqué of the Ottawa Ministerial on WTO Reform', 25 October 2018. www.wto.org/english/news_e/news18_e/dgra_26oct18_e.pdf.
[7] Australia, Brazil, Canada, Chile, European Union, Japan, Kenya, Korea, Mexico, New Zealand, Norway, Singapore and Switzerland.

monitoring and transparency of members' trade policies which play a central role in ensuring WTO members understand the policy actions taken by their partners in a timely manner'.[8]

Building on this momentum, Canada introduced a proposal that positions transparency as a key component strengthening the WTO's deliberative functions. Recalling the WTO's mandate to 'facilitate the implementation, administration and operation, and further the objectives',[9] Canada suggested that the WTO might share information about domestic measures and their impacts, build its capacity and the opportunity for deliberation, and make use of opportunities and mechanisms with which to address specific trade concerns (STCs).[10] The broad understanding of transparency set out in this proposal, which led to discussions in specific committee contexts,[11] is close to that set out in this book. Aiming, however, at the WTO as a whole rather than only the SPS and TBT Committees, the Canadian vision may lack some of the specific insights that are necessary to enhance the benefits of transparency in the SPS and TBT contexts.

Also aiming to strengthen transparency, five Members under the leadership of the United States[12] introduced a more specific proposal focusing on enhancing notification practices under the different WTO agreements.[13] While notification is already more actively practised under the SPS and TBT Agreements than under other WTO agreements, the proposal nevertheless includes suggestions to enhance SPS and TBT notifications as well.[14] In particular, the Members propose that a 'Working Group

---

[8] 'Joint Communiqué of the Ottawa Ministerial on WTO Reform', 2.
[9] Under Art. III.1 of the Marrakech Agreement. See ibid.
[10] WTO, 'Strengthening the Deliberative Function of the WTO' (JOB/GC/211, 14 December 2018).
[11] Global Affairs Canada, 'Improving the Deliberative Function of WTO Bodies', 24 January 2019. www.canada.ca/en/global-affairs/news/2019/01/improving-the-deliberative-function-of-wto-bodies.html.
[12] Argentina, Costa Rica, European Union, Japan and the United States.
[13] WTO, 'Procedures to Enhance Transparency and Strengthen Notification Requirements under WTO Agreements' (JOB/GC/204/Rev.1, 2019).
[14] The other agreements covered by the proposal include: Agreement on Implementation of Article VI of the GATT 1994 (Anti-dumping); Agreement on Subsidies and Countervailing Measures; Agreement on Safeguards; Understanding on the Interpretation of Article XVII of the GATT 1994 (State Trading); Agreement on Implementation of Article VII of the GATT 1994 (Customs Valuation); Agreement on Import Licensing Procedures; Agreement on Rules of Origin; Agreement on Preshipment Inspection; Decision on Notification Procedures for Quantitative Restrictions (G/L/59/Rev.1, 2012); Agreement on Trade-Related Investment Measures; and Section 1 of the Agreement on Trade Facilitation.

on Notification Obligations and Procedures' be established to regularly assess Members' compliance with notification obligations, to take appropriate steps to reinforce this compliance and to make recommendations on ways in which the WTO might encourage more Members to comply with their obligations. In addition, the proposal suggests that administrative sanctions be imposed on those countries who do not provide complete notifications and do not seek assistance from the WTO Secretariat to do so.[15]

Overall, these proposals confirm that transparency is high on Members' agendas. The follow-up on the Ottawa Declaration[16] and positive reactions to the US proposal[17] demonstrate a strong commitment among WTO Members to transparency and suggest that Members are ready to increase their efforts.

These different proposals will be discussed in this chapter insofar as they provide insights into ways of ensuring more effective transparency mechanisms as a substitute for and complement to dispute settlement.

I Improving the Availability of Information

Centralised access to information, as ensured by notifications, is an essential attribute of the SPS and TBT transparency framework, laying the groundwork for all the other functions of transparency: it enables easy access to information on WTO Members' domestic measures, gives timely notice to other Members of measures to come, and paves the way for dialogue between the regulating Member and any potentially affected Member. In situations in which tensions persist, notifications and STCs have significant potential to place all WTO Members on an equal footing when it comes to awareness of measures that might affect them and which could be contrary to WTO law. The public accessibility of notifications through the WTO Secretariat helps to level the playing field among Members who may otherwise be unequally able to afford to seek out that information.

---

[15] WTO, 'Procedures to Enhance Transparency and Strengthen Notification Requirements', 3.
[16] Several countries agreed to begin analysing and discussing how the deliberative functions of certain WTO bodies could be improved and enhanced. See Global Affairs Canada, 'Improving the Deliberative Function of WTO Bodies'.
[17] Thirty-seven Members took the floor to react positively to the proposal, highlighting the importance of transparency as a fundamental pillar of the multilateral trading system: WTO, 'Goods Council Considers Revised Transparency Proposal to "Reinvigorate" the WTO', November 2018. www.wto.org/english/news_e/news18_e/good_12nov18_e.htm.

Access to notifications has recently been boosted by ePing, a new tool developed by the WTO Secretariat jointly with the United Nations Department of Economic and Social Affairs (UNDESA) and the International Trade Centre (ITC). However, there is still room for improvement and the system has yet to reach its full potential.

A   Deliver More Information about More Domestic Regulations: Reinforcing Members' Notification Practices

Members increasingly notify under both the SPS and TBT Agreements, and these notifications continue to represent a substantial share of all notifications to the WTO. However, some Members still do not notify and STCs may consequently be raised against non-notified measures. This suggests that there are undoubtedly measures that qualify for notification under the SPS and TBT Agreements, which deviate from international standards and have significant trade effects, but which are not notified. If more Members are to notify, there must be incentives encouraging Members to improve their compliance with transparency obligations, support for those Members who do not yet or only rarely notify and support for those who do to do so more effectively or more systematically.

1   Enhance the Incentives for Transparency

Incentives for transparency may be strengthened by means of both 'carrots' and 'sticks' – that is, by raising awareness about the benefits of transparency and by providing some forms of sanction in cases of non-compliance. The WTO and WTO Members have explored both options.

The 'sticks' for transparency are still relatively weak. Indeed, dispute settlement is not as significant a threat in relation to transparency as it is for other WTO obligations, because transparency claims are not as systematically raised in requests for consultations as are the more substantive provisions of the SPS and TBT Agreements. The mere absence of notification may not result in sufficiently significant trade losses to justify raising a dispute. Nevertheless, one Member's failure to notify may be harmful for other WTO Members, in particular in preventing Members and stakeholders from exercising their right to comment on draft SPS or TBT measures. A proposal on enhancing notifications envisages administrative sanctions for Members who have failed to notify after a year, which sanctions include the Member being ineligible to preside over any WTO body, the Member being ignored during trade policy reviews, the Member being required to make an additional contribution to the WTO budget, the WTO Secretariat submitting annual reports of the Member's notifications to the Council for Trade in Goods and the Member being subject to additional reporting requirements ahead of meetings of the WTO General Council.[18] These sanctions would be likely to provide a very strong incentive motivating Members to notify. They are, however, suitable for countries who choose not to notify in bad faith, but much less so for those countries that do not (yet) notify only because they lack the institutional structure and appropriate capacity to do so. Indeed, the least-developed countries (LDCs) in particular are typically less active notifiers and would therefore risk sanctions – sanctions that would exclude them from the regular work of WTO bodies and policy discussions, and thereby disadvantage them yet further. This is also true of a large number of developing Members that are not among the active notifying Members. It therefore seems unlikely that the WTO membership will accept the proposal. In particular, developing countries with more structural barriers to notification and fewer systematic mechanisms with which to identify the right measures to notify are likely to be firmly against such sanctions.

Not only is a system of sanctions a disproportionate response to Members who find it difficult to identify the measures that they should notify, but also it is unsuited to the general purposes of transparency as set out in the SPS and TBT Agreements. Indeed, this proposal promulgates a very binary vision of transparency that fails to reflect the complexity of transparency obligations. To merely view transparency obligations as 'complied with' or 'not complied with' and imposing sanctions as soon as there is a lack of compliance is to ignore the key purpose of transparency – namely, to facilitate access to and availability of effective information. To that end, strong incentives are needed to motivate Members' compliance with their transparency obligations.

The effect of the transparency framework – that is, raising awareness of measures that are currently non-notified – is itself such an incentive. More specifically to the SPS and TBT context, the WTO Secretariat could help to increase information about STCs raised in relation to non-notified measures. This would have the dual effect of making the information publicly available and further motivating the regulating Member to notify. In the absence of 'reverse notification' procedures under the SPS and TBT Agreements, an STC about a non-notified measure is the best source of information that WTO Members have about such measures. Indeed,

---

[18] WTO, 'Procedures to Enhance Transparency and Strengthen Notification Requirements', 3.

the STC itself serves as a reverse notification, offsetting the regulating Member's lack of transparency, and arguably, if a Member feels sufficiently affected by a measure to raise a concern in one of the Committees, the measure is likely to be of interest to other Members as well. However, finding out about the measure in Committee minutes does not deliver *timely* information to the potentially affected Members and the private sector, not least because the minutes are not issued immediately after the Committee meeting.

Once again, the Secretariat could play a role in making information about these STCs against non-notified measures more visible. When receiving intentions to raise STCs, the Secretariat could ask the concerned Member whether the STC is related to a notification and if not, the Secretariat might take steps to draw Members' attention to the non-notified measures. To some extent, shining a spotlight on those who fail to notify might encourage more Members to do so in the first instance.

2 Support Those Members Who Never or Only Rarely Notify to Do So

The WTO Secretariat is already making significant efforts to support Members in building capacity to submit notifications by means of the technical assistance that it provides, particularly to enquiry points, and the exchange of information in Committee meetings.[19] The high share of notifications from developing countries suggests that these efforts have been fruitful.

While the WTO Secretariat cannot tell Members which specific measures to notify, because this goes well beyond the Secretariat's mandate and is each Member's individual responsibility, it might nevertheless provide support to Members by helping them to fill the gaps in incomplete notifications.

On the one hand, the Secretariat could help to complete relevant information about domestic regulations. For this, it could encourage developing countries and LDCs to submit incomplete notifications rather than no notifications at all, undertaking to support them subsequently, for example by confirming the relevant Harmonized System (HS) codes that apply to the affected products or by helping the notifying Member to identify the regions or countries likely to be affected by the measure.

---

[19] See the different options for technical assistance and steps to request it listed by the Secretariat in WTO, 'WTO TBT Enquiry Point Guide: Making Transparency Work', June 2018, 80. www.wto.org/english/tratop_e/tbt_e/tbt_enquiry_point_guide_e.pdf.

Positive incentives from other WTO Members are also essential towards enhanced transparency. In particular, Members aware of the absence of a notification could inform the relevant country's enquiry point and bilaterally encourage the regulating Member to notify. When informing the enquiry point, the concerned Member might inform the WTO Secretariat in parallel, which might then help by systematically delivering reminders until the regulating Member notifies its measure or by offering the necessary technical assistance if the notification has not been submitted for capacity reasons. Finally, as the five Members led by the United States recently proposed, the WTO Secretariat could submit the notification in lieu of the Member if another Member were to request that it do so.[20]

On the other hand, the Secretariat could bridge the gap between notifying Members and the relevant international standardising organisations for information by informing the Member of the relevant standards or of the right format of notification in the specific instance. Indeed, correctly identifying the relevant international standard with which the measure conforms is said to be one of the major barriers to notification.[21] The WTO Secretariat could therefore consider a collaboration with the international standardising organisations, providing support to developing-country Members about relevant international standards related to notified draft measures. In this way, a measure notified as incomplete, referring to an international standard without clarity on which one or on the ways in which it conforms to the international standard, might be complemented with the support of the body responsible for the relevant international standard.

B   Broaden the Range of Information Available

The information currently available on domestic measures is essentially about Members' draft measures. To improve Members' understanding of each other's domestic regulatory frameworks, a more complete insight into the subsequent phases of the regulatory process, up to adoption of the measure, would be useful, to include sharing the comments on the notified draft.

---

[20] WTO, 'Procedures to Enhance Transparency and Strengthen Notification Requirements', 3.
[21] WTO, 'Analysis of the Replies to the Questionnaire on Transparency under the SPS Agreement', G/SPS/GEN/1402, 20 March 2015.

1 Improve Information about the Entire Regulatory Policy Cycle

Notifications remain limited to draft measures and follow-up notifications of addenda, corrigenda or revisions remain infrequent. Members have only limited access to the adopted measures and very little insight into the changes that result from comments made by other Members bilaterally or in discussions within the Committees. As already noted, while the Committees recommend that Members notify their adopted measures, very few of them do so in practice.

To encourage Members to share information about adopted measures, the WTO Secretariat could send automatic 'reminders' to Members after the date of adoption set out in the original notification, asking the Member to update the status of their notified draft and seeking more comprehensive information on any subsequent drafts. A brief summary of the status of the measure could then be included on the SPS and TBT electronic information management systems (IMSs), allowing all Members to have a clear overview of the measures in force across the whole membership. Indeed, if such information were to be made available for enough SPS and TBT measures, the outcome may be a searchable database on the import and export requirements in force among WTO Members, which could be filtered by type, territory, etc.

2 Improve Information about the Trade Effects of Regulations

One of the major shortcomings of the WTO's information system as it stands is the difficulty of estimating the trade effects of domestic measures, even when they are notified[22] – an estimate that both the regulating Member and its trading partners find difficult when dealing in the abstract with the trade effects of regulatory drafts. To better estimate these effects, WTO Members may benefit from leveraging existing regulatory policy that allows them to estimate the benefits and costs of regulations, through both regulatory impact assessments (RIAs) and stakeholder consultation.

a **Encourage the Use of Domestic RIAs when Estimating the Trade Effects of a Measure** Regulatory impact assessments are an essential tool in evaluating the impacts of domestic measures and all Members of the Organisation for Economic Co-operation and Development (OECD)

---

[22] Robert Wolfe, 'How Can We Know (More) About the Trade Effects of Regulation?', E15 Initiative/ICTSD/WEF, 25 August 2015. https://papers.ssrn.com/sol3/papers.cfm?abstract_id=2800641.

use them. While the commonplace cost–benefit analysis conducted during the RIA focuses mostly on domestic social and economic factors, an increasing number of OECD countries also use RIAs to identify the likely trade costs of draft regulations.[23] Insofar as the SPS and TBT Agreements both require an evidence basis for domestic regulations to avoid measures being arbitrarily conceived, the two Committees could further encourage WTO Members to use RIAs systematically to prevent the adoption of measures that impose unnecessary costs of trade. This is standardly the case in Mexico, for example, where the RIA process includes specific questions on the trade effects of regulations and serves to alert trade authorities in government when a draft may have an impact on trade, which alert triggers an SPS or TBT notification.[24]

More broadly, sharing the results of RIAs in SPS and TBT notifications could allow Members to share information about the potential impacts of their measures. In particular, including RIAs in the notification process could be a useful means of encouraging feedback on the domestic RIA and therefore may improve the ability of Members to estimate the effects of their regulations beyond the border. The TBT Committee suggested such a mechanism in its draft Non-exhaustive List of Voluntary Mechanisms and Related Principles of Good Regulatory Practice (GRP), which remains under discussion in the TBT Committee at time of writing.[25] Given the delay in adopting this document, a recommendation to this effect in both the SPS and TBT Committees could usefully motivate Members to notify their RIAs.

b **Improve Dialogue with the Private Sector** The private sector can play an important role in supporting Members to make effective use of the SPS and TBT transparency tools, by providing them with information about the trade effects of regulations. This can help Members to make comments on notifications, to launch STCs or to raise disputes, as we have already seen. However, to date, only major corporations have tended

---

[23] OECD, *OECD Regulatory Policy Outlook 2018* (Paris: OECD, 2018), 134. www.oecd.org/governance/oecd-regulatory-policy-outlook-2018-9789264303072-en.htm.

[24] OECD, *Review of International Regulatory Co-operation of Mexico* (Paris: OECD, 2018), 62–9. www.oecd.org/publications/review-of-international-regulatory-co-operation-of-mexico-9789264305748-en.htm.

[25] A first draft of this document was circulated in February 2013 and the latest draft to date was circulated in December 2014.

to have the level of knowledge about both the trade-restrictive measures and their inconsistency with regard to WTO obligations necessary to allow them to encourage their government to adjudicate.[26]

While it remains important to maintain the filter of government both at the Committee level and prior to dispute settlement, systematic dialogue with the private sector is essential. This is the main medium through which Members become aware of potentially trade-restrictive measures at a time when they can take action – that is, communicate with the regulating Member to encourage constructive amendment of the draft measure. The WTO's ePing system is an important source of information for the private sector, including small and medium-sized enterprises (SMEs) from developing countries and LDCs. Presumably, this should therefore considerably improve the dialogue between the private sector and WTO Member governments.

In addition, WTO Members should be encouraged to engage regularly with representatives from their exporting industries to raise awareness of the WTO system and of the rights and obligations that Members have under the SPS and TBT Agreements. Some Members have three committee meetings at the domestic level that 'mirror' proceedings in the WTO's SPS and TBT Committees. Such regular dialogue between Member governments and the private sector seems to be the minimum activity required if either is to be certain of having an overview of the trade effects of issues on the Committee agenda. More broadly, the various stakeholder engagement procedures that already exist in the domestic context and allow stakeholders to consult on regulatory drafts could further be built on to draw out evidence about the trade effects of the regulations. Such stakeholder engagement should nevertheless be based on sound principles to ensure its quality and to widen participation among representative samples spanning the Members' economy.[27]

---

[26] Dirk De Bièvre, Arlo Poletti and Aydin Yildirim, 'About the Melting of Icebergs: Political and Economic Determinants of Dispute Initiation and Resolution in the WTO', in Manfred Elsig, Bernard Hoekman and Joost Pauwelyn, eds, *Assessing the World Trade Organization: Fit For Purpose?* (Cambridge: Cambridge University Press, 2017), 125.

[27] See e.g. Principle 2 of OECD, 'Recommendation of the Council on Regulatory Policy and Governance' (2012). www.oecd.org/governance/regulatory-policy/49990817.pdf; OECD, 'Draft Best Practice Principles on Stakeholder Engagement in Regulatory Policy' (2017). www.oecd.org/governance/regulatory-policy/public-consultation-best-practice-principles-on-stakeholder-engagement.htm.

3 Enhance Information about Bilateral Dialogue

The WTO Secretariat indicates that Members allow, on average, 60 days for comments to be made on a measure – and this is the period that the Secretariat recommends. To extend to the entire membership the benefits of the bilateral discussions that take place by means of comments on notifications, the Secretariat could encourage Members to publish the comments they have both made and received, other than when they consider comments to be too politically or economically sensitive to be disclosed. Indeed, the European Union (EU) already takes this approach towards its TBT measures.

In the context of the TBT Committee's seventh triennial review, Korea proposed that Members disclose comments and that the Secretariat take a more active role in facilitating better follow-up on those comments:

> [Korea] proposes that the WTO Secretariat adopt a WTO-administered system for administering comments on notified measures. Through the adoption of such system, the WTO may look over the enquiries that have been raised and encourage the Member that has received the enquiry to respond to it in a timely and appropriate manner. It is Korea's view that an adoption of the WTO-administered system could be useful in making enquiry points function more effectively and efficiently.[28]

Other Members did not follow up on this proposal and it therefore did not result in a recommendation. Indeed, the requirement that the WTO Secretariat monitor all comments and follow up with non-responding Members individually would place a high burden on the shoulders of the Secretariat staff. However, merely publishing comments on notifications on the TBT and SPS IMSs, making them visible across the whole membership, may have a positive impact, encouraging regulating Members to respond to those comments. If Members were to share the appropriate information with the WTO Secretariat, it could then directly link notifications, comments on the notifications and any STCs raised. Such a link would introduce a new level of transparency into the 'disputing pyramid', and it would offer Members an overview of the regulatory situation in any given instance and of the regulatory dialogue taking place to try to address any issue arising.

II Enhancing the Scope and Benefits of Regulatory Co-operation

The multilateral regulatory co-operation that takes place within the SPS and TBT Committees is probably the most frequent and inclusive mechanism supporting Members in the development of their domestic

---

[28] WTO, *Seventh Triennial Review: Submission from the Republic of Korea* (G/TBT/W/419/Rev.1, July 2015), para. 3.1.

measures – and yet its potential is largely under-exploited. While an average of 40 STCs are discussed per SPS Committee meeting and 150 per TBT Committee meeting, each is approached very much on its own merits, resulting at best in changes to specific measures but no further cross-cutting discussions to promote the WTO's negotiation agenda. Further efforts could therefore be made, in particular by the WTO Secretariat, to ensure that this platform serves all WTO Members equally and to improve the effects of the multilateral dialogue by widening participation to include different stakeholders and experts.

A   *Use STCs to Channel Efforts towards Regulatory Co-operation on Priority Issues and between Like-Minded Countries*

The regulatory dialogue that takes place as a result of SPS and TBT transparency obligations is crucial in preserving Members' regulatory autonomy while encouraging co-operation in the implementation of the SPS and TBT Agreements. As such, the spontaneity of the discussions and the truly multilateral opportunity that the two Committees offer for dialogue between any two or more WTO Members is an invaluable opportunity to reduce regulatory divergence. This is all the more so in an interconnected world fragmented by global value chains, in which trade does not take place only with neighbouring countries.

The STC discussions represent an invaluable source of evidence on the issues and sectors that are most commonly subject to STCs, and which require close co-ordination between Members to avoid unnecessary barriers to trade. Members tacitly acknowledge this by convening thematic sessions back to back with the TBT Committee meetings on issues that are often subject to STCs.[29] Such thematic sessions do, however, remain time-bound and the substance depends on individual Members' priorities. There is scope for Members to make much more of these STC discussions, more closely and more systematically monitoring the issues raised. While it is important to maintain a certain level of informality about the topics of regulatory co-operation, those topics should be Member-led, driven by Members' legitimate concerns about regulatory divergences and inconsistencies with WTO obligations.

The WTO Secretariat is well placed to deliver this mechanism, given its oversight of discussions taking place in both SPS and TBT Committee meetings, its technical expertise on the subject matter and its political

---

[29] This has taken place e.g. on food labelling in November 2016: see www.wto.org/english/tratop_e/tbt_e/tbtnov16_e.htm.

independence of Members' priorities. In this sense, the Secretariat could valuably help Members to identify priority issues on which regulatory co-operation is needed, to deliver regular updates within the two Committees and to highlight areas in which regulatory co-operation between countries could help them to address these issues. Based on this independent account, all WTO Members would have the same comprehensive view of the scope for co-operation and could take the initiative to co-operate more closely with other WTO Members who have declared similar concerns to their own. These Members could co-operate, for instance, by concluding mutual recognition agreements (MRAs) with other like-minded countries. And should the issues seem sufficiently significant, the Members might use these as a launch pad for negotiations towards plurilateral agreements.

B Enhance the Scope of Regulatory Co-operation to Allow for the Better Balancing of Trade and Non-trade Considerations

International regulatory co-operation (IRC) can have important implications for reducing the costs of international trade. However, such co-operation remains, first and foremost, subject to the authority of regulators who have their own policy objectives, which may be very distinct from trade considerations. Nevertheless, the two communities have a lot to learn from each other and, in particular, while the trade community can benefit from increased co-ordination between regulators, the regulatory community can benefit from the tools for regulatory co-operation and information exchange that already exist under the SPS and TBT Agreements. As such, better co-ordination between the two communities can be mutually beneficial, would support the purposes of transparency under the SPS and TBT Agreements, and could ultimately help Members to manage their own conflicts.

At the same time and while not within the scope of the WTO Agreements, non-trade considerations necessarily influence discussions between WTO Members and can be important factors feeding into trade concerns and disputes. Broadening discussions in SPS and TBT Committees to include such considerations could therefore help to make the IRC that takes place through STCs more comprehensive and effective in addressing Members' overall concerns.

1 Better Co-ordinate Trade and Regulatory Communities

We saw in Part I that various principles set out in the SPS and TBT Agreements aim to rationalise WTO Members' policy interventions, calling for dialogue and co-operation among WTO Members. Indeed, regulatory co-operation can be an important way in which regulators reduce regulatory divergence and therefore reduce cost impacts on trade, in line with the WTO's core objective. However, regulatory co-operation can also pursue other objectives, such as managing risks and externalities that cross borders – typically, transboundary air pollution or outbreaks of disease, improved administrative efficiency or simply knowledge flows.[30] There are therefore important incentives for regulators to co-operate that reach beyond the trade objectives and account for the policy realities of the interconnected world. Co-operation remains, however, a nascent principle in regulatory policy, happening mostly on an ad hoc basis, and most regulators are ignorant of the tools that enable such co-operation.[31] This is less true in the WTO, where such tools have been set up under the SPS and TBT Agreements and are extensively used by Members, as seen throughout this book. Comments on notifications and STCs can offer opportunities from which not only trade policy-makers but also regulators can benefit – in particular feeding into domestic stakeholder engagement policies and helping the Member to identify any unexpected costs of its regulatory proposals. In this sense, co-ordination between trade and regulatory communities can mutually benefit both, allowing them to exchange essential information about foreign regulations and exposing them to feedback from foreign peers. Indeed, the eighth triennial review of the TBT Committee recommended that Members be encouraged '[t]o discuss good practices for domestic coordination and engagement with regulators, including sharing information about how Members effectively communicate with regulatory agencies to ensure that all relevant notifications are made'.[32] In similar vein, Hoekman notes that 'the WTO (and trade agreements more generally) could be used as a focal point for encouraging regulators to interact with each other and to consider co-operation that enhances their joint ability to attain regulatory objectives at lower cost'.[33]

Such co-ordination at the Member level could foster a more active role for domestic regulatory oversight bodies in bringing together all relevant actors, including regulators and trade policy authorities, to discuss

---

[30] OECD, *International Regulatory Co-operation* (Paris: OECD, 2013), 77. www.oecd-ilibrary.org/governance/international-regulatory-co-operation_9789264200463-en.
[31] OECD, *OECD Regulatory Policy Outlook 2018*, 124.
[32] WTO, 'Eighth Triennial Review of the Operation and Implementation of the Agreement on Technical Barriers to Trade under Article 15.4' (G/TBT/41, 19 November 2018), 20.
[33] Bernard Hoekman, ' "Behind-the-Border" Regulatory Policies and Trade Agreements', *East Asian Economic Review* 22, no. 3 (2018): 271.

regulatory matters pending, to identify feedback received not only through domestic stakeholder mechanisms but also through WTO transparency channels, and to discuss information about foreign regulatory initiatives that may be of relevance.

2 Include Non-trade Considerations in the Discussion

One notable absence in the dialogue that takes place in the SPS and TBT Committees is that of those representing non-trade considerations. The WTO is an organisation aiming to facilitate trade, and the SPS and TBT Agreements are specific areas of trade in goods to which the WTO aims to reduce barriers. However, the two Agreements also notably require a balance with non-trade-related objectives and protection of Members' regulatory autonomy. The regulatory dialogue that takes place at the early stages of Members' domestic regulatory process is an invaluable opportunity to balance the *a priori* opposing interests with trade and other policy objectives. This is an idea in line with the 'New WTO Think' that Mavroidis and Bollyky advocate, which 'remains rooted in the original rationale of the GATT [General Agreement on Tariffs and Trade] (or GATT-think) of reducing the negative externalities of unilateral action and solving important international coordination challenges, but is more inclusive of regulators and non-state actors and more flexible and positive in its means'.[34]

Taking non-trade considerations into account is all the more important given that concerns that also relate to wider societal concerns have been driving the most recent TBT cases in particular.[35] Addressing such matters through co-operative efforts while the measure is still in draft phase would have significant value where Members are genuinely seeking to adopt the best measure available.

To include consideration of non-trade interests in the scope of the SPS and TBT Committees in line with the existing obligations under the Agreements, the Secretariat might enhance the role played by other international organisations – in particular international standardisation bodies. Indeed, while the WTO takes a negative integration approach, it works with organisations that do not, and the SPS and TBT Agreements

---

[34] Thomas J. Bollyky and Petros C. Mavroidis, 'Trade, Social Preferences and Regulatory Cooperation: The New WTO-Think', RSCAS Research Paper No. 2016/47, 2 December 2016, 5. https://papers.ssrn.com/sol3/papers.cfm?abstract_id=2879329.

[35] Wolfe, 'Letting the Sun Shine in at the WTO: How Transparency Brings the Trading System to Life', Staff Working Paper No. ERSD-2013-03, 22 November 2013, 24. http://papers.ssrn.com/sol3/Delivery.cfm?abstractid=2229741.

explicitly include obligations to accept international standards and to participate in such organisations.

The SPS Agreement suggests that Members might ask international standardising bodies for their opinions on a specific matter.[36] Most relevant organisations have observer status in the TBT and SPS Committees, and they can therefore participate in the discussions. In addition, some organisations ask to participate in the Committee meetings to provide an opinion on a matter and hence provide an 'independent' perspective on a concern of Members. This is the case, for instance, with the World Health Organization (WHO), which provides its opinion regularly in the context of TBT STCs relating to tobacco,[37] or the Organisation for Animal Health (OIE), which intervenes on issues regarding animal health, such as avian influenza.[38]

More systematic consultations with standardisation bodies during Committee meetings – particularly during the discussion of STCs regarding those bodies' standards – would enhance the link between the SPS and TBT objectives of harmonisation and the existing international standards. The position of the expert standardising body in the STCs would enhance the effectiveness of the regulatory co-operation by improving understanding of the relevant international standard.

C Support Developing Countries' Participation in Regulatory Dialogue

Influencing trading partners to amend those regulations that have an adverse effect on trade requires a Member to have the capacity to estimate the impacts of foreign regulations on its trade, and to submit comments on notifications and launch STCs. Yet the trends in country group participation in relation to both SPS and TBT STCs still show that developing countries are more active only in supporting concerns and that LDCs are virtually absent from discussions. More in-depth technical assistance from the WTO Secretariat could specifically focus on helping these Members with the 'demand side' of information – that is, helping them to make comments on notifications and raise STCs. Training Members to identify those measures that may have trade effect – the very first major step in the 'disputing pyramid' – would help to equalise the benefits of transparency and would ultimately grant *all* Members equal access to dispute settlement, if it proves necessary in any given instance.

---

[36] Article 12.6 SPS.
[37] See e.g., in the TBT Committee, 'Australia – Tobacco Plain Packaging Bill 2011' (ID 304).
[38] See e.g., in the SPS Committee, 'India – Restrictions Due to Avian Influenza' (ID 185).

Conclusion of Part III

As we have seen, only a very small fraction of specific trade concerns (STCs) eventually end up in formal disputes, arguably because the transparency framework has allowed Members to effectively manage conflicts at an informal level. The majority of all SPS and TBT disputes are discussed in the SPS and TBT Committees before, during or after the formal dispute is raised, and this is especially true of disputes that focus on SPS or TBT issues. Developing countries in particular tend to launch STCs before or in parallel to dispute settlement procedures, whereas the EU and the United States raise formal requests for consultations in the TBT Committee without first passing through Committee discussions. This confirms that WTO Members truly view the Committees as a valuable forum in which to work through disputes regarding domestic regulatory matters and, often, a privileged space with regard to costly formal dispute settlement procedures. The behaviour of the EU and United States confirms that they may have other means of managing trade conflicts or gaining information to build disputes that does not require them to raise STCs as systematically as other Members.

By improving the disclosure of information and the regulatory co-operation that is facilitated by the SPS and TBT transparency mechanisms, the tensions between Members could be yet further reduced, reserving the dispute settlement system for exceptional cases.

Nevertheless, the existence of the dispute settlement system is undeniably a crucial way of enforcing WTO law when tensions regarding potentially WTO-inconsistent measures persist. It is therefore important that, in addition to acting as a conflict management tool, transparency equalises Members' access to dispute settlement and improves Members' chances of settlement after consultations have been initiated and before a panel is established. Recalling that information about other Members' regulations, resources and alternative fora is the determining factor that allows Members to launch formal disputes, the variety of transparency tools available within the SPS and TBT frameworks provides Members with valuable ways of climbing the 'disputing pyramid'.

In general, the transparency tools of the SPS and TBT Agreements appear to have untapped potential to prevent disputes and allow more WTO Members to access formal dispute settlement. In particular, they have the potential to further improve the availability of information and enhance the scope and benefits of the regulatory co-operation that takes place within the SPS and TBT framework – and various initiatives to enhance transparency within the WTO confirm that momentum is high among Members willing to move in this direction.

CONCLUSION

Jagdish Bhagwati refers to transparency as the 'Dracula effect', saying that 'exposing evil to sunlight helps to destroy it'.[1] Does transparency under the WTO Agreements on the Application of Sanitary and Phytosanitary Measures (SPS Agreement, or SPS) and on Technical Barriers to Trade (TBT Agreement, or TBT) ensure a 'Dracula effect', helping to prevent and address WTO-inconsistent practices? Or does it fuel more disputes? In other words, does transparency act as a substitute for or a complement to dispute settlement – or both?

An examination of Members' transparency practices in the SPS and TBT Committees shows that transparency can fulfil the three functions of dispute settlement: it can embed security and predictability into the multilateral trading system; it can preserve Members' rights and obligations; and, to a certain extent, it can even clarify existing provisions. It delivers security and predictability through an increasingly efficient source of centralised information that offers insights into Members' domestic regulations before their entry into force, granting Members and their industries time to adapt to new requirements. It allows Members to play the role of 'watchdogs', aiming to preserve their own rights and to verify other Members' compliance with their obligations by means of bilateral and multilateral dialogue on draft measures. This Member-driven 'surveillance' is all the more efficient because it takes a co-operative form and is as useful for the regulating Member, who benefits from inputs into its measures, as it is for the affected (or potentially affected) Member, who may convince the regulating Member to amend the measure in light of its concerns. Finally, transparency may even help to clarify existing provisions – not from a legal point of view, because that level of interpretation remains the sole responsibility of the WTO's Dispute Settlement Body (DSB), but

---

[1] Jagdish N. Bhagwati, *Protectionism* (Cambridge, MA/London: MIT Press, 1988), 85.

from a practical point of view: co-operation among Members may help them to collaboratively determine what the right approach is under the Agreements.[2] Informally, then, transparency can help Members to implement their SPS and TBT obligations, fulfilling the functions of dispute settlement. This is all the more so when considering that the main objective of dispute settlement is finding a mutually acceptable solution[3] and, as Mavroidis argues, that the WTO dispute settlement system aims to achieve co-operation between WTO Members rather than to punish offenders.[4]

Part I offered an overview of the legal framework established by the SPS and TBT Agreements, explaining why transparency has a specific function within that framework. The negative integration approach pursued by the two Agreements, complemented by provisions requiring a certain 'quality' in the domestic regulatory process, calls for strong transparency of draft regulations. This unique transparency framework under the SPS and TBT Agreements tackles the ambiguity that the negative integration approach engenders, aiming to deliver knowledge of domestic requirements and predictability by ensuring that Members disclose their proposed measures, and by encouraging and enabling international regulatory co-operation (IRC) on each one.

The focus on *ex ante* transparency in these two Agreements fosters a dialogue before measures have entered into force, thus opening the way for multilateral regulatory co-operation that can be beneficial for both the regulating and the concerned Members. The opportunity to voice concerns and the obligation to take these concerns into account help Members to work towards regulations that satisfy both the legitimate objectives of the former and the trade interests of the latter. Ultimately, this *ex ante* transparency, together with the regulatory co-operation in relation to the legal framework established under the SPS and TBT Agreements, fosters better compliance with those Agreements.

---

[2] Scott notes in this regard that '[i]n the course of their repeated interactions, Members arrive at settled (though not necessarily authoritative, from the point of view of the dispute settlement bodies) understanding of the meaning of the agreement in context': Joanne Scott, *The WTO Agreement on Sanitary and Phytosanitary Measures*, 54.

[3] Article 3, §7 DSU.

[4] '... what matters most to them is a spirit of co-operation and restraint of trade wars, rather than punishment of the culprits': Petros Mavroidis, 'Dispute Settlement in the WTO: Mind over Matter', RSCAS Working Paper No. 2015/34, 2015, 1. http://cadmus.eui.eu/bitstream/handle/1814/35980/RSCAS_2015_34.pdf?sequence=1.

Part II introduced the 'disputing pyramid' which comprises all of the domestic regulations with effects on trade at its base up to the very few formal disputes that are raised at its peak. It showed that the transparency tools set out within the SPS and TBT Agreements lay the groundwork for various sources of information on domestic regulations, and that the WTO Secretariat's centralisation of all of this information represents a tremendous boost to Members' access to that information at minimum cost. Overall, three sources of complementary information were presented – namely, notifications, regulatory dialogue and the private sector.

Notifications constitute an undeniably significant source of information, because they provide timely information centralised within the WTO and therefore accessible equally to all Members. No bilateral or regional initiative, however ambitious it may be, can ensure such multilateral benefits from disclosure of information. Nevertheless, a few gaps in the available information still remain and there are no guarantees that all measures affecting trade are indeed notified. In fact, a number of specific trade concerns (STCs) are raised each year against non-notified measures, suggesting that notifications may not be sufficient. To a certain extent, the STCs therefore complement non-notified measures by means of a *de facto* 'cross-notification' by concerned Members – but this necessarily implies that a Member has obtained the information somehow, again implying search costs for the Member raising the concern. And once the concern is raised, the information benefits are extended to the entire WTO membership through the Committee discussions, but this information may arrive too late in the regulatory process, after unnecessary trade effects have already had a negative impact on trading partners.

The private sector – that is, industry representatives and trading companies – may provide invaluable information on the trade impact of measures. As such and as is the case in relation to disputes, the private sector is at the heart of many STCs that take issue with harms on specific firms or industries. However, since dialogue with the private sector is not formalised within the WTO and depends largely on Members' own prerogatives and resources, this source of information is unevenly accessed among Members. The new electronic alert system put in place by the WTO Secretariat, jointly with the United Nations Department of Economic and Social Affairs (UNDESA) and the International Trade Centre (ITC), may help to facilitate communication with the private sector.

Nevertheless, the extent of the private sector's involvement in STCs remains relatively low, suggesting that specific firms' trade losses are not necessarily the key predictor of whether a Member will raise an STC.

As seen in the detailed discussion on the substantive content of STCs, the low cost of raising an STC means that Members need to be less invested in an issue before raising it as an STC than they must be if they are to pursue a dispute. There may therefore be STCs raised on public policy aspects of regulatory co-operation even when no industry is apparently experiencing significant trade loss.

Members' practices in relation to STCs confirm that transparency can serve as a substitute for dispute settlement, allowing Members to enter into in-depth dialogue about domestic regulations before they are adopted or before their trade effects escalate. A closer look at the issues discussed in STCs shows that the functions of this mechanism are threefold: it allows Members to gain more information, to influence other Members' regulations and to address practical issues they encounter when attempting to implement another Member's requirements. While these functions may overlap within the same concern, there seems to be a distinction between the TBT Committee, in which Members most commonly use STCs to obtain further information on a domestic measure or to influence their trading partners' draft measures, and the SPS Committee, in which Members overwhelmingly try to address issues with implementation, thus aiming to influence their trading partners' measures, but usually after they have been directly affected. Overall, STCs largely focus on the obligations of transparency, necessity, international standards or non-discrimination under the SPS and TBT Agreements, emphasising that the STCs are a mechanism targeted at Members co-operating to uphold these core principles.

Part III compared STC discussions and requests for consultations made to the DSB in an effort to observe the complementarity between the two mechanisms. The number of disputes that are preceded by transparency efforts is significant – and even more so when we look at those disputes that are focused on major SPS and/or TBT claims. Our analysis confirmed that there is an overall tendency to address concerns in the Committee before escalating an issue to formal dispute settlement. This is particularly true of developing countries, which tend to use STCs in both Committees before resorting to dispute settlement. Overall, STCs tend to be more about understanding a measure, while disputes are about whose interpretation of an obligation is correct. What is common to both SPS and TBT provisions is that necessity and the scientific rationale of measures are more frequently raised in STCs than in requests for consultations. This underlines the importance that transparency plays in understanding inherently subjective elements of domestic measures – namely, the rationale behind them, and the supporting role that regulatory dialogue plays in striking the right balance between achieving these objectives and complying with obligations under the SPS and TBT Agreements. In the rather marginal cases in which recourse is ultimately had to dispute settlement, it tends to be because the parties to the dispute cannot reach an agreement informally and need a third party to offer a legal interpretation. This is strikingly the case for risk assessment under the SPS Agreement: a high share of requests for consultations raise the issue, although it is much less frequently raised in STCs.

Overall, the comparison of STCs and requests for consultations highlights that transparency enables discussions to be prospective: they allow Members to co-operate and reach an agreement before a measure is implemented, or before the resulting trade costs become too significant. A dispute, however, is necessarily retrospective – the measure has to be in place and causing harm before a dispute can be launched – and yet the remedy is not retroactive.[5]

Building on the premise that transparency is used as a complement to dispute settlement, Part III further examined how transparency can feed into dispute settlement – in other words, whether the information acquired through the SPS and TBT transparency mechanisms can provide a sufficient basis on which Members can identify WTO-inconsistent measures and therefore raise a formal dispute. We recalled existing literature that explains Members' adjudication practices in terms of unequal access to information, unequal resources and especially legal capacity, and we also considered the issue of alternative fora in which to address the issue. We argued that:

- the WTO's centralisation of information significantly reduces the search costs that lead to disparities in access to information;
- the regulatory dialogue that takes place within the Committees allows Members to better evaluate the impacts of a measure and therefore to more easily identify potentially restrictive measures; and
- STCs allow all Members to try to find a negotiated solution to resolve the conflict before it escalates to a formal dispute.

Based on these findings, further research is still required into the effects of transparency and into the factors that justify dispute settlement. These two issues require extensive research into specific cases,

---

[5] Robert Wolfe, private communication with the author.

as opposed to the overarching approach that was adopted in this book. Indeed, while the analysis here illustrated Members' current transparency practices and suggested that both information and regulatory dialogue help Members to understand each other's measures, further research could also provide evidence on the concrete consequences of STCs at the domestic level. Factors such as the timing of comments on notifications and STC discussions with respect to the development of the domestic measure, the respective countries involved, and the sectors and industries affected could be considered when evaluating the effectiveness of an STC. Through case studies into particular issues that have been raised in the Committees, such research could indicate to what extent the inputs from other Members were indeed incorporated into the drafts and therefore under which specific circumstances STCs are truly a valuable tool for IRC.

That being said, the evidence gathered in this book already shows that transparency can be both a complement to and a substitute for dispute settlement, ultimately offering all Members the same opportunities in ensuring the implementation of the Agreements. The importance of transparency within the WTO should not be under-estimated and it is no surprise that authors have called it the 'Third Pillar' of the WTO[6] or the 'real jewel' in the WTO 'crown'.[7] Although the SPS and TBT Agreements require a particular level of transparency, giving it a significant place in Committee practice, the lessons learned under these two Agreements could be valuable for other WTO provisions – particularly those concerning non-tariff barriers to trade.

The lessons we can learn from transparency under the SPS and TBT Agreements might also be valuable beyond the WTO. Other organisations may benefit from the WTO's experience in enabling regulatory co-operation: the centralisation of information by the WTO Secretariat, combined with the transparent dialogue within technical committees, are a crucial foundation for effective information and dialogue, to the benefit of the entire WTO membership. The role that transparency plays in conflict management and dispute prevention would be of particular

---

[6] Erik Wijkström, 'The Third Pillar: Behind the Scenes, WTO Committee Work Delivers', E15 Initiative, 15 December 2015.
[7] Petros C. Mavroidis and Robert Wolfe, 'From Sunshine to a Common Agent: The Evolving Understanding of Transparency in the WTO', RSCAS Research Paper No. PP 2015/01/Columbia Public Law Research Paper No. 14-461, 25 April 2015, 1. http://papers.ssrn.com/abstract=2569178.

use to other international organisations that have neither the institutional framework nor the mandate to pursue formal dispute settlement.

In times when multilateral negotiations are difficult and dispute settlement remains a costly and burdensome process, we may recall that the 'third pillar' of the WTO is standing strong and is deserving of more attention. The rich dialogue and increasing transparency that the SPS and TBT Agreements facilitate demonstate the crucial role of the WTO's institutional framework for taming unnecessary barriers to trade, while protecting the variety of domestic policy approaches. Investing further in this framework to make transparency truly effective is therefore essential to the everyday conduct of international trade.

APPENDICES

Appendix A Methodology

The empirical evidence on which this book relies is largely drawn from analysis of minutes of meetings of the two Committees – specifically, in-depth analysis of the minutes related to all specific trade concerns (STCs) over five years (2010–2014). Throughout the rest of the book, the trends on different transparency tools span a broader time frame and use more up-to-date data. The broader trends confirm that 2010–2014 serves as a representative sample period.

The author coded the minutes to identify general trends and compiled a database that allowed for comparison of the different concerns raised in both the Committees. The categories tracked in the database related to both the process and the substantive content of the Committee discussions. In terms of process, the database looks at the entire 'disputing pyramid', as described throughout Part II, tracking the use of notifications, comments on notifications, STCs, requests for consultations, panel reports and Appellate Body reports. In terms of content, the database tracks issues citing Members' major legal obligations under the WTO Agreements on the Application of Sanitary and Phytosanitary Measures (the SPS Agreement, or SPS) and on Technical Barriers to Trade (the TBT Agreement, or TBT) – namely, the necessity of domestic regulations, discrimination, the adoption of international standards, transparency, and special and differential treatment of developing-country Members, with more specific issues among these flagged when relevant. This classification differs from that used by the WTO Secretariat in its TBT and SPS Information Management Systems (IMSs) (http://tbtims.wto.org and http://spsims.wto.org), because the IMS data does not support comparison of the SPS and TBT concerns and does not provide sufficient detail for an in-depth analysis of the issues discussed. The author shared this database with the WTO Secretariat to ensure that it was factually correct.

It is similar, *mutatis mutandis*, to the database developed by this author and a co-author for a related article.[1]

In addition, the author developed a specific questionnaire to survey the informal role played by the private sector in helping WTO Members to process their trading partners' TBT and SPS notifications and in raising trade concerns. The author shared the questionnaire with the WTO Secretariat and her PhD supervisor to confirm its relevance. The author submitted the questionnaire to TBT country delegations and it served as a basis for interviews with 12 delegates in particular (Brazil, Canada, Chile, China, European Union, India, Kenya, Peru, Russia, South Africa, Trinidad and Tobago, and Uganda). This sample aimed to reflect a representative cross-section of countries at different levels of development. The country delegates interviewed were selected based on their active participation in TBT Committee discussions. The results of this survey and the interviews are referred to in Chapter 4, on the role of the private sector in measuring impacts of domestic regulation.

Finally, beyond continuous exchanges with her PhD committee, the author also conducted a number of thematic interviews with TBT delegations and WTO Secretariat staff (namely, Lauro Locks, Devin McDaniels, Gretchen Stanton, Ludivine Tamiotti, Erik Wijkström and Christiane Wolff), as well as other practitioners on international trade law and policy (namely, Véronique Bastien, Alejandro Jara, Iza Lejárraga, Niall Meagher, Roland Mollerus, Denise Prévost and David Shark), to test her arguments.

Appendix B Interviewing the Private Sector about TBT Transparency

This survey was conducted during December 2014 and January 2015 by means of interviews in person or by phone with WTO Member State delegations to the TBT Committee. These delegates were those most involved in the TBT Committee – in most cases based in their countries' capital cities, but in some cases based in Geneva. The same questions were a starting point for discussion with all Members, albeit slightly adapted to suit the Member's level of development.

---

[1] Marianna Karttunen and Devin McDaniels, 'Trade, Testing and Toasters: Conformity Assessment Procedures and the TBT Committee', *Journal of World Trade* 50, no. 5 (2016): 755–92.

1. Formal co-operation with the private sector:
   - Do you have an export alert system or other equivalent mechanism to ensure timely coordination with your industry representatives regarding WTO Members' notifications?
   - Who are the private sector representatives you are most in contact with? (Business associations, federations, unions, etc.)
2. Awareness on potentially trade-restrictive effect of notified measures:
   - To what extent does the private sector play a role in bringing to your attention potential trade-restrictive effects of newly notified measures by other Members?
3. Comments on notifications:
   - How many comments on notifications do you raise and which proportion originates from private sector concerns?
4. Incentive to raise a specific trade concern:
   - Which proportions of the specific trade concerns that you raise were brought to your attention by the private sector?
5. Drafting specific trade concerns:
   - Do you seek legal counsel in drafting STCs? If so, is it from a private law firm?
6. Awareness on non-notified measures:
   - Does the private sector play a role in bringing to your attention measures of other Members that have not been notified?

REFERENCES

Ala'i, Padideh. 'From the Periphery to the Center? The Evolving WTO Jurisprudence on Transparency and Good Governance'. *Journal of International Economic Law* 11, no. 4 (2008): 779–802.

Ala'i, Padideh. 'From the Periphery to the Center? The Evolving WTO Jurisprudence on Transparency and Good Governance'. *Contributions to Books*, 6 February 2010. http://works.bepress.com/padideh_alai/3.

Alemanno, Alberto. 'The Regulatory Cooperation Chapter of the Transatlantic Trade and Investment Partnership: Institutional Structures and Democratic Consequences'. SSRN Scholarly Paper, 27 August 2015. http://papers.ssrn.com/abstract=2651091.

Barrios Villareal, Andrea. *International Standardization and the Agreement on Technical Barriers to Trade*. Cambridge: Cambridge University Press, 2018.

Bhagwati, Jagdish N. *Protectionism*. Cambridge, MA/London: MIT Press, 1988.

Bianchi, Andrea, and Anne Peters, eds. *Transparency in International Law*. Cambridge: Cambridge University Press, 2013.

Blonigen, Bruce A., and Chad P. Bown. 'Antidumping and Retaliation Threats'. NBER Working Paper No. 8576, November 2001. www.nber.org/papers/w8576.

Bollyky, Thomas, and Petros C. Mavroidis. 'Trade, Social Preferences and Regulatory Cooperation'. RSCAS Research Paper No. 2016/47, 2 December 2016. https://papers.ssrn.com/sol3/papers.cfm?abstract_id=2879329.

Bown, Chad P. *Self-Enforcing Trade: Developing Countries and WTO Dispute Settlement*. Washington, DC: Brookings Institution Press, 2009.

Bown, Chad P. 'Trade Disputes and the Implementation of Protection under the GATT: An Empirical Assessment'. *Journal of International Economics* 62, no. 2 (2004): 263–94.

Bown, Chad P., and Bernard M. Hoekman. 'WTO Dispute Settlement and the Missing Developing Country Cases: Engaging the Private Sector'. *Journal of International Economic Law* 8, no. 4 (2005): 861–90. https://doi.org/10.1093/jiel/jgi049.

Boza, Sofia, and Felipe Fernández. 'Development Level and WTO Member Participation in Specific Trade Concerns (STCs) and Disputes on SPS/TBT'. SECO/WTI Working Paper No. 2014/17, 16 June 2014. https://papers.ssrn.com/sol3/papers.cfm?abstract_id=2618535.

Busch, Marc L., and Eric Reinhardt. 'Three's a Crowd: Third Parties and WTO Dispute Settlement'. *World Politics* 58, no. 3 (2006): 446–77.

Busch, Marc L., Eric Reinhardt and Gregory Shaffer. 'Does Legal Capacity Matter? A Survey of WTO Members'. *World Trade Review* 8, no. 4 (2009): 559–77. https://doi.org/10.1017/S1474745609990085.

Cappelletti, Mauro, and Bryant Garth. 'Access to Justice: The Newest Wave in the Worldwide Movement to Make Rights Effective'. *Buffalo Law Review* 27, no. 2 (1978): 181–292.

Chen, Sijie. 'China's Compliance with WTO Systemic Obligations: Institution-Related Impediments to Effective Implementation of GATT Article X'. *Amsterdam Law Forum* 4, no. 4 (2012): 26–50.

Coglianese, Cary. 'The Transparency President? The Obama Administration and Open Government'. *Governance* 22, no. 4 (2009): 529–44.

Coglianese, Cary, and André Sapir. 'Risk and Regulatory Calibration: WTO Compliance Review of the US Dolphin–Safe Tuna Labeling Regime'. *World Trade Review* 16, no. 2 (2017): 327–48. https://doi.org/10.1017/S1474745616000562.

Correia de Brito, Anabela, Céline Kauffmann and Jacques Pelkmans. 'The Contribution of Mutual Recognition to International Regulatory Co-operation'. OECD Regulatory Policy Working Papers No. 2, 31 August 2016. www.oecd.org/regreform/WP2_Contribution-of-mutual-recognition-to-IRC.pdf.

Crowley, Meredith, and Robert Howse. '*Tuna–Dolphin II*: A Legal and Economic Analysis of the Appellate Body Report'. *World Trade Review* 13, no. 2 (2014): 321–55.

Davis, Christina L. *Why Adjudicate? Enforcing Trade Rules in the WTO*. Princeton, NJ: Princeton University Press, 2012.

Davis, Christina L., and Sarah Blodgett Bermeo. 'Who Files? Developing Country Participation in GATT/WTO Adjudication'. *The Journal of Politics* 71, no. 3 (2009): 1033–49.

De Bièvre, Dirk, 'Governance in International Trade: Judicialisation and Positive Integration in the WTO'. MPI Preprints No. 2004/7, 28 July 2004. https://papers.ssrn.com/sol3/papers.cfm?abstract_id=566501.

De Bièvre, Dirk, Arlo Poletti and Aydin Yildirim. 'About the Melting of Icebergs: Political and Economic Determinants of Dispute Initiation and Resolution in the WTO'. In *Assessing the World Trade Organization: Fit For Purpose?*, edited by Manfred Elsig, Bernard Hoekman and Joost Pauwelyn, 120–46. Cambridge: Cambridge University Press, 2017.

Delimatsis, Panagiotis. 'Institutional Transparency in the WTO'. In *Transparency in International Law*, edited by Andrea Bianchi and Anne Peters, 112–41. Cambridge: Cambridge University Press, 2013.

Evenett, Simon J. 'Global Trade Alert: Motivation and Launch'. *World Trade Review* 8, no. 4 (2009): 607–9. https://doi.org/10.1017/S1474745609990061.

Felstiner, William L. F., Richard L. Abel and Austin Sarat. 'Emergence and Transformation of Disputes: Naming, Blaming, Claiming …'. *Law & Society Review* 15, no. 3/4 (1980–81): 631–54.

Francois, Joseph, Henrik Horn and Niklas Kaunitz. 'Trading Profiles and Developing Country Participation in the WTO Dispute Settlement System'. IFN Working Paper No. 730, 12 January 2010. https://papers.ssrn.com/sol3/papers.cfm?abstract_id=1534766.

Fung, Archon. *Full Disclosure: The Perils and Promise of Transparency*. New York: Cambridge University Press, 2007.

Galanter, Marc. 'Why the "Haves" Come out Ahead: Speculations on the Limits of Legal Change'. *Law and Society Review* 9, no. 1 (1974): 95–160.

Ghosh, Arunabha. 'Developing Countries in the WTO Trade Policy Review Mechanism'. *World Trade Review* 9, no. 3 (2010): 419–55. https://doi.org/10.1017/S1474745610000261.

Global Affairs Canada. 'Improving the Deliberative Function of WTO Bodies'. 24 January 2019. www.canada.ca/en/global-affairs/news/2019/01/improving-the-deliberative-function-of-wto-bodies.html.

Gruszczynski, Lukasz. 'The REACH Regulation and the TBT Agreement: The Role of the TBT Committee in Regulatory Processes'. In *Research Handbook on the WTO and Technical Barriers to Trade*, edited by Tracey Epps and M. J. Trebilcock, 424–53. Research Handbooks on the WTO. Cheltenham: Edward Elgar, 2013.

Guzman, Andrew T., and Beth A. Simmons. 'Power Plays and Capacity Constraints: The Selection of Defendants in World Trade Organization Disputes'. *The Journal of Legal Studies* 34, no. 2 (2005): 557–98.

Hart, Henry Melvin, Albert Martin Sacks, William N. Eskridge and Philip P. Frickey. *The Legal Process: Basic Problems in the Making and Application of Law*. Westbury, CT: Foundation Press, 1994.

Hoekman, Bernard M. '"Behind-the-Border" Regulatory Policies and Trade Agreements'. *East Asian Economic Review* 22, no. 3 (2018): 243–73.

Hoekman, Bernard M., and Michel M. Kostecki. *The Political Economy of the World Trading System: The WTO and Beyond*. Oxford: Oxford University Press, 2009.

Hoekman, Bernard M., and Petros C. Mavroidis. 'Enforcing Multilateral Commitments: Dispute Settlement and Developing Countries'. Working Paper, 14 September 1999. www.iatp.org/sites/default/files/Enforcing_Multilateral_Commitments_Dispute_Set.htm.

Hoekman, Bernard M., and Petros C. Mavroidis. 'The Dark Side of the Moon: "Completing" the WTO Contract through Adjudication'. November 2012. http://globalgovernanceprogramme.eui.eu/wp-content/uploads/2012/11/Hoekman-Mavroidis-MESSERLIN-FEST_FIN.pdf.

Hoekman, Bernard M., and Petros C. Mavroidis. 'WTO Dispute Settlement, Transparency and Surveillance'. *World Economy* 23, no. 4 (2000): 527–42. https://doi.org/10.1111/1467-9701.00288.

Horn, Henrik, Louise Johannesson and Petros C. Mavroidis. 'The WTO Dispute Settlement System 1995–2010: Some Descriptive Statistics'. IFN Working Paper No. 891, 16 November 2011. www.ifn.se/wfiles/wp/wp891.pdf.

Horn, Henrik, Louise Johannesson and Petros C. Mavroidis. 'The WTO Dispute Settlement System 1995–2010: Some Descriptive Statistics'. *Journal of World Trade* 45, no. 6 (2011): 1107–38.

Horn, Henrik, Petros C. Mavroidis and Håkan Nordström. 'Is the Use of the WTO Dispute Settlement System Biased?'. CEPR Discussion Paper No. 2340, December 1999. https://cepr.org/active/publications/discussion_papers/dp.php?dpno=2340.

Horn, Henrik, Petros C. Mavroidis and Håkan Nordström. 'Is the Use of the WTO Dispute Settlement System Biased?'. In *The WTO and International Trade Law/Dispute Settlement*, edited by Petros C. Mavroidis and Alan O. Sykes, 454–86. Cheltenham; Northampton, MA: Edward Elgar, 2005.

Horn, Henrik, Petros C. Mavroidis and André Sapir. 'Beyond the WTO? An Anatomy of EU and US Preferential Trade Agreements'. *The World Economy* 33, no. 11 (2010): 1565–88. https://doi.org/10.1111/j.1467-9701.2010.01273.x.

Horn, Henrik, Petros C. Mavroidis and Erik N. Wijkström. 'In the Shadow of the DSU: Addressing Specific Trade Concerns in the WTO SPS and TBT Committees – Entwined'. *Journal of World Trade* 47, no. 4 (2013): 729–59.

Howse, Robert. 'A New Device for Creating International Legal Normativity: The WTO Technical Barriers to Trade Agreement and "International Standards"'. In *Constitutionalism, Multilevel Trade Governance and Social Regulation*, edited by Christian Joerges and Ernst-Ulrich Petersmann, 383–96. Studies in International Trade and Investment Law. Oxford: Hart, 2006.

Howse, Robert. 'Democracy, Science, and Free Trade: Risk Regulation on Trial at the World Trade Organization'. *Michigan Law Review* 98, no. 7 (1999): 2329–57.

Howse, Robert. 'The *Tuna/Dolphin* Appellate Body 21.5 Ruling: A Decision That Could Threaten the Integrity and Efficiency of WTO Dispute Settlement'. *International Economic Law and Policy Blog* (blog), 2015. https://worldtradelaw.typepad.com/ielpblog/2015/11/the-tunadolphin-appellate-body-215-ruling-a-decision-that-could-threaten-the-integrity-and-efficiency-of-wto-dispute-settl.html.

Howse, Robert, and Henrik Horn. 'European Communities – Measures Affecting the Approval and Marketing of Biotech Products'. *World Trade Review* 8, no. 1 (2009): 49–83.

Hudec, Robert E. *The GATT Legal System and World Trade Diplomacy*. Salem, NH: Butterworth Legal, 1990.

Karttunen, Marianna, and Devin McDaniels. 'Trade, Testing and Toasters: Conformity Assessment Procedures and the TBT Committee'. *Journal of World Trade* 50, no. 5 (2016): 755–92.

Kende, Mathias. *The Trade Policy Review Mechanism: A Critical Analysis*. International Economic Law. Oxford: Oxford University Press, 2018.

Koebele, Michael. 'Article X TBT'. In *WTO: Technical Barriers and SPS Measures*, edited by Rüdiger Wolfrum, Peter-Tobias Stoll and Anja Seibert-Fohr, 307–14. Leiden/Boston, MA: Martinus Nijhoff, 2007.

Laird, Sam. 'The WTO's Trade Policy Review Mechanism: From Through the Looking Glass'. *The World Economy* 22, no. 6 (2003): 741–64. https://doi.org/ https://doi.org/10.1111/1467-9701.00230.

Lejárraga, Iza. 'Multilateralising Regionalism: Strengthening Transparency Disciplines in Trade'. OECD Trade Policy Paper No. 152, 26 June 2013. doi:10.1787/5k44t7k99xzq-en.

Marceau, Gabrielle, and Joel P. Trachtman. 'A Map of the World Trade Organization Law of Domestic Regulation of Goods: The Technical Barriers to Trade Agreement, the Sanitary and Phytosanitary Measures Agreement, and the General Agreement on Tariffs and Trade'. *Journal of World Trade* 48, no. 2 (2014): 351–432.

Mavroidis, Petros C. 'Dispute Settlement in the WTO: Mind over Matter'. RSCAS Working Paper No. 2015/34, 2015. http://cadmus.eui.eu/bitstream/ handle/1814/35980/RSCAS_2015_34.pdf?sequence=1.

Mavroidis, Petros C. 'Driftin' Too Far from Shore: Why the Test for Compliance with the TBT Agreement Developed by the WTO Appellate Body Is Wrong, and What Should the AB Have Done Instead'. *World Trade Review* 12, no. 3 (2013): 509–31. doi:10.1017/S1474745613000013.

Mavroidis, Petros C. 'Last Mile for Tuna (to a Safe Harbour): What Is the TBT Agreement All About?'. *European Journal of International Law* 30, no. 1 (2019): 279–301. https://doi.org/10.1093/ejil/chz002.

Mavroidis, Petros C. 'Regulatory Cooperation: Lessons from the WTO and the World Trade Regime'. E15 Initiative Policy Options Paper, 22 January 2016. www3.weforum.org/docs/E15/WEF_Regulatory_Cooperation_Lessons_ WTO_WTR_report_2015_1401.pdf.

Mavroidis, Petros C. 'Surveillance Schemes: The GATT's New Trade Policy Review Mechanism'. *Michigan Journal of International Law* 13, no. 2 (1991): 374–414.

Mavroidis, Petros C. *The General Agreement on Tariffs and Trade: A Commentary.* Oxford Commentaries on International Law. Oxford/New York: Oxford University Press, 2005.

Mavroidis, Petros C. *The Law of the World Trade Organization (WTO): Documents, Cases & Analysis*, 2nd edn. American Casebook Series. St. Paul, MN: West, 2013.

Mavroidis, Petros C. *The Regulation of International Trade, Vol. 1: GATT.* Cambridge, MA/London: MIT Press, 2016.

Mavroidis, Petros C. *Trade in Goods.* Oxford: Oxford University Press, 2012.

Mavroidis, Petros C., and André Sapir. 'Dial PTAs for Peace: The Influence of Preferential Trade Agreements on Litigation between Trading Partners'. *Journal of World Trade* 49, no. 3 (2015): 351–72.

Mavroidis, Petros C., and Erik N. Wijkström. 'Moving out of the Shadows: Bringing Transparency to Standards and Regulations in the WTO's TBT Committee'. In *Research Handbook on the WTO*, edited by Tracey Epps and Michael J. Trebilcock, 204–37. Cheltenham: Edward Elgar, 2013.

Mavroidis, Petros C., and Robert Wolfe. 'From Sunshine to a Common Agent: The Evolving Understanding of Transparency in the WTO'. RSCAS Research Paper No. PP 2015/01/Columbia Public Law Research Paper No. 14-461, 25 April 2015. http://papers.ssrn.com/abstract=2569178.

Mavroidis, Petros C., and Robert Wolfe. 'Private Standards and the WTO: Reclusive No More'. RSCAS Research Paper No. 2016/17, 2016. https://cadmus.eui.eu/bitstream/handle/1814/40384/RSCAS_2016_17.pdf?sequence=1.

Melillo, Margherita. 'Informal Dispute Resolution in Preferential Trade Agreements'. *Journal of World Trade* 53, no. 1 (2019): 95–127.

Miller, Richard E., and Austin Sarat. 'Grievances, Claims, and Disputes: Assessing the Adversary Culture'. *Law & Society Review* 15, no. 3/4 (1980): 525–66. doi:10.2307/3053502.

Mitchell, Andrew, and Elizabeth Sheargold. 'Regulatory Coherence in Future Free Trade Agreements and the Idea of the Embedded Liberalism Compromise'. In *Future International Economic Integration: Embedded Liberalism Compromise Revisited*, edited by Gillian Moon and Lisa Toohey, 137–58. Cambridge: Cambridge University Press, 2018.

Moïsé, Evdokia. 'Transparency Mechanisms and Non-tariff Measures'. OECD Trade Policy Papers No. 111, 1 April 2011. www.oecd-ilibrary.org/content/workingpaper/5kgf0rzzwfq3-en.

Nadakavukaren Schefer, Krista. 'Corruption and the WTO Legal System'. *Journal of World Trade* 43, no. 4 (2009): 737–70.

Neubauer, David W., and Stephen S. Meinhold. *Judicial Process: Law, Courts, and Politics in the United States.* Boston, MA: Cengage Learning, 2012.

OECD. 'Draft Best Practice Principles on Stakeholder Engagement in Regulatory Policy'. 2017. www.oecd.org/governance/regulatory-policy/public-consultation-best-practice-principles-on-stakeholder-engagement.htm.

OECD. *International Regulatory Co-operation*. Paris: OECD, 2013. www.oecd-ilibrary.org/governance/international-regulatory-co-operation_9789264200463-en.

OECD. 'International Regulatory Co-operation and Trade: Understanding the Trade Costs of Regulatory Divergence and the Remedies'. 24 May 2017. www.oecd.org/gov/international-regulatory-co-operation-and-trade-9789264275942-en.htm.

OECD. *International Regulatory Co-operation: The Role of International Organisations*. Paris: OECD, 2016.

OECD. *OECD Regulatory Policy Outlook 2015*. Paris: OECD, 2015.

OECD. *OECD Regulatory Policy Outlook 2018*. Paris: OECD, 2018. www.oecd.org/governance/oecd-regulatory-policy-outlook-2018-9789264303072-en.htm.

OECD. 'Recommendation of the Council on Regulatory Policy and Governance'. 2012. www.oecd.org/gov/regulatory-policy/49990817.pdf.

OECD. *Review of International Regulatory Co-operation of Mexico*. Paris: OECD, 2018. www.oecd.org/publications/review-of-international-regulatory-co-operation-of-mexico-9789264305748-en.htm.

OECD. 'Synthesis Report on Trade and International Regulatory Cooperation'. COM/GOV/TAD(2016)1, 2016.

OECD/WTO. *Facilitating Trade through Regulatory Co-operation: The Case of the WTO's TBT/SPS Agreements and Committees*. Paris: OECD, 2019. www.oecd.org/gov/facilitating-trade-through-regulatory-co-operation-ad3c655f-en.htm.

Ostry, Sylvia. 'China and the WTO Transparency Issue'. *UCLA Journal of International Law and Foreign Affairs* 3, no. 1 (1998): 1–22.

Pagani, Fabrizio. 'Peer Review: A Tool for Co-operation and Change'. OECD SG/LEG(2002)1, 11 September 2002. www.oecd.org/dac/peer-reviews/1955285.pdf.

Palmeter, David, and Petros C. Mavroidis. *Dispute Settlement in the World Trade Organization: Practice and Procedure*. 2nd edn. Cambridge: Cambridge University Press, 2004.

Park, Nohyoung, and Myung-Hyun Chung. 'Analysis of a New Mediation Procedure under the WTO SPS Agreement'. *Journal of World Trade* 50, no. 1 (2016): 93–115.

Pauwelyn, Joost. 'Minority Rules: Precedent and Participation before the WTO Appellate Body'. In *Establishing Judicial Authority in International Economic Law*, edited by Laura Nielsen and Henrik Palmer Olsen, 141–72. Cambridge: Cambridge University Press, 2016.

Pauwelyn, Joost, and Weiwei Zhang. 'Busier than Ever? A Data-Driven Assessment and Forecast of WTO Caseload'. *Journal of International Economic Law* 21, no. 3 (2018): 461–87. doi:10.1093/jiel/jgy035.

Peters, Anne. 'Towards Transparency as a Global Norm'. In *Transparency in International Law*, edited by Andrea Bianchi and Anne Peters, 534–607. Cambridge: Cambridge University Press, 2013.

Pollack, Mark A., and Gregory C. Shaffer. *When Cooperation Fails*. Oxford: Oxford University Press, 2009.

Prévost, Marie Denise. *Balancing Trade and Health in the SPS Agreement: The Development Dimension*. Nijmegen: Wolf Legal, 2009.

Prévost, Marie Denise. 'Transparency Obligations under the TBT Agreement'. In *Research Handbook on the WTO and Technical Barriers to Trade*, edited by Tracey Epps and Michael J. Trebilcock, 120–63. Research Handbooks on the WTO. Cheltenham: Edward Elgar, 2013.

Qureshi, Asif H. 'The New GATT Trade Policy Review Mechanism: An Exercise in Transparency or "Enforcement"?'. *Journal of World Trade* 24, no. 3 (1990): 142–60.

Rigod, Boris. *Optimal Regulation and the Law of International Trade*. Cambridge: Cambridge University Press, 2015.

Scott, Joanne. 'Cooperative Regulation in the WTO: The SPS Committee'. NYU Global Law Working Paper 03/06, 2006.

Scott, Joanne. *The WTO Agreement on Sanitary and Phytosanitary Measures: A Commentary*. Oxford Commentaries on the GATT/WTO Agreements. Oxford: Oxford University Press, 2009.

Shaffer, Gregory C. *Defending Interests: Public–Private Partnerships in WTO Litigation*. Washington, DC: Brookings Institution Press, 2003.

Stevenson, Angus, ed. *Oxford Dictionary of English*. 3rd edn. New York: Oxford University Press, 2010.

Tamiotti, Ludivine. 'Article 2 TBT Agreement'. In *WTO – Technical Barriers and SPS Measures, Vol. III*, edited by Rüdiger Wolfrum, Peter-Tobias Stoll and Anja Seibert-Fohr, 210–34. Max Planck Commentaries on World Trade Law. Leiden/Boston, MA: Martinus Nijhoff, 2007.

Tongeren, Frank van, Véronique Bastien and Martin von Lampe. 'International Regulatory Cooperation, a Trade-Facilitating Mechanism'. 15 December 2015. http://e15initiative.org/wp-content/uploads/2015/09/E15-Regulatory-Coherence-van-Tongeren-Bastien-von-Lampe-Final.pdf.

Trebilcock, Michael J., Robert Howse and Antonia Eliason. *The Regulation of International Trade*, 4th edn. Abingdon/New York: Routledge, 2013.

Van den Bossche, Peter, and Werner Zdouc. *The Law and Policy of the World Trade Organization*. Cambridge: Cambridge University Press, 2013.

Weiler, Joseph H. H., and Henrik Horn. '*EC – Trade Description of Sardines*: Textualism and Its Discontent'. In *The American Law Institute Reporters' Studies on WTO Case Law: Legal and Economic Analysis*, edited by Henrik Horn and Petros C. Mavroidis, 551–78. American Law Institute Reporters' Studies. Cambridge/New York: Cambridge University Press, 2007.

Wijkström, Erik N. 'The Third Pillar: Behind the Scenes, WTO Committee Work Delivers'. *E15 Initiative*, 15 December 2015.

Wijkström, Erik N., and Devin McDaniels. 'Improving Regulatory Governance: International Standards and the WTO TBT Agreement'. *Journal of World Trade* 47, no. 5 (2013): 1013–46.

Wolfe, Robert. 'How Can We Know (More) about the Trade Effects of Regulation?' E15 Initiative/ICTSD/WEF, 25 August 2015. https://papers.ssrn.com/sol3/papers.cfm?abstract_id=2800641.

Wolfe, Robert. 'Letting the Sun Shine in at the WTO: How Transparency Brings the Trading System to Life'. Staff Working Paper No. ERSD-2013-03, 22 November 2013. http://papers.ssrn.com/sol3/Delivery.cfm?abstractid=2229741.

Wolfe, Robert. 'Protectionism and Multilateral Accountability during the Great Recession: Drawing Inferences from Dogs not Barking'. *Journal of World Trade* 46, no. 4 (2012): 777–814.

Wolfe, Robert, and Terry Collins-Williams. 'Transparency as a Trade Policy Tool: The WTO's Cloudy Windows'. *World Trade Review* 9, no. 4 (2010): 551–81.

WTO. 'A Compilation and Summary of the Responses Received to the Questionnaire for a Survey to Assist Developing Country Members to Identify and Prioritise Their Specific Needs in the TBT Field'. G/TBT/W/186, 14 October 2002.

WTO. 'Actions Regarding SPS-Related Private Standards'. G/SPS/55, 6 April 2011.

WTO. 'Ad Hoc Consultations and Resolution of Trade Concerns'. G/SPS/GEN/781, 2007.

WTO. 'An Analysis of the Priorities Identified by Developing Country Members in Their Responses to the Questionnaire for a "Survey to Assist Developing Country Members to Identify and Prioritise Their Specific Needs in the TBT Field"'. G/TBT/W/193, 2003.

WTO. 'Analysis of the Replies to the Questionnaire on Transparency under the SPS Agreement'. G/SPS/GEN/1402, 20 March 2015.

WTO. 'Australia – Measures Affecting the Importation of Salmonids: Notification of Mutually Agreed Solution'. WT/DS21/10, 1 November 2000.

WTO. 'Communication from Mexico'. G/TBT/GEN/Add.22, 2016.

WTO. 'Decisions and Recommendations Adopted by the Technical Barriers to Trade Committee since 1 January 1995'. G/TBT/1/Rev.8, 2002.

WTO. 'Decisions and Recommendations Adopted by the WTO Committee on Technical Barriers to Trade since 1995'. G/TBT/1/Rev.10, 2011.

WTO. 'Decisions and Recommendations Adopted by the WTO Committee on Technical Barriers to Trade since 1995'. G/TBT/1/Rev.12, 2015.

WTO. 'Eighth Triennial Review of the Operation and Implementation of the Agreement on Technical Barriers to Trade under Article 15.4'. G/TBT/41, 19 November 2018.

WTO. 'Fifth Triennial Review of the Operation and Implementation of the Agreement on Technical Barriers to Trade under Article 15.4'. G/TBT/26, 2009.

REFERENCES

WTO. 'Fourth Triennial Review of the Operation and Implementation of the Agreement on Technical Barriers to Trade under Article 15.4'. G/TBT/19, 14 November 2006.

WTO. 'Goods Council Considers Revised Transparency Proposal to "Reinvigorate" the WTO'. November 2018. www.wto.org/english/news_e/news18_e/good_12nov18_e.htm.

WTO. 'Guidelines to Further the Practical Implementation of Article 5.5'. G/SPS/15, 2000.

WTO. 'How to Apply the Transparency Provisions of the SPS Agreement: A Handbook Prepared by the WTO Secretariat'. September 2002. www.wto.org/english/tratop_e/sps_e/spshand_e.pdf.

WTO. 'Implementation-Related Issues and Concerns'. Doha WTO Ministerial 2001: Ministerial Declarations and Decisions, CN – WT/MIN(01)/17, 2001.

WTO. 'Joint Communiqué of the Ottawa Ministerial on WTO Reform'. 25 October 2018. www.wto.org/english/news_e/news18_e/dgra_26oct18_e.pdf.

WTO. 'Notification Template' (G/SPS/N, undated). www.wto.org/english/tratop_e/sps_e/transparency_toolkit_e.htm.

WTO. 'Notification Template' (G/TBT/N, undated). www.wto.org/english/tratop_e/tbt_e/tbt_notifications_e.htm.

WTO. 'Overview Regarding the Level of Implementation of the Transparency Provisions of the SPS Agreement'. G/SPS/GEN/804/Rev.7, 6 October 2014.

WTO. 'Overview Regarding the Level of Implementation of the Transparency Provisions of the SPS Agreement'. G/SPS/GEN/804/Rev.11, 11 October 2018.

WTO. 'Overview Regarding the Level of Implementation of the Transparency Provisions of the SPS Agreement'. G/SPS/GEN/804/Rev.12, 17 October 2019.

WTO. 'Procedure to Encourage and Facilitate the Resolution of Specific Sanitary or Phytosanitary Issues among Members in Accordance with Article 12.2, Decision Adopted by the Committee on 9 July 2014'. G/SPS/61, 2014.

WTO. 'Procedure to Enhance Transparency of Special and Differential Treatment in Favour of Developing Country Members'. G/SPS/33, 2004.

WTO. 'Procedure to Monitor the Process of International Harmonization'. G/SPS/11, 1997.

WTO. 'Procedure to Monitor the Use of International Standards: Proposal by Argentina'. G/SPS/W/255, 2010.

WTO. 'Procedures to Enhance Transparency and Strengthen Notification Requirements under WTO Agreements'. JOB/GC/204/Rev.1, 2019.

WTO. 'Questionnaire on Transparency under the SPS Agreement'. G/SPS/GEN/1382, 2 February 2015.

WTO. 'Recommendation on Coherent Use of Notification Formats'. G/TBT/35, 2014.

WTO. 'Recommended Procedures for Implementing the Transparency Obligations of the SPS Agreement (Article 7)'. G/SPS/7/Rev.3, 2008.

WTO. 'Regulatory Cooperation between Members: Background Note by Secretariat'. G/TBT/W/340, 2011.
WTO. 'Review of the Operation and Implementation of the SPS Agreement'. G/SPS/53, 3 May 2010.
WTO. 'Revision of the Procedure to Monitor the Process of International Harmonization, Decision of the Committee'. G/SPS/11/Rev.1, 2004.
WTO. 'Sanitary and Phytosanitary Measures: E-Learning'. February 2014.
WTO. 'Second Triennial Review of the Operation and Implementation of the Agreement on Technical Barriers to Trade'. G/TBT/9, 13 November 2000.
WTO. 'Seventh Triennial Review of the Operation and Implementation of the Agreement on Technical Barriers to Trade under Article 15.4'. G/TBT/37, 2015.
WTO. 'Sixth Triennial Review of the Operation and Implementation of the Agreement on Technical Barriers to Trade under Article 15.4'. G/TBT/32, 2012.
WTO. 'Strengthening the Deliberative Function of the WTO'. JOB/GC/211, 14 December 2018.
WTO. *Technical Barriers to Trade*. The WTO Agreements Series. Geneva: WTO, 2014.
WTO. 'Thematic Session of the TBT Committee on Transparency: Moderator's Report'. G/TBT/GEN/167, 17 June 2014.
WTO. 'Third Triennial Review of the Operation and Implementation of the Agreement on Technical Barriers to Trade'. G/TBT/13, 2003.
WTO. 'Twentieth Annual Review of the Implementation and Operation of the TBT Agreement'. G/TBT/36, 23 February 2015.
WTO. 'Twenty-First Annual Review of the Implementation and Operation of the TBT Agreement'. G/TBT/38, 2016.
WTO. 'Twenty-Fourth Annual Review of the Implementation and Operation of the TBT Agreement'. G/TBT/42, 25 February 2019.
WTO. 'Twenty-Third Annual Review of the Implementation and Operation of the TBT Agreement'. G/TBT/40, 12 March 2018.
WTO. 'Updating the Decisions and Recommendations Taken by the Tokyo Round Committee on Technical Barriers to Trade Regarding Procedures for Notification and Information Exchange'. G/TBT/W/2/Rev.1, 21 June 1995.
WTO. 'Updating the Listing of Notification Obligations and the Compliance Therewith as Set Out in Annex III of the Report of the Working Group on Notification Obligations and Procedures'. G/L/223/Rev.26, 13 March 2019.
WTO. 'Working Procedures of the Committee, Adopted by the Committee Meeting at Its Meeting of 19–30 March 1995'. G/SPS/1, 1995.
WTO. 'WTO TBT Enquiry Point Guide: Making Transparency Work'. June 2018. www.wto.org/english/tratop_e/tbt_e/tbt_enquiry_point_guide_e.pdf.
WTO SPS Committee. 'Summary of the Meeting Held on 26–27 June 1995'. G/SPS/R/2, 18 July 1995.

WTO SPS Committee. 'Summary of the Meeting Held on 8–9 October 1996'. G/SPS/R/6, 14 November 1996.
WTO SPS Committee. 'Summary of the Meeting of 19–20 March 1997'. G/SPS/R/7, 29 April 1997.
WTO SPS Committee. 'Summary of the Meeting Held on 15–16 October 1997'. G/SPS/R/9, 15 December 1997.
WTO SPS Committee. 'Summary of the Meeting of 30 June–1 July 2011'. G/SPS/R/63, 12 September 2011.
WTO TBT Committee. 'Attachments to TBT Notifications'. G/TBT/GEN/65, 14 December 2007.
WTO TBT Committee. 'Minutes of the Meeting Held on 21 April 1995'. G/TBT/M/1, 28 June 1995.
WTO TBT Committee. 'Minutes of the Meeting of 29 June 2001'. G/TBT/M/24, 14 August 2001.
WTO TBT Committee. 'Minutes of the Meeting of 23 March 2004'. G/TBT/M/32, 19 April 2004.
WTO TBT Committee. 'Minutes of the Meeting of 30–31 October 2013'. G/TBT/M/61, 5 February 2014.
WTO TBT Committee. 'Minutes of the Meeting of 5–6 November 2014'. G/TBT/M/64, 5 November 2014.

INDEX

Agreement on Application of Sanitary and Phytosanitary Measures. *See* SPS Agreement
Agreement on Technical Barriers to Trade. *See* TBT Agreement

barriers to trade
  non-tariff. *See* non-tariff trade barriers
  tariff. *See* tariffs
bilateral trade agreements (BTAs)
  enquiry points, 85
  notification requirements in, 59
  private stakeholders as addressees, 77
  transparency provisions in, 17–18
Brandeis, Justice Louis, 1

cigarettes, 2, 59–60
conformity assessment
  mutual recognition of, 114–15
  procedures (CAPs), 27, 29
    costs, 29
    definition of, 29
    examples of, 29
    objective of provisions on, 29

developing countries
  asymmetry between private parties from developed Members and from, 71
  importance of transparency for private actors in, 69
  making regulations known, 47
  ability to request special assistance through comments on notifications, 89
  Secretariat raising attention of, 74
  Members' engagement in transparency, 141–42
  special needs of, 203–5
dispute settlement
  good offices of chair as tool of dispute prevention, 96–97
  notifications and Members' access to information, and, 71
  resources for accessing adjudication, 253–60
    Members' legal capacity, 256–60
    Members' relative resources, 254–56
    overall resources of country, 253–54
  SPS Agreement, and, 1, 9
  TBT Agreement, and, 1, 9
  transparency, and, 10, 71. *See also* transparency as complement for dispute settlement; transparency as substitute for dispute settlement
  equalising access to process, 2
  notifications, effects of, 71
  WTO Dispute Settlement Body. *See* WTO Dispute Settlement Body (DSB)

electronic tools
  e-mails to Members, use of, 81–82
  enhancing effectiveness of transparency, 81–83
  importance of, 82

316

INDEX

increase in use of/ePing, 82–83
online tools to publish/notify trade measures, encouraging use of, 8
publication of notices, use of internet for, 65, 66
WTO Secretariat's role in ensuring availability by, 144–47
  disseminating information through e-mail alerts and online databases, 145, 147
  notification through electronic Notification Submission System, 144–45
emergency notifications, 75–76, 80–81
enquiry points
  bilateral nature of dialogue with, 93–94
  bridging gap between regulators and traders, 93–94
  failure to provide information, effect of, 91
  importance of, 89
  objectives of, 90
  obligation to establish, 84–85, 89–94
  private sector, and, 85, 91–92
  providing information
    Members and other interested parties, to, 91–92
    proposed/adopted regulations, on, 89–91
  regional trade agreements, and, 85

GATT
  Article X, 11, 14, 49
    disclosure and due process, 12–14
    general transparency provision, as, 5, 12–13
    governments' regulatory policy, and, 13
    obligation of publication, 66
    objectives, 13
  barriers created by domestic regulations, and, 21
  exceptional cases under Article XX, 23, 26, 31
  objectives of measures, consideration of, 26
  SPS and TBT Agreements, and, 47, 49
  discriminatory measures, restrictions on, 3
  measures 'beyond border', 3
  measures of 'general application', interpretation of, 54–55
  non-discrimination obligation, 38
  regulatory autonomy principle, based on, 23
  specific trade concerns (STCs), 95–96
  tariffs
    focus on reducing in first years of, 5
    progressive reduction of, 21
    schedules of concessions, 5
    trade barriers, as, 2–3
  transparency
    Article X (general transparency provision), 5, 11, 12–14, 49, 66
    Article XI (quantitative restrictions), 5
    disclosure and due process, 12–14
    ex post, 51, 53
    general commitment to notify, nature of, 53
    measures in early stages of GATT, 5
    objectives in early negotiations, 47, 49
    public availability of information on domestic regulations, 49
    publication obligations, 54–55, 66, 68–69
General Agreement on Tariffs and Trade. *See* GATT
global value chains, 2
Good Regulatory Practices (GRPs), 115–18
  discussion of, 122
  importance of, 116

Good Regulatory Practices (*cont.*)
  Organisation for Economic Co-operation and Development (OECD), 115–16
  SPS and TBT Agreements, 116–18
governments
  citizen participation in democratic process, 12
  domestic frameworks, WTO transparency and, 16–17
  first-generation transparency as 'decentralised' transparency, 6
  GATT Article X, and, 13–14
  holding accountable through open access, 5, 12

harmonisation
  SPS Agreement, under, 105–9
    exceptions to obligation, 108–9
    monitoring of process, SPS Committee, 124
    objective of, 106
    obligation to base domestic measures on international standards, 106–7
    obligation to participate in standardising bodies, 107–8
  TBT Agreement, under, 109–12
    deviations from international standards, 111
    differing approaches across Members, 112
    identification of international standards, 110
    importance of international standards to facilitate trade, 109–10
    Members' role in preparation of standards, 112
    nature of obligation regarding international standards, 110–11

impact assessments. *See* regulatory impact assessments (RIAs)
information
  availability of, 5–7, 47–49
  centralising by WTO Secretariat. *See* WTO Secretariat
  centrality to regulatory dialogue, 155–65
  enabling dialogue, 7–8, 83–99
  exchange of, 121
  improving availability of, 278–86
    broadening information available, 282–86
    encouraging use of domestic RIAs to estimate trade effects of regulation, 283–84
    enhancing incentives for transparency, 279–81
    enhancing information about bilateral dialogue, 286
    improving dialogue with private sector, 284–85
    improving information about entire regulatory policy cycle, 283
    improving information about trade effects of regulations, 283–85
    increasing information about domestic regulations, 279–82
    supporting notifications by Members who rarely notify, 281–82
  making regulations known/available to interested parties, 47–49
  need for more accessible sources of, 6
  new technologies, use of. *See* electronic tools
  private sector
    obtaining information from, 252–53
    role of in chain of information, 269–71
  sensitive, political difficulties related to, 150
  sharing, 1
  international regulatory co-operation, 100, 101, 118, 129, 177, 288, 295
  international standards, 37, 51–52, 57–59, 69, 72, 85, 101, 103, 104–12, 115, 122, 124, 149, 175, 181, 185, 199–201, 202, 203, 207, 210, 213, 222, 224–26, 258, 276, 282, 291, 297

INDEX 319

legitimate objectives, 34–37, 57, 68, 70, 72, 80, 102, 111, 116, 191–93, 197, 204, 259, 295

mutual recognition of domestic requirements, 112–15
   conformity assessment, TBT Agreement, 114–15
   equivalence of international and foreign regulation, 113–14
   forms of, 112–13
   'rules', examples of, 113

non-discrimination. *See* non-tariff trade barriers: SPS and TBT Agreements
non-tariff trade barriers
   domestic regulations, 21
   GATT. *See* GATT
non-tariff trade barriers: SPS and TBT Agreements, 22
   justification of domestic measures, 30–38
      balancing regulatory autonomy and free trade, 23–24
      justification of domestic measures, 30–38
      legal principles applying to domestic regulations under SPS and TBT Agreements, 23–45
      prohibition of discrimination within limits of regulatory autonomy, 38–45
      scope of SPS and TBT Agreements, 25–30
      SPS Agreement: necessity of domestic measures, 32–33
      SPS Agreement: scientific evidence, 33–34
      TBT Agreement: measures pursuing legitimate objectives, 36
      TBT Agreement: risks that non-fulfilment would create, 37–38
   prohibition of discrimination within limits of regulatory autonomy, 38–45
      non-discrimination under SPS Agreement, 38–42
      non-discrimination under TBT Agreement, 42–45
   scope of SPS and TBT Agreements, 25–30
      measures under SPS Agreement, 25–27
      TBT measures: CAPs, 29
      TBT measures: standards, 30
      TBT measures: technical regulations, 27–29
notification authorities, 73–74

Organisation for Economic Co-operation and Development (OECD)
   Good Regulatory Practices (GRPs), 115–16
   international regulatory co-operation (IRC), 101, 115

private sector
   asymmetry between private parties from developed Members and developing Members, 71
   enquiry points, responses from, 85, 91–92
   importance of transparency for, 69
   improving dialogue, 284–85
   obtaining information from, 252–53
   private stakeholders as addressees, 76–77
   bilateral and regional trade agreements, in, 77
   role in providing comments to notifications, 86, 88–89
   role in chain of information, 269–71
   role in measuring impacts of domestic regulations, 166–73
      assessing impact of notifications, 169
      drafting STCs, 169–70
      existing processes to co-operate with private sector, 170–72

private sector (*cont.*)
　forms of collaboration with private sector, 170–73
　initiative addressing STCs, 169
　private sector's role in trading system, 166–67
　STCs citing private sector, 167–68

reasoned transparency. *See* transparency
regional trade agreements (RTAs)
　enquiry points, 85
　notification requirements in, 59
　　private stakeholders as addressees, 77
　transparency provisions in, 17–18
regulatory co-operation enabled by SPS and TBT institutional framework, 118–28
　downstream activities of policy cycle, regulatory co-operation in, 124–28
　data collection and policy analysis, 121
　developing of rules, standards and guidance, 122–23
　discussion of Good Regulatory Practices (GRPs), 122
　exchange of information, 121
　negotiating of international agreements, 123
　opportunities for co-operation through SPS and TBT Committee work, 119–28
　regulatory co-operation in downstream activities of policy cycle, 124–28
　regulatory co-operation in upstream activities of policy cycle, 121–23
　upstream activities of policy cycle, regulatory co-operation in, 121–23
　dispute settlement, 127–28
　monitoring of implementation, 124–26
　monitoring of process of harmonisation, 124
　STCs, discussion of, 125
　Trade Policy Review Mechanism (TPRM), monitoring by, 125–26
　WTO, SPS and TBT Committees, 118–19
regulatory co-operation under SPS and TBT Agreements, 100–28
　Good Regulatory Practices (GRPs), 115–18
　importance of, 116
　Organisation for Economic Co-operation and Development (OECD), 115–16
　SPS and TBT Agreements, 116–18
　harmonisation under SPS Agreement, 105–9
　exceptions to obligation, 108–9
　objective of harmonisation, 106
　obligation to base domestic measures on international standards, 106–7
　obligation to participate in standardising bodies, 107–8
　harmonisation under TBT Agreement, 109–12
　deviations from international standards, 111
　differing approaches across Members, 112
　identification of international standards, 110
　importance of international standards to facilitate trade, 109–10
　Members' role in preparation of standards, 112
　nature of obligation regarding international standards, 110–11
　institutional framework enabling regulatory co-operation. *See* regulatory co-operation enabled by SPS and TBT institutional framework
　international standards, adoption of, 104–12
　characteristics of positive integration in SPS/TBT Agreements, 105

INDEX 321

harmonisation under SPS
   Agreement, 105-9
harmonisation under TBT
   Agreement, 109-12
SPS/TBT Agreements reducing
   regulatory heterogeneity,
   104-5
mutual recognition of domestic
   requirements, 112-15
   conformity assessment, TBT
      Agreement, 114-15
   equivalence of international
      and foreign regulation,
      113-14
   forms of, 112-13
   'rules', examples of, 113
nature of international regulatory
   co-operation (IRC),
   101-4
   co-operation, nature of, 102-3
   costs reduction, regulatory
      co-operation contributing
      to, 102
   definition of, 101
   OECD, and, 101
   trade liberalisation, regulatory
      co-operation contributing
      to, 102
regulatory co-operation
   encouraged under SPS and
   TBT Agreements, 104-18
   adoption of international
      standards, 104-12
   Good Regulatory Practices
      (GRPs), 115-18
   mutual recognition of domestic
      requirements, 112-15
   transparency, and, 100
regulatory impact assessments (RIAs)
   ex ante, 61
   use of, 61
regulatory transparency. See
   transparency

significant effect on trade, 59-60
   information about relevant
      measures in WTO
      context, 59-62

publication of draft regulations
   where potential for
   significant effect, 59-60
specific trade concerns (STCs)
   comments on notifications to STCs,
      from, 162-65
   domestic regulatory process,
      contribution to, 185-205
   concerns involving opportunity
      to comment, 187-88
   concerns with time to adapt,
      189-90
   discrimination, 201-3
   international standards, 199-201
   questioning necessity of
      measure, 190-99
   rationale behind measure, 192-96
   restrictive requirements, 197-99
   special needs of developing
      countries, 203-5
   timely opportunity to discuss
      and influence measures,
      186-90
   using STCs for regulatory
      co-operation on priority
      issues, 287-88
evolving Committee practice,
   95-99
   good offices of chair, 96-97
   practice under GATT, 95-96
   practice under WTO, 96-97
   STCs in Committee discussions
      today, 98-99
GATT, under, 95-96
general trends regarding disputes,
   220-33
   issues raised in STCs and
      disputes, 224-28
   participating Members, 228-33
increasing importance of, 94
Members raising, 7-8
multilateral dialogue between all
   WTO Members, as, 15,
   94-97
notifications to STCs, from, 156-58
practical impediment to trade,
   addressing, 205-7
private sector

specific trade concerns (STCs) (cont.)
  drafting STCs, 169–70
  initiative addressing STCs, 169
  STCs citing, 167–68
  regulatory co-operation and, 125
  source of information, as, 158–60
  text of agreements, 94–95
  transparency, information clarification, 178–85
    lack of transparency in draft measure, 181–85
    request for clarification on scope of requirements, 180–81
    request for information, clarification, 178–81
    request for update on status of draft measure, 179–80
  understanding domestic regulation of WTO Members, 175–78
  when transparency is enough, 207–13
    resolved STCs: international standards, scientific justification, and control, inspections and approval procedures, 210–11
    resolved STCs: procedural questions/practical impediments to trade, 208–12
    resolving concerns regarding large or small trading nations, 211–12
    resolving practical impediments to trade, 209–10
    STCs assumed to be resolved due to short discussion/long periods of inactivity, 212–13
SPS Agreement
  discriminatory or restrictive practices, 3
  dispute settlement, and, 1, 9
  domestic measures, justification of appropriate level of protection, meaning of, 33
    criteria for necessity of measure, 32
    necessity of measures as core discipline, 31
    necessity of SPS measures, 32–33
    scientific evidence, 33–34
  enabling dialogue between Members, 7–8
  GATT, and. See GATT
  good offices of chair, 96–97
  harmonisation. See harmonisation
  measures defined by their purpose, 25–27
  nature/definition of SPS measures, 25
    determining purpose of, 26
    objective of, 26–27
  nature of SPS Agreement, 3
  negative integration approach, nature of, 3
  non-discrimination under SPS Agreement, 38–42, 44–45
    consistency of protection, 39–42
    SPS Committee guidelines, 40–42
    test, 38–39
    transparency, importance of, 41
    warning signals of discrimination, 41
  non-tariff trade barriers. See non-tariff trade barriers: SPS and TBT Agreements
  regulatory co-operation. See regulatory co-operation under SPS and TBT Agreements
  scope of SPS Agreement, 25
  STCs, Members raising. See specific trade concerns (STCs)
  transparency. See transparency/transparency obligations under SPS and TBT Agreements

tariffs
  GATT, and. See GATT
  trade barriers, as, 2–3
TBT Agreement
  discriminatory or restrictive practices, 3
  dispute settlement, and, 1, 9

enabling dialogue between
    Members, 7–8
GATT, and. *See* GATT
harmonisation under. *See*
    harmonisation
nature of, 3
necessity to fulfil legitimate policy
    objectives, 34–38
  measures pursuing legitimate
    objectives, 36
  necessity of measures as core
    principle, 31
  risks that non-fulfilment would
    create, 37–38
  steps to determine necessity of
    measure, 35–36
negative integration approach,
    nature of, 3
non-discrimination under TBT
    Agreement, 38, 42–45
  absence of general exception
    clause, 43
  establishing measure as
    discriminatory, 42
  legitimate regulatory
    distinction, concept of,
    43–44
non-tariff trade barriers. *See* non-
    tariff trade barriers: SPS and
    TBT Agreements
regulatory autonomy of Members,
    importance of, 42
regulatory co-operation. *See*
    regulatory co-operation
    under SPS and TBT
    Agreements
scope, 55
STCs, Members raising. *See* specific
    trade concerns (STCs)
TBT Committee discussions on
    REACH Regulation, 16
TBT measures: conformity
    assessment procedures
    (CAPs), 27, 29
  costs, 29
  definition of, 29
  examples of, 29
  objective of provisions on, 29

TBT measures: standards, 27, 30
  definition of, 30
  private, 30
  voluntary regulations of, 30
TBT measures: technical
    regulations, 27–29
  characteristics defining, 28
  definition of, 28
  document, meaning of, 28
  governmental nature of, 30
  mandatory character of
    measures, 28–29, 30
  transparency. *See* transparency/
    transparency obligations
    under SPS and TBT
    Agreements
tobacco. *See* cigarettes
Tokyo Round Standards Code, 47
Trade Policy Review Mechanism
    (TPRM), 11
  criticisms of, 15
  enhancing enforcement of WTO
    obligations, 10
  establishment of, 7
  monitoring by, 280
  peer reviews under, 14–15
  purpose of, 7
  role as 'guardian' of transparency in
    multilateral trading system,
    14–16
  WTO Secretariat, and, 15
transparency
  complement for dispute settlement.
    See transparency as
    complement for dispute
    settlement
  important trend in international
    law, as, 12
  information. *See* information
  provisions in bilateral
    and regional trade
    agreements, 17–18
  reasoned transparency, meaning
    of, 4
  regulatory transparency, meaning
    of, 4
  role in implementation of TBT and
    SBT Agreements, 1

transparency (cont.)
　social order, contributing to, 2
　substitute for dispute settlement. See transparency as substitute for dispute settlement
　TPRM, and. See Trade Policy Review Mechanism (TPRM)
　trading system, improving operation of, 2
　WTO, transparency in. See transparency/transparency obligations in WTO
transparency as complement for dispute settlement, 1, 9, 217–91
　alternative fora/negotiating capacity, 273
　enhancing scope and benefits of regulatory co-operation, 286–91
　　better co-operation between trade and regulatory communities, 288–90
　　enhancing regulatory co-operation to balance trade/non-trade matters, 288–91
　　including non-trade considerations in discussion, 290–91
　　using STCs for regulatory co-operation on priority issues, 287–88
　general trends regarding SPS and TBT STCs and disputes, 220–33
　　Committee discussions preceding majority of SPS disputes, 220–23
　　issues raised in STCs and disputes, 224–28
　　participating Members, 228–33
　　TBT Committee discussions complementing dispute settlement, 223–24
　general trends regarding SPS and TBT STCs and disputes: participating Members, 228–33
　　Members active in SPS STCs and disputes, 229–32
　　Members active in TBT STCs and disputes, 232–33
　improving availability of information, 278–86
　　broadening information available, 282–86
　　encouraging use of domestic RIAs to estimate trade effects of regulation, 283–84
　　enhancing incentives for transparency, 279–81
　　enhancing information about bilateral dialogue, 286
　　improving dialogue with private sector, 284–85
　　improving information about entire regulatory policy cycle, 283
　　improving information about trade effects of regulations, 283–85
　　increasing information about domestic regulations, 279–82
　　supporting notifications by Members who rarely notify, 281–82
　information about other Members' regulations, 266–71
　　role of private sector in chain of information, 269–71
　　SPS and TBT transparency to improve information disparities, 266–69
　information about WTO-inconsistent measures, 250–53
　　better capacity to detect deviations, 250–51
　　difficulty of identifying SPS and TBT measures at origin of trade effect, 251–52
　　obtaining relevant information from private sector, 252–53
　information and dialogue towards mutually acceptable solution, 217–18
　lack of alternative fora to address trade frictions, 260–64

INDEX

informal dialogue, 261–62
preferential trade agreements (PTAs), 262–63
requests for consultations, 264
resources, 272–73
resources for accessing adjudication, 253–60
Members' legal capacity, 256–60
Members' relative resources, 254–56
overall resources of country, 253–54
SPS and TBT requests for consultations: overview of transparency steps, 233–46
disputes that emerged out of nowhere, 243–46
major SPS and TBT disputes and transparency, 235–43
transparency and disputes, 219–20
whether current interaction between transparency and dispute settlement is best it can be, 274–78
transparency as substitute for dispute settlement, 1, 9
base of WTO disputing pyramid: centralised access to measures of WTO Members, 138–55
Members' notification practices: engagement in SPS/TBT transparency, 138–47
shortcomings of notifications systems, 147–54
use made of notifications by other Members or stakeholders, 154–55
centralised information to regulatory dialogue, 155–65
comments on notifications to STCs, from, 162–65
notifications to STCs, from: WTO framework, 156–58
role of regulatory dialogue in improving understanding of measure, 159–61
STCs: source of information, 158–60
explanation of 'pyramid' metaphor, 132–35
main counterpart in private sector, 172–73
Members' notification practices: engagement in SPS/TBT transparency, 138–47
disseminating information through e-mail alerts and online databases, 145, 147
increase in notifications means increase in transparency, 139–41
Members' engagement in transparency by development status, 141–42
notification through electronic Notification Submission System, 144–45
opportunity for comments on notifications, 142–44
Secretariat's role in ensuring availability by electronic tools, 144–47
opportunities for dialogue, 131–32
preventing conflicts by *ex ante* transparency, 131
private sector's role in measuring impacts of domestic regulations, 166–73
assessing impact of notifications, 169
drafting STCs, 169–70
existing processes to co-operate with private sector, 170–72
forms of collaboration with private sector, 170–73
initiative addressing STCs, 169
private sector's role in trading system, 166–67
STCs citing private sector, 167–68
shortcomings of notifications systems, 147–54
political difficulties related to sensitive information, 150
practical difficulties involving resource constraints, 148–49
remaining information gaps from notifications, 150–54

transparency as substitute for dispute settlement (*cont.*)
  remaining practical difficulties in notifications, 147–50
  STCs: domestic regulatory process, contribution to, 185–205
    concerns involving opportunity to comment, 187–88
    concerns with time to adapt, 189–90
    discrimination, 201–3
    international standards, 199–201
    questioning necessity of measure, 190–99
    rationale behind measure, 192–96
    restrictive requirements, 197–99
    special needs of developing countries, 203–5
    timely opportunity to discuss and influence measures, 186–90
  STCs: practical impediment to trade, addressing, 205–7
  STCs: transparency, information clarification, 178–85
    lack of transparency in draft measure, 181–85
    request for clarification on scope of requirements, 180–81
    request for information, clarification, 178–81
    request for update on status of draft measure, 179–80
  STCs: understanding domestic regulation of WTO Members, 175–78
  what Members need to know to prevent disputes from arising, 174–75
  when transparency is enough, 207–13
    resolving practical impediments to trade, 209–10
    resolving STCs: international standards, scientific justification, 210–11
    resolving STCs: large or small trading nations, 211–12
  resolving STCs: procedural questions/practical impediments to trade, 208–12
  STCs assumed to be resolved due to short discussion/long periods of inactivity, 212–13
transparency tools in SPS and TBT Agreements, typology of, 62–99
  centralised transparency/access to information, 62–63, 71–83
    electronic tools to enhance effectiveness of transparency, 81–83
    notifications: Members' rights to access information, 71–81
  centralised transparency: notifications/Members' access to information, 71–81
    addressees of notifications, 74–77
    content of notification obligation, 72–73
    dispute settlement, and, 71
    emergency notifications, 75–76, 80–81
    establishment of notification authorities, 73–74
    follow-up to original notification, 79–80
    Members as addressees of notifications, 74–76
    no requirement to notify adopted regulations, 78–79
    private stakeholders as addressees of notifications, 76–77
    SPS format for notifications, 73
    TBT format for notifications, 73
    timing of notification obligation, 77–79
  collaborative transparency: enabling dialogue among WTO Members, 63, 83–99
    basis of, 83
    obligation to establish enquiry points, 84–85, 89–94

INDEX

responding to enquiries and comments: transparency that fosters dialogue, 84–89
STCs: mechanism of multilateral regulatory dialogue, 94–99
collaborative transparency: obligation to establish enquiry points, 84–85, 89–94
  bilateral nature of dialogue with enquiry points, 93–94
  bridging gap between regulators and traders, 93–94
  enquiry points providing information on proposed/adopted regulations, 89–91
  failure to provide information, effect of, 91
  importance of, 89
  objectives of enquiry points, 90
  private parties, responding to, 91–92
  providing information to Members and other interested parties, 91–92
  regional trade agreements, and, 85
collaborative transparency: responding to enquiries and comments, 84–89
  additional procedures specific to SPS Agreement, 89
  comments on notifications, 86–89
  obligation to respond to enquiries, 84–86
  obligation to take comments into account, 86–88
  private sector's role in providing comments, 86, 88–89
collaborative transparency: STCs, 94–97
  evolving Committee practice, 95–99
  increasing importance of, 94
  text of agreements, 94–95
comprehensive system of transparency of domestic regulations, 62
electronic tools to enhance effectiveness of transparency, 81–83
  e-mail to Members, use of, 81–82
  importance of electronic tools, 82
  increase in use of electronic tools/ePing, 82–83
right-to-know transparency, 62, 63–71
  ensured through obligation of publication, 63
  publication of adopted regulations, 66–71
  publication of notice, 63–66
right-to-know transparency: publication of adopted regulations, 66–71
  adopted regulation, nature of, 67
  full transparency throughout domestic regulatory cycle, ensuring, 66
  location of publication, 68
  scope of obligation as inclusive as possible, 66–67
  targeting of publication, 68–71
  timing for publication of adopted measures, 67–68
right-to-know transparency: publication of notice, 63–66
  content and location of obligation to publish notice, 64–66
  internet, use of, 65, 66
  SPS Committee publication requirements, 65
  TBT Committee publication requirements, 64–65
  timing of publication of notice, 66
transparency/transparency obligations in WTO
  case study of right-to-know, targeted and interactive transparency in WTO, 8–11
  domestic frameworks, WTO transparency and, 16–17
  ex post transparency as dominant dynamic, 53

transparency/transparency obligations in WTO (cont.)
  fragmentation of production cycles in multilateral trading system, 2
  GATT. See GATT
  information/dialogue centralised by WTO Secretariat. See WTO Secretariat
  overview of transparency in WTO, 4–8
    first-generation transparency as 'decentralised' transparency, 6
    forms of transparency as three-generation process, 4–5
    information technology tools enabling centralised transparency, 8
    interactive/collaborative transparency: information enabling dialogue, 7–8
    need for more accessible sources of information, 6
    right-to-know transparency: availability of information, 5–6
    targeted transparency: access to information, 6–7
  purpose of transparency requirements, 3–4
  reasoned transparency, 4
  reasons for, 2
    allowing Members to monitor implementation of Agreements, 2
    regulatory co-operation, enabling, 3
  regulatory transparency, 4
transparency/transparency obligations under SPS and TBT Agreements
  absence of international standard: information only about measures presumed divergent, 57–59
    bilateral/regional trade agreements, notification requirements of, 59
    conformity of regulations to international standards, effect of, 57–58
    international standard criteria, criticism of, 57–58
    SPS Committee encouraging notification of compliant measures, 58
    TBT Committee encouraging notification where no international standards, 59
  active use by Members of developed transparency framework, 8–9
  allowing Members to monitor implementation, 2
  case study of right-to-know, targeted and interactive transparency, 8–11
  core principle under SPS and TBT Agreements, transparency as, 46–47
  dialogue on draft measures between Members to encourage regulatory coherence, 50–51
    consultations reinforcing transparency, 51
    ex ante transparency, 51
    obligation of notification, 51
    opportunity/right to comment on draft measures, importance of, 50
  ensuring implementation of TBT obligations, 10
  making regulations known/available to interested parties, 47–49
    obligation of publication, 48
    TBT and SPS Agreements publicity obligations compared, 48
  proposed regulations: broad range of measures under transparency framework, 54–57
    SPS measures or regulations, 54–55
    TBT Agreement: CAPs, 55–56

INDEX

TBT Agreement: transparency of standards, 56–57
TBT Agreement: transparency of technical regulations, 55–56
purpose of transparency under SPS and TBT Agreements, 3–4, 47–51
  dialogue on drafts between Members to encourage regulatory coherence, 50–51
  information: making regulations known/available to interested parties, 47–49
  predictability: allowing traders time to adapt to new measures/costs, 49–50
regulatory co-operation, enabling, 3
scope of transparency obligations: proposed regulations, 51–62
  absence of international standard: information only about measures presumed divergent, 57–59
  ex post transparency as marginal aspect of transparency obligations, 53
  proposed regulations: broad range of measures under transparency framework, 54–57
  proposed regulations: emphasis on *ex ante* transparency, 52–53
  scope of basic *ex ante* transparency obligations, 52
  significant co-ordination between authorities at domestic level, 51–52
  significant effect on trade: information about relevant measures in WTO context, 59–62
  transparency obligations applying to measures having effect on trade, 51–52
  existence of potential for significant effect, determining, 60–61
  impacts on trade, determining, 61
  publication of draft regulations where potential for significant effect, 59–60
  regulatory impact assessments, use of, 61
  trade-facilitating measures, treatment of, 61–62
SPS and TBT Agreements transparency tools. *See* transparency tools in SPS and TBT Agreements, typology of

Uruguay Round (1986–1994), 6, 10

World Trade Organization (WTO)
  Dispute Settlement Body. *See* WTO Dispute Settlement Body (DSB)
  GATT. *See* GATT
  legal system, strength of, 2
  Secretariat. *See* WTO Secretariat
  SPS Agreement. *See* SPS Agreement
  TBT Agreement. *See* TBT Agreement
  TPRM. *See* Trade Policy Review Mechanism (TPRM)
  transparency obligations in. *See* transparency/transparency obligations in WTO
WTO Dispute Settlement Body (DSB)
  costs of, 9, 10–11
    transparency tools helping to overcome start-up costs, 11
  enforcement between sovereign states, achieving, 2
  major achievement of WTO, as, 9
  nature of, 9
  regulatory co-operation, and, 127–28
    preventing disputes, 128

WTO Dispute Settlement Body (DSB) (*cont.*)
   resources for accessing adjudication, 253–60
      Members' legal capacity, 256–60
      Members' relative resources, 254–56
      overall resources of country, 253–54
   transparency. *See also* transparency as complement for dispute settlement; transparency as substitute for dispute settlement
      dispute settlement, and, 10, 71
      equalising access to, 2
      notifications, effects of, 71
WTO Secretariat
   centralisation of information and dialogue, 3, 7, 49, 71
   data collection and policy analysis, 121
   electronic tools to enhance effectiveness of transparency, 81–83
      disseminating information through e-mail alerts/online databases, 145, 147
      e-mails to Members, use of, 81–82, 145, 147
      importance of, 82
      increase in use of electronic tools/ePing, 82–83
      notification through electronic Notification Submission System, 144–45
      online tools to publish/notify trade measures, encouraging use of, 8
      Secretariat's role in ensuring availability by, 144–47
   Members' notification obligations, 6, 7, 71
   notification authorities, 74
   notifications
      addressees of, 74–77
      electronic tools to improve effectiveness of transparency, 81–83
      Members, 71, 74–76
      regulatory co-operation preventing disputes, 128
      TPRM, and, 15
      transparency obligations under TBT Agreement, description of, 62

For EU product safety concerns, contact us at Calle de José Abascal, 56–1°,
28003 Madrid, Spain or eugpsr@cambridge.org.

www.ingramcontent.com/pod-product-compliance
Ingram Content Group UK Ltd.
Pitfield, Milton Keynes, MK11 3LW, UK
UKHW020254090825
461507UK00021B/959